Robert Toomb

Robert Toombs

The Civil Wars of a United States Senator and Confederate General

MARK SCROGGINS

McFarland & Company, Inc., Publishers
Jefferson, North Carolina, and London

Library of Congress Cataloguing-in-Publication Data

Scroggins, Mark.
Robert Toombs : the civil wars of a United States
senator and Confederate general / by Mark Scroggins.
p. cm.
Includes bibliographical references and index.

ISBN 978-0-7864-6363-3
softcover : 50# alkaline paper 

1. Toombs, Robert Augustus, 1810–1885.
2. Legislators — United States — Biography.
3. United States. Congress. Senate — Biography.
4. Generals — Confederate States of America — Biography.
5. United States — History — Civil War, 1861–1865 — Biography.
6. Georgia — History — Civil War, 1861–1865 — Biography.
7. United States — Politics and government —1815–1861.
8. Georgia— Biography.
I. Title.

E415.9.T6S38 2011 328.73'092092 — dc23 [B] 2011020762

British Library cataloguing data are available

On the cover: Robert Toombs, 1859, and flag detail (Library of Congress)

Manufactured in the United States of America

McFarland & Company, Inc., Publishers
Box 611, Jefferson, North Carolina 28640
www.mcfarlandpub.com

To
Sweet Pickle
and
Mr. Wonderful

Contents

Preface and Acknowledgments

At times during this project, I was convinced that I was every bit as frustrated with Robert Toombs as some of his colleagues must have been when he was on one of his political rampages. Toombs was a born politician in both the positive and negative senses of the word. He could be kind, pushy, funny, arrogant, charming, eloquent, sarcastic, dedicated, slovenly, candid, manipulative, and a host of other dispositions that his mood or the circumstances required. But no one got to the top levels of the nineteenth century political world — or today's — without the abilities Toombs had, for better or worse.

Toombs had plenty of better *and* worse in his character. He did both good and harm to the South and to the nation. He tried for years to find compromise with the North as his more extreme Southern colleagues demanded splitting the country. Yet as the Civil War approached, he enthusiastically helped tear Georgia out of the Union and nailed it into the Confederacy. After the war, he lounged in his own bitterness, resentful at the loss of the Confederacy, the government, the new economy, and the whole damn thing. In the end, he was a failure.

I have tried to explain him, the things he did and why he did them against the backdrop of American history in the nineteenth century. But most of all, I have tried to tell an interesting story about an interesting man in an interesting time. I hope I have succeeded.

But whatever success I have achieved in writing this book would not have been possible without a vast network of extremely helpful archivists, family, and friends across the country. Any omissions that follow are due simply to the author's neglectfulness and exhaustion that comes after a long writing project.

Relatively few of Toombs' letters have been left behind, and they have been scattered in numerous library collections across the country. Most were published in Ulrich Phillips' massive *The Correspondence of Robert Toombs, Alexander Stephens, and Howell Cobb* that was issued in 1913 by the American Historical Association. But there are a few small manuscript collections as well. The largest and richest is at the Hargrett Rare Book and Manuscript Library at the University of Georgia in Athens. Special thanks are due to Chuck Barber, head, manuscripts and assistant director of the Hargrett Library, who was instrumental in making and sending copies of Toombs' correspondence to me. I also owe a good deal of gratitude to Gilbert Head, university archives associate, for his patience and persistence in pursuing my sometimes muddled questions and requests, especially about Robert Toombs' years at the University of Georgia.

Another small collection of Toombs correspondence exists at Duke University. I'd like to thank Janie C. Morris, research services librarian at the Rare Book, Manuscript, and Special Collections Library, for finding and sending correspondence to and from Toombs in their collection, Tim Pyatt, university archivist, Rare Book, Manuscript, and Naomi L. Nelson, director. Another collection of letters is at the Special Collections & Archives Department at the Robert W. Woodruff Library at Emory University. Graduate assistant Sarah Stanton was invaluable in finding, copying, and sending Toombs material to me as was Elizabeth Chase, coordinator for Research Services, Manuscript, Archives, and Rare Book Library.

Numerous other archivists and historians helped me along the way. Without their aid and assistance, the book would not have been as rich in the details of Toombs' life. Jewell Anderson Dalrymple, reference coordinator at the Georgia Historical Society, and Nora E. Lewis supplied many miscellaneous items concerning Robert Toombs. Also, special thanks go to both Gail DeLoach, who has helped me with this and various other projects, and Steve Engerrand at the Georgia State Archives. Ann Graham, president of the Demosthenian Society, enthusiastically checked the society's records for traces of Toombs. Much thanks goes to Julianna Spallholz in Special Collections at the Schaffer Library at Union College in Schenectady, New York, and Ellen H. Fladger, head of Special Collections, who provided invaluable material about the university and Toombs' student days there. I am grateful to Claire McCann, manuscript librarian at the Margaret I. King Library at the University of Kentucky, who provided copies of correspondence between Toombs and John J. Crittenden and Matthew Turi at the University of North Carolina at Chapel Hill.

Wilbur E. Meneray, assistant university librarian for Special Collections, and Leon C. Miller, head, Louisiana Research Collection at the Howard-Tilton Memorial Library at Tulane University, was kind enough to send the telegram traffic between Toombs and Jefferson Davis when Davis offered Toombs the secretary of state portfolio. Sam Fore in the Manuscripts Division, South Carolina Library, University of South Carolina, provided me copies of the Toombs Letterbook consisting of correspondence between Secretary of State Toombs and his commissioners in Washington, D.C.

Budge Weidman at the at National Archives in Washington was kind enough to share copies of documents about the life of one of Toombs' former slaves, Garland White, and Robert Toombs' Confederate service files. Her work with the Civil War Conservation Corps (CWCC) is a wonderful ongoing project, staffed by volunteers that is arranging the compiled service records of each soldier who served with the United States Colored Troops during the Civil War. Special thanks are also due to Meg Hacker at the National Archives and Records Administration in Ft. Worth, Texas, for putting me on the track of the original files for Garland White.

I can't say enough about the courtesy of Marty B. Fleming, historic site manager, and Marcia N. Campbell, interpretive specialist, at the Robert Toombs House State Historic Site in Washington, Georgia. They sent great information to me about the Toombs home site and the town of Washington, Georgia, and patiently answered my endless email queries and phone calls. Mr. Fleming was also extremely generous with his time and resources when I made my pilgrimage to Toombs' hometown. Thanks, Marty. Others who provided invaluable help include Amy C. Schindler, university archivist and acting Marian, and Alan

McLeod, director of the Special Collections Center at the College of William and Mary; and Donna Stapley, assistant to the director at the University of Virginia Library.

Most of the research was conducted in Houston, Texas, through the fabulous public library system and the various university libraries in the area. The Alfred Nuemann Library at the University of Houston, Clear Lake, is a wonderful facility, rich in reference material and microform collections (with the added advantage of its being very near my home). The Fondren Library at Rice University was also a resource I used many times. The Houston Public Library's Main Branch in downtown Houston was simply a great source, especially the people in the interlibrary loan department. Houston Public Library's Clayton Genealogy Library is a true treasure for genealogists and historians alike. The many trips I made to this facility were always richly rewarding.

There have been three major biographies written about Robert Toombs. The first was by Pleasant Stovall, who is the only biographer that had the pleasure and luck of knowing his subject personally. Stovall's book was published in 1892 and has the feel of being written by the court historian, though it is filled with valuable anecdotes about Toombs' achievements and escapades. Ulrich Phillips also produced a biography in 1913. It is an aloof nuts and bolts political biography that drew on his work on Robert Toombs' papers that were published in *The Correspondence of Robert Toombs, Alexander Stephens, and Howell Cobb* mentioned above. The third and best known biography so far is William Thompson's *Robert Toombs of Georgia* published in 1966. It is a well researched and well written book that is balanced with sympathy and criticism.

Besides the traditional sources, I also conducted much of the research through the Internet. Several websites were invaluable and this project may not have been worth doing without them. The Making of America websites by Cornell University and the University of Michigan are wonderful tools for researchers in nineteenth century history. Both sites together contain almost four million pages of images from period books and articles. I was also very fortunate that the Augusta *Chronicle* has put the images of almost its entire run of newspapers online. The Atlanta *Constitution* was also available online through Ancestry.com. Other notable electronic sources for this project were the *Congressional Globe,* which has gone online through the Library of Congress American Memory website. The Digital Library of Georgia project has also put online Ulrich Phillips' massive *The Correspondence of Robert Toombs, Alexander H. Stephens, and Howell Cobb,* selected letters from Robert Toombs to his wife, Julia, and rare books pertaining to the history of Georgia.

Finally and most of all, this project would not have been possible without the support and understanding of my many friends and family. Much credit goes to Professor Robert Smith, Professor Ronald Gaddie, Dr. Ben Alpers and Sue Schofield, all of the University of Oklahoma, who encouraged me to pursue the project further when I thought it was not worth pursuing. Joanne Sprott, indexer and proofreader extraordinaire. Steve Candler, my friend and colleague, gave valuable advice about photographs and lots of laughs.

I have to mention Jing Li (Ms. Jean) and InAe Jennings for entertaining a rambunctious and curious three-year-old boy during the many hours it took to work on this book. I am grateful to Tammy Yang for the same reason. Thanks to Hong Chen and Simon Huang for their computer help on the technical side. And most of all my wife, Miranda Wenjian Xing-Scroggins, for her love, support, patience, and to Mike Scroggins for just being there.

Portions of chapters 3 and 4 appeared in the master's thesis "Sliding to Secession: Robert Toombs and Disunion."

Oh, I'm a good old Rebel,
Now, that's just what I am.
For this "fair land of freedom"
I do not care a damn.
I'm glad I fit against it—
I only wish we'd won;
And I don't want no pardon
For anything I've done.

By Major James Innes Randolph

Introduction

On January 15, 1861, former U.S. senator Robert Toombs and his wife, Julia, left Washington, D.C., and boarded the train for their home in Washington, Georgia.

Toombs had resigned from the Senate only a week before. He was usually not a reflective man, but as the train pulled away he couldn't help but think about the last fifteen years he had spent in Congress. He had feared from the beginning that war with Mexico would tear the Union apart over the issue of slavery. The fight over whether the new territories won from Mexico would be slave or be free had separated the North from the South.

For Toombs, it was only right that at least some of those territories have slavery. He had fought for that proposition with everything he had. The Constitution, Congress, and the Supreme Court had all vindicated slavery. But traitors in the North — abolitionists, Republicans, even members from his own former Whig party — had argued every point, had thrown up every political obstacle they could get their hands on, had done everything they could to subvert the law and undermine the South's rights to expand its institutions.

He had fought like hell, had put his political reputation on the line more than once, and all for what? Abolitionists, Republicans, and other enemies had tried to start a war in Kansas over slavery, had even paid crazy old John Brown to start a war in Virginia. Toombs was convinced that there had been any number of conspiracies to choke slavery and everything else in the South to death. Instead, the Union had died by the hands of the South's political foes.

It had finally come to this. Despite his fire and brimstone political rhetoric, his bullying and blustering, Toombs had been a Unionist in his heart. He had remained one as long as he could. He wondered if spending the majority of his political career trying to work out some compromise to appease the North had been worth it. The political crisis he long feared had arrived. The Union was ended. The Union was no more.

The one thing that countered his bitterness was the promise of a new future, a new beginning. While the railway car clattered and bounced and swayed, he pondered what lay ahead. South Carolina had left the Union. Florida, Alabama and Louisiana had followed. Now all eyes were on his state of Georgia. Georgia was on the brink and could go either way. But Robert Toombs had left the Union and if he had anything to say about it, he was going to take Georgia with him.

A new nation was being born. The struggle might be long and hard. But he had no doubt that this new confederacy of Southern states would grow into something mighty, a strapping new republic that would overwhelm its originator and take its place at the table with the powers of Europe, perhaps even compete with them for their empires.

And like Washington and Jefferson, he was going to be one of its founding fathers. There was even serious talk that he might be elected as the new nation's first president. He knew that he was more suited for a legislative office than an executive office, but still, the idea appealed to him. At any rate, he knew he had a place in the new nation's destiny and that his fate was tied to whatever happened.

Content at that thought, Robert Toombs settled back as the train rolled south to his home in Washington, Georgia.

1

Georgia

It was a long way from Washington, Georgia, to Washington, D.C., and back again. It had also been a long road for Toombs' forefathers. Like many Southerners, Toombs liked to romanticize his ancestors' gallantry. He was proud that they had defended King Charles the First against Oliver Cromwell's Roundheads during England's Great Rebellion. Unfortunately for the Toombs clan, they were caught on the wrong side of power when Charles was beheaded in 1649. In retaliation, Cromwell's Parliament imposed heavy fines and confiscated the Royalists' property to pay for the civil war. This may have been why the Toombs family fled England and landed in Virginia sometime in the 1650s. There they settled in for several generations as yeoman farmers.[1]

Toombs' paternal grandfather, Gabriel Toombs, temporarily carried on the family's cavalier tradition by enlisting in the Virginia Militia during the French and Indian War. During that war, the French, the British, and their Native American allies on both sides fought for domination and the vast resources on the North American continent. Virginia governor Robert Dinwiddie lit one of the sparks for the war when he accused French trappers of encroaching on the lucrative fur trade and tried to run them out of the Ohio Valley.

Hostilities officially broke out in the spring of 1656. The Virginia Militia was put under the supervision of the by-the-book General Edward Braddock. Braddock and his two British regiments had been in America just long enough to develop a loathing for the "slothful and languid disposition" of the Virginia volunteers. At the disastrous Battle of the Wilderness at Fort Duquesne in 1755, the 450 Virginians in Braddock's force fought bravely enough. But they had no chance against the French and their Native American allies. The Virginia Militia could not mount an effective fight under Braddock's regimented leadership, despite the presence of the general's young aide named George Washington. The French and the Native Americans took cover behind rocks and trees and easily picked off British troops as they tried desperately to stay in formation under blasts of gunfire and hails of arrows. The Virginians wanted to counterattack with "Indian tactics" but British officers refused to let them. At one point, confused British soldiers poured friendly fire on a contingent of militia which was firing from behind a fallen tree. It was a disaster for both the British and the Virginia militia.[2]

So Gabriel limped back home to Caroline County. Apparently, that was enough of the Toombs' cavalier tradition for him. He resumed keeping his tavern, operating the ferry across the Mattaponi River, and acting as the overseer on the tollway from "Widow Bell's to Gouch's road." As a tavern keeper, Gabriel was a well-known and respected member of the community. But he was also a bit of a rascal who had his share of brushes with the law. For instance, in April of 1765, a Ruth Sale brought charges against him for an unspecified offense. Gabriel did not bother to show up in court. He lost the case and was fined seven pounds. A grand jury also found him guilty in November of the same year for not listing land he owned in St. Mary's Parish. Between keeping his tavern, collecting tolls, and his legal skirmishes, Gabriel and his wife, Ann, raised a brood of children, six of which survived into adulthood: Dawson, Mary, Elizabeth, Ann, Sally, and the future senator's father, Robert.[3]

Robert Toombs Sr. was apparently born sometime in the 1740s. Although surrounded by the political turmoil of the 1760s and 1770s, he was not moved to action until 1779 when he joined the Virginia Militia. He served until 1782 and retired as a major. Like so many other Revolutionary War veterans, Major Toombs and his family left their home to seek opportunity and fortune in their newly won country. The Toombs clan was probably lured to Georgia by the state's liberal headright and bounty land laws. Major Toombs may have been associated with George Matthews, a Virginian who went to Georgia to fight the British. After the war, Matthews developed a taste for land speculation and persuaded the obliging Georgia legislature to reserve two hundred thousand acres of real estate exclusively for Virginia families.[4]

Georgia officials were eager to attract settlers after the Revolution ended. They especially wanted to populate the unsettled parts of the state with veterans. The Spanish in neighboring Florida and disgruntled Native Americans were a constant threat. Georgia politicians went out of their way to recruit homesteaders who had fought in the Revolutionary War. These veterans had fearsome reputations. They knew how to form militias instantly and knew how to intimidate enemies who might be thinking about raids and invasions. In 1781, the Georgia legislature passed an act that gave 250 acres of tax exempt land to any man who could prove he had served during the Revolution "provided such person or persons cannot be convicted of plundering or distressing the country." Two years later, a generous headright law granted two hundred acre plots to veterans who agreed to homestead on the frontier and pay two shillings a year per hundred acres. This headright law applied only to George Matthew's Virginians. It was a lure hard for an ambitious veteran to resist.[5]

Georgians were also aggressively removing Native Americans from their midst. State officials took three million acres of prime land from the Creek and Cherokee nations because these tribes had supported the British during the war. Then the land was thrown open to white settlers. Between 1783 and 1790, the population of Georgia more than tripled. By the time Major Toombs arrived, the state was rapidly filling with frontiersmen, settlers, businessmen, horse traders, land speculators, and other wily wheeler-dealers.

Robert Toombs believed his father landed in Georgia in 1784. Most of the Toombs family, including old Gabriel, came along with the major. On 17 May 1784, both Major Toombs and Gabriel signed up for bounty land grants in Washington County. Gabriel petitioned for 213 acres. But Major Toombs had probably been issued a Continental Certificate that entitled him to a larger grant and he asked for 939 acres. By 1787, he was living in Wilkes County. He owned two hundred acres of taxable land and four slaves.[6]

The state legislature had carved Wilkes County out of the hilly Georgia wilderness on 5 February 1777. Named after John Wilkes, the turbulent British politician who backed the Americans during the Revolution, the county initially encompassed 391 square miles with almost 1.3 million acres waiting to be given away as head-right land. It was the first public land to be offered in the new state. The rich soil and its proximity to the South Carolina border attracted a lot of land-hungry settlers. The Toombs clan and many of their Virginia neighbors settled in and around the small town of Washington which had been chartered in 1779. Washington was on the edge of the frontier, but the area was already gaining a reputation as a cosmopolitan and bustling economic center since Wilkes County already contained a third of Georgia's population. By 1790, the citizens could brag about several schools and a brand new log courthouse.[7]

Despite a constant stream of settlers, the economy in Georgia grew sluggish just after the Revolution. In 1790, Major Toombs defaulted on his taxes. His crops may have failed or he may have been away when the tax list was compiled. But failure to pay his taxes did no harm to his standing in the community. He was elected first lieutenant in the local militia in 1791. He also slowly acquired more assets. By 1793, he listed ten slaves and 260 acres.[8]

That same year, at Nathaniel Greene's plantation in Wilkes County, a tutor named Eli Whitney patented the cotton gin. Before 1793, cotton was not a practical commercial crop. Growing it ruined the soil. Separating the seed from the fiber was laborious and expensive. Cotton growers just could not compete commercially with indigo, tobacco, or rice. But Whitney patented his invention and cotton gins spread across the South like wildflowers. In 1790, only two million pounds of cotton was produced in the South. Ten years later the number was closer to twenty million pounds. The new cotton economy brought prosperity, people, and a few internal improvements such as roads and canals to the South. It also planted the seeds of the sectional tension that brought four years of bloody slaughter a generation or two later.[9]

Any planter who was acquisitive for land, had some managerial skills, a knack for business, and a proper share of good luck could make a fortune planting indigo, rice, tobacco and the new get-rich-quick crop of cotton. Major Toombs' fate was not much different. In less than twenty years after his arrival in Georgia, he owned 640 acres and eighteen slaves. Along the way, he married his first wife, a Miss Sanders, in neighboring Columbia County. But she died soon after the marriage. There were no children. The major was in his mid-to-late fifties, an old man by late eighteenth century standards, when he took his second wife. For whatever reason, he traveled back to Culpepper County, Virginia, and married thirty-year-old Sarah (Sally) Catlett on 17 February 1798. Major Toombs either stayed in Virginia almost the whole year or went home then returned for the dowry. But in October, he was in Culpepper County to petition the court to take five slaves back to Georgia with him "in consequence of his intermarriage with Sarah Catlett."[10]

Lawrence Catlett Toombs was the only child born to Major Toombs and Sally. Then Sally was dead a few years later. So Major Toombs threw his energies into accumulating more land and more slaves. He did not miss his chance when Georgia held lotteries to give away additional tribal land taken from the Creek Nation. Thanks to a new law passed by the Georgia legislature in 1803, every free white male over twenty-one years old and who had lived in Georgia for three years was eligible for a draw. Major Toombs took two draws, indicating he was married and had at least one child. By the next year, he owned almost a thousand acres in Wilkes and Greene counties and thirty-eight slaves.[11]

After Sally's death, the well-to-do major married Catherine Huling. Like the Toombs family, the Hulings were transplants from Virginia who had thrived on the Georgia frontier. Catherine's family ran a small plantation with a little over five hundred acres and thirty slaves. Catherine was "a most excellent Christian woman," a devout Methodist "of strong and exalted piety" who "gave generously of her own means to her family and friends." She was also a devoted mother.[12]

Catherine Huling Toombs gave birth to five children in quick succession: Sara Ann Elizabeth Toombs, James Huling Toombs (who was killed in a hunting accident when he was a boy), Augustus, and Gabriel. Robert Augustus Toombs arrived on July 2, 1810, the youngest of the five children. The Toombs offspring were children of privilege and by all accounts nurtured by loving parents. Young Robert was an active and rambunctious kid. He was a healthy child but so small and slender that his nickname was "Runt." What people noticed most about him were his dark, intense eyes and his shock of auburn hair. He loved horses and was probably riding before he could walk.[13]

Robert Toombs lost his father when he was only four years old. Major Toombs was well into his sixties or mid-seventies when he died late in 1814. The major bequeathed to his family an estate of twenty-two hundred acres, forty-five slaves, and about $35,000 in cash, bonds and property. His first-born son, Lawrence Catlett, received three hundred acres of land, several slaves, and shares in the Bank of Augusta. The rest of the property was divided among the other children —"born or to be born to my present wife"— and was to be given to them as they came of age. His final wish was that his children "be Well educated and decently maintained."[14]

Robert Toombs never really knew his father and probably had few real memories of him. But he always spoke of this distant figure with "the tenderest regard." Toombs' lifelong friend Alexander Stephens wrote years later: "His father's energy, enterprise, and honesty were the attributes that seemed to claim his strongest veneration." Robert Toombs may have inherited his business acumen and his eye for a deal from his father and his sense of duty and generosity from Catherine. But he seems to have gotten a wide streak of orneriness from Grandfather Gabriel.[15]

Runt was an energetic and mischievous kid. He was an excellent horseman and was fond of foxhunts. He once rode sixty miles and attended a dance that same night. Even as a boy, he loved to ride. He had a reputation for galloping through Washington, his auburn hair flying, one of his older brothers hanging on behind for dear life. If the town authorities complained, no one in his family noticed. His mother claimed that Robert "grew up almost without her knowledge, so little trouble had he given her."[16]

Catherine and hired tutors probably educated her brood in the three R's when they were small children. The minister of the local Presbyterian Church, Alexander Hamilton Webster, tutored young Robert. When he was twelve years old, Robert and brothers Gabriel and James were enrolled in the Wilkes County Academy. The academy was an old field school, so called because these schools usually sat in worn out fields that could no longer grow crops. Wilkes County Academy was one of the first schools chartered by the state legislature. It was sort of a private prep school for children of Georgia elite. The fine two-story building was constructed in 1797 and accommodated both the school and a church. If the school was typical of most southern academies, it offered curricula well beyond reading, writing, and 'rithmatic, emphasizing science and business. Perhaps this is where Toombs got hooked on literature. He had a passion for Shakespeare, Cervantes, ancient classics (especially Plato), and other literary works that stuck with him for the rest of his life. He usually could not resist sprinkling his speeches and letters with a literary or poetic fragment or two. He also had an acerbic literary wit. Milton was overrated because he was indecipherable in places, a friend once complained. Toombs said that was one Milton's greatest defects: "he was *blind*, and never learned to write for fools."[17]

After he graduated from Wilkes Academy, Catherine took Robert to Athens and enrolled him in Franklin College — the forerunner of the University of Georgia. Though the college had been chartered by the Georgia legislature in 1785, it took the board of governors sixteen years to actually authorize any buildings. The first facility was not erected until 1801. The site was chosen when one of the trustees, John Milledge, donated 633 acres he had purchased from a speculator named Daniel Easly. The school was named Franklin College after Benjamin Franklin.[18]

The college had nine buildings on thirty-seven fenced acres with over one hundred students by the time fourteen-year-old Robert Toombs arrived on campus. Franklin College became a success thanks mostly to the work of the college's third president, Moses Waddel. Waddel was a dour-faced minister from South Carolina who was appointed president in 1819. He was an intensely religious disciplinarian who especially disapproved of novels and dancing. He was known to peek out his windows with a spyglass to catch students sneaking away from campus.[19]

Washington Academy had prepared Toombs well for his oral entrance exams. He parsed his Cicero, Virgil, the Greek Testament. He passed his English exam and was "well acquainted with arithmetic." But after Franklin College accepted Robert Toombs as a student on July 31, 1824, the stolid old school would never quite be the same.[20]

Franklin College's curriculum was based on traditional studies of Latin, Greek, and mathematics. There were dollops of natural philosophy and weekly "forensic disputations," which were usually political or legal debates. Toombs lugged the standard textbooks around campus: Ruddiman's *Latin Grammar*, Pike's *Arithmetic*, perhaps most importantly, Duncan's *Logic* and Blair's *Rhetoric*. He attended mandatory prayer at sunrise. He said his Latin and Greek recitations until breakfast at nine o'clock. Recitations began again at ten and lasted until noon. After lunch was study hall from two until five. Freshmen and sophomores could read library books only in the library. Novels were strictly forbidden. The curriculum followed Yale's academic model but Franklin College was also a farmyard of political activity. It was taken for granted that the students were being groomed for political leadership. The rigors and discipline of student life were meant to prepare the pupils for the rough and tumble of Georgia politics.[21]

Toombs spent his freshman year quietly, probably because his mother stayed with him and "relieved him of the usual loneliness which overtakes a student." Why she left her other children in Washington is unknown. Perhaps young Robert was prone to mischief and she wanted to keep an eye on him. But she must have returned to Washington after the first year. During his sophomore year, the fifteen-year-old Toombs quickly earned a reputation for gambling, drinking, fighting, foul language, and other hell-raising that has been generously enhanced into legend.[22]

But maybe the pranks and misconduct were not entirely the young Toombs' fault. Athens was a typical college town of about a thousand permanent residents that was divided almost evenly between blacks and whites. But when school was in, the town filled up with frisky students full of adolescent energy and mischief. The college's prudential committee did its best to shield the kids from temptation. It forbade gambling and banned merchants from selling liquor near campus. But the town still had its corners of vice. As for the faculty, they regarded policing the students as an unpleasant waste of time that was not in their job description. All of that was just fine with young Robert Toombs. He was an indifferent student and more interested in opening a bottle than his textbooks. By May of 1825, he was boarding with L.A. Erwin in Athens while the Toombs estate was being charged for his room and board as well as his tavern bill.[23]

Toombs found his studies tedious. But he thrived in the Demosthenian Literary Society. Three juniors, James Jackson, Williams Rutherford and Augustus Clayton, are thought to have founded the Demosthenians on February 5, 1803. The society was named after the Greek orator Demosthenes and was formed for "the promotion of extemporizing, or extemporary speaking." The Demosthenes' arch rival, Phi Kappa, was founded by Joseph Henry Lumpkin in 1817. Both societies were dedicated to the art of debate and oratory.[24]

Almost every Franklin College student belonged to one of the debating societies. Membership was crucial if a young man wanted to make a reputation — sort of like joining a modern fraternity. Although there were no classes on Saturday, the college rules required students to stay in their rooms until noon if they were not a Demosthenian or a Phi Kappa. Each fraternity began its proceedings in its respective hall at nine o'clock on Saturday morning. There might be a break for lunch but a good debate could go late into the night. The meetings generally consisted of formal debates about philosophy, history, religion, and of course, politics. No record exists of the debates Toombs participated in. But the Demosthenians must have been formative in the rhetorical style that he used and became so famous for in the years to come.[25]

The Demosthenians kept Toombs busy, but he still found time to make trouble during his sophomore year. For some reason, two brothers named Junius and Granby Hillyer were both called "Bull" by the other students. Toombs apparently added a few "various shameful and obscene remarks" to their nickname. On September 16, Junius and Granby jumped Toombs and gave him a beating.

Toombs was enraged and he was not about to let go of an insult. A few days after the fight, he burst into the Hillyers' room. He hurled a heavy wash bowl at Granby. More seriously, he pointed a pistol at Junius. The gun may or may not have been loaded, but another student wrestled it away from him. A day or so later, Toombs tried to attack the Granby brothers with a knife in one hand and an axe in the other. Again, a student intervened. The next day, Toombs ambushed them with a club and another pistol. He apparently managed to get a few licks in on Junius before he was restrained. Despite brandishing an arsenal of weapons, Toombs never seriously hurt either of the Granby brothers. He may have been truly infuriated at them for the beating. Or he may have just been blustering, as he did so well later in his political life. Whatever he was trying to prove, it caused him serious trouble with school authorities.[26]

The faculty met on September 20 and expelled Toombs immediately. "Dismissed Toombs," Dr. Waddel wrote curtly in his diary. But the next day, Toombs sent a letter of apology acknowledging "the impropriety" of his conduct. The letter was also accompanied with a remarkable petition from both the Demosthenians and Phi Kappas. The petition asked that his expulsion be remitted or at least the punishment be mitigated. Somehow, this fifteen-year-old had politicked virtually the entire student body to prevent his being sent home. Reluctantly, perhaps, the university readmitted him. But the faculty put Toombs on probation for the rest of the term. The administration disapproved of students who "resort to weapons of a deadly nature." Even though he got away with it, the faculty warned the students not to behave like Toombs had or they would meet "the utmost disapprobation." Brandishing weapons was a crime "that will always be punished to the utmost extent of the law."[27]

There may have been some justification for Toombs' rampage. The same day they expelled Toombs, the faculty voted to have the Hillyers "publicly admonished" by President Waddel. The Hillyers were also put on probation and were to be dismissed immediately if they got into any more trouble. Later, the brothers were sentenced to three months in

Franklin College's Grammar School. This institution was initially opened to help remedial students who were unprepared for the rigors of college academics. But it quickly became an exile for troublemakers.[28]

There were a few other scrapes with college authorities. In 1825, President Waddel noted in his diary that he "spoke to Toombs about swearing." In September of 1827, Toombs and his roommate, William Rembert, were warned about "indulging in loud laughter and boisterous conversation in their room." They were told to be quiet but "upon admonition waxed worse and worse." The boys were fined two dollars apiece.[29]

Toombs took the Demosthenians Society's authority no more seriously than he did Franklin College's. He was fined numerous times for skipping tribunals, missing meetings, going out without permission, eating in the hall, and several times for disorder. He was also fined a dollar for "not accepting clerk's office," twenty-five cents for "reading in the hall," and twelve and a half cents for "being out too long." Toombs paid his fines in full.[30]

By 1828, Franklin College had as much as it could stand of Toombs. The first resolution the long-suffering faculty passed in their January meeting expelled the troublesome student. Toombs again submitted a letter asking the faculty to readmit him, thinking that if it worked the first time it would work again. But the half-hearted letter of apology had no sway. The faculty was fed up with his authority flouting, frat boy antics. They could do "nothing more in his case." But Toombs laughed them off. He already had other plans.[31]

Despite his escapades, Toombs is one of the university's favorite alumni. His student days are legendary. One story has a proctor discovering him as he is drinking and gambling with some friends. All of the students flee except for the inebriated Toombs who wobbily exclaims: "The guilty flee when no man pursueth, but the righteous are as bold as a lion!" In another story, Toombs was again caught gambling by an alert proctor. Before he could be reported, Toombs hurriedly ran to Dr. Waddel and asked for an honorable discharge from the college. Waddel scribbled the letter and sent Toombs on his way. Later that day, Dr. Waddel ran into Toombs who was still walking around on the campus.

"Robert Toombs," Waddel said, "you took advantage of me early this morning. I did not then know that you had been caught at the card table last evening."

Toombs puffed out his chest and arrogantly replied that Dr. Waddel was no longer addressing a student of Franklin College "but a free-born American citizen."[32]

Another tale that got better with every telling says that after Toombs achieved fame as a senator and orator, Franklin College offered him an honorary degree. Thanks but no thanks, Toombs replied. "When I was unknown and friendless, you sent me out disgraced, and refused me a diploma. Now that I would honor the degree I do not want it." This sounds like a smart aleck remark Toombs actually might have made. But the story is apocryphal. Even though he was expelled, he harbored no bitterness. In 1859, he was appointed to the board of trustees, served on it for twenty-five years, and often donated his time and money generously to the college.[33]

The most famous story of Toombs' outlandish college days is the legend of the Toombs Oak. In this story, Toombs was expelled just before his graduation in 1828. Supposedly, the vindictive student spent almost an entire year in Athens until graduation ceremonies began in August. Commencement was a special occasion in Athens. Proud parents, important alumni, and local and state dignitaries clattered onto the hot, dusty college campus. Horses, buggies, and fancy coaches brought hundreds of people to town for four days of music, speeches, eating, drinking, handshaking, and backslapping. The program was usually made up of juniors making their finest orations on the first day, the seniors speaking the next.

Then the best orator the college could find — usually a well-known politician — capped off the celebration with a grand commencement address.[34]

During the commencement for the class of 1828, speakers were delivering the most elaborate and eloquent rhetoric they could muster in the college chapel. Toombs took his revenge under an oak tree that stood only twenty yards from the front door. He piled up some old boxes, climbed onto the improvised rostrum, and began speaking. His speech was said to be so powerful, so persuasive, and so funny that the audience began to drift out of the chapel to hear what was going on. Everyone soon abandoned the chapel and gathered under the oak tree to hear this fabulous young orator. The tree was forever after known as the Toombs Oak. It is said that lightning struck the old tree the day Toombs died. It decayed throughout the 1890s until it collapsed. It was finally cut down in 1908.[35]

It is a good story, but it never happened. Listeners probably drifted in and out of the chapel all the time during commencements. The chapel was built in 1808, but after twenty years of neglect, it deteriorated into a shabby structure that had fallen into disrepair. By the time Toombs' speech was supposed to have lured the audience outside, "not half of the crowd could get into the chapel," one spectator wrote, "and not half of those succeeded in entering could hear the orators." A sundial was erected where the Toombs Oak stood in 1908 to commemorate the nonevent. Then a new historical marker was added in 1987 to mark the spot where Toombs never made one of his most famous speeches.[36]

By the time Franklin College expelled Robert Toombs, he was already a thousand miles away at Union College in Schenectady, New York. Union College was one of the oldest colleges in the state. Established in 1795, its name expressed its nondenominational charter and was a symbol of the unity of the new nation. In only thirty-five years, the institution had grown from a humble academy to the fourth largest college in the country. It trailed behind only Harvard, Yale, and Princeton. By the time Toombs enrolled in 1828, the college sat on a one hundred-acre site with North and South College buildings and attached colonnades. President Eliphat Nott saw to the rapid growth with unflagging energy and political influence.[37]

Nott was an outspoken advocate of liberal education. He minimized Union College's emphasis on the traditional curriculum of Latin and Greek classics. He favored instead history, science, modern languages, and mathematics. He was also lenient towards the student body. He encouraged and supported fraternities such as Kappa Alpha (1825), Sigma Phi (1827) and Delta Phi (1827). Yet Nott was every bit the disciplinarian that Franklin College's president Waddel was. "Not the least disorder is allowed in or about the edifice," he proclaimed proudly. He kept his students busy the entire week with collegiate and religious exercises. "On the [Sabbath] day no student goes from the yard except to church, and even then he walks with his professor in procession, sits with him, and with him returns. Perhaps no college has ever furnished such complete security to the manners and morals of youth."[38]

Students at Union College could choose between the classical or scientific curriculums. Seniors who took the classical course studied intellectual and natural philosophies, astronomy and two sessions of Hebrew. Those who opted for the scientific route took the same courses except Hebrew classes were replaced by anatomy and physiology or studying the law texts of Blackstone and James Kent's influential volumes, *Commentaries on American Law*. Physical education was also encouraged and students were "drilled, during play hours, by an experienced military officer." Students who did not want to participate in gym could devote "their hours of recreation to agricultural pursuits." The dress code was simple: a gray coat with a collar, gray pantaloons, and a gray overcoat "of domestic manufacture." To be accepted at Union College, students had to furnish "evidence of good moral character." Transfer students were also required to have "a regular dismission or letter of request."[39]

Seventeen-year-old Robert Toombs arrived on campus as a senior in the winter of 1827. He was one of twenty-eight transfer students from the South. How Toombs furnished evidence of good character is not known. Whoever was in charge of admissions was probably not aware of his record at Franklin College. But his rap sheet would have predicted little. Toombs opted for the scientific course so he could study law. He applied himself seriously and turned out to be a good student. He scored a poor sixty in botany, mineralogy, and technology, but got an eighty in Virgil, and a solid one hundred in his studies of Blackstone.[40]

He also joined the Delphian Institute Society. The Delphians were a fraternity similar to the Demosthenians at Franklin College, dedicated to debate and oratory. Students sympathetic to slavery formed the Delphians' in 1819 as a splinter group from the Philomathean Society. Obviously, the Delphians' pro-slavery sympathies attracted more Southern students than other fraternities on campus. Quartered in the anti-slavery North, Southern students who belonged to the Delphians were more tightly knit and secretive than other fraternities. Yet not all members were Southerners. Of the forty-eight Delphians in 1828, only twenty of them were from the South. Five were from Georgia, including Toombs' chum and fellow troublemaker from Franklin College, William Rembert. Though no legends followed from Toombs' stay at Union College, he was a gifted orator and was said to have "uncommon abilities of speech and reason."[41]

Toombs received his A.B. degree in July of 1828. He ranked third out of the 83 graduates in his class. He may have been pressured by his family to quit horsing around and earn a degree. Or perhaps the college's lenient attitude was more to his liking. Whatever the reason, Toombs applied himself and flourished under President Nott's regime. His expenses totaled $49.78, including six dollars for graduation fees, two dollars for commencement, forty dollars for tuition, and a three-cent fine for missing one of his orations. The regular tuition had been cut in half for Toombs. The economic depression that swept through the South in the 1820s depleted the Toombs' fortune; and there is some evidence that the estate had been mismanaged. In any case, Toombs was considered a "Charity Student" at Union College.[42]

Toombs started classes as a junior at the law school at the University of Virginia a month and a half later. The university was established at Charlottesville nine years earlier by the venerable Thomas Jefferson. Jefferson put his hand to everything from the architecture to the curriculum. The university finally opened its doors on March 7, 1825. Jefferson paid particular attention to establishing the law school. At the time, it was one of the few universities in the country that had a school of law.[43]

After considering a list of prominent men such as Francis Walker Gilmer and Attorney General William Wirt, Jefferson settled on John Tayloe Lomax of Fredericksburg to preside over the law school. Lomax was born in Virginia in 1781. He went to St. John's College, served as a commissioned officer in the War of 1812, then set up his law practice in Fredericksburg after the war was over. Although Jefferson was acquainted with the Lomax family, John Tayloe Lomax came to his attention through James Madison.[44]

Jefferson personally appointed Lomax dean of the law school in April of 1826. The salary was fifteen hundred dollars a year plus twenty-five to fifty dollars for every enrolled student. Lomax was to give a two-hour law lecture every other day during the ten and a half month session. Jefferson also reminded Lomax that there was some urgency in opening the law school for "several students have left and others contemplate leaving us." Lomax took up his duties on July 5, 1826, the day after Jefferson died.[45]

At a time when most professors taught solely through lecture, Lomax assigned his students to read Blackstone, Kent, and lesser known works in the law. Professor Lomax realized no law school could "form a complete lawyer." But he believed his course would "enable the student with proper dilligence to acquire a valuable fund of information upon the subjects of ... jurisprudence, and to supply himself with facilities for making further advances."[46]

Tuition for the law school was sixty dollars, in cash, in advance. The curriculum consisted of Professor Lomax's assigned exercises from the law texts while he supplied explanations "as will best illustrate the subject in hand." Professor Lomax must have been a tough teacher. But he also had a dissident streak that a twenty-year-old like Toombs could admire. Toombs thought so much of his old professor that some twenty-five years later, when he filled out an alumni form for Union College's alumni catalogue, he mentioned he "studied under Judge Lomax."[47]

Like most educational institutions, discipline at the University of Virginia was a problem. Jefferson had drawn up a lenient code of conduct for his students. But he naively expected them to behave like gentlemen anyway. Many professors, though, were as bad as the students. They ignored rules they did not want to enforce. They neglected calling the roll or reporting absences. The local hotelkeepers were also sometimes forced to conspire with the students in making mischief. If the students were not pleased, they could always find somewhere else to stay.[48]

Toombs more or less behaved himself, but he managed to get into some trouble with school authorities. On January 1, 1829, the faculty reported that Toombs and several students "had on various occasions violated the enactments with regard to wearing uniforms." University regulations required students to wear a "coat, waistcoat & pantaloons of cloth of a dark gray mixture at a price not exceeding $6. per yard." Students had to wear this outfit on the Sabbath, during examinations, at "public exhibitions in the University," and "whenever they appear without [the university's] precincts."

The faculty censured a few of the students for violating the dress code. But Toombs was not one of them. However, at one faculty meeting, Professor Lomax protested the school's authority to enforce these rules. He argued that the dress code could not be enforced because the requirements were too vague. Students had no way of knowing whether it was to be interpreted as "a recommendation, permission, or as compulsory."[49]

In early February, an epidemic swept through the campus. One student died of "typhus fever" and nine others were sick. Forty-four students left and eighteen more vacated the dorms. Out of 117 students, almost two-thirds of them were sick or leaving. The "ordinary exercises of the schools of the university" were suspended until March 5 and the remaining students were permitted to temporarily withdraw. The administrators urged the professors to aid and advise the remaining students as much as possible, but academic life had effectively stopped. Toombs probably fled with other students. He may have returned to Georgia or he might have stayed with relatives in nearby Caroline County. But he was back on campus a few months later.[50]

That summer, Toombs' name came up in a boisterous incident. On the night of June 24, some tipsy students were returning from a rowdy party in Charlottesville. A member of the faculty named Dr. Harrison complained that the students made "a disturbing noise" and one of the drinkers called Toombs' name. Dr. Harrison investigated the commotion and found a student named Mr. Carr "apparently intoxicated." Later, around midnight, there was a knock on the professor's cellar door and he heard "indecent propositions made to a female servant." The faculty met the next day to discuss the incident. Several students were directly questioned. Toombs was not interrogated, but Carr was immediately dismissed from the university.[51]

Robert Toombs graduated from the School of Law at the University of Virginia at the end of the term. He was fourteenth in his graduating class, tied for last place. Out of a possible score of 310, he got a dismal seventy-seven.[52]

Still, he was armed with a law degree and a lot of ambition. He went home to Georgia and immediately tried to establish himself as a lawyer. At the time, becoming an attorney was based as much on social connections as ability. An aspiring lawyer would usually apprentice with an established attorney who agreed to take him on. The law student did everything from sweeping floors or running errands to writing briefs or assisting in cases. Sometimes there was a bit of directed reading or a law lecture in between chores. But the impatient Toombs had been to law school and he wanted to get started. Somehow — probably through connections with the Cobb family — the nineteen-year old got his name on a list of young men petitioning the Georgia Senate for admission to the bar. Despite the fact that state law required an attorney to be at least twenty-one years old, the act was passed on December 19, 1829. The same day, Toombs petitioned the Elbert County Superior Court for a license to practice law.[53]

In March of 1830, the youngster took the bar exam. William H. Crawford, who had been a congressman, senator, secretary of war under James Madison, secretary of the treasury under James Monroe, and a leading presidential contender in 1824, was spending his retirement as the Northern Circuit Superior Court judge. The solicitor general of the Northern Circuit, Frank Hardeman, administered the oral exam. They grilled the young man about basic precepts of the law. His application to the bench was approved on March 17, 1830, and Toombs took his oath. His law license was issued the next day and signed by Judge Crawford.[54]

Toombs set up his own law practice in Washington, Georgia. He picked up cases where he could and began riding the Northern Circuit around Wilkes, Columbia, Greene, Elbert, Franklin, and Oglethorpe counties. Georgia's ten circuits were divided into a superior court administered by one judge and inferior courts administered by five judges. Court sessions took place twice a year in adjacent counties and lasted five days each. The Northern Circuit was filled with particularly hungry and ambitious young lawyers who were out to make names for themselves in state and national politics. Competition was stiff and fools were quickly devoured by the likes of Charles Jenkins, Joseph Henry Lumpkin, Frances H. Cone, Alexander Stephens, and Howell Cobb.[55]

At first, Toombs' legal career appeared about as promising as his motley academic career had been. Older and more experienced lawyers considered him an inept slacker. One attorney recalled that Toombs was lazy about his law practice during his first four or five years. Despite this, a few old hands saw something promising in the kid. Prominent attorneys such as Francis Cone and Frank Hardeman took pains to make sure that Toombs served as their junior in important cases. Judge William H. Crawford saw to it that cases Toombs was working on were on his docket. Toombs "reached excellence in law" one biographer wrote "by slow degrees of toil." But he was being mentored by and apprenticing under some of the best legal and political talent in Georgia.[56]

Still, at first, Toombs was disorganized in the courtroom and did not know how to plead before a jury. "In his first forensic arguments his rapid utterance was as indistinct as if he had mush in his mouth," a friend wrote years later. Then Toombs learned how to bring the same oratory talents he displayed in college to the courtroom. "After a year or two of practice he developed both power and attractiveness," the writer recalled.[57]

Toombs worked hard and rapidly learned the legal system through on-the-job training. He was known as a quick study who had an intuitive ability to immediately absorb and analyze large bulks of material. As he matured, he got a reputation for finding the key legal point in the debris of any judicial argument. He had a "lightning-like perception" of the strong and weak points in a case. He also took great pride in being a member of the legal profession. Whenever he was asked to identify his occupation — in answering the census for instance — he never described himself as a planter or congressman or U.S. senator. His answer was simply "attorney at law." Within a few years, he was one of Georgia's most talented and highly paid legal talents. By the 1870s, it was rumored that he would not touch a case for less than five thousand dollars.[58]

Alexander Stephens said that, contrary to popular opinion, Toombs always prepared thoroughly for legal cases, speeches, or political debates. "He has always been a close and hard student," Stephens recalled from Fort Warren prison years later. "He can acquire more in less time than any one I ever saw," Stephens said. Whether he was reading a report, a novel, or the classics, Toombs could seize the ideas, "gleaning the vital part from the general verbiage by a process rapid as intuition." Another lawyer stated that Toombs gave "diligent attention" to "every detail of preparation of his cases." Someone else said more bluntly that Toombs could "strip a case of its toggery and go right for its vitals." While an average Georgia lawyer's salary was about three thousand dollars a year, within ten years Toombs was pulling down a remarkable five thousand dollars per session from his cases in Elbert County alone.[59]

On the other hand, Toombs had a nimble wit and knew how to improvise. One of Toombs' neighbors claimed that one time when Toombs was on the circuit, he tore his pants. "The way he mended them was remarkable," the neighbor wrote. Toombs "*inked* his drawers, which answered every purpose."[60]

The young attorney rode up and down the circuit, traveling back and forth over the dusty roads of Georgia, law books and legal briefs in his saddlebags. He built his practice slowly and put up at hotels, taverns, and inns of varying quality with his fellow lawyers. He litigated squabbles over debts, property disputes, drew up land deeds for buyers and sellers, wrote up mercantile partnerships, and liquidated estates. Toombs also began establishing a reputation as a sarcastic individualist who went his own way when it pleased him. Once, a ruthless client asked Toombs if he could win his case in court. Toombs replied, "Yes, you can recover the suit, but you ought not to do so. This is a case in which law and justice are on opposite sides."

When the client insisted on pursuing the case anyway, Toombs told him to hire someone else for his "damned rascality."[61]

Another time, one of Toombs' colleagues called him aside. What should I charge my client? he asked Toombs. "Well," Toombs said, having heard the lawyer plead the case, "I should have charged a thousand dollars; but you ought to have five thousand, for you did a great many things I could not have done."[62]

Toombs' quickly shed the disjointed ramblings that cost him cases in his early years. One of Toombs' colleagues recalled a murder case that took place in 1837. During the trial, an inexperienced defense lawyer bungled his case so badly that the crowd in the courtroom started heckling him. It was his first case and the young attorney got so flustered that he could only ramble and blabber during his summation. The crowd howled down the novice and started calling for a conviction.

Amid the shouting and yelling and jeering, Toombs sauntered to the edge of the jury box. He held up his hand for quiet. Then he scolded the mob as "bloodhounds eager to slake their accursed thirst in innocent blood." He rebuked them for their vindictiveness and "brought them back to their proper behavior." Then Toombs handed the jury back to the defense lawyer. The accused was acquitted. The story may be apocryphal, but Toombs' oratory talents are not.[63]

Toombs also knew when a minimal defense could win. During a case in which a widow's inheritance was disputed, Toombs rose before the judge. "May it please your honor," he said, "seizing, marriage, death, dower" and sat down. There was a burst of laughter in the courtroom as the gavel fell. Toombs won the case.[64]

While he was riding the circuit and building his law practice, Toombs fell in love with Martha Julianna DuBose. The DuBose family were Huguenots who came to South Carolina in the 1600s and had drifted into Georgia over the years. Julia's father, Dr. Ezekiel DuBose, was a wealthy planter who served in South Carolina's House of Representatives for over twenty years before briefly being elected to the state senate. In 1811, he settled in Lincoln County, Georgia, and lived there until his death in December of 1819.[65]

Julianna, or Julia as she was called, was the eighth of eleven children. Born on May 15, 1813, in Lincoln County, Georgia, she was the youngest female in the family. Like her future husband, she was reared in a world of Southern privilege. But unlike him, she grew up around men constantly seeking elective offices and political favors. She observed and learned from the wives who collaborated with them. Julia was no naïf when it came to politics. She was not considered a great beauty but it was said that no one could forget her dark, liquid eyes when they met her. Toombs and Julia were also related through marriage: Toombs' half-brother, Lawrence Catlett Toombs, had married Julia's sister Elizabeth Harriet DuBose in 1826. Robert and Julia Toombs were married on November 18, 1830. He was twenty. She was seventeen.[66]

People who knew Julia said she was benevolent, pious, and serious. She thrived in the social whirl of political wives. She entertained lavishly and graciously and was utterly devoted to her husband, children, and extended family. But Julia had a catty side. Mary Chesnut noted in her diary that Julia called a party President Buchanan gave for members of Congress in 1861 "excretable." She detested the wife of Texas congressman John Henninger Reagan and made fun of her for her lack of polish and education. And when Jefferson Davis fell ill in August of 1861, Julia insisted he was faking and pronounced it "humbug."[67]

Above all, Julia was a capable and savvy woman. Toombs depended on her to advise him and to manage financial and plantation matters since he had to be away from home so often. She must have also been a strong, patient, and self-possessed woman to put up with the rambunctious and occasionally crude Toombs during their forty-three-year marriage. Julia was there when he needed someone to confide in and someone to complain to since he often found himself surrounded by people he considered fools — which was most of the time.

For his part, Toombs absolutely adored her. He loved her as deeply as any man ever loved a woman. "I know for whatever success in life I may have had, whatever evil I may have avoided, or whatever good I may have done," he wrote her on her fortieth birthday, "I am mainly indebted to the beautiful, pure, true-hearted little black-eyed girl, who on the 18 of November, 1830, came trustingly to my arms, the sweetest and dearest of wives."[68]

When he was not courting Julia, Toombs rode the circuit where he met men who became valuable business and political connections. His colleagues were some of the most talented and ambitious men in Georgia. Charles J. Jenkins, George W. Crawford, Howell

Cobb, Herschel Johnson, and Toombs all embarked on their legal and political careers at about the same time. He also worked with some of his college cronies such as Joseph Henry Lumpkin and the same Junius Hillyer he had terrorized at Franklin College. All were rising stars in Georgia politics.

One of these important men was Alexander Stephens. Toombs and Stephens did not meet until they were in their mid-twenties. But Stephens had followed in Toombs' footsteps like a younger brother. Stephens was two years younger than Toombs, born on February 12, 1812, near Crawfordville in Taliaferro County. Stephens lost his mother a few months after his birth. His father died in the spring of 1826 and his stepmother a few weeks later. Stephens was an orphan three times over by the time he was fourteen years old. He was sent to live with his uncle until 1827 when he was enrolled at Toombs' old alma mater, the Wilkes County Academy. While there, Stephens stayed with Toombs' old tutor, Alexander Hamilton Webster.

Stephens suffered another loss when Webster, who became his benefactor and mentor, died in early 1828. With the financial help of the Georgia Education Society he enrolled in Franklin College that summer, just six months after Toombs was expelled. At first, Stephens studied for the ministry. But he was not sure if he truly had the calling. Unlike Toombs, Stephens was a model student. His grades were always excellent and he did not get a single fine or demerit during his four years at Franklin College. But instead of joining the Demosthenians, Stephens joined the Phi Kappas and was elected president of the society twice. Maybe the verbal jousts called him to politics instead of the pulpit. At any rate, Stephens likely heard stories about Toombs' antics. Stephens graduated in 1832 and spent several months teaching and tutoring before returning to Crawfordville to study law. He passed his bar exam on July 22, 1834, and signed up to ride the same circuit as Toombs, litigating cases in Wilkes, Columbia, Greene, Elbert, Franklin, and Oglethorpe counties.[69]

Stephens vividly recalled the first time he saw Robert Toombs. It was his first day in the Washington Courthouse in Wilkes County. He had been a circuit lawyer for exactly one week. Although they had never met, Stephens must have known Toombs by his reputation. "Toombs was at court the first time I was admitted: I was not introduced to him, however." A week later, they got to know each other although Stephens did not remember the exact circumstances. The acquaintance "soon grew into intimacy" and before long they were riding the circuit together, partnering on law cases, sharing rooms on the road, and investing in business deals. Toombs often looked after his friend's affairs when Stephens was away. In 1838, Toombs even loaned Stephens money for a trip to Florida for his health. "Our personal relations have never been interrupted from the first day of our acquaintance," Stephens recalled many years later.[70]

It was a very unlikely friendship. Toombs and Stephens could not have been more opposite in temperaments or natures. Stephens was frail and gloomy, a melancholy hypochondriac obsessed with death. He never married, was prone to long spells of brooding, and was as morbid as an undertaker. One biographer called him a "child of despair." Toombs said that Stephens "never looked as if he had two weeks' purchase on life." On the other hand, Toombs was robust, profane, and lived as if he were a force of nature. He enjoyed his family life and his worldly pleasures: good wine (sometimes too much), good cigars, telling a ribald tale, and the gregarious, convivial world of politics. But Toombs and Stephens fit together like a fist in a glove. Toombs loved Stephens with an almost "pathetic tenderness," Jefferson Davis' wife wrote years later, "and, in all matters of importance, Mr. Toombs came up, in the end, on Mr. Stephens' side."[71]

Whatever mysterious forces attract and bind life-long friendships can never be understood or fully explained. But Toombs and Stephens may have seen something in the other that each one lacked, a case of the whole being bigger than two parts. As different as they were, they had great respect for each other's talents and gifts. And they genuinely liked each other's company. But part of what glued their friendship together was similar social and political philosophies. Both were arrogant about their intellect, though Stephens was more vain about his intellectual snobbery and rectitude; Toombs simply scoffed at those he considered beneath him or dismissed them with a snide remark. Socially, they were both on the road to becoming wealthy planters. Professionally, they were both extremely ambitious. Politically, they both aligned with their state's interests — whatever they happened to be — and never ceased fighting political battles for Georgia before or after the Civil War. Their friendship lasted for over fifty years.

In 1836, war flared up on Georgia's borders. Georgians and Native Americans had clashed for generations. But ultimately, the Native Americans were pushed farther and farther south as whites encroached on their land. Many Native Americans gave up their hunting traditions and established prosperous farms and plantations in northern Florida. But a series of deceitful and callous treaties first confined them to reservations and then removed them from their homes entirely. The Treaty of Moultrie Creek in 1823 restricted them to the southern interior of the Florida Peninsula; then the Indian Removal Act of 1830 removed them to the west. Finally, the Treaty of Payne's Landing signed in 1832 gave the Seminoles three years to leave Florida altogether.

In Alabama, the Creek Nation was also threatened with removal. They knew of the Seminoles' plight and attempted to march east to unite with them and possibly drive the whites out of the area — or at least convince the federal government that removal would not be worth the carnage. The resisters, led by Seminole chief Osceola, began a guerilla war that reached from Florida across the entire southern half of Georgia into Alabama.

In western Georgia, there had been an escalating series of attacks and counterattacks between the Creeks and the Muscogee County militia around Columbus on the Georgia-Alabama border. In May, the Creeks rampaged across that area and attacked a ferry and a mail coach. The state was in an uproar. "The wild savage, frenzied by the smell of blood in its nostrils, is prowling the wilderness," shrieked the Columbus *Herald*, "skulking around plantations leveling the deadly rifle at the breast of the white man, scalping the unoffending wife and mother and beheading the innocent and unsuspecting babe!" The Macon *Messenger* squalled that the "Creek Indians ... are all in arms and killing every white person they have fallen in with." The Columbus *Enquirer* gave lurid accounts of Indians "scouring the country in all directions from their hiding place, or headquarters, indiscriminately butchering our neighbors, men, women, and children, plundering their houses, destroying their stock, and laying waste to their farms."[72]

The conflict became so bad that Governor William Schley issued a general order pleading for volunteers from all over the state. He called for three battalions of militia to serve for three months to protect settlers from the "tomahawk and scalping knife." The day after Governor Schley issued his proclamation, three hundred Creek Indians burned the small village of Roanoke and slaughtered most of its men, women and children.[73]

All of this was too much for Robert Toombs. He had no military experience except for brief musters in his local militia called the Washington Guards. These annual musters were a combination of amateur military maneuvers, county fair, political rally, and parades. The local "soldiers" would commence their "drills," shouting "Shoulder — Arms!" and march around awhile. Afterwards, there would be auctions, barbecues, horse races, wrestling matches, shooting contests, and the unavoidable stump speeches. It was hardly rigorous military training.[74]

Still, Toombs volunteered for service with the Washington Guards. Sixty men from Wilkes and Lincoln counties composed the militia. On May 31, they elected Toombs captain. The militia mustered in on June 5 and was put under the command of Colonel William Porter's 1st Georgia Volunteers.[75]

The Washington Guards arrived in Columbus in early June. None other than General Winfield Scott, who was stationed in Columbus, commanded the volunteers and a few token federal forces. "One third of the Georgia troops at least were without supplies," one of the local newspapers reported, but Scott outfitted them with plenty of rations when they arrived. Scott intended to carry out a carefully choreographed offensive using Georgia and Alabama troops to attack Creek camps from the south and east. This would cut off the Creeks' chance to rendezvous with the Seminoles in Florida. But before Scott could execute his plan, General Thomas Jessup routed the Creeks at Big Spring on June 15. Three hundred warriors were captured along with their chief, Eneah Mathla.[76]

Although the Second Seminole War lasted another six years, Jessup's victory ended most of the hostilities in Georgia. It also ended Toombs' military career for the next twenty-five years. In a public letter, Scott praised the Georgia volunteers with the "highest approbation." Although some of the Georgians were inactive "for the want of arms," Scott gave credit where credit was due, especially to the detachments that were "ready to oppose an obstinate resistance to superior [Creek] numbers." Whether the Washington Guards were in battle or directly commanded by General Scott or even saw any Indians is unknown. Toombs' men may have been assigned to simply camp somewhere on the Chattahoochie River to make sure no Creeks got into Florida. The Washington Guards probably mustered out as scheduled on 12 July and headed home. But the experience gave Toombs bragging rights as a genuine Indian fighter.[77]

Despite his beginnings as a lackluster student and his early days as an underachiever at the bar, his reputation as a successful lawyer was growing. He had the appropriate political views as far as important politicians were concerned. And now he had the requisite military experience required for a Southern politician. He was, by Georgia political standards, a young man on the move.

2

Milledgeville

In the early 1830s, political parties in Georgia had only a limited formal structure. They were not much more than casual alliances of cronies who had competing local, political, and financial interests. That legacy was handed down by two political heavyweights from Georgia, John Clark and George M. Troup. John Clark was born in 1766 and fought in the Revolution when he was a teenager. After several military exploits with the Georgia militia, he served in the Georgia House and then was elected governor twice in the early 1820s. Clark's political followers were generally small farmers, trappers, and working people who lived on the unsettled northern and western Georgia frontier where towns and wealthy slaveholders were rare.

Clark's rival, George Michael Troup, was from a well-known if not-well-off family. Troup was born in 1780, educated at Princeton, and became a successful lawyer in Savannah. He had a long political pedigree, serving as a state legislator, congressman, and senator before winning a series of terms as governor, succeeding John Clark in the late 1820s. As governor, Troup was a reformer and, unlike Clark, backed publicly financed education and internal improvements. Troup's partisans lived mostly in Middle Georgia and along the coast where the political culture was more urban and more sensitive to agribusiness and commerce.

Georgia's town-versus-country political heritage also grew out of the remnants of the old Democratic-Republican Party. The Democratic-Republican Party claimed the mantle of Jefferson; but it was actually created by James Madison. The party dominated national politics until the 1820s. The members preached states rights, a weak central government, and were opposed to a national bank. But the War of 1812 split the party in two. The Old Republican faction adhered to Jefferson's principles: an agrarian economy, a weak federal government, and strict interpretations of the Constitution. The nationalist faction advocated a strong central government, a hefty military, and high tariffs to protect American manufacturers. In Georgia, both sides wrestled in annual elections for seats in the state legislature. Clark's faction clung to Jefferson's Old Republican ideals; the Troupites more or less advocated the nationalist program. They were also dedicated opponents of John Clark and Andrew Jackson. On November 13, 1832, the Troup Party adopted the official sounding name of State Rights Party.[1]

Georgia remained fairly immune to national issues until South Carolina nullified the Tariff of Abominations in 1832. These tariffs had put high fees on iron, British wool, distilled liquor and foreign manufactured goods. Consumer items were usually expensive in the South since there was not much industrialization. The tariffs increased the price for Southerners who wanted to wear fancy clothes and drink fine whiskey.

Jackson's vice president, John C. Calhoun, led the revolt. He urged his home state of South Carolina to declare the tariffs null and void and to simply ignore them. "Distempered brains of disappointed ambitious men," President Andrew Jackson snorted about the "nullies." When Jackson threatened to use force to collect the tariff, he set off a firestorm throughout the South.[2]

Almost overnight, Jackson changed from a hero to a "hypocrite, usurper, and tyrant — the most daring, reckless and dangerous of usurpers — and the most self-willed, heartless and bloody of tyrants." The South Carolina legislature responded to Jackson's Force Bill by threatening to leave the Union if Jackson used coercion. In the end, Congress passed the Force Bill anyway but pacified South Carolina with a law that gradually reduced the duties on textiles.[3]

In Georgia, the nullification crisis forced the State Rights Party into a peculiar balancing act. Most Georgians were nauseated at the tariff and Jackson's heavy-handed threats. But they had no desire to follow South Carolina out of the Union. However, State Rights politicians were still guilty by association. One of their stars, John M. Berrien, was Jackson's attorney general. Berrien, a prosperous lawyer and rice planter from Savannah, denounced the tariff while at the same time keeping his distance from nullification. State Rights leaders had to explain over and over that opposing the tariff was not the same as nullification. The Clarkites, now calling themselves the Union Party, depicted their State Rights opponents as disloyal nullifiers who were anxious to commit treason over a few dollars.[4]

Robert Toombs cast his first national vote for Andrew Jackson in 1832. But like so many Georgians, he soured on Old Hickory after the nullification crisis. He rode the circuit and tended his law cases, made the occasional stump speech and mingled with important State Rights Party officials. By 1834, he was probably helping organize State Rights Party activities in Wilkes County and even on the state level. Toombs was only twenty four years old. Still, he had been groomed for leadership. He was slowly being initiated into politics.[5]

The reason Toombs was attracted to the State Rights Party was no mystery. His resume closely resembled those of men like Charles Jenkins, George W. Crawford, Alexander Stephens, Stephens' half brother Linton, and other bright young promising Georgians. Many of these future State Rights stars were educated in the North. Most of them were lawyers and on their way to becoming affluent planters. These men were blessed in their own way with a gift for words and they knew how to use them. They were calculating and shrewd, each dedicated to a vision of what the South was and could become. Most State Rights men worshipped the past. They considered themselves the intellectuals and nobility of their political and social world. Like most of his colleagues, Toombs was smart, well read, at times eloquent, and he was not shy about flaunting it.

State Rights members believed one of the reasons state government existed was to encourage business, commerce, education, and internal improvements. They scoffed at the Union Party's *laissez-faire* attitudes. State Rights politicians carefully designed their rhetoric to attract common folk. Yet their policies usually appealed to merchants, professionals, bankers, and prosperous planters. State Rights men were appalled at Andrew Jackson's followers. They trusted state government but distrusted political parties. Thomas Jefferson once divided men into two kinds of political animals: the first distrusted the people and thought power was best in the hands of the higher classes. The other, he said, had confidence in voters' honesty and good judgment. Toombs and the State Rights Party generally agreed more with the first part of Jefferson's statement than with the second. So throughout his long life, Toombs usually found himself and his party in the minority, an "outsider as insider," one historian called him.[6]

Toombs went to Georgia's very first State Rights convention in June of 1835 as a delegate from Wilkes County. It was his first formal venture in state politics. The convention selected fiery judge Charles Dougherty for governor. Only 34 years old, Dougherty had been a successful lawyer in Athens before he was elected as the judge for the Western Circuit. The convention also nominated George Rockingham Gilmer for an open seat in Congress. Gilmer had served several times in the Georgia legislature, had been elected four times to the House of Representatives and was governor from 1829 until 1832. He was best known for forcing the Cherokee Nation onto the long Trail of Tears.

The convention passed a slate of resolutions. One reassured voters who were still nervous about South Carolina's secession threats that the party was devoted to "preservation of the Union, and the sovereignty of these States — to the perpetuation of American liberty — to the vindication of the constitution." The convention also endorsed Tennessee's Hugh Lawson White for president.

Unfortunately for the State Rights Party, Charles Doughtery and George Gilmer both failed to realize national issues were encroaching on Georgia's provincial politics. The Union Party raised the specter of nullification against their State Rights opponents. State Rights men tried to paint Union Party candidates as minions of the unpopular Andrew Jackson. But Dougherty lost the governor's race to William Schley by two thousand votes and the State Rights Party was hopelessly defeated for seats in the state legislature and U.S. Congress.[7]

As the presidential election of 1836 approached, the Democrats settled for Andrew Jackson's vice president, Martin Van Buren. The recently formed Whig coalition was leery of national parties, so it put three regional candidates on the ticket: Daniel Webster in the North, William Henry Harrison in the West, and Hugh Lawson White in the South. Born in 1773, White had been a popular judge in Tennessee, served in the Georgia Senate, and had been a United States district attorney. He was elected to the U.S. Senate in 1825 as a Jackson Democrat but broke with Jackson over political patronage. White was moderate when it came to state's rights. But he won the South's support with his outspoken dislike for Martin Van Buren.

The Whigs hoped to throw the election into the House of Representatives with their three separate candidates. With some luck and lots of political arm twisting they thought they might squeeze out a victory. In Georgia, the Union Party aligned with the national Democrats. But the State Rights Party still kept its distance from the Whigs. While there was little difference between the two state parties on some matters — almost everyone agreed about slavery and keeping the tariffs high — both sides fought a vicious campaign over encroaching federalism and local issues such as how to pay for internal improvements and where to spend state revenue.

As national issues intruded, Georgia moved away from the politics of personality. But that did not protect the candidates from personal attacks. Democrats accused Hugh Lawson White of being a lawyer for several abolitionist organizations, called him a traitor because of his break with Jackson, and it was said that he had escorted a black woman to the polls in Knoxville, Tennessee. Whigs and the State Rights Party called Van Buren an aristocrat, a political intriguer, an abolitionist, and spread rumors that he would let black men vote.[8]

On election day, Georgia overwhelmingly picked Hugh Lawson White for president. But Van Buren carried the national ticket by 170 electoral votes. Georgia's State Rights candidates did a little better than in past elections. They managed to win a congressional seat when William C. Dawson replaced the deceased John Coffee. But the State Rights Party was still in the minority in the Georgia Assembly. If there was any consolation, they lost the election by 3500 fewer votes than the year before. The slight gains indicated to some party leaders that political success was to be found by shunning alliances with national parties and concentrating on local concerns. Others thought partnering with the Whig Party or other anti–Democratic organizations was the way to go. It was an argument Whigs never fully resolved and it helped spell disaster for the party twenty years later.[9]

The election gave the Georgia legislature one important new member. Alexander Stephens won the seat from Taliaferro County. Stephens' first effort in the legislature established him as one of the bright young stars in Georgia politics. Georgia had struggled to build a decent transportation system for years. In 1826, a state committee known as the Board of Public Works tossed aside plans to build a series of roads and canals and recommended a network of railroads instead. Governor Wilson Lumpkin loved the idea. He envisioned a mesh of railroads tying Georgia together as well as connecting it with the rest of the country. He thought the state should finance a vast "trunkline"—or the "great snout" as its opponents derisively called it—that private railroad companies could patch into with local and branch lines.

This proposed railroad was to start at the Tennessee border near Rossville and intersect with branch lines to Athens, Milledgeville, and other destinations. Both political parties favored railroad schemes. The argument centered on who would pay the monumental costs: taxpayers or businessmen. Union Party members and Democrats thought railroading was best left to the private sector. State Rights men believed it should be built by state funds.[10]

As usual, the legislature debated the issue incessantly. But then the chamber turned to listen to a cadaverously thin young man with a high shrill voice. Yes, the initial four million dollar investment might be a burden to the state coffers, Stephens agreed. But millions more tax dollars would be brought in since property values along the line would soar. The state, he said, was guaranteed at least three hundred thousand dollars a year in revenue.

Stephens was through speaking half an hour later. When he finished, politicians in the chamber enthusiastically applauded the strange looking young legislator. They could already hear the coins clinking as they fell into the treasury. Stephens made his reputation that day. The bill that finally passed established the Western and Atlantic Railroad and pulled all the other railroad companies together that were already constructing lines or vying for state contracts. It also authorized the companies to receive state funds which naturally increased the value of company stocks. Stephens was given much of the credit for the bill's success. But it was no accident that he was one of its most ardent proponents. Stephen's mentor, Dr. Thomas Foster, was a stockholder in the Georgia Rail Road and Banking Company, and Stephens' best friend, Robert Toombs, was one of the board's commissioners.[11]

By now, Robert Toombs' prospects were extremely bright. His law practice, business interests, and land holdings were prospering. And his family was growing. His first daughter, Mary Louisa (Lou) was born in 1834. Two years later, Sarah (Sallie) joined the family. In January of 1837, he purchased a house and 136 acres in Washington, Georgia, for five thousand dollars. The house had been built in 1797 by Dr. Joel Abbott. Dr. Abbott was a prominent resident of Washington who had served in the state legislature and four terms in Congress before passing away in 1826. To buy the house, Toombs apparently liquidated much of his other land holdings and sold off many of his slaves a year or two before. But by 1837 he had moved Julia, Lou, and Sallie and most of his fifty-three slaves into his stately new home.[12]

Like a lot of young Southern lawyers and planters, Toombs set out for a seat in the state legislature. Charles J. Jenkins, who was also a Union College alumni and went on to a long career in the state legislature before becoming speaker of the Georgia House, had held office there for a few years. John B. Lamar, who would later go on to serve in Congress, was also preparing for a run at the Georgia legislature. And his best friend, Alexander Stephens, was already running for a second term as the representative from Taliaferro County. Toombs' friends may have talked him into running for office or he may have heard the call on his own. Whatever the case, Toombs was elected as a delegate to the State Rights convention from Wilkes County. In May, he traveled to the convention in Milledgeville.[13]

The convention met just as the country was plunging into the Panic of 1837. It was the worst economic crisis the nation had ever experienced. In 1833, Andrew Jackson destroyed the Second Bank of the United States by vetoing its re-charter. When the U.S. Bank closed its doors, the federal government's funds were distributed to other banks throughout the country. Local bankers were suddenly swimming in federal money. Many of them recklessly gambled their new riches on land speculation, internal improvement schemes, and assorted wild investments. The country rode a wave of artificial prosperity. Then Jackson issued the Specie Circular, an executive order requiring federal land offices to accept only gold or silver and not bank script (paper money issued by banks). Although the federal government did not issue paper money, local and state banks did, usually distributing more script than the gold or silver in their vaults could back.

Most of the boom was fueled by bank script. When the economy contracted, thanks in part to Jackson's executive order, financial institutions came up short. Their vaults quickly emptied when customers wanted to exchange bank notes for gold or silver. Banks, in turn, tried to collect loans from merchants and farmers and businessmen who could not pay. Businesses went bust. Farms were liquidated. Banks across the country stopped issuing script or closed their doors.[14]

In the South, much of the prosperity was based on a mirage anyway. The cotton economy was fueled by credit and rampant land speculation that was often little more than a game of chance. During the panic, money tightened. Internal improvement projects were cancelled or went broke. Deflation swept the region. Cotton proctors who once paid exorbitant prices for a bale of cotton refused to extend any more credit. Farmers and planters had to sell off land or equipment or other assets to pay expenses. Slaves that sold for fifteen hundred dollars before the panic brought only two hundred dollars afterwards.[15]

Georgia did not suffer as much as some places in the South. Though the state was somewhat insulated from the ravages of the panic, it still hurt the economy badly. In April of 1837, there were 36 banks operating in the Georgia; by the end of May, only seventeen remained open. By the end of that summer, the Central Bank of Georgia was the only institution still paying out funds.

The Central Bank was a bold but short-lived experiment. The Georgia legislature set it up in 1828 as a state-owned corporation. The bank was authorized to disburse funds, receive taxes and other state revenue, issue script, exchange specie, and make and collect small business and agricultural loans. The authorities hoped it would stabilize the currency and somehow generate significant additional funds for the government. The Central Bank was not just a state-run savings and loan; it was a sort of secondary state treasury.[16]

The bank was controlled by three directors appointed annually by the governor. Bank officials could not borrow money from the bank, could not do business with each other, and could not be officers at other banks. Like all banks in the state, the Central Bank of Georgia had to submit an annual detailed report to the governor. In addition, a joint legislative committee reviewed the report every year and made recommendations, usually, as it turned out, for the political benefit of whatever political party was in power.[17]

The State Rights Party wasted no time in exploiting the lousy economy and the unpopularity of Martin Van Buren, the new Democratic president who had inherited the financial mess from the Jackson administration. They even began calling themselves the State Rights and Republican Party to attract dissatisfied Union Party members and those who wanted to disassociate themselves from the unpopular president. When they opened their convention in May, they unanimously appointed John M. Berrien president. Berrien was an old dog in Georgia politics. He was born in New Jersey in 1771 but was brought to Savannah when he was only a year old. Educated at Princeton, he established a successful Savannah law practice, was quickly elected as a circuit judge, then a state senator, then to the U.S. Senate in 1825. In 1829, Andrew Jackson selected him as U.S. attorney general. But Berrien resigned in 1831 over the Peggy Eaton affair. He returned to Savannah to resume his law practice and to train the next litter of young politicians. By the middle of the next decade, he would be mercilessly pushed out of the way by some of those same young pups.[18]

At the convention, the delegates vigorously criticized the Union Party's mismanagement of Georgia's Central Bank. They poured scorn on Jackson and Van Buren and nominated perennial candidate George Gilmer once more for governor. Berrien summed up the looming fight in his opening speech as a contest between the "advocates and opponents of federal misrule."[19]

The Union Party re-nominated Governor William Schley for another term. They went right to work distorting Gilmer's record. They criticized him for recommending gold-rich land be withheld from the state lottery. They claimed he was soft on Native Americans since he advocated allowing them to testify in court. And it was said he would let the sons of rich men avoid the draft in the state militia because he supported excusing students at Franklin College from military service. "Imbecile, wavering and inconsistent," snorted one editorial.[20]

State Rights men gleefully blamed the Union Party and the Democrats for the disastrous Panic of 1837. They tied opposition candidates to Van Buren's coattails at every opportunity. They also accused the Central Bank's administration of malfeasance, favoritism in making loans, and cronyism. State Rights newspapers insinuated that a vote for Schley endorsed the destruction of the Bank of the United States, the sickly economy, nepotism, abolitionism, and other sorts of knavery.[21]

By spring, Robert Toombs was campaigning for the Wilkes County seat in the Georgia legislature against Nicholas Wylie, a wealthy planter and political non-entity. "Captain" Toombs campaigned hard throughout the district. With endless stump speeches, tedious handshaking, and immense barbecues, he stuck fast to his State Rights talking points. He criticized the way the Central Bank was being run and anything else having to do with the Union Party or Democrats. He was a popular candidate even though Wilkes County was not traditionally a State Rights district. At one Independence Day celebration, he was introduced as a "soldier, orator and statesman, and is deserving of any appointment the state or U.S. can confer upon him."[22]

Toombs won his seat in October. It was a "close and animated" election. Wilkes County stuck with its Union Party ways and Toombs was the only State Rights Party member in the three member delegation from the district. Governor William Schely also won the tally in Wilkes County by a whisker-thin thirty-four votes. But most counties abandoned the Union Party and the State Rights nominee George Gilmer won the governor's chair by only 762 votes. Democrats lost majorities throughout the South thanks to the economic depression, and the Union Party kept its majority in Georgia, perhaps because the state had not felt the economic crisis as severely as some other places.[23]

When Toombs arrived in Milledgeville, it was a city of about 2100 residents, almost equally divided between whites and slaves. Like any capital city, it was renowned for its lavish social scene and imposing capitol building which had been completed in 1807. Its Gothic Revival brick walls were eight feet thick and were laid out in a parallelogram. Lacking a dome, it glowered over the town like a university or a cathedral instead of the seat of government. Milledgeville was also a town with a reputation for gambling, cockfights, horse races, and bordellos. Hogs, cattle, and other livestock foraged for whatever they could find in the unlit dirt streets and among the ramshackle buildings. Thirsty legislators could meet at the Big Indian Tavern for a ten-cent drink and a high stakes game of faro. Or they could walk a few blocks to the bordello district.[24]

Toombs took his seat in the legislature on Monday, November 6, 1837. The Georgia legislature was forever and endlessly incorporating churches, schools, and towns and arguing about dispensing money for roads, ferries, bridges, railroads, and other concerns, important and mundane. Toombs was assigned to the Judiciary Committee and to several lesser committees during his first session. These committees had to draw up reports on arcane matters such how to tax slaveholders who owned slaves in counties where they did not live and where to put election precincts. But the legislature's most pressing concerns were the economy and the Central Bank.

In his inaugural address, Governor Gilmer attacked Central Bank president Tomlinson Fort and the other administrators. He vowed that those who had received political patronage from the Union Party "could scarcely expect to escape the same rule of conduct to themselves." Governor Gilmer also urged the legislature not to penalize banks that had withdrawn or stopped paying specie. He wanted the legislature to "compel" those banks to begin issuing money as soon as possible. Governor Gilmer acknowledged that it had been "useful" for the banks to suspend specie payment. But he urged the Union Party legislature to resume payments "as soon as the state of its commerce and its exchanges will permit."[25]

According to the Central Bank's annual report, that might not be any time soon. Fort and his gang had illegally borrowed $230,000 and the funds were almost exhausted. The report also asked the legislature to let the bank to borrow $160,000 more. The shortfall was due, in part, to the federal government's refusal to pay all surplus revenues it owed to the bank. Still, the bank — and thus the state — were almost broke. The legislature overwhelmingly passed a resolution condemning the management of the bank. Then it authorized the bank to borrow $150,000 to make up the shortfall.[26]

It was a humiliating circumstance for the bank's president, Tomlinson Fort. Fort was born in 1787. He trained as a doctor and practiced medicine in Milledgeville for nearly forty years. He was a state legislator from Baldwin County until 1825 then served one term in the U.S. House of Representatives. In 1830, he decided the Union Party needed a strong local advocate. So he went into the newspaper business and bought the weekly Milledgeville *Federal Union*. It became a loud voice for the Union Party.[27]

Union Party members generally agreed with the national Democratic machine: they were against national banks. State Rights members, on the other hand, had a variety of positions. Some were former Union men who had split with the party over Jackson's Bank War and had some sympathy for some kind of centralized federal monetary system. Others liked the concept of banks but were rabidly against the government meddling with the money supply. Still others were somewhere in between. Overall, most Georgians favored some kind of banking system because of the importance of cotton and other cash crops. Toombs was moderate about banking. He generally advocated for privately owned local banks. But he was suspicious of government involvement when it came to money. He was appalled at Van Buren's Independent Treasury proposal that would let the federal government deposit funds in its own vaults around the country instead of in local banks. So he did his best to undermine the Union appointed administration in the Central Bank.

Toombs generally supported his party and Governor Gilmer on banking issues. His first attempt at legislation was a bill he introduced on December 6 that tried to "restrain, prevent, and make penal" any financial institution in the state from issuing notes that could not be redeemed after sixty days. The intent was to loosen credit and encourage banks to issue specie again. After some amending, the bill passed a few weeks later. Toombs also voted for a resolution that made the Central Bank call in enough loans to pay financial distributions to counties that had not been paid what they were owed. But when Governor Gilmer vetoed the bill authorizing the Central Bank to borrow money to cover its obligations, credit tightened in Georgia even further. As it turned out, the State Rights Party took the blame for shriveling the state's credit system while average Georgians could barely make ends meet.[28]

Despite the tight economy, Governor Gilmer also urged the state to keep paying for internal improvement programs. Like the national Whig Party, State Rights politicians generally favored government spending on the infrastructure. During his first years in the legislature, Toombs generally supported spending public funds for internal improvements, although in this session he voted against opening roads in Union County. But he voted with the State Rights Party for such things as a bridge across the Chattahoochie River between Clarksville and Dahlohenga, the erection of a state lunatic asylum, and for funds to hire an engineer to survey the Chattahoochie River between "West Point to Winn's ferry" opposite Hall County. He also voted with his party to apportion $350,000 to the Western and Atlantic Railroad, although the bill failed by a large majority. Toombs was learning how to take care of his constituents back in Wilkes County as well. He introduced petitions from "sundry citizens," a bill to incorporate Rehoboth Academy and Baptist Church, and presented a petition on behalf of a Revolutionary War soldier named Issac Hopkins for an unspecified request. His largess with government money would soon end.[29]

The legislature adjourned on December 5 and Toombs headed home. He resumed his law practice and overseeing his plantation. He also looked after some of Alexander Stephens' business interests. When one of Stephens' numerous ailments flared up, Toombs loaned him money to travel for his health. "He attended to nearly all the business that my brother could do while I was away," Stephens recalled.[30]

The Georgia Constitution called for annual elections for state representatives. So by summer, Toombs was back on the campaign trail for the 1838 contest. The economy had recovered a bit and many banks in Georgia were issuing paper money again. It was a congressional election year, so Toombs and his political colleagues tried to marry the panic from the year before to Van Buren and his Independent Treasury bill. The Union Party and Democrats across the country accused the Whigs and State Rights men of having no principles other than reestablishing a National Bank. "A shadowy vagueness of noncommittalism overspreads all its expositions of its doctrines of future policy," shuddered one Democratic journal.[31]

State Rights men may have had principles, but they were short on party discipline. Some of their candidates like Edward J. Black, Walter T. Colquitt, and Mark A. Cooper supported the Treasury Bill. But most State Rights men sneered at Van Buren's Credit System. Despite their incoherence, every State Rights candidate for Congress won at the polls and the party made healthy gains in state offices. Wilkes County voters disliked the idea of the federal government interfering with their money. They also disliked the federal government keeping federal money in federal bank vaults. So they put their marks in the State Rights column for every state legislative and congressional candidate.

Toombs sneered along with those who hated Van Buren's treasury scheme. That was enough for the voters to re-elect him to the legislature. Nationally, the Whig Party swept the majority of state legislatures but the Democrats carried a small majority in Congress. In Georgia, the Union Party still held a razor-thin majority. Toombs served only on the Judiciary Committee. More significantly, he proved to be a friend of corporations, especially the Western and Atlantic Railroad. He voted for bills to allow the operation to borrow up to three million dollars. He also backed Governor Gilmer's request to allow more state bonds to be issued so the railroad could be completed. His attitude would drastically change when he was an old man. In his later years, Toombs would find himself fighting many battles with the powerful railroad corporation he helped establish.

The legislature handled no big issues in this session. Few politicians were brave enough to tackle anything controversial with a congressional campaign on the immediate horizon. So Toombs concerned himself with small matters such as voting against appointing eleven additional members to the University of Georgia's board of trustees at state expense and removing obstructions in the Chattahoochee River. Toombs also voted for relief for soldiers who were wounded in the recent Creek War and for a bill to protect steamboat and stagecoach companies from paying damages caused by neglectful pilots and drivers. For his constituents in Wilkes County, he shepherded a bill through the legislature to incorporate the Washington Railroad and Banking Company.[32]

Although the Georgia economy had bounced back a bit in 1838, it quickly stagnated again. Banks suspended specie payments by the spring and summer of 1839. To make matters worse for the State Rights Party, it had a difficult time finding a nominee for governor. The young, dynamic John B. Lamar refused the nomination; William C. Dawson, who was serving in the House of Representatives, declined. So, perhaps against his wishes, the convention once again nominated Charles Dougherty, who had been the party's candidate in 1835 but had lost to William Schley. The Union Party selected Charles McDonald, a prosperous planter and railroad man who made his home in Macon.[33]

The State Rights campaign focused on the evils of Van Buren and his Democrats more than local issues. At a Fourth of July rally in Crawfordville, for instance, Stephens called the Democrats "wolves in sheep's clothing," "Judas-like traitors," and a party full of "falsehood, corruption, and treachery." Union flacks smeared Dougherty in turn and implied State Rights men were linked with the aristocratic Northern Whigs. The Union Party had also captured several former State Rights organizers who went on to endorse Charles McDonald. The State Rights Party was seriously wounded going into the campaign anyway due to a nasty split over reapportionment. The party took a drubbing in the election. McDonald defeated Dougherty by 2,000 votes and the Union Party held large majorities in both the House and Senate.[34]

The politicians accomplished little in the legislature in 1839. The presidential election year was close and they wanted to get on with campaigning. Still, a few significant issues were addressed. On December 12, Toombs introduced a dubious amendment to the annual bank bill that proposed all the Central Bank's already strained funds be used to retire the state's debt "before any part thereof shall be used for the purpose of banking." The Union majority in the House defeated the amendment 101 to 79. Toombs also tried to get a branch of the Central Bank established in Milledgeville. When the bill was sent back from the Senate, he tried to get it reconsidered. The speaker of the House declared Toombs' motion out of order. Toombs argued energetically, but the Union-controlled House defeated the young legislator.[35]

Another issue that occupied Toombs was a serious quarrel between Maine and Georgia. In the spring of 1837, a schooner named *Boston* left Rockland, Maine, with a cargo of lime. The ship was taking water when it pulled into port in Savannah. So the captain hired a shipwright named James Sagurs to repair leaks in the hull. Sagurs put a young slave named Atticus on the job. When the ship put to sea a few weeks later, Atticus somehow stowed away on board. Sagurs traveled to Maine to recover his property but he ran into all sorts of official and unofficial interference. Eventually, Sagurs dragged Atticus back to Georgia. But he was not satisfied and complained loudly to former governor William Schley, Governor Gilmer, the legislature, the newspapers, and anyone else who would listen.[36]

Georgia politicians knew a good issue when they saw one. Countless resolutions and bills were introduced to punish Down Easterners for appropriating a Georgia slave. On December 17, Toombs introduced a bill that would somehow protect the property of Georgians "from the aggressions of the people of the State of Maine" by confiscating the assets of people who had come from Maine to live in Georgia. He also proposed seizing "the persons of such citizens and inhabitants and other persons coming into this State, from the State of Maine." George Crawford, who had been Georgia's atorney general from 1827 to 1831 and was the representative from Augusta, offered a more serious substitute that quarantined ships from Maine when they arrived in port and required authorities to search the ships before they left. The bill passed overwhelmingly and made more sense than Toombs' attempt. But Toombs' message had been clear: do not interfere with the South's way of life. It was one of the first times Georgia took on a Northern state over the issue of slavery and one of Toombs' first shots at anti-slavery groups.[37]

In this session, Toombs changed his attitude about spending on internal improvements. When the economy was relatively healthy, he often favored money for new infrastructure projects. But with the economy tight and the state already in deficit, he kept a close eye on the treasury's purse. So he voted against repairs to a road between Dade and Walker counties, against distributing $60,000 of unappropriated money for a state school fund, and against state funds to build an asylum for the mentally ill, an appropriation he had supported just a year before.[38]

Toombs may have had few legislative victories, but he was quickly developing a reputation for making caustic speeches and possessing a blunt, acerbic wit. That made him a favorite for local reporters. One writer described Toombs as a formidable adversary in debate. "He is a bold, fluent, sarcastic speaker, ever ready and ever fortunate and clear in illustration."[39]

The Augusta *Chronicle* also profiled Toombs. "This member possesses high genius, a thorough acquaintance with mankind, and is distinguished by his physical and moral courage," the correspondent gushed. "Often eloquent, always sensible and convincing, he is a formidable adversary in debate." Toombs was "frank and careless in his manner — he appears to be wholly indifferent to rhetorical embellishment." The *Chronicle* let it slip that Toombs had been offered a place on the congressional ticket in the 1840 elections. "We have heard with regret that he has declined emphatically," said the paper. "Having a handsome fortune, we know no gentleman who could so well sacrifice something to the public; and no one [to] whom we would contribute more cordially to elevate." Toombs may or may not have been approached about running for Congress. More prominent men such as William Dawson and Thomas Butler King were also eyeing the race. Toombs — or his political mentors — also may have felt he was not quite ready for the national stage.[40]

State Rights strategists considered nominating the perennial candidate George M. Troup for the presidency in 1840. But this time Troup refused. So party leaders joined the national clamor for William Henry Harrison. For the first time, the State Rights Party officially affiliated itself with the Whigs. The Whigs sprang to life in 1834 as an opposition party to Andrew Jackson. Founded by Henry Clay, John Quincy Adams, and other talented politicians, the Whigs were always more of a coalition than a single cohesive force. Whigs generally agreed on a few key convictions: high tariffs to protect American manufactured goods, internal improvements financed with government money, sound monetary policies, and the supremacy of Congress over the president. But for the most part Whigs were bickering factionalists made up of pro-slavery zealots, abolitionists, pro-labor activists, anti-labor capitalists, Masons, former Anti-Masons, conservatives, reformers, elitists, and populists, all brought together by a common enemy — Democrats.[41]

In December of 1839, the Whigs held their first national convention. They met in Baltimore to nominate a presidential candidate. But they bypassed their two most famous leaders. Daniel Webster lacked appeal outside New England, and Henry Clay had already lost two presidential elections in 1824 and 1832 and carried too much political baggage. Webster's and Clay's politics were also a bit too old fashioned and stodgy for the younger party members' tastes. So the Whigs nominated William Henry Harrison.

Harrison was born in 1773, not in a log cabin as his press machine pretended, but to a well-to-do family in Virginia. He progressed through a series of nondescript political offices culminating in unremarkable terms as a congressman and senator from Ohio. He finally wound up as the clerk in the Common Court of Pleas. His military career was more distinguished than his political career. He was a major general in the War of 1812 and had some success against the British in Canada before resigning in frustration. But he was best known for a battle on the Tippecanoe River where he routed Tecumseh, a Shawnee chief who was leading the resistance against white incursion on Native American land. The battle was almost forgotten until Whig image makers picked it up and changed Harrison from a former Ohio politician and obscure court clerk into a brave Indian fighter defending pioneers on the Indiana frontier.

The 1840 political campaign was like no other in American history. Despite the fact that Harrison lived on a three thousand-acre estate in North Bend, Ohio, Whigs portrayed their sixty-eight-year-old candidate as a homespun farmer that spat out rustic wisdom along with his tobacco juice. Log cabins and hard cider were the symbols of the campaign along with the chanted doggerel "Tippecanoe and Tyler, too!" There was merchandise galore: Tippecanoe songbooks, Tippecanoe joke books, Tippecanoe handkerchiefs, even Tippecanoe shaving cream. Whig rallies became spectacles with endless conventions, parades as far as the eye could see, usually with portable log cabins and cider barrels in tow. Whig political rallies were measured not by attendance, but by the acre.[42]

Toombs worked tirelessly during the campaign. In May, he attended the Wilkes County convention for the State Rights Party, which was conveniently held not far from his home at the courthouse in Washington. He kicked the convention off by reminding the delegates how important it was to defeat Van Buren. The convention's resolutions declared that Jackson and Van Buren had brought "dismay and ruin" through their "corrupt and misguided" administrations. At the end of the evening, Toombs was the most prominent of the four man delegation going to the state convention.[43]

On June 1, he attended an Anti-Van Buren Convention in the chamber of the Georgia House of Representatives. John M. Berrien was appointed president and the usual resolutions praising "Old Tippiecanoe" and his running mate, John Tyler, were enthusiastically passed. A slate of candidates was also picked for the congressional ticket. But Edward J. Black, Walter T. Colquitt, and Mark A. Cooper, who had supported Van Buren's Sub-Treasury scheme, were struck as nominees for Congress. They were quickly absorbed by the Union Party. Toombs was appointed to a committee of eight to write an address to the voters of Georgia that recommended the electors for president and vice president and members of Congress "to their favorable consideration."[44]

Two months later, the official state convention was held in Macon. Van Buren was detested so much that the party temporarily called itself the State Rights and Anti-Van Buren Party. The convention was short on issues but had hoopla and silliness to spare. An estimated twelve thousand to eighteen thousand "hardy sons of Georgia" descended on Macon the day the convention began. The delegates tried to march to the convention hall with their portable log cabin and barrels of hard cider. "But it was soon perceived that it was impossible to form a grand civic procession in so short a time, and hence its organization was reserved until they should move it to the dinner table," a correspondent from the Augusta *Chronicle* wrote.[45]

The delegates finally crowded into the convention hall and kicked off the proceedings. John M. Berrien presided over continuous speeches, proclamations, and resolutions. When a resolution was offered by Absolon H. Chappell endorsing Harrison, Toombs chimed in with an amendment that declared any ends used to defeat Van Buren justified the means and he sarcastically invited members of the Union Party "to unite with us in the deliverance of our common country from the hands of the spoilers."[46]

Nor could the rains keep the crowds away from a September rally in Elbert. Thousands of soggy supporters came to eat free barbecue, drink hard cider, and admire the log cabin on wheels. One correspondent noted the "beautiful" cabin was "distinguished by every decoration which usually adorns those unostentatious 'temples of liberty.'" After the parade and dinner, the speeches commenced and lasted well into the night. Former governor George Gilmer addressed the crowd. Charles Dougherty, who had lost the governorship so badly to William Schley, said a few words. It was getting late by the time Toombs was asked to speak. Uncharacteristically, he hesitated. But the crowd, unwilling to "forego the pleasure they anticipated from his address" cried "Go on!"

So Toombs launched into a denunciation on the evils and chicanery of the Democrats. He was especially harsh about the subtreasury bill that had been passed by Congress earlier that summer. "By the brilliancy of his wit, humor, anecdote, and argument, he gained and fastened the attention of the vast crowd," the *Chronicle* gushed about Toombs' two-hour long speech, "whose ardor in the good cause seemed to rise with the progress of the speaker as repeatedly evinced by the most rapturous and deafening applause."[47]

Harrison won the November election by a landslide. Van Buren carried only seven states and got sixty electoral votes to Tippecanoe's nineteen states and 234 votes. Harrison also got 145,000 more popular votes than Van Buren. The Whigs held Congress with a majority of six in the Senate and a healthy 31 in the House of Representatives. It was the highest turnout for a presidential election to that time. The Whigs triumphed thanks to the shaky economy, the drab Van Buren, and the Democrats' inability to match the clever marketing of the Whig image makers. The tactics of the campaign were ironic for a party of primarily upper middle class and wealthy men who were appalled by the Democrats' vulgar, plebian supporters. But they set out to appeal to a wider electorate than ever before and succeeded. The election had particularly profound consequences for Georgia. By expelling the likes of Black, Colquitt, and Cooper—who had always harbored Unionist sympathies—the usually fractious State Rights Party became, at least temporarily, more cohesive. The party also moved closer to alignment with the national Whigs, even though partnering with any national parties chafed against good states rights thinking.[48]

Georgia's State Rights candidates rode Harrison's coattails into office. With the exception of Wilson Lumpkin and Albert Cuthbert, every congressman in the Georgia delegation was from the State Rights Party. Georgia voters also gave the party a rare majority in both houses in Milledgeville. Toombs became chairman of the Finance Committee. He was also on the Committee on the State of the Republic and the Judiciary Committee once more.[49]

The State Rights lawmakers, heady with victory, saw their majority as a mandate to ignore the Union Party and ram their economic reforms through the legislature. By now, Georgia was in the depths of a full blown depression. The Central Bank's funds were nearly exhausted and it had suspended specie payments again. The last legislature, over strenuous objections by the State Rights Party, had empowered the bank to issue notes anyway. The Union legislature hoped issuing notes would prop up internal existing improvement projects, allow borrowers to pay off loans, and otherwise stimulate the state economy. But the depreciated notes threatened to cause yet another financial collapse and to put the state into deficit. An editorial in the Augusta *Chronicle* lamented that a few years before, Georgia had been "opulent in her public resources," and "credit unsurpassed by any other State in the Union." The *Chronicle* called for the State Rights legislature to pass "speedy, radical reformation."[50]

But Democrat Charles McDonald was still governor. In his annual message, he recommended the legislature raise taxes. He also wanted the lawmakers to authorize the state to buy out individual stockholders in the Central Bank and sell its bank stock at a discount. This scheme would pump badly needed money into state coffers and relieve the economic crisis, at least temporarily. State Rights men disingenuously claimed they wanted no part of Governor McDonald's plan. Toombs used his new powers on the Finance Committee to influence a conservative fiscal policy and he spearheaded the opposition to the governor's proposal. He chaired the special committee that was authorized to repeal the Central Bank's charter if necessary. The committee could also recommend the best way to resume the "speedy payment of the debts of this State and the restoration of her credit." But first, Toombs inquired into the management of the Central Bank. It was a chance to reform the state's economic system and at the same time take a dig at the Democrats who were running the state's bank.[51]

According to the scathing report, which Toombs probably wrote, the bank was seriously decapitalized by wasteful appropriations and too much overhead. The bank had also put too much undervalued specie into circulation "as *money,* [that] were in fact worth fifteen or twenty percent less than *money.*" Except for raising taxes, the committee recommended a similar proposal to the governor's plan: Georgia should sell its stock in the Central Bank and in the Bank of Augusta and pay the state debt immediately. The committee also recommended repealing the Central Bank's charter and putting a new one in place to prevent "similar public evils" from happening again. Although the bank's charter remained unchanged, most of the committee's recommendations were passed by the legislature, including a prohibition against the Central Bank from issuing notes it could not redeem. State Rights men had claimed they wanted no part of Governor McDonald's plan, but in actuality, they wanted no part in letting him share the credit.[52]

Toombs' recommendations tried to put some stability into Georgia's banking system. But they did little to relieve voters' financial suffering. To add insult to Georgia's already injured economy, floods ruined the most of the 1840 cotton crop. Planters begged Governor McDonald for financial assistance. So he sent a special message to the legislature asking for some "constitutional measures for the relief of the people." But, the governor warned, the money could not come from the already strained finances of the Central Bank. Nor could the state easily afford a special session of the legislature. "I venture to place the matter before you," Governor McDonald wrote jauntily to the legislature, "not doubting that all will be done by you that can be, to avert the consequences of a calamity that could not have been foreseen, and that no prudence could have guarded against."[53]

State Rights legislators knew a rat when they smelled one. The request came almost too late in the session for any action. If no legislation passed, Democrats could claim their opponents were indifferent to the economic suffering of their fellow Georgians. If the State Rights dominated legislature funded the governor's request, the Democrats would take credit for it in the next election. The governor had just handed his party a wonderful issue to bash State Rights candidates with in the next election. Upon receiving the message, Toombs immediately offered a resolution requesting that the governor "suggest to the consideration of this House, at his earliest convenience, some definite measure for the relief of the people."[54]

A select committee was formed to examine the problem. Meanwhile, the governor issued another message that reemphasized the need for a "constitutional" way to give the people relief. Once again, he emphasized the Central Bank could not compensate planters for their losses. And the state could not afford a special session of the legislature. "If you should determine against [a relief bill]," the governor wrote, "I shall have the expression of the Legislative opinion that no measure of the sort is demanded by our constituents."[55]

The committee issued bad news a week later. The report acknowledged the planters' financial trouble. But the report argued that the benefits for a few special interests did not outweigh the greater public good. "We deem it unwise, impolitic, and unjust, to use the credit, and pledge the property and labor of the whole people, to raise money to supply the private wants of a portion only, of the people." Guarding the public treasury was one of the "most important and delicate powers, which a free people confide in their representatives," the report continued, and "should be jealously guarded, sacredly protected, and cautiously used, even for the attainment of the noblest public ends and never for the benefit of one class of the community, to the exclusion or injury of the rest."

The report said that using public money to help only cotton planters was illegitimate to the spirit of free government: "The proposed measure violates these admitted truths, asserts the untenable principle, that governments should protect a portion of the people, in violation of the rights of the remainder." Besides, the state could not provide "popular wants with money, because she has none." Toombs believed using government money for relief pitted the interests of one group against another and that was simply wrong. In short, the state was broke and there was nothing the legislature could do.[56]

Toombs was not willing to give tax money to rich planters but he was more than willing to use his position in the majority for some very partisan politics. Two weeks after the session began he attached a preamble to Governor McDonald's endorsement of President Van Buren's Independent Treasury bill: "The recent defeat of Martin Van Buren for the Presidency of the United States, is an event which should diffuse joy and gladness throughout this Republic." Toombs listed reasons that ranged from Van Buren's use of patronage, the Panic of 1837, and his stands against slavery. The administration was "marked by folly, corruption, imbecility, wicked principles, and worse practices." On the other hand, William Henry Harrison "will be ardently devoted to the noble and patriotic purpose of bringing back the administration of our government to its pristine purity, and to the promotion of the prosperity, the happiness, and the glory of our whole country."[57]

Unlike his first few years in the legislature, Toombs voted for very few internal improvements anymore. The economy had stagnated and revenues were tight. So he vigorously watched over the state's funds. He opposed internal improvements simply because the state had very little money and he thought deficit spending was unwise. To his way of thinking, the best course his party could take was to shore up the banking system, keep the state out of a deficit, and stabilize the economy. So he voted against reimbursing citizens seeking money from the state for lost or damaged property during the Creek Wars. He voted against a new tax bill for the next year. But he did vote for a bill to force the state to pay appropriations from the sale of college lands (with interest) into Franklin's College's endowment fund that had previously been put into state coffers.[58]

If the State Rights Party thought bank reform and tightening the state budget during a financial crisis was going to win votes in the 1841 elections, the leaders badly miscalculated. Toombs' refusal to help planters after the failure of the cotton crop was political suicide. The Union Party cheerfully reminded voters that Governor McDonald had asked for financial assistance while the State Rights legislature ignored him. Governor McDonald was reelected and took a strong Union majority into the legislature with him. Even Wilkes County went all Union again that year.[59]

The political defeat was academic for Robert Toombs. For whatever reason, he did not run for political office that year. Perhaps he sensed the political slaughter and chose to remain on the sidelines. Or he might have been laying the groundwork for his run for Congress. He could have had personal reasons. Still, he was active in the campaign and stumped hard for State Rights candidates and their gubernatorial nominee, William C. Dawson.[60]

The euphoria over the victories in 1840 quickly skidded into despair for the Whig Party. In frosty Washington D.C., William Henry Harrison delivered a two-hour inaugural address without an overcoat. He was dead after less than a month in office. When Vice President John Tyler took Harrison's place, the Whigs and Georgia's State Rights Party thought one of their own was still in the White House. Tyler had been a Democrat but he broke with Jackson over the nullification crisis. Tyler resigned from the Senate instead of expunging Andrew Jackson's censure. The Whigs immediately embraced him. Tyler was put on the ticket in 1840 to attract states rights and strict constructionist votes as well as to balance the ticket for the South.

But Tyler still had Democratic sympathies. He was not a nationalist like so many Whigs were. He was avid about states' rights. He opposed high tariffs and federal subsidies for internal improvements. Tyler may have called himself a Whig, but Henry Clay considered him a "president without a party."[61]

A quarrel immediately broke out between Tyler and the Whig-dominated Congress.

The Whig program included repeal of Van Buren's Independent Treasury bill, establishing a new national bank, and increased tariffs. In the late summer of 1841, Tyler vetoed two national bank bills. A few days later, the Whig Party expelled him. Tyler retaliated by purging Whigs from patronage-given offices and appointing Democrats in their place. Tyler and the Whigs were at war. Rumors about impeachment began circulating.[62]

Despite the Whig turmoil, the Georgia State Rights convention assembled on June 14 in Milledgeville. But for all intents and purposes the party was now solidly allied with the Whigs. The party even called the gathering the Whig and State Rights Convention. Toombs was on hand and probably helped write the main address. It was long on praise for Henry Clay and endorsed him for president even though the election was still two years away. Admittedly, the nomination was premature. But the State Rights men could not "repress the expression of their admiration of the character and public services of Henry Clay of Kentucky." Daniel Webster was still in the hated Tyler's cabinet as secretary of state. So Clay seemed like the only one who could heal the party after the disastrous loss of Harrison and Tyler's renegade administration. It was a warm endorsement for a man who had been left out in the cold by his party only two years earlier.[63]

The Union Party had already adhered to the Democratic national machine and knew how to nationalize the issues. So the early endorsement gave the Union Party plenty of time to tie Clay to the State Rights Party's tail. Unionists pounded State Rights candidates about Henry Clay, the tariff, and their failed promises to improve the economy. Unfortunately, State Rights men had little to campaign on. Whigs had controlled Congress in Washington, D.C., and the economy was still in a shambles. All the State Rights Party could do was campaign against corruption in the Central Bank and insult the various Union candidates. Edward J. Black was a "thorough-paced demagogue." John B. Lamar was "nominated principally on account of his family and name." And John H. Lumpkin was a man whose "ability is moderate, his information limited." Whig papers went to great lengths to tie their opponents to the national party, reporting on Democratic chicanery as far away as New England. Georgia politics had finally turned away from local concerns and was fully ensnared in national politics.[64]

On election day, the Whigs kept the U.S. Senate by a slim majority of three. But they lost the House to the Democrats. In Georgia, the State Rights Party—or Whigs as they were openly calling themselves now—were narrowly defeated in the House but overwhelmingly lost the Senate. "The Locofoco [Democrat] majority is a result, we regret to say, which has been produced by the folly of our professed friends," the Augusta *Chronicle* whined, lamenting losses even in usually safe Whig counties.[65]

If it was any consolation, the Whigs carried Wilkes County and Toombs was sent back to the legislature. Despite being in the minority, he was made chairman of the Judiciary Committee and served on a select committee to examine redistricting in the state. He stayed busy heckling the Union majority and trying to see his legislative initiatives through. "The calendar was strong with a heterogeneous collection of bills proposing stay laws," Toombs wrote to a friend. Stay laws were designed to postpone payments on contracts by people with too much debt to pay. When the stay law bill was referred to a select committee, the committee endorsed it. But Toombs signed the minority report that strongly denounced altering contracts. The bill "works moral wrong and political injustice," the report said. The stay law failed.[66]

Toombs not only tried to force debt-ridden citizens to pay their contracts, he also tried to force the debt-ridden state to pay its contracts as well. Georgia had passed a law in 1836 that authorized construction of a railroad "communication" line to run from the Tennessee

River to the Chattahoochee. The proposed line would go through Athens, Milledgeville, and terminate at Columbus. The bill also required the state to buy a quarter of the stock in railroad companies as soon as half of the company stock had been sold. When the Monroe Railroad and Banking Company met the requirement, Governor McDonald certified the company's eligibility for state funds.[67]

But the legislature balked at the $200,000 stock purchase and tried to kill the legislation. Toombs and thirty of his Whig colleagues entered a protest in the House Journal. The protestors "would not impugn the motives of any man," but trying to kill the legislation was "nothing more or less than repudiating a debt due by the State." The State Rights legislators called the proposal unprincipled, unworthy of the legislature and dissented on what they regarded as a "violation of the plighted faith of the State." The portion requiring the state to buy stock was repealed. The Whigs lost, but nobody was going to renege on a contract under Toombs' watch without a fight.[68]

Toombs also got into a scrap over John M. Berrien. In 1841, the Georgia legislature had elected Berrien to the U.S. Senate (state legislatures elected U.S. senators until the Seventeenth Amendment passed in 1913). Berrien and the state legislators had been openly quarreling ever since. The Democratic legislature was especially miffed when Senator Berrien supported Whig programs. It specifically instructed him to change his votes on the national bank bill, the tariff, repeal of the independent treasury, and even his vote for a $25,000 stipend for William Henry Harrison's widow. Berrien refused. So the legislature censured him.

In the legislators' view, they had elected him; he was their instrument and should play whatever tune they called for. Berrien saw it differently. In a lengthy editorial published in September of 1842, he explained that as a U. S. senator, he was a representative to the nation, not an officer of the government of Georgia. He carefully justified each of his controversial votes. Then he took a dig at the South by frankly admitting that Northern states were well ahead in "improvements" while "much of ours is still in a wilderness state." The reason was simple: the South focused on growing cotton while the North had diversified its economy. He urged Whigs to shake themselves out of their stupor and "speak through the ballot box" to unseat Democrats. The address was designed to rally Whigs, bring them to the polls, and to put a finger in the eye of the Democrats. Berrien did not bring enough Whigs to the polls but he certainly irritated his opponents.[69]

In December, the Union majority drew up resolutions once again censuring Senator Berrien. Berrien was in the "palmy days of his intellect" and "no longer a fit and proper representative of the State," according to the Democratic legislature. Toombs lashed out and loyally defended the senator. At a Whig caucus the day before, he submitted a set of counter-resolutions that reaffirmed the party's support for Berrien. "The State legislature [is] not the custodian of a senator's conscience," he said. When the legislature voted on the censure, there was not a quorum. The Democrat from Bibb County suggested that the chair decide if the motion would carry. Toombs appealed to the chair and complained bitterly. But the Union majority passed the censure by a wide margin.[70]

As usual, the Central Bank was also an issue. It was assumed the bank's charter would not be renewed and the institution would quietly expire. When a bill passed that temporarily prolonged the bank's existence and used state funds to pay the unliquidated debts, Toombs and thirty-five of his associates entered another protest into the record. The banking experiment had utterly failed, the report said. The list of "melancholy grievances" inflicted by the bank included "pecuniary loss," "incalculable distress," that it contributed to the "destruction of public credit," and "sullied the honor and good faith of the State." The depreciated currency had also "endangered the social system," and created a "universal and heavy taxation to sustain public credit." The protesters were particularly incensed that public money was appropriated "not for the legitimate purpose of supporting their Government, but to support a rotten, exploded system of Banking." The minority report was convincing enough to sway the Democratic majority. Toombs voted against the final bill to close the Central Bank because of a provision that required Georgia to absorb the bank's debt. But the legislature finally put the bank out of its misery.[71]

The session was barely over before the Whigs began planning for the next elections. The Democratic Party—or "Locofocos"—had "exhibited itself in its most odious form," Toombs wrote to Senator Berrien. Toombs was still outraged at the way the legislature treated his mentor. He believed the censure was nothing more than political posturing. However, he thought the Democrats had miscalculated and his party could take advantage of it. No one truly believed senators were representatives of the state legislature, yet Democrats were "foolish enough to incorporate it in their creed & make it a fundamental principle of Democracy." The young legislator assured the elder statesman that he was more popular than ever. "Nothing could be so disastrous to you or them," he wrote, "as to think for a moment of being driven from your position by the clamor or insults of such a body of men as the democratic [sic] party of Georgia, who are a combination of the vilest crew of desperate, unprincipled scoundrils [sic] that ever deceived and betrayed an honest people." Neither man knew that within a few years Toombs himself would be trying to drive Berrien out of office.[72]

Toombs ran into some locofocoism of his own. In one of his speeches in the legislature, Toombs had accused Governor McDonald of robbing the public treasury. If this was so, asked Democratic newspapers such as the Milledgeville *Federal Union*, why hadn't there been an inquiry? Where was a special committee to investigate the allegation? Had Toombs, who made the allegations, neglected his duty?

Toombs quickly backed away from the his own accusations. He was not accusing the governor of personally profiting, he explained in the Augusta *Chronicle*. He was accusing the governor of misusing money from one state fund to buy iron for the Western and Atlantic Railroad when he should have used revenue from another fund. It was only a technical violation of the law. To bring an investigation "would have ended in nothing else but a useless consumption of the time of the Legislature, and consequently an unnecessary drain upon the exhausted Treasury." Toombs had gotten trapped in his own hyperbole. It would not be the last time it happened.[73]

As usual, the Whigs met in June for their state convention in Milledgeville. The delegates criticized the Democrats for "the evils that afflict our people," nominated George W. Crawford for governor, reaffirmed their support for Senator Berrien and even endorsed him as Henry Clay's running mate in the approaching presidential election. The convention also launched Alexander Stephens into the national spotlight and nominated him for the congressional seat from the Seventh District.[74]

The Whigs fought an aggressive campaign. Since the national economy was finally stabilizing and improving, they tried to give the credit to their slight majority in the Senate. In Georgia, the Whigs promised to keep the tariff high and tried to convince the voters that their opponents' tariff proposal was too low, the distribution of the proceeds from public land sales would be unfair in the hands of Democrats and their treasury scheme would bankrupt the country. At their state convention, the Democrats denounced banks, promised lower tariffs, and tried to tie local affairs to national issues: "A stranger could scarce discover that there is such a State as Georgia," one editorialist sniffed after the Democrats' convention.[75]

Toombs stormed the campaign trails of Georgia. He spoke in Oglethorpe, Windsor, wherever he was invited. It was even rumored that the Democrats cancelled a political debate because they did not want to "let that d[amne]d fellow Toombs speak." Toombs was a formidable antagonist. He blasted Democratic "pilferers and plunderers" at every chance. "The Democratic Party is strongly marked with blunders and disasters, weakness and wickedness, unsteadiness of purpose and vacillations in policy," said Toombs at one rally. Not only that, there was "wasteful extravagance and timid temporary expedients, a disregard of the public interests in official appointments, and contempt for the sanctity of private contracts and the public faith."[76]

The Whigs won the majority in both houses of the Georgia legislature. Whig George W. Crawford won the gubernatorial election and Stephens was sent to the House of Representatives in Washington. Toombs was chairman on the State of the Republic Committee and on the Committee on Internal Improvements. But the session was a quiet one because the presidential campaign was approaching and the politicians wanted to get out and campaign for their candidates. The only notable legislation was Toombs' bill to establish a supreme court in Georgia. The bill passed in the House, but was killed in the Senate by three votes. Toombs believed trying to establish the court was an unpopular move for his party, "but benefitted [sic] the country." After its defeat he was surprised to hear "the general regret expressed at its loss among the people."[77]

Toombs also introduced a bill that established county taxes to provide more funds to educate the poor. Most Whigs strongly believed in public education and the party prompted members to promote schools whenever they could. Georgia's progressive ideals about education were often met with a lack of innovative ideas. After the War of 1812, some state leaders proposed a public school system open to all children, rich and poor. Yet lawmakers were usually stingy with money for education. So by the 1830s, a "poor school" structure had been imposed.

In the poor school system, the state distributed funds for education to counties based on a census of "poor children and indigent parents." Children whose parents could not pay more than fifty cents above the poll tax qualified as charity students. But county officials usually paid for certain poor children to go to field schools or private schools or sometimes pay for a tutor. Some children benefited; many did not.[78]

The Committee on Public Education and Free Schools looked into Toombs' bill to raise taxes to increase funding to educate poor children. The committee's report thrashed earlier legislatures for not distributing existing money to fund public schools. Toombs, who had been considered a charity case during his college years, authored a bill that authorized fixed amounts of stock from banks as well as what was left of the assets of the Central Bank to be set aside to partially pay into the system. The final bill passed with an easy majority.

Toombs also submitted numerous petitions from constituents for relief, requests for reimbursements from the state, and he voted against a bill "for the protection and preservation of the rights and property of married women."[79]

"We have passed all the important measures of the session," he boasted to a constituent, "some of them by close vote but we have as yet failed in nothing." "The session passed off well," Toombs wrote to Alexander Stephens. "We succeeded in everything but the Court." All and all, Toombs was pleased with his party and his prospects for the future. "The session is decidedly popular with all classes. The people are better pleased than they have been for many years with their legislature, and I begin to think our power in Georgia is tolerably firmly fixed."[80]

Toombs served in the legislature for only seven years. He entered into the rough political game at a transitional time. National issues encroached on Georgia and the rest of the South. Democrats and Whigs then absorbed local political alliances into their large national parties. Partisan positions hardened. But Toombs left quite an impression. He was a good Whig who had worked hard and effectively fought Democrats for every inch of political and legislative ground. His blunt and sarcastic persona grated against the caricature of Whigs as a party of fops and elitists. But it caught the attention and approval of some prominent leaders. Important national issues were on the horizon and each came with both glory and troublesome aspects. Whig leaders knew a political brawler like Toombs would be useful. Toombs wanted to join his friend Alex Stephens in Congress anyway. So he began to work towards a slot on the national ticket.

3

House

In 1844, Robert Toombs made his debut on the national political scene. He had worked hard for his party in Georgia, even serving as chairman of the Whig State Central Committee. The Whigs are "full of hope and energy, and the spirit of [1840] is already rife among them," he wrote enthusiastically to Senator Berrien. "I doubt not we shall achieve a brilliant victory in November for Mr. Clay." Toombs was optimistic about Whig prospects although there was little collaboration among the various Whig organizations. "We have no committees of the party in existence authorized to concentrate their movements," he complained.[1]

It was not surprising the Whigs found it hard to cooperate. Like Georgia's old State Rights Party, the one thing Whigs unanimously agreed on was defeating Democrats. Their unity was always fragile, their positions sometimes ephemeral. Yet despite their disagreements and their almost perpetual minority status, the Whigs attracted some enormously talented men. Henry Clay, Daniel Webster, and John Quincy Adams always kept the Democrats on the run.

In May, the thirty-four-year-old state representative was elected as a delegate to the national Whig convention in Baltimore. President John Tyler had been a fiasco for the party. So to no one's surprise, the Whigs nominated Henry Clay for president and selected former New Jersey senator and mayor of Newark Theodore Frelinghuysen for vice president. Although the Georgia delegation failed to get John M. Berrien the second spot on the ticket, Toombs enthusiastically stumped for Clay and Frelinghuysen and Whig issues from Georgia to Boston. He argued endlessly that the high Whig tariff that passed in 1842 was good for national industry and was especially good for cotton. He also vigorously defended the constitutionality of the National Bank.[2]

In a debate with Democratic senator George McDuffie, Toombs cleverly turned the Democrats' argument against them by pointing out that they did not mind federal funding for projects in their districts. McDuffie was a grouchy old politician from South Carolina who passionately favored state sovereignty and just as passionately hated tariffs. McDuffie also had a reputation as a fiery debater. His style was like "harnessed lightning," one observer said. But Toombs, wearing a tobacco stained shirt, bested McDuffie during the debate. "Democrats were very strict [constitutional] constructionists when it was necessary to accomplish their political purposes," Toombs scolded, "but always found a way to get around these doubts when the occasion required." McDuffie was later heard to say: "This wild Georgian was the Mirabeau of this age."[3]

As far as the wild Georgian was concerned, the most dangerous issue for Southern

Whigs was annexing Texas. President Tyler and Sam Houston, president of the little Republic of Texas, both desperately wanted Texas in the Union. However, slavery was built into the Texas Constitution and Congress had no appetite to take on the issue. Nor was anyone willing to antagonize Mexico over the breakaway republic. To Mexico, Texas was a rebel state that had no business flirting with its powerful northern neighbor. Frustrated with the indecisiveness of American politicians, Sam Houston made some appealing — and well publicized — enticements to France and Great Britain. If the United States didn't want Texas, he declared, the only thing to do was to invite a rival power to build an empire along the Pacific. Houston likened Texas to "a bride adorned for her espousal."

President Tyler and Secretary of State John C. Calhoun did not let the bride stand at the altar long. On April 12, 1844, Tyler signed a treaty written by Calhoun and Houston that took possession of Texas as a new slave territory. The treaty was submitted to the Senate but defeated a few months later by a coalition of seven Democrats and twenty-eight Whigs. The Senate's failure to deal with Texas — and its slavery — guaranteed that it would be *the* issue in the 1844 campaign.

For the most part, Whigs opposed territorial expansion. More land would make the country too large to govern and drain resources away from internal improvements, they argued. Many Southern Whigs also feared slavery would not last in Texas and migration would leech power away from the old South. In April, Henry Clay published a letter that laid out his nuanced — some called it disingenuous — position. Annexing Texas compromised "the national character," he wrote, "involving us certainly in a war with Mexico, probably with foreign powers, [was] dangerous to the integrity of the Union, inexpedient in the present financial condition of the country, and not called for by any general expression of public opinion." It was good Whig policy but a disastrous miscalculation.[4]

Clay's Raleigh Letter was popular in the North. But he had to do a lot of political contortion to conserve his support in the South. Clay tried to explain that he was not personally against annexation, but "without war, with the common consent of the Union, and upon just and fair terms." Cautious Whigs shook their heads and tried to bury the issue under arguments about internal improvements, the National Bank, and the tariff. But Toombs supported Clay's position and spoke out. It did not matter if Mexico was weak and the acquisition easy, he said. The question was: "Is it right, is it just, is it the policy of this country to enlarge its territory by conquest?" Toombs thought not. He said countries that went to war without a just cause, for pride and glory, were "enemies to the human race and deserve the execration of all mankind." To Toombs, Texas was just a land grab. He would rather have "the Union without Texas than Texas without the Union."[5]

It was a surly lecture. But none other than Henry Clay liked what he heard. Clay had met the political fledgling at a dinner in Augusta and was so impressed that he "insisted I should make the race in the Whig interest," Toombs recalled forty years later. So Toombs pitched his hat into the ring and stumped throughout the Eighth District with his Whig arguments. The Democrats resorted to insinuating Toombs was an abolitionist. Accused of calling slavery "a moral and political evil," Toombs admitted he may have said something like that. But while the Democratic press had "affected fear and pretended suspicion" of the young Whig, his views on slavery were well understood. "I have no language to express my scorn and contempt for the whole crew [of Democratic reporters]," he snorted to a friend. During the campaign, Toombs berated the Democrats for using the slavery issue to scare voters. It was a "bugbear ... kept up to operate on the fears of the timid and the passions and prejudices of the unsuspecting."[6]

But the 1844 elections were a calamity for the Whigs. The odds never favored them to begin with. The Democrats charged Clay with all types of sins and transgressions, including indulging himself at the gambling table and the brothels. On the other hand, Democratic candidate James Polk had been a governor and speaker of the House, but he was still too obscure for the Whig machine to successfully caricature. The Whigs had also not shaken off the fiasco of President Tyler. Perhaps most importantly, the Democrats supported Manifest Destiny. While the Whig platform droned on and on in praise of Henry Clay and Theodore Frelinghuysen, the Democrats promised that the "reoccupation" of Oregon and "re-annexation" of Texas were "great American measures."[7]

So the Democrats won an enormous majority in the House and Senate. Georgia sent a Democratic delegation to Congress and gave its presidential votes to Polk and George M. Dallas. However, Toombs unseated the unpopular Edward J. Black, the apostate Whig who had defected to the Democrats over Van Buren's Treasury scheme in 1840 and who had been in and out of Congress for several years. Though the young Whig was an excellent campaigner and a master on the stump, it is striking that he won the election. The Eighth District was not a Whig stronghold. Toombs' Whiggish position against the annexation of Texas was especially unpopular. Still, he defeated Black by over thirteen hundred votes. It must have been a sweet victory.

Toombs had to wait almost a year before taking his seat in Congress. In the meantime, he practiced law and managed his plantations. Although suffering from a severe spell of "rheumatism," he dispensed political advice to his friends from his sickbed. He urged Alex Stephens to vote to repeal duties on iron for railroads to encourage internal improvements and "cheapen internal transportation which benefits all classes and especially agricultural classes." About Texas, he confessed to Stephens that annexation gave him "considerable trouble." But Toombs was a practical politician and, as was often the case, his public statements differed from his private thinking. Publicly, he supported Clay and had insinuated Texas was a land grab. But upon "the best reflection I can give it ... would decide it in favor of the popular will." He believed that it would be best for "public safety and the safety of the Union" to admit Texas as a single slave state with the option of severing it into four different states sometime in the future.[8]

Toombs knew the clash over Texas was going to cause a divisive sectional argument and a nasty issue for his party. "Our Northern Whig friends are foolishly, not to say wickedly, narrowing it down to a simple question of pro & anti-slavery. Nothing could be more unfortunate." He hoped the issue would be quickly settled to protect the country and Southern Whig interests. The agitation only embittered the feelings between the North and the South and gave "strength to the abolition movement & to the Southern Democracy, for clamour [sic] is the livelihood & agitation the stock in trade of both of those heartless, unprincipled factions." Yet he saw little hope the issue would be settled thanks to the Whigs in the North: "Texas was too strong for us when we were united; so hopeless is the contest when we are divided among ourselves."[9]

Although still in great pain from his "rheumatism," Toombs fired off a letter praising a speech Stephens gave in Congress a few weeks before. Stephens favored annexing Texas not to expand slavery, but to expand the political power of the South. Stephens' position was a counter-argument to Southern Whigs who feared annexation would cause mass migration to the Southwest, rendering old slave interests impotent. Stephens' argument was well received in Georgia. Toombs had said he would go along with whatever was popular, but he still had misgivings. He could see nothing but "evil to our party and the country that can come out of this question in [the] future." Toombs agreed that annexing Texas would add influence to the slave states, but believed that in every other respect "it will be an unmixed evil to us." Toombs, still a believer in Whig principles, still a nationalist, was far from the radical he would become only a few years later.[10]

But his prophecies came to pass. Tyler ignored Congress and sent a message to Sam Houston saying that consent of the Texians was all that was needed to bring Texas into the Union. Houston gladly consented. On March 3, 1845, Tyler performed his last official act as president: he signed the bill that brought Texas into the Union as a territory—with slavery. The new president, James K. Polk, let the measure stand. Texas became the twenty-eighth state nine months later. It was the last slave state to enter the Union. It only took fifteen short years for the controversies unleashed by the issues surrounding Texas to destroy the Whig Party and tear the country apart.

Toombs traveled to Washington when the Twenty-Ninth Congress convened on December 1, 1845. In the 1840s, Washington, D.C., was a notoriously awful place to work. Pennsylvania Avenue was a dirt strip that choked with mud whenever it rained. Street lamps were lit only when Congress was in session. The thin light illuminated pigs and cows or feral dogs and cats rummaging for something to eat among the rows of shops and taverns crowded together with ugly government buildings, monotonous brick row houses, squalid hovels, and the occasional vacant lot.[11]

Robert Toombs was in some ways like Washington, D.C. itself: self-important, unkempt, stately, and yet charismatic all at the same time. "At first sight, he appeared a person of insufferable self-conceit, and holding a sort of contempt of everyone around him," one writer noted. "He apparently bestowed the least attention in the world to his dress; his clothes fitting very ill, and not of spotless neatness, his hair seldom smooth, his boots unblackened, and perfect independence from the requirements of social refinement." Although never as popular as the likes of Stephen A. Douglas or William Henry Seward, Robert and Julia Toombs quickly gained a reputation for Southern hospitality and hosting lavish parties. Sometimes they spent up to eighteen hundred dollars a month on entertainment alone. Toombs could be remarkably charming, but he could also be a stuffed shirt, a snobbish and arrogant pompous ass. "He was haughty, imperious, and overbearing, intolerant, and impatient of contradiction," recalled a colleague years afterwards. "At first site, he impressed one unfavorably, and a feeling of dislike instinctively arose," said another. "But this impression was much lessened when he addressed the Senate, or when you met him in social circles."[12]

There was just something magnetic about Toombs. His speaking style could make the most seasoned politicians stop what they were doing and take notice. During one floor debate, he was denouncing a routine army appropriation bill as the House members talked, told jokes, read books, gossiped, and wrote letters or speeches. Amid the clamor, Toombs bellowed on. But eventually, he began to compare the American Army with the British Army. "Look at Great Britain," he said. "Look at that vast and magnificent empire, on whose territories it may be truly said, without exaggeration, that the sun never sets." As he spoke, various congressmen quit talking, put down their books, stopped writing, and all turned to listen. Several moved closer to hear what he was saying. "Soon a little crowd was collected on the floor of the House to hear every word."[13]

Democrats in the first session of the Twenty-Ninth Congress held a sixty-six seat majority in the House and a slim majority in the Senate. The Texas crisis had simmered down for now, but the first important issue Toombs dealt with as a freshman representative was the Oregon question.

Congressman Robert Toombs. Engraving from a Mathew Brady daguerreotype, probably late 1840s (courtesy of Georgia Archives, Vanishing Georgia Collection, wlk153).

The border of Oregon sat along the forty-ninth parallel with joint American and British occupation. An 1827 provision allowed either country to terminate the agreement simply by giving a notice of withdrawal. In the summer of 1843, a small group of Americans met at Champoeg in an old Hudson Bay Company warehouse, set up a temporary government complete with a provisional constitution, and called for the United States to extend its sovereignty over the entire territory. The British disputed the border, claiming the Columbia River should mark the northern boundary of the American claim instead of the forty-ninth parallel. But hotheaded Democrats demanded the entire region, roughly from northern California to central Canada. In his first annual message in December of 1845, Polk urged Congress to end joint occupation within a year. The thinking was that obtaining Oregon would counterbalance annexing Texas. But the border dispute caused hostile posturing in both Congress and Parliament.

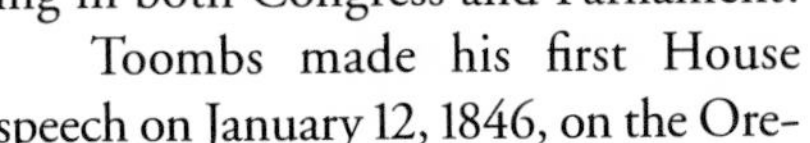

Toombs made his first House speech on January 12, 1846, on the Oregon question. He scoffed at the prospect of war or peace. The real questions were what rights did the United States have to Oregon and the appropriate time to terminate joint occupancy. Every other question was "incidental and subordinate" and had been blown out of proportion. Toombs said he believed Americans had no right to the Oregon Territory up to the 54' 40" parallel. Based on the history of exploration and title grants in the region, he believed the demands of extremist Democrats were flawed because of vague claims and treaties negotiated by Britain and Spain years before. Both sides were stuck with the Convention of 1818. Even if American immigrants poured into the area and filled its towns and villages with "palaces of government" and raised "temples of justice," it would make no difference. "Should we settle the country a thousand years hence, we must still come back to the question of the title of the convention of 1818."

Whether the disputed boundary stopped at the Columbia River or the fifty-fourth parallel, Toombs favored authorizing the president to give the British notice whenever it was expedient. Since the president conducted foreign relations, Toombs said he trusted Polk to do the right thing and "would not give just cause or complaint" if joint occupation ended. Besides, settlers who "wanted to build houses, to bring their flocks and herds, to enclose and cultivate their farms ... and enjoy all the privileges of owners of the soil" were flooding into Oregon. Therefore Toombs said he favored letting Polk terminate joint occupancy so the boundary question could be settled as soon as possible.[14]

Toombs claimed during his speech that he was speaking "with all candor and frankness." However, he was even more candid and frank in a letter to Georgia governor George W. Crawford a few weeks after the speech. "Mr. Polk never dreamed of any other war than a war upon the Whigs," Toombs sneered. Polk was "playing a low grog-shop politician's trick. He would be as much surprised and astonished and frightened at getting into war with England as if the Devil were to rise up before him at his bidding."

Polk was the "vilest poltroon that ever disgraced our government," a "sharp district politician without statesmanship or patriotism." Toombs thought Congress would reject giving notice to Britain. If the Whigs handed the question back to Polk, Toombs said, it would take the issue away from the Democrats. Polk had "raised the devil" and Toombs "wished to put upon him the responsibility of putting him down." As for Oregon itself, Toombs did not "care a fig about *any* of Oregon, and would gladly get ridd [sic] of the controversy by giving it all to anybody else but the British if I could with honor." Toombs thought the country was already too large, "and I don't want a foot of Oregon or an acre of any other country, especially without 'niggers.'"[15]

Some Georgians may have wanted Oregon, but few wanted war. Stephens had "no disposition to speak upon" the subject and wanted Polk to negotiate with England. Even Georgia Democrats doubted if a war was really necessary, although one crowd at a Democratic rally swore they would support Polk and fight even though they did not know "on which side of the Rocky Mountains Oregon was."[16]

When the resolution to give Polk the authority to terminate the agreement with Britain came up for a vote in the House on February 12, Toombs sparked controversy by voting against it. The Democratic press back in Georgia wasted no time jumping on him for hypocrisy. But Toombs defended his actions by claiming he voted against the resolution because the title to Oregon was not "clear and unquestionable" and he preferred some form of arbitration. Polk had rejected any arbitration, but Toombs suspiciously neglected to mention his outrage in his speech. Publicly, Toombs was being a statesman who was trying to expand the borders to look out for the best interest of the country. Privately, he was also trying to kill an issue that had hurt the Whigs terribly in the last election.[17]

In late April, Congress authorized Polk to terminate the joint occupation. On June 6, Britain's foreign secretary offered to accept termination if the border between the United States and Canada extended along the forty-ninth parallel. Great Britain was dealing with a Sikh uprising in its eastern empire and the Irish famine. So the government wanted to rid itself of the expense of Oregon. Polk, on the other hand, was not interested in provoking another war with Great Britain. He put on a great show of reluctance, but he approved of the treaty that was signed on June 15, 1846.

Another pivotal event came in late April. For several months, General Zachary Taylor had occupied the left bank of the Rio Grande which the United States claimed as the southern border of Texas. The Mexicans claimed the border stopped 150 miles north at the Nueces River. On April 24, a squad of 63 American dragoons was checking out an abandoned *hacienda* when they ran into 2000 Mexican soldiers. Sixteen Americans were killed and the rest were taken prisoner. Polk received the dispatch two days later. The outraged administration called it an ambush; the Mexicans saw it as resisting an invasion. Polk sent a declaration of war to Congress on May 11 claiming that Mexico had invaded American territory "and shed American blood upon the American soil." Two days later, Congress passed the declaration; the vote in the House was 174 to 14. In the words of General Taylor, "hostilities may now be considered as commenced."[18]

Most Democrats saw the war as another validation of their Manifest Destiny. Most Southern Whigs saw the war as ruthless Democratic imperialism against an inferior neighbor, a Goliath pounding on a David. Many Whigs feared — correctly as it turned out — an American victory would dismember the country over the slavery question. One week after the war opened, Toombs took to the House floor. He hated what Whigs derisively called "Mr. Polk's war" and he no longer publicly found Polk's foreign policy insight very trustworthy.

Although Toombs voted for commencing hostilities, he was outraged that John H. Lumpkin, the Democrat from Georgia's Fifth District, had attached a statement endorsing Polk's actions to an appropriations bill. "Even this occasion must be consecrated to party," Toombs howled, "and a preamble placed before the bill to cover the usurpations of the Executive." And if those who criticized Polk were to be branded destitute of patriotism, then he hoped "there were but few patriots in the country."

The real question to Toombs was not supplies for the troops or where the border was located. The issue was whether Polk had overstepped his authority by provoking Mexico. Toombs cited evidence that the Texas border ended at the Nueces, far north of where Zachary Taylor had encamped on the Rio Grande. As long as the army remained at Corpus Christi, nobody objected, he said. But marching the army to the Rio Grande "was contrary to the laws of this country, a usurpation of the rights of this House, and an aggression on the rights of Mexico." Toombs angrily told his colleagues they could "make the most" of his declaration.

Polk's war message had called for the Mexican government to pay large claims made by U.S. citizens. Toombs said that failure to pay debts was no justification for war. "If the failure to pay honest debts was a just cause for killing men the infliction of the penalty might commence at home among our non-paying States." Despite denouncing Polk and his Democrats, Toombs assured his colleagues that Whigs "were as ready as any gentlemen" to vote to send troops and supplies. In short, he was against the war but supported the troops. Toombs spoke with so much force and passion that the entire House gave him their undivided attention.[19]

Whigs damned and cursed Polk's shaky pretext for the war and criticized his mismanagement of the conflict at every opportunity. Alexander Stephens made an argument similar to Toombs,' saying Polk possessed no legal right to order General Taylor into the disputed area. Henry Clay warned that two countries as different as the United States and Mexico could not exist under one government. In Canada, the French "were still a foreign land in the midst of British provinces." Every Irishman, according to Clay, hated "with a mortal hatred, his Saxon oppressor." Several months later, a skinny congressman from Illinois named Abraham Lincoln echoed Toombs and Stephens when he asked Polk to verify the precise spot where "American" blood had been shed on "American" soil.[20]

To the Whigs' horror, the war went splendidly. In June, John C. Fremont and his volunteers captured the city of Sonoma in California; in July, 250 sailors took Monterey, California's capital, without firing a shot. By August, American forces controlled Los Angeles. A mere three months after fighting began, Polk asked Congress for a secret appropriation of two million dollars to finance a peace settlement. With only two days left in the session to consider the request, a group of Northern Democrats proposed a measure devised to keep slavery out of any new territory gained from Mexico after the war. When the "Two Million Dollar Bill" came to the floor, David Wilmot of Pennsylvania introduced this proviso. It passed eighty-five to seventy-nine in the House, but was filibustered to death in the Senate. Toombs voted against it. But Congress adjourned without further action.[21]

The Wilmot Proviso was hotly debated for the rest of the summer and autumn. It was written about on editorial pages, discussed in parlors, and argued about around cracker barrels. To many Northerners, the proviso was a gallant proposal, a righteous manifestation of their anti-slavery philosophy. But to Southerners, it was a nasty taunt and a gratuitous insult to their way of life. Southern boys were shedding their blood in this war just like Northern boys. Wasn't the South entitled to the spoils the same as their Northern brethren? As war with Mexico drew to a close, the impending question loomed: would America's new territories be slave or free?

The South opposed the proviso unanimously. Southern Democrats argued that the measure was a dire threat to the expansion of slavery. Southern Whigs argued it was a political contraption that endangered Southern rights. But the Wilmot Proviso found strong Whig and Democratic support on the other side of the Mason-Dixon Line. To keep the always fragile unity in the Whig family, party leaders agreed to condemn dissecting Mexico. If no territory were confiscated after the war, the Whigs reasoned, it would be impossible to inflict the Wilmot Proviso on the South.

Toombs returned home from Washington, D.C. in August, just in time for another campaign season to begin. His votes on major issues pleased his constituents. His attempt to keep the Democrats from lowering the tariff drew particular praise. Rolling back taxes and spending just before an election was an old Democratic trick, Toombs claimed. "Sound, practical, common sense views," the Augusta *Chronicle* clapped. Lengthy portions of his tariff speech were even quoted in the influential Whig journal *American Review.* Not bad for a freshman congressman.[22]

Toombs was easily re-nominated. The Democrats threw whatever they thought would stick at him. They accused him of being soft on slavery since he was in the same party as the abolitionist John Quincy Adams. They criticized him for his vote against lowering the tariff. They even accused Toombs of ducking his Democratic opponent, R.W. Flournoy, although neither man seemed keen to debate. But Toombs strolled to an easy reelection.[23]

He traveled back to Washington on December 28, late for the Second Session of the Twenty-Ninth Congress. Two weeks later, on January 8, 1847, he delivered his only major speech of the session. But it was a stem-winder. The pretext was a reply to a bill that authorized ten additional regiments for the war. Toombs was against it because it let the president appoint military officers. He preferred a measure that allowed volunteers to elect their own officers. The president had already appointed six brigadier generals and their only merit, according to Toombs, was that they were Democrats. Polk's appointed accomplices were nothing more than "a set of adventurers whom the soldiers would not elect."

Then Toombs went on the attack. Polk had attempted to silence debate, assailed Whig patriotism, and shut down Whig presses. Polk's "want of capacity and imbecility" gave the country "victories without advantages." It was Polk's fault that the Mexican Army had slipped away after losses at Palo Alto and Resaca de la Palma. Polk misused good Whig generals like Winfield Scott and Zachary Taylor and refused to give them enough reinforcements to fight the war effectively. "We are as far from conquering a peace as we were the day we started in this unfortunate war."

Toombs wanted a peace settlement that forced Mexico to pay every penny of U.S. claims. But he would "not take an inch of their territory." Mexico did not have to be dismembered. Toombs' scheme would seize Mexican ports, impose new taxes, and vigorously collect revenue. With Oregon, the American government had shown "a moderate and reasonable spirit of compromise.... But now it seemed we had found somebody we could whip, and we were determined to take enough out of her." Toombs knew that some might accuse him of giving "aid and comfort to the enemy." But, he said, he did not care. Taking land from Mexico was unjust, unprincipled, and un-American.

Up to this point, Toombs followed the usual Whig script. But then he turned his attention to the Wilmot Proviso. He had never seen anything "so well calculated to disturb the peace of the country." If the Wilmot Proviso was a Democratic trick to make political mischief, then the damage could be controlled. But if the backers of the proviso persisted, then the South would have to look after its own rights.

For the first time, Toombs invoked the specter of secession. The South would stay in the Union only if it was treated with "perfect equality," or "they would not stay in it at all," he said. The South wanted only "evenhanded justice." With no irony, Toombs said it would degrade the North to keep the South in an inferior position. The South had the right to carry its "institutions" wherever it went, "into all parts of the republic; they had a right to make their own laws while organized as territories, and when they became States, to choose for themselves whether they would have slavery or not."[24]

"It was decidedly one of the best speeches I ever heard Toombs make, and I have heard him make some fine displays," Stephens wrote from Washington, D.C., to his half-brother, Linton. "He had fully prepared himself, was calm and slow, much more systematic than usual, and in many points was truly eloquent." Stephens was quite pleased with his friend's speech and predicted that Toombs was "destined to take a very high position here."[25]

Toombs' speech was consistent with Whig strategy: criticize Polk, support the troops, and emphasize the heroics of fighting Whig generals. And if you were from the South, criticize the hell out of the Wilmot Proviso. For Toombs especially, the issue was as clear as a glass pane in a window: he believed Congress simply had no right to impose legislation that restricted slavery on the South. Like many moderate Southerners, he had no doubt the South had a theoretical right to secede. But he devoted much of his political energy to avoiding sectional scuffles. Only when threatened by legislation hostile to his Southern institutions — especially the peculiar one — did he lash out furiously. It was the driving force in his political life for the next decade and a half. Toombs was beginning to find it difficult to remain loyal both to the Union and to the South.

Toombs' speech was full of good Whig doctrine, but Alexander Stephens articulated Whig policy more clearly a few weeks later. On January 22, he introduced resolutions that declared the war was not being waged to dismember Mexico or for "acquisition of any portion of her territory" and that hostilities should end as soon as "an honorable peace" could be obtained. The resolutions failed, but Stephens' "No Territory" scheme was highly praised and adopted by Whigs, both North and South. "A courageous move," the *National Intelligencer* crowed. Stephens was a man not to be "deterred from doing what he knows to be right." "The position taken by Messrs. Stephens and Toombs on this important question is truly elevated," the Augusta *Chronicle* fawned, "and one which commands the admiration and respect of the patriots of the land." Some Whigs who had supported the Wilmot Proviso now backed "No Territory." Henry Clay even endorsed it. Stephens' resolutions were soon attached to every appropriation bill possible.[26]

Toombs remained mostly quiet for the rest of the session, perhaps to let Stephens keep the spotlight. Toombs and Stephens returned to Georgia early in March. Toombs tended his law practice, ran his plantations, and threw his considerable energies into establishing a public corporation to build a railroad branch line from Washington, Georgia, to intersect with the central railroad. Toombs was on the committee to negotiate and no doubt wield political influence with the Georgia Railroad. The spur was finally built in 1853 from Washington to Barnett.[27]

Toombs also did some politicking. He tried to shore up Whig support wherever he could. He even wrote to the volatile South Carolina Democrat John C. Calhoun. Senator Calhoun had come out loudly against Polk and the war. He also had some sympathy for the Whigs. Calhoun had proposed a set of pro–Southern resolutions stating that Congress could not deprive the South of its rights in the new territories and that people in the territories should be free to set up whatever form of government they wished. Toombs admired them greatly.

Toombs reminded Calhoun that he disliked the idea of appropriating Mexican territory. "I can see nothing but evil to come of it. And now I do see clearly how it can be well avoided to some extent." Appealing to the foxy old senator's political vanity, he wrote, "Our policy upon this whole Mexican question it is now evident will be in your hands. The Whigs and your friends will undoubtedly be able to control the next house [sic] of Representatives and upon this question I think the Senate."[28]

The Georgia Whig convention met at Milledgeville in July. Whigs denounced the Wilmot Proviso and extolled Whig officers in the field, especially Zachary Taylor. The convention even recommended that Taylor be given the Whig nomination for president in the 1848 election. But in the state elections, the Whigs' man for governor, Duncan L. Clinch, was defeated by Democratic stalwart George W. Towns. But the party took a small majority in the state legislature and reelected John M. Berrien and William C. Dawson to the Senate.[29]

Toombs returned to Washington for the opening session of the Thirtieth Congress. The Whigs held a seven-seat majority in the House, so Toombs could indulge his two favorite themes: touting Southern Whig policy and jabbing his finger in the administration's eye whenever he got the chance. His first action was submitting a resolution that stated neither the "honor or the interest of this Republic demands the dismemberment of Mexico, of the annexation of any portion of her territory ... as an indispensable condition to the restoration of peace." Toombs also questioned President Polk's right to withhold correspondence and instructions he had given a foreign minister that had negotiated with Mexico. Toombs thought the matter should be turned over to a congressional committee, although "he was not satisfied what that committee should be."[30]

Just like when he was in Georgia's House of Representatives, Toombs took up the fight against government largess. He was almost a fanatic in trying to force fiscal control on the government. He argued against everything from printing contracts to reducing a military company from a hundred men to its pre-war level of sixty-four men. In debating the annual salary of the Patent Office inspector, Toombs was determined to fix the amount at fifteen hundred dollars per year. When asked by Thomas Henley of Indiana if he could learn in three months enough technical ins and outs to decide upon the application for a patent "for a churn or a washing machine much less for improvements on a steam engine," Toombs replied that he did not think he could "learn to shoe a horse in three years; but it was not a reason why he should pay $500 for it."[31]

Despite his thriftiness, Toombs could still send pork to his state. He asked the Committee of Commerce to inquire into establishing a port of entry at Augusta and asked for federal funds to remove a number of shipwrecks from the Savannah River near Fort Pulaski.[32]

On February 2, 1848, the war with Mexico ended when the Treaty of Guadelupe Hidalgo was signed. Under the treaty, the Mexican-American border was relocated along the Rio Grande and Mexico gave up 500,000 square miles of the California and New Mexico region. In return, the United States agreed to pay fifteen million dollars to Mexico — half of what the U.S. tried to buy the land for before the war — and assumed $325 million in U.S. claims against the Mexican government. The war had cost a hundred million dollars and thirteen thousand American lives (only seventeen hundred of which were killed in battle; the rest died of disease).[33]

With the war over, politicians turned to the next presidential election. Whig leaders brushed off their military hero formula that had given them their only presidential victory with William Henry Harrison and started ginning up support for Zachary Taylor. As early as 1846, there had been talk of giving "Old Rough and Ready" the Whig nomination, despite the fact that Taylor had no political experience, held no discernable political views, and had never even *voted* in a presidential election.

Still, Taylor was Toombs' kind of Whig. The general had over a hundred slaves on his Louisiana plantation, was a Southerner by birth, and had no political record to run against. Southern Whigs assumed it was a safe bet that Taylor would be sound on Southern issues. Backing the insurgent Taylor was also a way for "Young Indians" like Toombs and Stephens to move old chiefs like sixty-six-year-old senator John Berrien out of the way and advance in the political tribe.[34]

But most importantly, Taylor could win.

Meanwhile, seventy-year-old Henry Clay was vying for his fourth Whig nomination. But he had little support from his party. Southern Whigs thought Clay had been too weak on Southern rights, not to mention he carried years of Whig baggage and, most unforgivably, lost the election in 1844. Clay also refused to gracefully get out of the way of Taylor's nomination. On April 10, he released a statement saying he would be available as a presidential candidate when the Whigs held their convention in Philadelphia. It was the first time anyone had publicly sought the office instead of waiting for "friends" to urge it upon him. To nineteenth century political eyes, Clay looked arrogant, egotistical, and disdainful of the process.[35]

"Clay has behaved very badly this winter," Toombs wrote to a friend in April. "His ambition is as fierce as at any time of his life, and he is determined to rule or ruin the party." Toombs believed Clay had sold out to anti-slavery Whigs in the North. Yet Clay was still popular in pockets of Georgia. "I find myself a good deal denounced in my district for avowing my determination not to vote for him." But "it gives me not the least concern. I shall never be traitor enough to the true interests of my constituents to gratify them in this respect. I would rather offend than betray them."[36]

Toombs also published a letter in the Augusta *Chronicle* that said Clay's nomination would cost the Whig Party the election, and "secure the continuance in power of the weak, profligate, and treacherous administration of Mr. Polk." On the other hand, General Taylor was "a sound Whig" who had devoted his life to defending the principles of his country. "Much of his life has been spent remote from civilized men, protecting the homes and the firesides of our frontier population," Toombs gushed. "To the remote forest, to the distant and vast prairie, to the gloomy everglade, he has been called, by duty, to privation, to toil, and to danger." Toombs was frustratingly silent on Taylor's political qualifications, but the country would hear from Taylor himself in "due season, in reference to these opinions."[37]

Toombs spent the spring doing everything he could to defeat Clay's nomination. "Mr. Clay occupies a position towards the strong anti-slavery men of the North that would make his election the greatest possible danger to the South," Toombs wrote a few weeks later, "and I shall never do any act to aid it, whatever may be the consequences personally to me." Toombs even threatened to leave politics if Clay got the nomination and "quietly drop into my former pursuits [the law and running his plantations] so congenial to my tastes, my interests, and mental preparation." But as long as he was a public servant, he vowed to maintain "the public interest and my own honor at any and every hazard of the popular displeasure."[38]

Toombs was called away from Washington and politics in May. His mother, Catherine, was gravely ill. Toombs rushed home only to find that he was too late. His mother died two days before he arrived. "She seemed to dwell in an atmosphere of love and good will, which pervaded all her words and actions," eulogized the Augusta *Chronicle*, "and no opportunity of conferring kindness or bestowing relief was suffered to pass unimproved by her."[39]

Despite his loss, Toombs, Stephens, and other Young Indians spent the summer talking up their candidate. They were instrumental in grooming the old general for his new political career and getting the Whig nomination for him. After Taylor made a series of political gaffes, a friend named Major W.W.S. Bliss visited John J. Crittenden, Stephens, and Toombs at their rooms in Washington. They discussed their candidate's shortcomings — specifically his lack of political knowledge. Crittenden, Toombs and Stephens then laid out Taylor's views point by point and Crittenden drafted letters for the presidential candidate to sign. The letters appeared a few days later in the New Orleans *Daily Picayune.* Known as the Allison Letters, they reassured Whig voters that Taylor would be conservative with the veto and would follow the will of Congress on important Whig issues like the tariff and internal improvements. Taylor, according to the letters, was "a Whig, but not an ultra one," whatever that meant. When Toombs counted the electoral votes, he reported to John J. Crittenden in late September that things "are not as good as I had hoped or expected." Still, he believed Taylor would be the next president. "Every day of my own time shall be given to that object until the sun goes down on the 7th Nov.," he vowed.[40]

In a public letter written to the Milledgeville *Southern Recorder*, Toombs admitted that some objected to Taylor because the "party harness does not fit him well." Still, Taylor was "a Whig in principle" and even refused to bind himself to those he agreed with. "These things commend him to my approbation and support." And Toombs disingenuously assured his readers that he held no regard for "the opinions which have been manufactured for General Taylor by either his Whig or Democratic enemies, or both combined."[41]

If Toombs believed in the policies that he had crafted for Taylor, he was having second thoughts about the man himself. Sentiment against Taylor was growing in the North and he feared the men who were nominated and instructed to vote for him "will set about to manage him out of it." Toombs had tried to tell the naive Taylor about this kind of political back-stabbing, but Taylor had "nobody to blame but himself, for I candidly and honestly warned him of the treachery, and designated the traitors," Toombs wrote to James Thomas. "But his insane ambition blinded him, and he must drink the bitter draft of disappointment which I would have gladly (from the recollections of the past) dashed from his lips."[42]

In May, the Democrats met in Baltimore and picked Lewis Cass as their candidate. Cass had been a general during the War of 1812, served as governor of the Michigan territory, as Andrew Jackson's secretary of war, and resigned from the Senate to run for president. A few weeks later, the Whigs held their convention in Philadelphia and nominated Taylor. No one was surprised, but some old-line Whigs were disgusted. Daniel Webster called Taylor "an illiterate frontier colonel." "Great God," one Henry Clay supporter wrote. "I feel disgraced that I was ever called a Whig."[43]

If Toombs was less than enthusiastic about his candidate, he was still enthusiastic about the prospects of his candidate's victory. The Young Indians had been busy counting votes and Toombs confided to George W. Crawford that "all our private information is of the most cheering character & I have adopted the general opinion here that we shall carry it by a large majority." Toombs was giddy over splits in the Democratic Party. Martin Van Buren had led a faction of dissidents out of the Democratic convention and out of the party over slavery. These anti-slavery Barnburners — derisively named after the apocryphal farmer who burned down his barn to get rid of the rats — nominated Van Buren while the regular Democrats, called Hunkers, nominated Lewis Cass. Whigs were sure the split in the Democratic ticket would certainly give Taylor the presidency.[44]

As for his own reelection to the House of Representatives, he had nothing but confidence. County conventions across the state were passing resolutions praising Toombs and calling for his re-nomination. Toombs thought his victory was a sure thing and he was doing everything he could for the ticket. "If the Whigs of the 8th [District] want my services in the campaign they can have them." And when Taylor won Georgia with a crushing majority from Whigs and cross-over Democrats, then "all my political objects will have been achieved & my ambition satisfied."[45]

On July first, Toombs made a stump speech on the hot and muggy House floor supporting Taylor. He listed the woes of the national economy and blamed the Polk administration. Not only had the president spent millions of dollars on the war and millions more on the peace; he but had also brought the country discord and sectional strife. "These are some of the bitter fruits of the election of Mr. Polk, and the success of the Democratic party," Toombs lamented.

The country needed a patriot and "the public marked General Zachary Taylor as that man." Toombs bragged about Taylor's non-partisan disposition and reiterated Taylor's sentiments as spelled out in the Allison Letters, including his promise to be sparing with the veto. Taylor refused to be considered a "mere party candidate, and put himself upon the support of those of his countrymen who concurred with him in opinions." Under a Taylor administration, "we shall no more see patronage and power doing the work of reason and argument in Congress." As for the Democrats' nominee, Lewis Cass, the noise and confusion of the campaign "have already so perplexed the old gentleman, that he despairs of being able to understand himself."[46]

On July 12, a sectionally balanced committee of four Whigs and four Democrats grappled with how to establish governments for Oregon, California, and New Mexico. John M. Clayton, a Whig from Delaware, was appointed chairman. Four days later, the committee submitted the Clayton Compromise Bill. The bill organized Oregon with its existing anti-slave laws, but gave the territorial government authority to alter them. It also organized California and New Mexico, but forbade the territorial governments from establishing laws for or against slavery. The legality of slavery was to be referred to the territorial courts, with a provision for appeals to the Supreme Court.

After twenty-one hours of debate, the Senate passed the bill. Though the compromise was popular throughout the South, Stephens spiked the Clayton Compromise in the House. According to Stephens' logic, Congress could not prohibit slavery in any U.S. territory. Congress and local legislatures, however, could constitutionally *establish* slavery. The South had just as much right to put its institutions in the new territory as the North, Stephens wrote, and he would never surrender that right by a vote. Not incidentally, this was also a way to further isolate Senator Berrien, who voted for Clayton's bill.[47]

Toombs reluctantly supported the compromise before it was killed. This was one of the few times he was not politically aligned with his friend from the Seventh District. But on substance, he agreed with Stephens. "We ought never to surrender the territory either directly or covertly [to the North] until it shall be wrested from us as we wrested it from the Mexicans," he wrote on August 25 to Andrew J. Miller, shortly after Congress adjourned. "Such a surrender would degrade and demoralize our section and disable us from effective resistance to future aggression. It is far better that the new acquisition should be the grave of the Republic than of the rights and honor of the South; and from the present indications 'to this complexion must it come at last.'"[48]

Toombs later said that he would have voted against the final bill and that he disagreed with Stephens only on procedural matters. Whatever the reason, the old dogs in the party were still critical of pups like Toombs and Stephens. Berrien's friends warned that Stephens and Toombs had "all banded together to advance themselves" by directing "the action of the Whig party."[49]

Stephens bore the brunt of the attacks by both Democrats and dissatisfied Whigs. "Traitor to the South" was one of the politer epithets hurled at him. Stephens' doubtful political career may have been salvaged when he was stabbed several times during a brawl with Judge Francis Cone, a Georgia Democrat with whom Stephens had traded more than a few hot words. A rumor had circulated that Cone had called Stephens a traitor. The perennially frail Stephens had publicly threatened to "slap his jaws" to repay the insult. In September, Cone followed Stephens to the Atlanta Hotel in Atlanta, Georgia. An argument escalated until Stephens whacked Cone with an umbrella. Cone, in a blind rage, stabbed Stephens several times.[50]

"You have doubtless heard that Stephens was cut down by a cowardly assassin," Toombs wrote to Crittenden. "His invaluable services have been thus far wholly lost in the campaign, which has thrown double duty on me." Toombs complained that he had not had enough time at home since Congress adjourned, but "Stephens was getting well slowly — the muscles connecting his thumb and forefinger of his right hand were cut asunder.... His physicians are still under some apprehension that he [will] have to lose the hand to escape lockjaw, tho' the chances of such a calamity are daily lessening."

The political contest was heated among editors and candidates, "but there is so little excitement among the people that one can hardly tell which way the current is moving." Toombs reported that Democrats did not attack the popular Taylor, "but furiously denounce Fillmore all the time." After the Whig convention, Democrats discovered that their vice presidential nominee, Millard Fillmore, had consistently voted against the gag rule in Congress. In 1838, he had even written a sympathetic letter to abolitionists supporting the end of slavery in Washington, D.C. and the interstate slave trade. "We were turning the tide very well on to him until that infernal letter of 1838 to the abolitionists was dug up. That has fallen upon us like a wet blankett [sic] and has very much injured us in the State."

Still, Toombs was confident that Georgia would go for Old Zach, but by a "*hard close* vote." Henry Clay's supporters — Berrien's friends — were doing nothing to help. "Some of them would be glad to lose it with the hope of breaking down Stephens and myself in the State," Toombs complained. "They will lessen my vote in my district some two or three hundred unless I can get them from the Democrats. I think I shall do so." Had Clay not announced himself as a candidate back in April, "there would not have been even a contest in Georgia, the friends of Clay being the only men here who ever dared to attack Taylor."[51]

As for his own re-nomination to Congress, he won it easily. Toombs accepted it with a long public letter that summed up the events that had occurred since he had been in the House. He missed no opportunity to criticize Polk, Polk's foreign policy, the Wilmot Proviso, and Democrats in general. The results of the war with Mexico had brought conquered territories and "reluctant people" under the U.S. flag along with political turmoil. "We have exchanged foreign war for domestic discord," he fumed.[52]

Toombs kept a backbreaking schedule during the campaign. He stumped in both his and Stephens' districts for Taylor. In less than a week, he gave speeches at Fenn's Bridge, Sparta, Warrenton, and Appling. "I think Mr. Toombs has had the weight of the canvass long enough," Stephens wrote to Julia, "and though he has done gallant service, this but inspires me with the wish to lend all aid in my power." "Julia complains a good deal at my absence," Toombs wrote to Crittenden, "but she is becoming herself warmly enlisted for 'Old Zach.'"[53]

The attack on Stephens gave Whigs a sympathy card to play during the election. Stephens was a frail, sickly man while Cone was brawny and robust. Whigs successfully depicted the attack as a political Goliath's attempt to assassinate a principled David. At the statewide Whig convention in Atlanta, rumors circulated that Stephens would make an appearance. The crowd roared when Stephens hobbled to the speaker's stand. "Stephens! Stephens! Stephens!" Stephens was not able to make a speech, but he told a short anecdote and urged everyone to vote for Zachary Taylor and to give him a good Whig Congress.[54]

Toombs and Stephens carried the campaign for Taylor everywhere they could, even to New York City. They were sure a crowd of Yankees would be hostile to Southern slaveholders telling them how to vote. So before his speech, Toombs and a congressional clerk named Samuel J. Anderson paid two hundred dollars to some local toughs for crowd control. According to Stephens, "Toombs, who was able to make himself perfectly at home in such a crowd" made the arrangements.

That night, Toombs walked on stage. "Fellow citizens of New York" was no sooner out of his mouth than loud cries of "Slaveholder! Slaveholder!" and "Hurrah for Clay!" were shouted from the audience. But Toombs' hired muscle grabbed the hecklers and flung them out the door. After the commotion, Toombs commenced his speech. Whether the audience was intimidated or genuinely interested in what Toombs had to say about Zachary Taylor, it was quiet and orderly the rest of the night. When Toombs finished, the crowd applauded and stomped and shouted "Three cheers for old Zach!"[55]

In October, Toombs and Stephens carried their districts by overwhelming majorities. But turnout was light for the presidential campaign a month later: Taylor narrowly defeated Democrat Lewis Cass and Free Soil candidate Martin Van Buren. Taylor eked out a win in Georgia by only two thousand votes. "I have worked hard and feel amply rewarded," Toombs wrote to Crittenden.[56]

It was a victory Toombs and his friends would regret.

After Taylor won the election, Southern Democrats accused Southern Whigs of sacrificing Southern rights. Taylor's sentiments about the Wilmot Proviso were unknown and Southern Democrats hinted darkly that Whigs would support him if he signed it. To add to Southern Whigs' distress, both parties in the North resolved to pass the proviso just to stamp out the freshly hatched Free Soil Party. So Southern Whigs were especially vulnerable to the charge of being soft on Southern rights.

When Congress convened in December, Whig congressman Daniel Gott of New York introduced a resolution in the House that prohibited slavery in Washington, D.C. Angry Southern legislators from both parties, incited by John C. Calhoun, formed a fifteen-member committee and held private meetings in the Senate Chamber. A five-man subcommittee, also led by Calhoun, issued a report that listed the major transgressions against slavery Congress had passed from the founding of the country to the proposed Wilmot Proviso. Calhoun ultimately called for a new Southern Rights Party to guard Southern interests. Most Southern Whigs, conservative by temperament and with no use for yet another rival party, wanted nothing to do with the exercise. They also feared the inflammatory rhetoric in Calhoun's Southern Address would only encourage the Northern majority to attack the South even more.

Toombs and Stephens were in the testy meeting. Both were decidedly hostile to Calhoun's report. Stephens quickly resigned from the committee. But Toombs stayed on to have the argument. He told Calhoun that uniting the South was neither possible nor desirable until Southerners were serious about dissolving the Union. Whigs were not ready to ask people "to look anywhere else than their own government for the *prevention* of apprehended evils." The Whigs had brought Taylor into power and they were not about to let him do anything to inflame a rebellion. Southern opposition could not be sustained by acting only on a hypothesis. "We intend to stand by the government," Toombs told Calhoun, "until it committed an overt act of aggression upon our rights, which neither we nor the country ever expected." Most of the Whigs on the committee saw the report as a political trap and even some Democrats thought Calhoun too extreme and refused to support it.

Calhoun's Southern Movement was "a bold strike to disorganize the Southern Whigs and either destroy Genl. Taylor in advance or compel him to throw himself in the hands of a large section of the [D]emocracy at the South," Toombs complained to Crittenden. Toombs, Stephens, and other Southern Whigs had attended the meeting to try to control the agenda and crush Calhoun's scheme. Toombs believed that Calhoun's strategy was based "not on the conviction that Genl. T. can *not* settle our sectional difficulties, but that he *can* do it." Toombs later bragged that he and his Whig friends had "completely foiled Calhoun and his miserable attempt to form a Southern party." The caucus wrangled over Calhoun's Southern Address until "a weak milk and water address to the whole Union" was drafted. This version was rejected and Calhoun's address was adopted by a measly thirty-six to nineteen on a party line vote. Twenty-four Whigs and seventeen Democrats — including Georgia's Howell Cobb — refused to sign. Toombs sewed the discord that foiled Calhoun's attempt to unify the South and the effort ended in division and bickering.[57]

But like any good politician, Toombs was willing to do a little horse-trading. He was willing to accept Daniel Gott's resolution against Washington, D.C.'s hated slave pens. "We will try to trade them off to advantage," Toombs wrote. "No honest man would regret their annihilation, if done rightly." By sacrificing the slave trade in Washington, D.C., Toombs hoped to encourage Northern Whigs to fight off the Wilmot Proviso. Also, since Americans with gold fever were streaming into California, Toombs was optimistic that these "legacies of the Polk administration" would be easy to adjust. "The temper of the North is good, and with kindness, and patronage skillfully adjusted, I think we can work out of the present troubles, preserve the Union, and disappoint bad men and traitors."

Toombs had earned some say in Taylor's cabinet picks. But he could not resist slamming Henry Clay again and urged Crittenden to keep him out of the Senate if possible. Clay was deeply hostile to Taylor and was "determined to come here and to make a party of his own, and perhaps join the Free-soilers." Toombs was also suspicious of Daniel Webster. He suggested getting someone in the cabinet such as New England industrialist Abbott Lawrence, who would be "much more easily managed." Toombs also urged Crittenden to accept a position in the cabinet. "The sentiment is universal here that it is of the first importance to the success of Genl. T's administration and to the country that you should come."[58]

Toombs' optimism evaporated within a few days. "The longer it remains on hand the worse it gets," he wrote to Crittenden. Toombs threw his support behind a bill by Virginia congressman William B. Preston that erected California and a portion of New Mexico west of the Sierra Membres into a state as soon as their constitutions were written. Toombs thought this was the most politically feasible. That region could not be a slave country; "we have only the point of honor to save; this will save it, and rescue the country from all danger from agitation."

Toombs acknowledged that he did not know Taylor's opinion on the matter, but he was sure Taylor would accept nothing less than protection of slavery in other new states. "I have a strong opinion in favour [sic] of [the bill's] propriety and practicality, and with a perfect knowledge of the hopes, fears, cliques, and combinations of both parties, I do not hesitate to say now is the very best time to force it to a settlement." Since it was widely believed that New Mexico and California were unsuitable for the plantation system, Toombs and his colleagues knew slaveholders would be reluctant to migrate there. Still, he hoped any new states would be left alone to determine their own institutions. Besides, one free state was preferable to three or four.[59]

On February 7, Preston introduced his bill that called for all of the former Mexican territory to be admitted as one state. There was no reference to slavery to be found. The speech was "a very good one and its effect very happy," Toombs wrote to Crittenden. Toombs predicted the measure would pass easily in the House although he thought it would have difficulty in the Senate. Still, he believed a majority from both parties would support the bill. "I consider the question for all practical purposes as now settled whatever may be its fate this session." Toombs' prediction was a disastrous miscalculation.[60]

On February 27, a stipulation forbidding slavery in the new territory was attached to Preston's bill. It took the bill down to defeat. During an all-night session of name-calling and threats of fistfights, Congress could only agree to extend the tax laws over the new territory. "When this committee determined to put the prohibitory clause upon the amendment of the gentleman from Virginia," Toombs told the House in despair "all chance of pacification was at an end."[61]

The defeat of Preston's bill left Toombs profoundly disillusioned. Anyone with common sense knew that California could not support slavery. Yet extremist Free-Soilers, Democrats, and some Northern Whigs insisted on tying the Wilmot Proviso to all territorial legislation. Southerners responded by fire-eating. "Public feeling in the South is much stronger than many of us supposed," Toombs wrote to Preston. Passing "the Wilmot Proviso would lead to civil war" and even admitting California as a free state would create "bitterness of feelings."[62]

If Toombs no longer had faith in his Whig colleagues in the North, he could still look to the Taylor administration. Inauguration day was cloudy and cold. Rain and snow foreshadowed things to come. Taylor's drab inaugural address gave no indication of his polices for the nation, the slavery issue, or the new territories. His views on the Wilmot Proviso remained a mystery. But Taylor was canny enough to realize his limitations as a Washington outsider. He had relied on established political insiders such as Alexander Stephens and Toombs for advice on cabinet appointments and patronage matters. Crittenden suggested Taylor make Toombs secretary of war. But Toombs was not cabinet officer material and he knew it. He suggested George W. Crawford for the post instead. Crawford had "administrative qualities of an unusually high order," Toombs wrote to Crittenden, while "I have an unaffected repugnance to official station, and my interests harmonize with my inclinations in this respect. Politics with me is but an episode in life, not its business."[63]

While tending his other business, Toombs kept one eye on the drift of the new administration. He quickly grew alarmed at what he saw. Rumors circulated that Taylor's administration was hostile to letting slavery into any new western territories. Southern Whigs like Toombs feared anti-slavery Whigs like New York's William Henry Seward, Daniel Webster of Massachusetts, and Secretary of the Treasury William Meredeth were exerting improper influence over the politically naïve Taylor.

Still, Toombs was willing to give Taylor the benefit of the doubt for the time being. "Genl. Taylor is in a new position, his duties and responsibilities are vast and complicated, and besides, he is among strangers whose aims and objects are not known to him," Toombs wrote to Crittenden's daughter. Sure, Taylor would make mistakes, but Toombs had confidence that he was honest and sincere and could adjust his course along the way. He still had high hopes for Taylor, although he sounded like a man ready to be disappointed: "If I am mistaken in this, no man in the nation will more bitterly repent the events of the last eighteen months than I will, and I think in that event I shall have made my last Presidential campaign."[64]

Southern Whigs were beginning to be alarmed, embarrassed, and were starting to feel betrayed by Taylor. His prolonged silence concerning slavery expansion and the Wilmot Proviso left them in a no-win situation that fall. Southern Democrats exploited divisions in the Whig family by insinuating Taylor would sign the proviso. In Georgia, Toombs and Stephens worked hard to keep the Democrats from bludgeoning Whigs with the issue. They dominated the Georgia Whig convention, handpicked Edward Y. Hill as the gubernatorial candidate, rammed resolutions through cursing the Wilmot Proviso and expressed their full confidence in Taylor.[65]

In August, Taylor made some vague public statements that hinted the North did not need to worry about the extension of slavery. The remarks boosted Whig chances in Northern elections, but it shattered Whig morale in the South. Whigs suffered heavy losses in the fall elections. Congress, state legislatures, and the Georgia governor's race fell to the Democrats. Shaken by the slaughter at the hands of the Northern Democratic–Free Soil coalition, Southern Whigs ran from the party like rabbits from the hounds. Those left standing were now hell-bent on bringing California and New Mexico into the Union without the Wilmot Proviso.

The fall elections encouraged Northern Whigs to talk enthusiastically about passing the proviso. Then in September, California delegates met in a small schoolhouse in Sacramento and wrote a state constitution. On November 13, 1849, they ratified the controversial document that banned slavery.

Toombs was now determined to find out once and for all where the administration stood on a host of issues. He met with Taylor a few days before the first session of the Thirty-first Congress convened. Toombs confronted Taylor about letting the patronage fall into the hands of Seward. According to Toombs, Seward was trying to get the Whig nomination as president in 1852 or 1856. Toombs feared Seward would take over the New York Whig political machine and force the whole Northern Whig Party into Seward's "extreme anti-slavery position" which would destroy the party in the South. "I knew the effect of this policy would certainly destroy the Whig party and perhaps endanger the Union." Toombs talked with Taylor at length about the Wilmot Proviso. The old general said he would do nothing to advance the proviso, but "he gave me clearly to understand that if it was passed he would sign it."

The meeting was a disillusioning epiphany for Robert Toombs. "My course became instantly fixed and settled," he wrote to George W. Crawford. "As I would not hesitate to oppose the Proviso even [to] the extent of a dissolution of the Union, I could not for a moment regard any party considerations in the treatment of the question. I therefore determined to put the test to the Whig party and abandon its organization upon its refusal."[66]

Like many Southern Whigs, Toombs realized too late that Taylor was a Southerner by birth but a nationalist at heart. He had been a soldier all of his life and had fought for the nation in those years, not the North or the South. Taylor turned out to be a Whig, but not an "Ultra Whig" after all. A year earlier, Taylor's stance should have pleased Toombs and his Whig colleagues. Toombs was a practical compromiser who made every effort to keep the peace between North and South to preserve the Union. But in Toombs' eyes, the Northern wing of the Whig Party had become narrowly dogmatic about sticking the Wilmot Proviso to the South. Toombs was radically disillusioned with Taylor, the Whigs, and the prospects for his country. As of the fall of 1849, he was a Whig in name only.

Toombs attended the congressional Whig caucus on Saturday, December 1. About ninety Whigs were there to select their leaders and set up their political agenda. During the meeting, it became evident that most Northern Whigs were determined to graft the Wilmot Proviso onto territorial bills for New Mexico and Utah. So Toombs submitted a resolution he had drawn up with Stephens: "Resolved," it read, "that Congress ought not to pass any law prohibiting slavery in the territories of California or New Mexico, nor any law abolishing slavery in the District of Columbia."

Northern members were shocked at Toombs' resolution. William Duer of New York rejected the resolution on the grounds that voting for it would make the Whigs a sectional party. Whigs disagreed on many things, Duer said, so he did not expect someone like Toombs to "coerce individuals to think alike on such exciting questions." Even a few Southerners thought it was too audacious. During the heated discussion, Stephens made a passionate case for the resolution. The Northern majority should not be able to inflict the "mortification" of the Wilmot Proviso on the South. Southern members generally agreed with Toombs' concept, but asked him to withdraw the resolution. Toombs refused. So the caucus voted to postpone it. With that, Toombs, Stephens, Allen F. Owen of Georgia, and several other Whigs turned on their heels and bolted the caucus.

Toombs had caused a stir. The papers referred to it as "a sad occurrence" and "an unfortunate event," and a "sign of a bad omen." Privately, others were more candid. "I regretted Mr. Toombs introducing his resolution into the Whig caucus," Nathan Appleton of Virginia wrote. He thought it "ill-timed, and to a certain extent improper." As James G. King of New Jersey put it, it was no time to be "distracting ourselves when we had a common enemy to face." "Toombs is a spoiled child," John Winthrop wrote to John P. Kennedy a few days later, "jealous, impatient, and perverse. He had his own way in respect to the Cabinet, & now he must rule or ruin in the House."[67]

Most Whig journals back in Georgia did not see it that way. "Mr. Toombs and his associates, who we regret are not more numerous, are seeking preservation of the Union by maintaining the letter and spirit of the Constitution," an editorial in the Augusta *Chronicle* lectured. It was a resolution that would fight the "fanaticism" of the North and only tried to secure the equality of every section of the Union. Toombs owed it to his constituents "to decline an alliance with men who, while professing conservatism, were running to ... secure the countenance and support of the fanatics."[68]

Whatever anyone said about Toombs and his colleagues bolting the caucus, they could not help but notice that this was a different Robert Toombs from the one that came to

Washington in 1845, a different man who had punctured Calhoun's Southern Movement only the year before. Toombs and Stephens wanted to reorganize the Whig Party into their own "southern movement" by making the Wilmot Proviso a test of party loyalty. What was the advantage in giving up those slave pens in Washington, D.C., if the proviso was going to be rammed down the South's throat anyway? Some thought Toombs and Stephens were simply putting on a political charade while others believed they were just positioning themselves ahead of extreme Southern "fire eaters" like Calhoun or Berrien.[69]

But Toombs and Stephens had their own reasons for trying to reform the Whig Party. To their thinking, Taylor had double crossed them. They had helped put Taylor in the president's office and he refused to protect their political and economic interests from the Wilmot Proviso or from the Northern wing of their own party. "My southern blood ... is up," Stephens angrily wrote to his half brother, Linton. "I am prepared to fight at all hazzards [sic] and to the last extremity in vindication of our honor and our rights." So was Toombs.[70]

The First Session of the Thirty-first Congress convened on December 3. The same day, California applied for admission to the Union. In his only annual message, President Taylor urged statehood for California without delay. He also recommended admission of New Mexico as soon as it was ready. Taylor's scheme gave Whigs important political cover: Northern Whigs could give up the Wilmot Proviso while Southern Whigs could pronounce their honor vindicated.

Politically, Taylor's plan was brilliant. The only problem was it would not work. Now that California had actually asked for admission, a furor was set off in Congress. With free states and slave states precariously balanced at fifteen apiece, admitting California as a free state seemed one more outrage against the South.

Meanwhile, the House could not even elect a speaker. Georgia's Howell Cobb received the nod from a majority of Democrats and Robert Winthrop of Massachusetts carried most Northern Whig votes. Minor candidates split the difference. Neither Winthrop nor Cobb could get the necessary majority thanks to obstructionists like Toombs and Stephens. They were determined to drag their feet to keep the House from organizing. If Northern Whigs and the Democrat-Free-Soil coalition held, the Wilmot Proviso was a sure bet. To defeat the vile measure, Toombs set out to "prevent the organization of the House going into the hands of the Northern Whig party. I should have gone to any extent necessary to effect that object. They foolishly did it themselves." By now, he was determined to settle the proviso question "honorably to my own section if possible, at any rate and every hazard, totally indifferent to what might be its effect upon Genl. Taylor or his administration."[71]

On the fortieth ballot, W.J. Brown of Indiana was almost elected. Toombs boiled over when it was revealed that Brown had assured David Wilmot he was friendly to the proviso. But Brown had also told Southern Democrats he had made no promises to the Free Soilers.

Toombs spoke out on December 13, a day after R.K. Meade of Virginia and William Duer of New York had to be restrained from a fistfight. The Free Soilers were engaged in a secret and dishonorable conspiracy and were trying to acquire "advantages in the organization of the House by private pledges, concealed and intended to be concealed from the great majority of those whose votes were necessary to elect the person for whom they voted," Toombs raged. He refused to cooperate in electing a speaker until there were some guarantees for the South's security. But as long as the interests of his section were in danger, he was "unwilling to surrender the great power of the Speaker's chair without obtaining security for the future," he fumed. "I cannot see that my constituents have anything to hope from your legislation, but everything to fear."

Toombs said he loved the Union and the Constitution and was ready to make concessions and sacrifices. But if slavery was restricted in California and New Mexico, "purchased by the common blood of the whole people, and to abolish slavery in this District, thereby attempting to fix a national and degradation upon half the states of this Confederacy, *I am for disunion.*" [italics in the original].

For Toombs, it was a matter of justice. In an unusually emotional appeal, he explained the awkward political position he had been in over the last few years. "I have used all my energies from the beginning of this question to save the country from this convulsion," he said. He had resisted unnecessary and harmful agitation and hoped against hope that "justice and patriotism" would induce the North to settle the question. "I have planted myself upon a national platform, resisting extremes at home and abroad, willingly subjecting myself to the aspersions of enemies, and far worse than that, the misconstructions of friends, determined to struggle for and accept any fair and honorable adjustment to these questions. I have almost despaired of any such, at least from this House."

Only when he got assurances that his constituents' institutions would be protected would he quit obstructing organization in the House. "Grant them and you prevent the recurrence of the disgraceful scenes of the last twenty-four hours, and restore tranquility to the country. Refuse them, and as far as I am concerned, 'let discord reign forever.'"[72]

Stephens also sounded secessionist alarms. "The day in which aggression is consummated upon any section of the country, much and deeply as I regret it, this Union is dissolved." The Union was founded upon "justice and right," Stephens reminded his colleagues. "However much gentlemen may refuse to believe it ... the Union was formed for the benefit of all. We of the South who came into this union, came into it for mutual benefits as well as you gentlemen of the North."[73]

These were Toombs' and Stephens' most strident disunion threats yet. Less than a year before, the two Georgia moderates urged their Southern colleagues to let California come into the Union without slavery. Now Toombs was threatening disunion with the best of the rabid Calhounites. Toombs genuinely felt Southern honor was imperiled by allowing California to enter the Union as a free state. But he may have also been trying to outflank Senator Berrien — who supported Calhoun's Southern Movement — and Georgia Democrats on the slavery expansion issue. Whatever his motive, Toombs knew how and when to use an incendiary speech to its best effect — and when to back off — and he quickly gained the admiration of Southern fire-eaters.

Toombs' and his Whig colleagues obstructed the proceedings of the House for almost a month. Ballot after ballot was taken for a speaker without success. Even Toombs was nominated twice (receiving only one vote each time). He continued disrupting the House on the grounds that a new Congress could not adopt any rules until a speaker was elected. Even the Whigs' own *National Intelligencer* grew impatient: "We can only say that we share the universal and painful regret which is felt at the condition in which the House finds itself placed, and especially at the baleful elements which embitter the strife and render the difficulty an ominous one."[74]

In one raucous fight over whether the House could debate before voting for speaker, Toombs stole the floor. Amid hoots and jeers and calls for order and demands that he yield the floor and the clerk trying to tally votes, Toombs cried "I stand upon the Constitution of my country, upon the liberty of speech, ['order, order'], which you have treacherously violated, and upon the rights of my constituents; and your fiendish yells may be well raised to drown an argument which you tremble to hear." Members tried to shout him down but

Toombs would not yield. "I know my right!" he roared over and over again. "You may call the roll, but you cannot silence me! I stand on the constitution of my country, and on the liberty of speech!" The scribe for the *Congressional Globe* noted that, during Toombs' tirade, confused congressmen had gathered around the clerk's table "indiscriminately calling upon the Clerk to record their votes." Toombs loudly filibustered until his voice gave out. "Exhausted, hoarse, and panting for breath from his violent oratorical effort, he sank into his seat."[75]

Toombs caused commotion until December 22 when, after sixty-three ballots, Howell Cobb was elected speaker. The election "made me regret that my aspirations have been gratified," Cobb wrote to his wife. Then the House went on to waste another month wrangling over votes for the doorkeeper and clerk.[76]

Despite the turmoil, Toombs found solace in his books and he never lost his sense of humor. "Mr. Toombs loved books of the imagination, travels, anything that would help him (as the English ambassador once said of him) 'to utter some of his brilliant paradoxes,'" Varina Howell Davis recalled years later. Despite fighting fearsome political battles over the compromise and jumping to his feet twenty times a day in the House, he rose at dawn to study French. "He would sit with his hands full of the reporter's notes on his speeches for correcting, with 'Le Medecin malgre' lui' in the other hand, roaring over the play," Varina Davis wrote.

"I said to him 'I do not see how you can enjoy that so much.'

"He answered 'Whatever the Lord Almighty lets his geniuses create, He makes someone to enjoy; this plays take all the soreness out of me.'"[77]

While the House dithered with organizational matters, the Senate tried to deal with the national crisis. On January 29, 1850, Henry Clay offered eight resolutions to heal the "five bleeding wounds" of the nation. The resolutions proposed admitting California as a free state; organizing the remainder of the Mexican cession without restrictions on slavery; adjusting Texas' claim to disputed portions of New Mexico; prohibition of the slave trade — but not abolition of slavery — in Washington, D.C.; a declaration from Congress stating it had no authority to meddle in the interstate slave trade; and a severe fugitive slave law.

Clay defended his resolutions in the Senate on the fifth and sixth of February. The galleries were filled with spectators waving their fans as the temperature in the Senate Chamber soared to over a hundred degrees. Thin, ailing, his voice hoarse, Clay implored the North to compromise with the South. Clay pointed out that the North, as the most populous section of the country, could accept the spirit of the Wilmot Proviso without forcing it upon the South. Slavery could never take root in the disputed territories. "What more do you want?" he asked. "You have nature on your side — facts upon your side — and the truth staring you in the face."

But Clay had a warning for Southerners: their rights were best protected by the Constitution, he said. War would be "furious, bloody, implacable, and exterminating," he warned his Southern brothers. Going over the precipice was a "fearful and dangerous leap ... into the yawning abyss below from which none who ever take it shall return in safety."[78]

Alexander Stephens sat with his cloak spread on the floor by Clay's desk as the Great Compromiser spoke. Stephens wrote later that Clay was "a more remarkable man and much greater orator" than he had thought. There is no record of Toombs' sentiments immediately after Clay's speech, but there is no reason to believe he felt differently.[79]

Clay's Omnibus Bill gave moderate Southerners hope that sectional controversies would be put to rest once and for all. It also assured the South that they would not be collared with the Wilmot Proviso. On February 13, Taylor submitted California's free-state constitution to Congress and urged immediate admission. This time it was Stephens' turn to thwart House business at every step. Like other moderate Southerners, Toombs and Stephens wanted compensation for the South if California were admitted as a free state. They were determined the Wilmot Proviso *would not* be passed and the remaining territories would be free to draft pro-slavery constitutions without restrictions.

A few days later, an informal bipartisan meeting was held at Speaker Cobb's house. Toombs, Stephens, Kentucky Democrat Linn Boyd, Ohio Democrat William A. Richardson, Illinois Democrats John K. Miller and John A. McClernand made it clear they were there with the blessings of Democrat senator Stephen A. Douglas. When the meeting was over a compromise was struck to push Clay's plan through Congress. Toombs and Stephens agreed to support admission of California as a free state. In return, there would be no restrictive legislation on slavery in the territories and no attempts to abolish slavery in Washington, D.C. The Democrats agreed to offer the bill in both houses of Congress. It seemed like a workable deal. Everyone was optimistic that this was the best way to resolve the sectional conflict.

On February 23, Toombs, Stephens, and Thomas L. Clingman of North Carolina called on President Taylor to bring him up to speed on the plan. But Taylor hated Henry Clay's Omnibus Bill. Taylor's scheme was to admit California and veto any legislative packages that came with it. When the delegation told Taylor there would be a Southern Whig revolt if he did not modify his opposition to the Omnibus Bill, the meeting degenerated into an argument. Toombs, Stephens and Clingman may have insinuated that the South was ready to secede or Taylor may have misunderstood what they were trying to do. Maybe Taylor just wanted to shoot the messengers.

Whatever was said, Taylor snorted that California *would* come into the Union as a free state and as soon as he received the constitution from New Mexico, he would sign that, too. As for Texas, if Texans invaded New Mexico to establish slavery there, he would send federal troops and, if necessary, take the field himself.

Enraged at Taylor's obstinacy, Toombs, Stephens, and Clingman stomped out of the room and whisked by Senator Hannibal Hamlin of Maine who had been called about a patronage matter. "What are you doing here?" one of them asked brusquely. Before Hamlin could answer, he was admitted to Taylor's office.

"General Taylor was rushing around the room like a caged lion," Hamlin recalled years later. He paced the floor three or four times before he noticed Hamlin. "Did you see those damned traitors? They have been making demands concerning my administration, and threatened that unless they were acceded to, the South would secede," Taylor shouted. "But if there are any such treasonable demonstrations on the part of the Southern leaders, I will hang them." Taylor cussed and cursed them. "I will hang them as high as I hung spies in Mexico, and I will put down any treasonable movement with the whole power of the government, if I have to put myself at the head of the army to do it."

Taylor asked Hamlin what he was doing in the Senate to defeat the Omnibus Bill. Hamlin replied that he was doing everything he could to stop it. "Stand firm," Taylor said. "Don't yield; it means disunion, and I am pained to learn that we have disunion men among us." Disunion was treason, Taylor lectured Hamlin, and if "disunionists attempt to carry out their schemes while I am President," he threatened, "I will hang them."

Hamlin complimented Taylor for his determination and left. On his way out, he passed Thurlow Weed who was one Taylor's advisors. Taylor told Weed what had just happened and added that if Southern Whigs had presumed he would acquiesce to their demands simply because he was a slaveholder, they were wrong.

The date and exact details of this meeting are unclear. Perhaps Taylor misunderstood that Toombs and Stephens were devoting themselves to passage of the compromise bill to *save* the Union, not tear it apart. Perhaps Toombs and Stephens were simply relaying a message from ardent secessionists like Taylor's son-in-law, Jefferson Davis, and Taylor simply heard what he expected to hear. The picture about this event is blurry. Hamlin wrote his account some twenty-five years later and admitted he could not remember the exact date. In his memoirs, Thurlow Weed never mentioned meeting Clingman. He remembered only that Toombs and Stephens were there. Stephens denied an argument ever took place. He said it was an earnest discussion. Another possibility is that the men were recalling two or three different meetings and remembering them as the same one. At any rate, Taylor seemed more concerned about being bullied by the Southern wing of his party than reasoning with them.[80]

On February 27, Toombs spelled out his position on the House floor. In a long prepared speech, he railed against the North's "fixed purpose" to destroy the South's political rights by banning slavery from California and New Mexico. Toombs argued that since the Constitution gave special protection to slaveholders, the government was a pro-slavery government as well as a government that protected "persons and property." In Toombs' view, it was up to the states to declare what was and what was not property, not the national government. But if the government was hostile to property, "it becomes an enemy to the people, and ought to be corrected or subverted.... This is the only rule which can preserve the harmony of the Union."

In fact, he thought it was the duty of the federal government to protect property of citizens in any territory until a state government was established. And that meant the new territories won from Mexico. As for California, Toombs could not support the present admission bill now that the Wilmot Proviso had been stuck to it. The bill did nothing but establish another free state. This was exactly the situation he had dreaded all along. "I foresaw the dangers of the question," he reminded his colleagues. "I warned the country of these dangers. From the day that the first gun was fired upon the Rio Grande.... I resisted all acquisitions of territory." Toombs warned the North not to legislate against slave property. "The day you do it, you plant the seeds of dissolution in your political system." Paraphrasing the New Testament and foreshadowing Abraham Lincoln, Toombs warned "then the House will be divided against itself, and it *must* fall" (italics in the original).

Despite his threats and blustering, Toombs ended with a plea to his colleagues to pass legislation protecting slavery until the territories were admitted as states then leave it up to voters to establish slavery. "This demand is just. Grant it, and you ... perpetuate the Union, so necessary to your prosperity; you solve the true problem of Republican Government."[81]

Although Toombs openly threatened secession — something he had denounced just months before — his speech was praised for its moderation and restraint in some of the Whig press. The Richmond *Times* wrote that it was an "able, eloquent and *moderate*" speech that "commanded the attention of every member of the House. The effort will cause him to be held in higher estimation than ever." The New York *Sun* called Toombs the "ablest man of either party from the South" and noted "one might have heard a pin drop from the moment he commenced until the end of his hour." Stephens said Toombs' speech "created a perfect comotion."[82]

On March 4, Senator James Mason of Virgina read John C. Calhoun's rebuttal on the Senate floor. The dying Calhoun sat wrapped in flannel blankets and clinging to life by sheer will, staring at nothing with half closed but still defiant eyes. The only way the Union could be saved, Calhoun's speech declared, was for the North to allow slavery in California and New Mexico, a strictly enforced fugitive slave law, and no more agitation on the slavery question. The Union would not be saved by eulogies no matter how "splendid or numerous. The cry 'Union, Union, the glorious Union!' can no more prevent disunion than the cry of 'Health, health, glorious health!' on the part of the physician, can save a patient lying dangerously ill." But if the North was unwilling to part in peace "tell us so, and we shall know what to do, when you reduce the question to submission or resistance."[83]

Three days later, Daniel Webster replied in his Seventh of March speech. He spoke "not as a Massachusetts man, nor as a Northern man, but as an American." Webster agreed that the Wilmot Proviso was not needed in California and New Mexico because of "the law of nature, of physical geography ... the law of the formation of the earth" would not support slavery. Webster secured the ire of New England when he criticized abolitionists. Their only accomplishment was a counter-reaction that did not set free, but bound faster the slave population. Webster conceded that there were legitimate grievances, but he believed supporting the compromise could solve them. Northerners had a duty to return fugitive slaves; but he warned Southerners not to carry secession too far: "There can be no such thing as peaceable secession," he told his Southern colleagues. "I see that it must produce war, and such a war as I will not describe, *in its twofold character*."[84]

Toombs indicated he also would support some variations of Clay's compromise package. His favorite version was Kentucky senator John Bell's concoction to admit California as a free state and break Texas into two states. Residents could then vote to allow either new state to enter the Union slave or free. He thought Congress might go along with it, even though the present body was "the worst specimens of legislators" he had ever seen. Both Northern Democratic and Northern Whig congressmen were "jobbers, lucky serving-men, parishless parsons and itinerant lecturers ... who are not only without wisdom or knowledge, but have bad manners, and therefore we can have but little hope for good legislation." What was more, a large number of them valued their position chiefly "for the facilities it gives them for a successful foray upon the national treasury." Still, he thought there was a "tolerable prospect" for a settlement of the slavery issue except that the "Calhoun wing of the South seem to desire no settlement and may perhaps go against any adjustment which would likely pass."[85]

While the House went back to hemming and hawing about purchasing water rotted hemp for the Navy and arguing over the election of their doorkeeper, Democratic senator Henry S. Foote of Mississippi recommended that all variations of Henry Clay's compromise bill be submitted to a select committee. The bipartisan committee was composed of thirteen senators with Henry Clay as chair. On May 8, Clay presented the report. The report lumped most of the compromises back into one bill: admission of California as a free state, territorial governments for Utah and New Mexico without stipulations to slavery, and compensation to Texas for adjustment of the boundary with New Mexico. A separate item called for a harsh fugitive slave law that federalized the capture of runaway slaves and imposed harsh fines on anyone aiding an escaped slave. Finally, the report endorsed ending the slave trade in the District of Columbia. Clay knew his Omnibus Bill would alienate Northerners, but it would have support from Southern Whigs and just might keep the country—and the Whig Party—from tearing itself apart.[86]

But President Taylor remained hostile to Henry Clay and any compromise. He refused to let his plan be linked to other legislation. Rumors circulated that the same candidate who had promised to be conservative with the veto would veto any plan to admit California except his own. Toombs was appalled at the administration's intransigence and blamed it on Seward. He looked to Congress to adopt the committee's recommendations, but "the government in furtherance of their stupid and treacherous bargain with the North are endeavoring to defeat it." He still respected Taylor and hoped he would change his mind. "Taylor is an honest and well meaning man," he wrote to a friend, but was "in very bad hands."[87]

Extremists on both sides of the Mason-Dixon line opposed Clay's scheme: Northerners hated the Fugitive Slave Law; slaveholders hated giving away California and New Mexico. Stephen A. Douglas of Illinois did not think the Omnibus Bill could pass in its packaged form. But the extremists faced formidable foes that supported the package: Clay, Henry Foote, and the mighty Daniel Webster backed the compromise. The majority of the American people also favored the compromise. Despite the efforts of hardliners, the Omnibus Bill seemed destined to become law. Political heavyweights such as Texas' Democratic senator Sam Houston and ex-president John Tyler urged Congress to pass the bill. Bipartisan letters and petitions poured in from state legislatures and county meetings imploring lawmakers to pass the package. Georgia Whigs generally welcomed the compromise, although Berrien denounced it as soon as Clay made it public.

Now it was the Senate's turn to dither. Amendments, proposals to adjourn, calls for postponements, and rancorous debates wedged the Omnibus Bill in the Senate. Except for a small role with Stephens in establishing a short-lived newspaper called the *Southern Press*, Toombs remained on his good behavior. But antagonism soon bled into the House.

On June 13, during debate on James Doty's bill to admit California, Toombs took on the Northern wing of his party over an amendment to allow territories south of the Missouri Compromise line to establish slavery if they wished. Toombs accused Whigs who supported the Wilmot Proviso of being frauds. These Whigs said they supported Taylor's plan, but accompanied it with the "declaration that 'no more slave States shall be admitted to the Union.'" These hypocrites claimed to support state sovereignty for their domestic institutions, which was "the only sound principle in the [president's] 'plan.'" Yet that principle was "murdered in the House, and by the hands of its pretended friends." If congressmen from the North were counting upon the people of the South to submit to "acts of oppression," Toombs said, then "national rights may be defended and public liberty preserved." Toombs saw protecting property as any government's obligation. If it could not, then "it was the right and duty of the people to overthrow them and establish better ones. This is the solvent of tyrannies — the will to be free."[88]

On June 15, Toombs elaborated on the theme that states had the right to permit or exclude slavery. Southerners were obstructing the admission of California not because of the anti-slavery clause in its constitution, Toombs said, but because the North was attempting to tack the Wilmot Proviso on every territorial bill. After a quick review of how the principle of state sovereignty had been discarded, Toombs accused the North of only pretending to favor Taylor's plan for "sinister and temporary purposes." But this was only a pretense. "They will not find a right place to affirm it until they get California into the Union, and then they will throw off the mask and trample it under foot." He intended to drag off that mask before California was admitted.

The South had the right "to an equal participation" in the territories and had the right to enter them legally with their property, Toombs said. This right was worth a thousand such Unions, even if those unions were "a thousand times more valuable than this." Then

Toombs finished with a dire warning: if the government deprived the South of its rights, "then I am its enemy, and I will then, if I can, bring my children and my constituents to the altar of liberty, and like Hamilcar I would swear them to eternal hostility to your foul domination. Give us our just rights and we are ready ... to stand by the Union, every part of it, and its every interest. Refuse it and for one I will strike for *independence.*"[89]

Toombs had tiptoed to the edge of secession several times, but had always stepped back at the last moment. Now he sounded like a man ready to run with Southern fire-eaters and jump off with both feet. According to Stephens, Toombs' Hamilcar speech caused "a perfect commotion." The House must have been stunned to hear this political fire and brimstone coming from a man with such a reputation as a moderate. It was almost as if Toombs had been possessed by the spirit of the recently deceased John C. Calhoun. But whatever the effect, Toombs' remarks froze Doty's bill in committee for the next six weeks.[90]

Meanwhile, Taylor's obstinacy only made things worse. He had urged New Mexico to apply for statehood for months. As for the Texas-New Mexico boundary dispute, Taylor believed the Supreme Court could settle that later. Taylor's scheme also permitted Albuquerque and Santa Fe, which were in the disputed area, to remain under New Mexico's jurisdiction.

Texans did not see it that way. Texas governor Peter Bell began preparations to dispatch a band of Texans to Santa Fe to prevent federal jurisdiction from being imposed in the area. On June 17, Taylor delivered a special message to Congress stating that the federal government *would* maintain authority over the area until the dispute was adjudicated. If Taylor wanted to provoke both Southern moderates and Southern radicals to distract their attention from the Omnibus Bill, he succeeded. Fire-eaters urged their constituents to join their Texas cousins and defend the Lone Star State against the federal government. Sam Houston was already talking seriously about leaving Washington and leading another Texan army as he had twenty years before.

On July 1, a caucus of Southerners asked C.M. Conrad, Humphrey Marshall, and Robert Toombs to warn Taylor that he was courting desertion by what was left of his Southern Whigs if he continued this foolish policy. Taylor curtly told them he would not change his mind. Nor was he about to sacrifice support from eighty-four Northern Whigs just to appease twenty-nine Southern ones. A day or so later, Toombs and Stephens heard that Taylor had ordered Secretary of War George W. Crawford to authorize federal troops in the New Mexico territory to use force against any Texans who advanced on Santa Fe. Crawford refused, declaring he would never sign such an order. "Then," said Taylor, "I'll sign it myself."

Once again, Toombs rushed to the Executive Mansion and implored Taylor to change his mind. An armed clash in New Mexico would be disastrous, he told the president. But Toombs' pleas did no good. Taylor remained firm. He sneered at the idea that Texas had any legitimate claim to New Mexico. It would be immediate statehood for California and New Mexico or nothing.

Toombs went back to the House of Representatives and told Stephens what had happened. They left together, disillusioned and disheartened. When they ran into Secretary of the Navy William Ballard Preston, they asked him if he could exert any influence to change Taylor's mind. Preston would only say he supported Taylor. Frustrated and angry, Stephens blurted out: "If troops are ordered into Santa Fe, the President will be impeached."

"Who will impeach him?" Preston challenged.

"I will," replied Stephens.[91]

On July 4, President Taylor attended the dedication ceremony for the Washington Monument. During the festivities, he overindulged in cherries, cucumbers, and iced milk to cool off in the hot sun. Later that night, he developed a severe stomachache. Doctors were summoned and diagnosed the president with a serious case of "cholera morbus." Taylor might have pulled through had his physician not stuffed him with opium, epicac, and quinine. On the evening of July 9, Toombs, Stephens, and George W. Crawford stopped by the Executive Mansion to check on Taylor's condition, but they were sent away. A few hours later, church bells tolled as the message spread throughout Washington, D.C. Taylor was dead.

Mourning for Taylor had barely started when a letter appeared in the Philadelphia *Bulletin* claiming Toombs and Stephens had harassed the ailing president on his deathbed. According to the wide-spread account, they criticized the dying president severely for his California and Texas policies and threatened to censure him for his conduct in a burgeoning scandal known as the Galphin Claim.[92]

On July 13, Stephens responded to the accusation in a letter to the Baltimore *Clipper*. "I did not see General Taylor during his last illness, nor did my colleague, Mr. Toombs," Stephens protested. "The last interview I had with him was several days before his attack ... and I feel warranted in saying the same in relation to my colleague, Mr. Toombs."[93]

The new president, Millard Fillmore, was a more skillful and adept politician than General Taylor. Fillmore backed the Omnibus Bill enthusiastically. The ailing and weary Henry Clay left Washington in August to recuperate in Rhode Island's sea breezes while Senator Stephen A. Douglas, chairman of the Senate Committee on Territories, took charge of the Ominbus Bill. Douglas broke the bill back into five separate measures and steered each through the Senate. In the House, Toombs served as chairman of a Southern rights committee that was set up to ensure the South's interests were protected. Each of the fifteen slave states had one representative. The group produced a report laying out the minimum principles the South would accept, most notably the South would not support a bill prohibiting slavery in the territories and that if all else failed the Missouri Compromise line must be extended to the Pacific.[94]

But progress was slow going as the House slogged its way through the usual appropriations bills. "Congress gets on with its usual tardiness and gives no time for adjournment," he complained wearily in a letter to Julia. She usually accompanied Toombs to Washington, but she had left for Georgia in late July, probably because this session of Congress had been so tedious and protracted. "Time passes very languidly and I don't think I shall be able to stay away from you all longer than the first of September," the lonely Toombs wrote. He also dreaded that Stephens would soon abandon Washington for Liberty Hall, his plantation in Crawfordville. Toombs would have to do battle alone. "Washington is even duller than when you left," he wrote to Julia. "Every body [sic] who can go has gone off."[95]

Toombs was also having trouble with some slaves that he had brought with him. The slaves, one named Lousia and the other Garland White, were lured away by a New York abolitionist named William L. Chaplin. Chaplin was a member of the Anti-Slavery Society, an activist on the Underground Railroad, and owned abolitionist newspapers in Albany and Rochester. Chaplin had also been involved in a failed attempt to liberate almost eighty slaves by arranging for them to escape on a ship named *The Pearl*. But the ship grounded before it got out of the Potomac, the slaves were recaptured, and many of them were sold down the river.

"The free negroes [sic] I have no doubt have her [Louisa] concealed & perhaps confined, but I think it much more probable that we shall take her," Toombs gloated. He was less concerned with Garland: "I would not confine him because I did not care whether he ran away or not." Whatever Toombs thought of Garland, the runaways were caught when Chaplin tried to liberate them. A six man posse chased Chaplin's carriage out of Washington. The posse fired several shots into the interior that wounded the occupants. When they finally rode the carriage down, they shoved a fence rail through the spokes to keep their captives from escaping. They dragged Chaplin out and gave him a beating for good measure. Chaplin was arrested and held in Washington, D.C., for six weeks. His abolitionist friends raised the six thousand dollar bail but there was a jurisdictional dispute and Chaplin was again jailed in Maryland. Famed abolitionist Gerrit Smith paid five thousand dollars of the eighteen thousand dollar bond out his own pocket. But all the money was forfeited when Chaplin skipped bail and headed back to New York.[96]

In August, the Senate sent the five separate compromise bills to the House. The bills admitted California as a free state, New Mexico and Utah were organized without slavery restrictions, the Texas' boundary issue with New Mexico was settled, the slave trade — but not slavery — in Washington was abolished, and the tough Fugitive Slave Act was passed. But the details of congressional life "interests me so little that I am sure I could interest nobody else with them," Toombs wrote to Julia a few days later. He was anxious to get through with legislative business and go home to Julia's company and support. "It has been a month Monday since you left, which has taught me one lesson that I shall profit by," he wrote to her, "& that is that I shall not stay here without you, therefore you must make your visits all out this fall & prepare for coming back next winter."

Toombs was as "lonely as a hermit" and he missed her terribly.

> It's just 12 o'clock, the time I usually turn into my solitary bed which brings to my memory the joys that are past. Don't you miss our delighfull [sic] *Sunday afternoons?* I realize almost with pain your exquisite loveliness; do you understand how pleasant recollections produce pain? If you don't just imagine how badly I want to kiss you & cant. Write me every mail, burn this letter. I sent a thousand kisses. I wish you could send me your lips to kiss."[97]

Toombs was fed up with the usual grind of congressional business and yearned for his wife. "I begin to be more anxious to see you than save the republic," he wrote to Julia as the debates in the House dragged on. "The old Roman Antony threw away an empire rather than abandon his lovely Cleopatra, and the world for near twenty centuries have called him a fool for it," he wrote. "I begin to think that he was the wiser of the two & that the world was the fool and not him. And that he was a sensible man after all & that the world was well lost for love. I can imagine nothing in the world that I would take in exchange for the sweet embraces of my own fine, warm hearted lovely wife."[98]

The House finally began voting on the compromise measures in the first part of September. During the debate to organize the territory of New Mexico, Toombs gambled one last amendment to try to insure slavery would not be prohibited. His amendment proclaimed

> That no citizen of the United States shall be deprived of his life, liberty, or property in said Territory, except by the judgment of his peers and the laws of the land; and that the constitution of the United States, and such statutes thereof as may not be locally inapplicable, and the common law, as it existed in the British colonies of North America until the 4th day of July, 1776, shall be the exclusive laws of said Territory upon the subject of African slavery, until altered by the proper authority.[99]

Toombs' strategy backfired when the House adopted the first clause of his amendment, making it a potential anti-slavery measure. The second clause was defeated one hundred and thirty-four to sixty-four.[100]

Toombs voted aye to organize New Mexico territory on September 5th, no on the admission of California on September seventh due to "certain irregularities" in the application for statehood, aye on the Fugitive Slave Bill on September 12, and he missed the September 17 vote for abolition of the slave trade in Washington, D.C.[101]

In a final and revealing speech to the House, Toombs defended himself and his actions against accusations by James A. Seddon of Virginia who implied Toombs had conceded too much to the North. From the first day of the session, Toombs said, his only goal was to defeat hostile legislation against "our property." He was proud that he had spent the last two years fighting against what the South thought was "not only unnecessary, but almost treasonable to demand." If he had given away any Southern principles, he had not conceded them to the North. He had "conceded it to the public will, to the peace and tranquility of the Republic, trusting that future events shall prove that those who differed from me are wrong, a sense of national justice, purified by the fiery ordeal through which we have passed, will vindicate the right, and do justice to my country."[102]

At long last it was over. The session ended on September 30. After ten long months, the Union was rescued and the battle wearied politicians migrated back to their districts.

The compromise was popular throughout the South and Toombs and Stephens got much credit for its success. "They have never despaired," one letter to the editor of the Augusta *Chronicle* gushed, "and when repulsed and denounced by friends as well as foes, they remained firm and undaunted in the one great purpose of having this question settled upon the eternal principles of Truth and Justice." But it was still a hard sell in some places. Democratic governor George Towns led Southern Democrats in cheerfully denouncing it as a Whig surrender to the North. Southern rights extremists wrote fire-eating editorials and Southern rights associations hatched like mosquitoes in springtime. Toombs and Stephens were denounced as hypocrites, "unsound on the slavery issue," and "gravediggers."[103]

As a counterpoint to extremists, both North and South, a new political party sprang up. Coalitions of disaffected Democrats and Whigs, unhappy with extreme party positions and wild talk of breaking the Union apart formed the Constitutional Union Party. By the fall of 1850 the movement was gaining momentum, especially in the South. Whig heavyweights like Daniel Webster and novelist John Pendleton Kennedy were banging the drum enthusiastically for the new party. Even the Whigs' own Henry Clay announced in a speech to the Kentucky legislature that opposition to the compromise — especially resistance to the Fugitive Slave Law in the North — would lead to the formation of two new parties, one for the union and the other against the union. If that happened, "I announce myself, in this place, a member of that union party, whatever may be its component elements."[104]

Just before the first session of the Thirty-First Congress ended, Governor Towns called for a special state convention. This convention was scheduled to meet on December 10 to deliberate whether Georgia should leave the Union. Before the convention met, Toombs wrote a long public letter explaining his actions in the Congress and why disunion was unnecessary. Three criteria would have led him to secession: abolition of slavery in Washington, the prohibition of slavery in the territories, and failure to pass some sort of Fugitive Slave Law. He had staked his political reputation on these principles and fought hard for them. "Yet I am reproached for not giving 'aid and comfort' to a factious, foolish and untenable resistance to the government" by those who had "wasted scores of ink in attempting to demonstrate my 'unsoundness on the slavery question'" and who use "truth or error for its accomplishment, as best may suit the exigencies of the hour." Yet he was willing to let bygones be bygones. Toombs and Stephens had been greatly abused by the opposition but as far as he was concerned the issue was settled. Toombs had been a tough Whig partisan, a sly and crafty political infighter, who waged war for every inch of political ground. But now he was ready to ally with anyone, regardless of party label, who stood with him behind the compromise. "With no memory of past differences of opinion, careless for the future, I am ready to unite with any portion, or all of my countrymen, in defence [sic] of the integrity of the Republic."[105]

As soon as Toombs, Stephens, and Howell Cobb got back from Washington, they were off, campaigning through Georgia, stumping for the Compromise, urging voters to send pro-compromise delegates to the state convention. Toombs and Stephens appealed to their Whig constituents while Cobb campaigned among Democrats. "Old party lines [were] obliterated and forgotten," Stephens wrote to Crittenden.[106]

The Georgia Triumvirate chugged back and forth across the state on rickety trains, touting the benefits of the compromise and the great bands that tied Georgia to the Union. Toombs stumped all over the state — Milledgeville, Richmond, Elberton, Appling, Oglethorpe. Democratic charges of selling out to the North were untrue, he said. He had fought a hard fight against Northern aggression; the Wilmot Proviso had been defeated, Washington, D.C., still had slavery (he neglected to mention the slave trade had ended), and the South now had an effective fugitive slave law. Yes, California was a free state, but that had been left up to them. If the disunionists were honest, he said, they would see that Southern principles had been "strengthened, not weakened ... and will survive [the disunionists'] present zeal and future apostasy."[107]

Although sentiment for the Union was overwhelming in Georgia, Toombs and Stephens nearly set off a riot when they spoke in Columbus. "Toombs and Stephens have operated like sparks on a tinder box in this community," the Columbus *Times* reported. "They have raised the very dander of our people." Toombs was hanged in effigy. During his speech, fights broke out. Toombs, in turn, harangued the audience. One young man called Toombs a liar. Toombs replied with a sharp remark about the young man's father. "And out of this grew a blow or two, the drawing of a pistol or two, and the baring of several blades," the local reporter wrote matter-of-factly. "The crowd was a very fiery one that sat under Toombs and Stephens — we deem it fortunate there was no serious accident to report."[108]

Georgia elected delegates to the special state convention on November 25. Unionist candidates won overwhelming victories. Former Democrats and former Whigs had come together under one banner. Only ten of Georgia's ninety-three counties elected Southern Rights delegates. Two hundred and sixty-four delegates convened in Milledgeville on December tenth. Seventy-six-year-old Thomas Spalding of McIntosh, who had signed one of the state's earliest constitutions in 1798, was elected president of the proceedings. A committee of thirty-three was appointed to chew over what action — if any — should be taken. The Unionists at the convention drowned out the twenty-three Southern rights delegates, or Ultras. As a result, the Unionist resolutions prepared by the committee of thirty-three were adopted; they became known as the Georgia Platform.

The platform spelled out Georgia's — or more specifically, the Constitutional Union Party's — desire to "perpetuate the American Union." However, the platform warned Northerners that Georgia would stay in the Union, but only "with constitutional rights." The first three planks affirmed Georgia's acceptance of the compromise, although Georgians did "not wholly approve, [they] will abide by it as a permanent adjustment of the sectional controversy." The fourth plank warned Northerners to back away from abolishing slavery in

Washington, D.C. or restricting slavery in Utah and New Mexico. "The state of Georgia will and ought to resist even (as a last resort) to a disruption of every tie that binds her to the Union" The fifth plank declared that only strict enforcement of the Fugitive Slave Act would ensure the preservation "of our much beloved Union."[109]

Toombs tried to get the whole platform passed as one package. But the Ultras broke the platform into separate resolutions and tried to amend them to death. When the Ultras were accused of obstructing the proceedings, J.L. Seward observed that Toombs and Stephens used the same tactic in the House the year before. They "got the people of Georgia to the point of resistance," Seward wailed, then "they come home and ask [them] to submit to the injustice done them."[110]

There was no injustice as far as Toombs was concerned. In his speech, he was bursting with optimism. He warned that there would still be fights with Southern extremists and Free Soilers and abolitionists. But he sincerely believed the people would come together if the Union were truly in danger. The fight had been divisive, but he urged reconciliation. "If we reject our friends at the North," he said, "the end will then come." The only way the country would survive was to "band ourselves together and take counsel with those men and patriots every where [sic], how we may best maintain our own rights and the integrity of the Republic, now and forever."[111]

The Georgia Platform was debated for two days. The delegates voted. Then the Georgia Convention adjourned on December 14. Georgia would stay in the Union. The Compromise of 1850 was affirmed. Old political alliances in Georgia were severed and a new political party was born. Wags said the Georgia Convention was actually the Constitutional Union Party's first convention. One newspaper asked "how in the damn hell [Union Democrats] got into an omnibus with Bob Toombs and Alex Stephens?"[112]

At any rate, Southerners watched Georgia to see if they followed the secessionist tinge that had triumphed in June's Nashville Convention. But Georgia greeted the convention in Nashville with a big yawn. Most of the delegates stayed home. Georgia's support for the Union and the compromise curtailed the fire-eaters' passions. It appeared the Union was no longer in peril.[113]

Toombs headed back to Washington in late December for the second session of the Thirty-First Congress. He was barely unpacked and suffering from a cold when he found the Democratic caucus had voted against a resolution endorsing the compromise. It was "the strangest state of things here for four days that has ever been witnessed in this country, and really I am more at a loss for the interpretation thereof than I have ever been before," Toombs wrote to Howell Cobb. Toombs advised a group of Southern Whigs who called on him to write a strong compromise resolution of their own and withdraw when it failed. "My object was to cutt [sic] them all off from their national organization and therefore shut them out of the Whig national convention if one should be held."

This bit of political chicanery was apparently supposed to give exiled Whigs an excuse to join the new Constitutional Union Party. Instead, Northern Whigs double-crossed him by pulling away from Free-Soil Democrats — at the urging of Fillmore's cabinet — and passing the resolution. "This took everybody by surprise and created great fluttering in the Democratic ranks," Toombs said. "It is supposed here to be a Whig effort at nationalization. Such a result was neither intended nor expected by those Northern Whigs who voted for it; but they desired to cutt [sic] loose from their Free-soil allies at any and every hazard.... Therefore this movement will greatly strengthen and not 'Weaken our line.'"[114]

But Fillmore was working hard to steal the Union Party's message: the Compromise had been a Whig measure that saved the Union; most Whigs favored it. So who needed a Constitutional Union Party? Toombs acknowledged in his letter to Cobb that his "readings" of the situation might have been wrong. How the politically crafty Toombs missed Fillmore's flanking move is a mystery. Or maybe he was hoping for a powerhouse ticket headed by Henry Clay or Daniel Webster or his new political friend Howell Cobb in the 1852 presidential race. But Toombs' made a fatal miscalculation about his new party and his political future. Only six months before, Toombs was offering friendship to his former political enemies. Now he was turning his ploughshares back into swords.

The Second Session of the Thirty-First Congress was routine. As usual, Toombs tried to hold the line against federal openhandedness. He fought a harbor bill to clean up the Mississippi and appropriations for a new naval observatory. Mostly, he wanted to get away from Washington, telling Julia he hoped to leave by January 12 or so. In February, he was still there.[115]

Toombs had to decline an invitation to a Constitutional Union rally held to celebrate Washington's birthday. He sent his regrets but used the opportunity to pen a tough, partisan, and rousing public letter. Non-intervention with slavery in New Mexico and Utah had to be met with "singular unanimity and fervidness by the South." He urged Constitutional Unionists to stand firm against secessionists. "We can easily settle with them at the ballot box."

As for Whigs and Democrats, especially Northern breeds, they had degenerated into mere factions and hoped only to plunder the public. "Their success would benefit nobody but themselves, and would be infinitely mischievous to the public weal." Yet there was another menace: the anti-slavery principle William Henry Seward called "Higher Law." Seward had admitted that slavery was legal under the Constitution but said there was a "higher law" that took precedence over any laws of man. This doctrine was an "antagonism to our constitutional compact." If it was accepted as "a fixed fact," then "we have no other safety except in secession." Still, the Constitution and Union were worth a struggle. "Who will falter in this glorious conflict?"[116]

Toombs left Washington at the close of the session and prepared to take his family on a vacation in Europe. But he had to cancel. Events in Georgia made it necessary for him to remain at home and "again enter into the political arena," he sighed in a letter to Crittenden. The Georgia legislature had bumped the congressional elections up to 1851 to accommodate all the conventions and rallies that had been held the year before and Toombs got busy campaigning for his new party.[117]

On May 28, the State Rights Party held its convention in Milledgeville. Composed mostly of former Democrats with a few former Whigs thrown in, the convention adopted a resolution announcing a state had a "sovereign" right to secede from the Union. The convention selected former Democratic governor Charles J. McDonald as its gubernatorial candidate. McDonald was a confirmed fire-eater who had served as president of the second Nashville Convention in November. The State Rights' strategy was to sheer off enough of the electorate to split the Constitutional Union Party coalition.[118]

The Constitutional Union Party held its convention a few days later. Secession was a touchy issue, but thanks to Toombs, who was chairman of the Resolutions Committee, the party avoided the subject altogether. The platform mischaracterized the State Rights Party as a gaggle of secessionists, declared that the Union should be maintained, and rallied around the Georgia platform. To carry their banner, they nominated Howell Cobb for governor.

The candidates' position on the theoretical right to secede became *the* issue in the campaign. "Warn the good people of Georgia to beware of revolution — refer to France — and plant yourself against the factionists of S[outh] C[arolina]," the ailing Stephens advised Cobb. "The right of secession treat as an abstract question.... There was never a more bitter contest I expect in our state than will be this fall." Toombs also advised Cobb to show that secession was an "immateriality in the contest."[119]

At first Cobb tried to ignore the issue. It was a "mere dispute about words," as Toombs called it. But Cobb had to finesse his answers to stay on the good side of former Democrats and still appeal to former Whigs. "Wherever the fire-eaters have a chance," Toombs wrote to Cobb a few months later, "they will fight like the devil — though we shall whip them all over the state."[120]

Toombs stumped all over the state for Cobb, the Union Party, and his own reelection. "Don't you hear these howlings rolling over toward the rocky moutains [sic]?" he wrote to Cobb. Toombs predicted he would take his district by two thousand votes and Stephens would win by three thousand. He thought Cobb's prospects were good too. "I think you will whale him [McDonald] out by 16,000." Toombs made one more succinct remark: "I have announced myself in the field against Berrien." Toombs was going for the Senate seat.[121]

On election day, the Union Party demolished its opponents. Cobb won the governor's chair with over eighteen thousand votes and carried ninety-five of Georgia's 116 counties. Toombs won every county in his district, beating Robert McMillen 4,704 to 2,538. Union candidates left only eight seats in the Senate and twenty-seven seats in the House for State Rights Party members in the Georgia legislature.[122]

"I have been in the midst of an exciting political contest with constantly varying aspects," Toombs wrote to Julia. Judge Berrien's friends were working hard to defeat him, "but as yet I have constantly held the advantage over them." So Toombs was cautiously optimistic: "I think I can beat the whole combination tho' it is too close to be comfortable. It is impossible to give an idea of every varying scene, but as I have staked my political fortunes on success, if I am defeated in the conflict my political race is over, and perhaps I feel too little interest in the result for success."[123]

There was little for Toombs to fret about. He coveted Berrien's Senate seat and had tried for the last five years to outmaneuver the old guy. Now his hard work, sacrifices for his principles, threats, and political scheming paid off. One of the first acts the Georgia legislature performed when it convened was to elect Robert Toombs to the U.S. Senate.

Berrien knew he was finished the moment the Constitutional Union Party was formed and announced he would not seek another term in the Senate. Instead, Berrien hoped that his protégé, Charles Jenkins, would win the place instead of Toombs. But Berrien had grown out of touch with his constituents. He had opposed Clay's compromises yet he was against secession. He also desperately tried to ally with Democrats, but it was an uncomfortable fit. Berrien's term did not expire until March of 1853 and the legislature was roundly criticized for its action. "Mr. Toombs made Mr. Cobb Governor, Mr. Cobb made Mr. Toombs Senator, and Mr. Stephens is to have what he calls for at all hours," sniffed the Albany [Georgia] *Patriot*.[124]

At the end of May 1852, John Berrien resigned from the Senate, almost a year before his term was up. Governor Howell Cobb appointed Robert M. Charlton to finish the term while Toombs waited to take the seat on March 3, 1853. The New York *Times*, never one of Toombs' friends, noted snidely that "Mr. Toombs will bring, perhaps, greater zeal, but far less ability and influence to the same work."[125]

Toombs addressed a crowd at the Georgia statehouse in November, urging them to ally with Northern Democrats instead of Seward's Whigs. He promised that the Constitutional Union Party would remain independent and would send no delegates to either Democratic or Whig national conventions. The new party would wait, he said, for the candidates to be chosen and then determine if an endorsement would be made. But above all, an "indispensable condition" for the Union Party's support was support for the compromise. Toombs promised to appeal to sound men from both parties "to preserve the institutions of the South ... and the integrity of the Union."[126]

Then he was off to Washington. As usual, Democrats dominated both houses of Congress with overwhelming majorities. "We organized the house yesterday and elected all the officers," Toombs wrote to Julia. "Lynn Boyd [Democrat] of Kentucky [is] speaker. He is without qualifications of any sort for it. We shall therefore have a confused, disorderly house, during the whole Congress." Toombs and Stephens voted for Democrat Junius Hilyer for speaker. Toombs must have buried the hatchet along the way, because this was the same Junius Hilyer he had pulled a pistol on at Franklin College some twenty-five years earlier.[127]

Although Toombs and Stephens did not realize it, they were already political orphans. The compromise was a done deal, a fact of life. So the fair-weather politicians that joined the Unionists began drifting back to their old political alliances and mustering for new political battles. As one Boston Whig asked: "How can a party exist without an opposition?" Still, Stephens insisted optimistically that "the Whig party is dead. It made a galvanic struggle in caucus, but it may be considered as disbandonned [sic]." Another blow to the fragile Union Party came in January. Former Democrats in the Georgia legislature who were elected as Union Party candidates agreed to send a delegation to the Democratic national convention at Baltimore. "I do not know anything about Toombs," lamented a friend of Cobb's, "but if he is going with us he ought to come out and say so very soon."[128]

Toombs was uncharacteristically quiet and passive about the impending death of the Union Party. Perhaps he heard the party's funeral procession coming long before his colleagues. The Democrats were openly courting him anyway. The February issue of the *United States Democratic Review* raved about his "fiery southern heart" and his "ultra democracy of the constitution [sic].... Such fearless, energetic and talented statesman as himself, democratic policy imperiously needs at this hour, and we shall be happy to welcome him into the ranks."[129]

Toombs' only major appearance was at a Washington's birthday celebration at the Willard Hotel. Toombs lauded Washington's cautious words about entering into foreign entanglements. He exclaimed that this doctrine "never has been assailed until within the last few months.... I rejoice in the fact that this first assault upon the doctrine of Washington was not by an American [Great cheering]."

Toombs was alluding to Hungarian rebel leader Louis Kossuth. Kossuth, who had recently been ousted as president of Hungary, was in the midst of an international tour and urgently requesting aid for his country's struggle for independence from Austria. Toombs tore into Kossuth's cause, calling it a "dangerous departure from the established policy of our country." For Toombs, intervention in the affairs of another country was simply wrong. He saw no reason why his country should "turn knight-errant, imitate the knight of La Mancha, and travel up and down the world, revenging or righting the wrongs of all injured nations."

Toombs was no expert on the intricacies of foreign policy. But he may have been hitching a ride on the isolationists' train to make a larger point. At the conclusion of his speech, he could not resist mentioning that the country owed its peace and prosperity "and even safety, to the constitutional incapacity of the Federal Government to regulate or control the internal affairs of the separate states. This is our only safety."

The *National Intelligencer* praised Toombs' speech, but the New York *Times*, which had zealously advocated Kossuth's cause, saw through Toombs' rhetoric. The *Times* took the *Intelligencer* to task for publishing Toombs' remarks, sneering that the aim of the exercise was not to "magnify the memory or exalt the fame of Washington, but to prostitute both to the purposes of this new and somewhat remarkable organization."[130]

Toombs fell horribly ill in late March with "jaundice, pneumonia & rheumatism," Joseph Henry Lumpkin's wife reported. His daughter Sallie also seemed to be lying on her deathbed. Toombs was well enough to travel back to warm Georgia on April tenth. He looked "feeble, but ... gradually recovering." He also took special notice of Julia's fortieth birthday. "You are the same lovely & loving, warm hearted, sweet wife to me that you were when I made you my 'bonnie bride' nearly twenty three years ago," he wrote. "There is no other change except the superior loveliness & beauty of the full bloom ever the budding rose." He was able to return to Washington in late May. "My health is rapidly improving, and I now think I shall be 'myself again' in a few days," he reported happily to Cobb.[131]

Toombs was also gearing up for the conventions and the presidential election in the fall. He told Cobb that the resolution to send a Unionist delegation to the Democratic convention may be "for much good, and I apprehend no danger from it." He was leaning against giving Fillmore the nomination again and was even toying with the idea of joining the Democrats. Perhaps this was why he was strangely silent about the assaults on the Union Party. "The Democratic convention will unquestionably adopt the Compromise by a great majority. It will be full, fair and explicit. Of this I do not entertain a doubt."

Toombs favored the nomination of General Winfield Scott. He thought Fillmore's "friends" in the border states were really for Scott and would back him at the convention. Toombs was helping them by staying quiet in order not to "alarm the scoundrels, that they may carry out their treachery." Toombs preferred Scott because his nomination "cannot embarrass us under any circumstances." The "fire-eaters and free-soilers [sic] are rapidly knocking under, and will mostly fall into line." But Scott was soft on slavery and turned out to be more beloved as a general than as a politician. Toombs would quickly change his mind.[132]

The Democratic National Convention met at the Mechanic's Institute in Baltimore at the beginning of June. The Democrats were as fragmented as the Whigs, if such a thing was possible. At first, Democrats thought they were unified. But selecting a candidate that pleased every faction proved difficult as it was going to be for the Whigs. Finally, after forty-nine ballots, dark horses Franklin Pierce from New Hampshire and Senator William R. King of Alabama emerged with the nominations. The platform was a mundane document that spelled out everything the federal government could not do — internal improvements, establish national banks, and interfere with slavery. The platform did endorse the Compromise of 1850 and the Fugitive Slave Act and promised the party would aggressively resist any agitation about slavery.

The Whigs held their convention later that month in the same facility. As early as the fall of 1851, Constitutional Unionists had hoped disaffected Whigs and Democrats in the North would combine to win the presidency with Daniel Webster leading the ticket. But Democrats would have no trouble tying Webster's long record and his endorsement of the Fugitive Slave Act to his Whig tail. Fillmore was no good either: Northern Whigs believed he was spineless against the Southern wing of the party. By default, Whigs believed their only viable candidate was Old Fuss and Feathers, Winfield Scott.

Like Zachary Taylor, Scott should have emerged as a Whig hero. Southerners idolized his military conquests in the War of 1812 and in Mexico; and he had quietly lobbied for the compromise in 1850. But Southerners detested his Northern political mentors, especially the likes of William Henry Seward and Thurlow Weed. Still, the military hero formula was tried and true, so Whigs gave the nomination to Scott after fifty-three ballots. With some exceptions, such as a plank supporting internal improvements, the Whig platform was almost identical to the Democrats,' including an endorsement of the Fugitive Slave Law.

Unfortunately, Scott had a knack for getting into trouble when he talked politics. So his handlers urged him to take no positions during the campaign. The closest he came to making a definitive statement was on the eve of his nomination. He pledged to honor the "platform of principles which the Convention has laid down." His Northern handlers were aghast that their candidate was standing by the Fugitive Slave Law. There were plenty of public appearances after that blooper, but Scott alienated both the North and the South by saying nothing else about the compromise, the Fugitive Slave Law, or anything else of substance.[133]

Like most Southerners, Toombs revered the old general. In 1849, he had introduced a bill to create the rank of lieutenant general for Scott. But now Toombs and Stephens refused to endorse him. He had promised to uphold the Whig platform, but he refused to specifically support the compromise or the Fugitive Slave Law. Toombs assured Howell Cobb that Southern Unionists would not tolerate Scott if he were nominated. "He is the *favorite* candidate of the *Free-soil* wing of the Whig party," Stephens editorialized in the Augusta *Chronicle*, "and as such in my judgment he is not entitled to the support of any Southern man who looks to the protection of the rights of the South and the Union of the States" (italics in original).[134]

On July 3, Toombs took the House floor and made a stump speech against Scott's nomination. He assured his listeners that while his motives might seem partisan, they were no more than his public duty. He thought the Constitutional Union Party had settled the sectional crisis by supporting any politician from any section of the Union and from any party that endorsed the compromise. But the usual political interests had hoodwinked the American people by giving them a crop of candidates who needed "hired biographers and venal letter writers to inform the people who they were, and what were their opinions on public questions." Unlike a Washington, a Jefferson, or even a Jackson, these men needed "interpreters of letters to the public, cunningly contrived to mystify what they intended to elucidate."

Toombs, delighting in his role as a political independent, denounced national conventions, Democrats, Free-Soilers, and especially Whigs. Free-Soil Whigs had stolen control of the Whig Party. "The Whigs who supported General Scott for the nomination were the men who had been most active, by speech and pen, from the beginning of this excitement, in promoting sectional strife and discord." This was why Toombs could not support Scott. Scott had done nothing to make his position clear. "It does not require much writing for a man to say whether he likes the platform or whether he does not like it," Toombs smirked, "but he took a great deal of writing to get around it."

Toombs could not say it in public, but he had perpetuated the same trick in Zachary Taylor's campaign. The result had exploded in his face like a faulty musket. He was not willing to use that weapon again. General Scott was a man of honor and a great military leader, no doubt. But he was "unfit for the office ... and dangerous to the country." Scott was "painfully obscure where it was his duty to be plain, but sufficiently certain where obscurity would at least have been prudent." Toombs could not trust Scott, even if Scott was sincere in his principles, because "I will not trust him where it is not clear that they agree with mine."[135]

A few days later, the *National Intelligencer* published a joint statement signed by Toombs, Alexander Stephens, and several other former Whigs saying they could not and would not support Scott for president. Good riddance! cried the New York *Times* to Toombs and his bolter friends. "So long as they lie uncomplainingly in the dust, and smile wooingly upon the iron-shod heel that grinds their facile necks,— the Union is safe and the South aquiescent [sic]." The editors at the *American Whig Review* expressed regret that anyone might withdraw from the Whig Party over Scott's nomination, but claimed they were unaware "of any such feelings of dismay at this defection" and found in Toombs' and Stephens' threats "little cause for alarm."[136]

The congressional session ended on June 10 and Toombs headed home. Unfortunately, he found the Constitutional Union Party to be as fragmented and messy in Georgia as the Whigs and Democrats were in the rest of the country. At their state convention at Milledgeville, Cobb's ex–Democrats threw their support behind Pierce. The Toombs and Stephens men backed Daniel Webster, although Webster had not even consented to run. Conservative Whigs backed former governor George M. Troup. On the first day of the convention, the Webster forces — or the "Tertiam Quids," as Georgia papers called them — walked out. There was no hope of putting the fragments of the Constitutional Union Party together. On August 10, the party was officially disbanded.

The presidential campaign was a dull one. Both parties effectively removed any argument about slavery by endorsing the Compromise of 1850, so the only issues left were the personalities of the candidates. The Whigs attacked Pierce's war record and, referring to his occasional bouts with alcoholism, claimed he was the hero of many a well fought *bottle.* The Democrats resorted to calling General Scott names like "a carbuncled-faced old drunkard" who "grew up with epaulets on his shoulders, a canteen on his back, and a breastplate on *his rear.*"[137]

Webster stood no chance of winning the election but Alexander Stephens campaigned enthusiastically for him. Toombs made a few flabby speeches for Webster, but his heart was not in the campaign and for the most part he was content to stay home. The Tertiam Quid movement collapsed when Webster died ten days before the election.[138]

On election day, Pierce won with a devastating margin, carrying twenty-seven states and 254 electoral votes to Scott's measly four states and forty-seven electoral votes. The popular vote was a little closer: 1,601,474 for Pierce, 1,386,580 for Scott. Pierce carried Georgia by almost fifteen thousand votes. Toombs' candidate for governor, Charles Jenkins, lost to Democrat Herschel Johnson by five hundred votes. Georgians favored a Democrat who articulated support for the compromise instead of a Whig who articulate very little.

After the election, Toombs and his family retired to his plantation in the "wild and out of the way country" in Stewart County. He had bought the 1160 acre property back in 1839 and named it Roanoke after the Georgia village that had been destroyed during the Creek Wars twenty years before. Toombs and his family often used Roanoke as a vacation home. "The Presidential election went very much as I hoped and expected, except in Ten. and Kentucky," Toombs wrote to Crittenden. "I suppose it must have satisfied the Northern Whigs that free-soil don't pay any better at the North than at the South. They swore if their candidate had no other merit, he was certainly *available.*"

Toombs, was at his most jaundiced, fed up with the all the political hacks. "The Union [will] prove too much for the Politicians," he told a friend, "let them try and take it." To

Crittenden, he wrote that Pierce was a man without claims or qualifications, surrounded in the cabinet by "dishonest and dirty a lot of political gamesters" rather than the "canting hypocrites who brought out Genl. Scott." Still, Toombs preferred Pierce over Scott. There would be no peace or security with "Seward, Greeley and Co. in the ascendant in our national counsels," he wrote, "and we had better purchase them by the destruction of the Whig party than of the Union." Toombs gave no thought to crawling back to the Whigs like many of his Constitutional Union colleagues had. If the Whig Party was "incapable of rising to the same standard of nationality as the motley crew which opposes it under the name of the Democracy, it is entitled to no resurrection."[139]

Toombs missed almost a month of the Second Session of the Thirty-Second Congress, appearing in Washington on January 3 where he took rooms at Mrs. Duncan's Boarding House. It was a routine meeting that dealt with mundane affairs like banking reform in Washington, pension bills ("I object to the bill," Toombs cried in an intemperate mood, "and I object to pensions for anybody"), and swamp land titles. As usual, Toombs tried to keep the federal pocketbook closed tight. "I will give millions for proper legislation, but not one cent for jobs." The most significant event for Toombs during this lame duck Congress happened on February 24 when his credentials were presented to the Senate.[140]

If Toombs kept an eye on the public purse strings, he spared no expense on his daughter's wedding in April. Louisa was barely nineteen when she married William Felix Alexander. Three hundred people crowded into the Toombs home in Washington, Georgia, for the social event of the season. "Lou" was a beautiful, waif-like creature with dark eyes to match her dark hair. One guest at the wedding said she was the "prettiest bride I ever saw, and she reminded me of some of the romantic descriptions in novels of 'fair and fragile' brides." The Reverend George Pierce, Bishop of the Methodist Episcopal Church, South, performed the wedding service. James Buchanan was also present and claimed the right to "kiss the bride of the nation." Toombs was fond of his new son-in-law and regarded him as a son he never had. Felix Alexander was apparently a good match for Lou, but the marriage was all too brief.[141]

In May, Toombs once again turned his attention to local politics. "I did not give you an account of my speech," he wrote to Julia after a campaign stop in Montgomery, "but as you always want my opinion of them, I can say I was fortunate in having a lot of very dull speakers to show against & therefore the speech took remarkably well, better doubtless than it deserved." Toombs' reputation for oratory was legendary. But like any good showman, he knew when a performance measured up and when it did not. In this case, "I thought it a rather lucky hit."[142]

The Georgia Democratic convention was held in June. Howell Cobb's man, Herschel V. Johnson, was picked as candidate for governor. Toombs was as strong as ever in the state, but was still without a party or even a political label. On June 22, the Gubernatorial Convention of Republican Citizens met in Milledgeville. Toombs' puppet, John W. Sanford, presided over the convention. The convention gave their nomination to Charles J. Jenkins. Jenkins was a former Whig from Augusta who had served in the state legislature, as speaker of the Georgia House, and was state attorney general. Jenkins had some minor national fame by being Daniel Webster's vice presidential nominee in 1852.

What there was of a platform condemned both political parties, accused the Pierce administration of trying to wreck the Georgia Platform by giving too much patronage to Free-Soilers and abolitionists, and called on both Democrats and Whigs to vote for Jenkins. If Toombs was trying to revive the Union Party, it was a sorry effort. Sanford may have revealed more than he intended when he told the convention delegates they were there not "to save the Union again, *but to save ourselves*" (italics in the original]. The "Toombs Convention," the Milledgeville *Federal Union* growled, was "a transparent humbug perpetrated by Toombs and Stephens."[143]

The campaign was as dull as soap. Democrats painted Jenkins as a Whig, an aristocrat, and tried to tie him to the Algerine Law, a short lived but detested measure passed by the state legislature in 1841 that split the Augusta Board of Aldermen. Only those with a thousand dollars of property and who paid twenty-five dollars in city taxes could vote for aldermanic candidates. The opposition simply accused Johnson of being a secessionist. "Secessionism and radicalism hangs about their's and the neck of their candidate H.V Johnson like an incubus," puffed the Augusta *Chronicle*. "Judge Johnson is in principle, opposed to conciliatory measures," Toombs snorted in a speech at Oglethorpe, "he is a secessionist of the Nashville stripe, always ready to buckle on his armor for battle against the Union."[144]

But the candidates themselves spoiled the fun by traveling and dining together and even sharing the same rooms on the campaign trail. Toombs did his best to rally Whigs and former Unionist Democrats who were "enthusiastic for Jenkins and are preparing for an active canvass." The most exciting thing that happened during the campaign was a posse that pursued Toombs' horse and buggy for several miles thinking he had stolen it. But on election day, Toombs threw in the towel. "I am here in the bustle of novelties," he wrote to Julia from Milledgeville. "The Democrats have the complete ascendancy in both houses & carry every thing their own way." Herschel Johnson carried the election by a meager 510 votes. The Democrats also took six of eight congressional seats. The more or less reunited Democrats eked out a victory by exploiting the fragmented Whigs, Constitutional Unionists, and political independents like Toombs.[145]

Toombs was unable to attend the opening of the First Session of the Thirty-Third Congress due to sad personal business. "I feel that I must pour out my sorrow to some one and who else can I look to but to one who ever faithful & true[;] has had my whole heart from my youth till [sic] now," Toombs wrote to Julia. His brother-in-law and good friend, Henry Jefferson Pope, had passed away from yellow fever and Toombs was called upon to handle his affairs. It was one of the "dark and sad" times of his life. "The remains of my lost friend Mr. Pope came down on the cars this morning." When Toombs accompanied the body to the boat, he was uncharacteristically overwhelmed with grief. "Oh, it was so sad to see one whom so many people professed to love, in a strange place, conveyed by hirelings and deposited like merchandise among the freight of a steamboat on the way to his long home."

Pope's death hit him hard and he poured his sorrow out to Julia. "As I saw him placed in the appointed spot among the strangers and bustle of a departing boat, careless of who or what he was, I stole away to the most retired part of the boat, to conceal the weakness of friendship and relieve my overburdened heart with a flood of tears." Toombs, always the Southern gentlemen, felt "it would be a profanation of friendship even to be seen to feel in such a crowd. But for my overwhelming duty to the living I would have taken the boat and gone on with his remains."

Being executor of what was left of the estate was not a pleasant job either. Pope had apparently concealed his financial failings from his family. "He could not make money, and it really seemed that his every effort to do so plunged him deeper into debt," Toombs wrote to Julia. Toombs was the one who had to tell his family the estate was almost broke. "I would have done anything to have relieved them upon a full disclosure. He was idolized at home, and I have wept at the sorrows of the poor people in his employment, upon the very mention of his death." Toombs confessed to Julia that he knew he should control his grief, but "I could not find relief without pouring out my sorrows to you."[146]

Later that night, after getting Pope's body off after a long delay, Toombs wrote again to Julia. He was doing better but the experience made him too nervous to sleep. So he threw himself into his work by "examining papers and calculating in figures as a positive relief from reflection." However, work was no substitute for confiding in his dear wife. "Julia [,] it soothes me to write you just a few lines & therefore I write something to day [sic]."[147]

Despite the tragedy, the future was promising. The nation was prospering, the slavery question had been settled — or so it seemed, Toombs had a blissful family life, and a seat in the Senate was waiting for him. But the next seven years held much personal and political tragedy for Robert Toombs.

4

Senate

Robert Toombs took his seat in the Democratically controlled Senate for the first time on January 23, 1854. On that day, the Senate got one of the boldest and most powerful debaters the institution had ever seen. But along with his talents, Toombs brought an intellectual smugness and pomposity that was hard even for the largest nineteenth century political egos to tolerate. "In the street, he would strike you as a self-conceited, bullying, contemptuous person, with brains in the inverse proportion to his body, which was large and apparently strong," one writer recalled. But in private, Toombs was a courteous and hospitable gentleman, and if nothing else, "frank in the expression of opinion."[1]

Toombs could be haughty and intimidating when it served his purposes. But Stephens knew Toombs better than almost anyone and said that he was not a mean man. He could be acerbic and sarcastic, but there was "no malice in his nature." Toombs was impulsive and was ruled by an "undisciplined ambition." But as a "husband, father, master, friend or neighbour," [sic] he could not be beat.[2]

Toombs could also turn on his Southern charm at will. During social occasions, he had a way of putting strangers at ease. Many who met him described him as "dashing" or a man with a "commanding" presence. British journalist William Howard Russell said that Toombs was "unquestionably one of the most original, quaint, and earnest" Southern leaders that he had ever met. At forty-five years old, he was just over six feet tall, with hair that was still black, and broad shoulders. Though he was getting "stout," he still carried himself well.[3]

He was considered handsome, even though he was negligent about his "toilet and dress." Varina Howell Davis was taken with him. "His coloring was good, and his teeth brilliantly white, but his mouth was somewhat pendulous and subtracted from the rest of his strong face," she wrote. "His eyes were magnificent, dark and flashing, and they had a certain lawless way of ranging about that was indicative of his character." Mrs. Davis was particularly struck by his hands. She described them as "beautiful," and wrote that they were "kept like those of a fashionable woman."[4]

The day Toombs arrived in the Senate, Stephen A. Douglas of Illinois introduced a bill organizing the immense region east of Iowa and Missouri into two territories, Kansas and Nebraska. Organizing this vast area would give settlers a chance to gain legal title to some land, encourage building a railroad all the way to the Pacific Ocean, and not incidentally, unite fragmented Democrats behind a strong party measure. As a pacifier to Southern Democrats, the bill repealed the Missouri Compromise that had forever prohibited slavery

Senator Toombs. Daguerreotype taken in 1854, the year he entered the Senate. Courtesy of Georgia Archives, Small Print Collection, spc07-010b.

above the 36' 30" parallel. Instead, settlers in the territories could vote for or against the institution.

The North was outraged. "A measureless treachery and infamy ... founded on a gigantic and impudent falsehood" sniffed Horace Greeley, editor of the New York *Tribune.* The bill was "an atrocious plot" to exclude "immigrants from the Old World and free laborers from our own States, and convert it into a dreary region of despotism, inhabited by masters and slaves," Joshua Giddings ranted in a widely circulated editorial.[5]

The few Southern Whigs who remained in office were skeptical of any Democratic plan, whether it was good for slavery or not. But Toombs embraced it. "There cannot be a doubt as to the propriety and policy of repealing the Missouri Compromise," Toombs wrote to W.W. Burwell, editor of the Baltimore *Patriot.* But the North was using the measure cynically for its own purposes. The North had consistently "trampled" the idea of slavery above the 36' 30" parallel. During the fight over statehood for California, most of the North "repudiated and refused to recognize the Missouri Compromise; and even today the free-soil scoundrels who talk of the breach of compact repudiate it in principle (which was division on a line of latitude) and insist only on the prohibition." Toombs suspected this scheme was nothing more than packaging the Wilmot Proviso in a different wrapper. In principle, the Kansas-Nebraska Bill was an extension of the non-intervention principles of the Compromise of 1850. It would settle the territorial issue, which was what the public wanted, and offer a solution to "this dangerous question." If the bill failed, then "I see no hope in the future. Dissolution will surely come, and that speedily."[6]

Toombs buttonholed as many Southern Democrats and Southern Whigs as he could to get their support for Douglas' bill. He had turned his back on the Whigs in 1850, but he was still a loud voice in the party. He sincerely believed the Kansas-Nebraska bill would stop sectional conflict. But according to New York Whig Solomon Haven, Toombs also wanted to use the issue to break what remained of Southern Whigs from the Northern wing of the party. Perhaps he was also still trying to revive the Constitutional Union Party.[7]

On February 15, Toombs' efforts were threatened when the *National Intelligencer* came out against repeal of the compromise and urged Whigs to vote against the Kansas-Nebraska bill. Toombs quickly joined a meeting of Southern Whig senators in the lobby of the Senate. Several newspapers accused Toombs of trying to splinter the Whigs and give the Northern "debris" to those New Englanders "infected with the abolition itch." But as Toombs told the story a few months later on the Senate floor, the meeting was called only to counteract the damage the *Intelligencer* editorial was about to produce. Toombs had been elected to chair the "caucus" and submitted a resolution: "RESOLVED: That we disapprove of the course of the National *Intelligencer* upon the Nebraska bill, and that, in our opinion it does not truly represent the opinions of the Whig party of the South." The resolution passed unanimously and it was agreed that George Badger of North Carolina would announce the next day that Southern Whigs supported the measure.[8]

Toombs waded into the fight publicly on February 23. His first speech in the Senate was a combination of high oratory and invective against the unholy duo of Free-Soilers and Abolitionists. The Kansas-Nebraska Act was the best solution in the true spirit of the Constitution, Toombs said. At issue was nothing more than the same old troubling question: whether Congress could restrict slavery in a territory before it joined the Union.

Toombs maintained three points: first, the Kansas-Nebraska Act, with its popular sovereignty clause, was consistent with the Constitution. Second, it was a "wise, just, and proper" settlement of the slavery question. And finally, the Missouri Compromise should be repealed because it was "unconstitutional, unequal, and unjust."

As a diehard conservative, Toombs believed the national government could do nothing not authorized by the Constitution, and "there the question with me ends." Those who argued against the Kansas-Nebraska Act — namely Charles Sumner, Salmon P. Chase, and especially William Henry Seward, who were fighting the measure tooth and nail — had apparently not read or thought very deeply about the Constitution. "They had no use for it; and it was wise for them not to allude to it." To Toombs, it seemed every citizen had the indestructible right to carry into the territories an "equal right of enjoyment of the common domain." Quite simply, the Constitution gave no express power to prohibit slavery in the territories.

Throughout his speech, he berated and scolded Sumner and others for their opposition. He was outraged at their hypocrisy. They had not supported the Missouri Compromise in California and New Mexico, but were now clamoring for its protection because "as it is now presented, it is a naked question of prohibition ... and all the rest is but fraudulent pretexts with which to delude and deceive better but simpler people than themselves."

He summed up his position about midway through his speech. "You cannot crush out popular sovereignty to get rid of its abuses," he said. "It will outlive you and your follies, and prejudices. It is strong in the strength, and rich in the vitality, of truth. It is immortal. It will survive your puny assaults, and will pass on and mingle itself 'with the thought and speech of freemen in all lands and centuries.'"[9]

Toombs' first effort in the Senate was praised in the Southern Whig press. Even the

Democratic *Southern Banner* in Athens said the speech was "gratifying to the friends and advocates of popular sovereignty." But the Northern papers berated Toombs' lack of decorum. He was typical of the "ultra-slavery propagandists" who were "intolerant, domineering and insolent" and brought their "habits of the plantation" into the Senate Chamber, observed the disdainful New York *Times*. Southerners were using the "slave-driver's lash — differing a little in shape, and applied to Northern white men, instead of Southern slaves," the *Times* snorted, "but wielded for the same end, the enforcement of their will, and by essentially the means,— brute force instead of justice and reason." For good measure, the *Times* noted that Toombs "refused to listen to Messers. Sumner and Seward, when with an excess of courtesy, they ventured to congratulate him on his first senatorial speech."[10]

On March 4, after a seventeen-hour Senate session, the Kansas-Nebraska Act passed thirty-seven to fourteen. Several Whig and former Whig senators found something else to do that day in order not to commit the Whig Party one way or the other. Toombs was absent too, but he was laid up with a "catarrhal fever." Senator William C. Dawson, the senior senator from Georgia, noted for the record that Toombs was unable "from indisposition" to be in the Senate, but if he could have been there, he would have voted for the bill as well. Toombs called in sick.[11]

Suddenly, the Kansas-Nebraska Act was a test of loyalty for both parties. Northern Whigs opposed the bill, Northern Democrats were divided, and Southerners from both parties were only halfheartedly behind it or indifferent. Still Douglas and the Pierce administration bludgeoned their Democrats into moving it along while Northern and Southern Whigs committed fratricide, each wing accusing the other of being either a traitor or an abolitionist. The Kansas-Nebraska Act flew through the Senate, but it only crawled through the House.

"I am so utterly disgusted with politics & parties here that I can hardly think on the subject long enough to write a line," Toombs groaned to George W. Crawford. He was sure the bill would fail even though Democrats dominated the Congress because "many of its professed friends in the house [sic] are secretly trying to beat it." So the bill stayed bottled up in the House until Stephens broke it loose "and took the reins in my own hand and drove with whip & spur until we got the 'wagon' out of the mire," as he put it to James Thomas.[12]

Meanwhile, the Senate was grinding out the usual business of private relief bills, army appropriations bills, and other mundane matters. But Senator Toombs, now on the Committee of Indian Affairs, was more willing to spend money from the public treasury. He supported a resolution to pay spoliation claims to those who had suffered losses during attacks by Creek Indians in the 1830s. He also uncharacteristically supported printing 10,000 copies of President Pierce's veto of a bill to support the indigent insane by selling public land. The veto "was a matter of more consequence than any which we have had before us at this session," Toombs said. The Senate should evaluate the bill further, he thought, but the veto should be printed on the basis that it was "a very important document."[13]

But Toombs did not entirely forsake his role as a watchdog over public money. He strongly objected to printing thirty-seven thousand copies of the agriculture report from the Patent Office. "We go on printing the miserable stuff that is reported to us from the Patent Office," Toombs grumbled. "It ought to be stopped. It is a book nobody wants. As to mine, I am willing to give them away whenever they may be called for."[14]

The Kansas-Nebraska bill finally passed the House on May 22 by a whisker-close 113 to 110, but was kicked back to the Senate with a minor amendment. Toombs was delighted with the legislation, even if Kansas became a free state. "I say I do not care what may be the result of this measure," he remarked in the Senate on May 25 amid a nasty argument with Whig John Bell of Tennessee. "If it were to be applied to Kamtschatka, or the unexplored regions around the North pole, I would still say that the principle is right, and should be carried out."

The South had always hated the Missouri Compromise. But now that loathsome concession had been destroyed. Toombs acknowledged the Kansas-Nebraska Act had little support in the South so far. Though no petitions had been presented on its behalf, "the South speaks not in that way," he instructed his colleagues. "She speaks through her Representatives and Senators." Petitions were used only by "factious agitators, as a vehicle for slander, blasphemy, and impertinent interference with subjects with which they have no business, and on which they are without knowledge." Toombs praised the Kansas-Nebraska bill for destroying the Missouri Compromise and restoring "justice, equality, and the Constitution" to Southern slaveholders.[15]

President Pierce signed the Kansas-Nebraska Act into law on May 30. No one foresaw the consequences. What began as a modest bill to organize a bit of territory in the west inadvertently splintered the Northern wing of the Democratic Party, laid the foundation for Northern radicals to form a frighteningly successful party they called Republicans, and touched off a guerrilla war on the Kansas frontier. Perhaps most significantly, this bill not only caused a political famine in the Democratic Party, but it also starved the Whig Party to death.

Toombs broke away from Congress to wrap up some unpleasant business in early July. "I only sold twenty one of Mr. Pope's negroes [sic] they [sic] were his best hands and sold for very high prices, a good deal more than I expected." When he inspected his crops he found they were "very fine, but the corn is now wanting rain." Above all, he missed Julia.

"I do not think I have ever had you so constantly in my mind in my life as I have this trip," he wrote to her. "I have thought of you by the hour & memory has traced every linament of your face and forms from head to foot a thousand times. I know not why this has been so much the case this trip except I never saw you look more beautiful & cherfull [sic] & happy than the week before last [when] we parted." He missed her particularly on this trip and longed to be with her. "What a blessed thing is memory which enables us to enjoy over & over again the sweet charms & pure loveliness of absent dear ones."[16]

Toombs was in a reflective mood during this brief period. Maybe being in the Senate made him more philosophical, or perhaps closing Henry Pope's estate caused him to muse on human mortality. "I was happy to hear that you and Sallie were both so well & cherful [sic]" he wrote to Julia from his home in Washington, Georgia. "Lou says she believes you and Sis are as gay as lark & enjoy the thing very much as you are constantly writing her of company and gay scenes." He hoped so "for it is true wisdom to cast away care & enjoy all the innocent pleasure we can."[17]

The peaceful interval ended abruptly, for he was back in Washington, D.C., by mid-July. On the twentieth, he attacked a homestead bill that passed in the House in March. The bill granted 160 acres to settlers who had lived on public land for at least five years. Southerners generally opposed this kind of legislation, fearing it would lure slaveholders away from the South and entice Free Soilers to settle on public lands.

Congress had heard every conceivable scheme to give away the public domain, Toombs said, including "the imbecile conceit of giving it to the worthy and unworthy who have borne arms on the side of this country." Toombs favored a scheme that would grant a "proportionate" share of land to every citizen of the United States. That contrivance was impractical, so he supported a Democratic substitute, sponsored by Senator R.M.T. Hunter of Virginia, that required homesteaders to pay a minimum of twenty-five cents an acre after five years of occupation.

To Toombs, public lands were a trust for the American people. But Congress could not execute the trust because the members could not agree on a coherent policy. Now the question was whether land in the public domain should be used to benefit aspiring landowners or politicians in Congress, whether land should "be sold for votes or sold for money, in order to relieve the public treasury."

Even though Senator Hunter's bill sold public land for a pittance, it would put land in the hands of settlers and under the control of the states. This would prevent the federal government from "disturbing the proper and just considerations of those high questions of public policy which arise day after day in this great country." The House failed to reconsider the measure and the bill was defeated.[18]

Significantly, this was the third Democratic measure Toombs had supported since he arrived in the Senate six months before. He had backed Stephen Douglas' Kansas-Nebraska Act, he had supported Pierce's veto of the Indigent Insane Bill, and now he had bolstered a Democratic homestead bill. For all his posturing as a former Whig or a Constitutional Unionist or a political independent, Toombs was starting to walk and talk like a Southern Democrat ... or at least like a backer of Franklin Pierce.

He had even started to loosen the government's purse strings a little. But for all his newly found largess, Toombs closed his first session in the U.S. Senate by taking a tough stand against an ordinary internal improvements bill for rivers and harbors. "I deny your right to take from the honest laboring men of this country their money without compensation, and appropriate it to local objects," he told senators. "I said it was plunder. I will repeat it — it is plunder."[19]

The long session ended in August and Toombs trudged home. But all was not well and he found no more peace in Washington, Georgia, than he had in Washington, D.C. Louisa, his oldest daughter, was sick and Toombs was "quite anxious" about her. And a suitor Toombs disliked was courting his youngest daughter, Sallie. "There are some things in the stock of people I do not like," Toombs wrote to Julia. "Sallie would be very unhappy with the wrong sort of man, but I suppose she is but little inclined to be advised on such a matter," he sighed like almost every father has in the same situation.[20]

Toombs also had to close out more of Pope's estate. Pope's property sold for a good price, he wrote to Julia from Columbus, Georgia. "I was very fortunate in getting them [slaves] well situated and all the families together. There was not a single case of separation of husband & wife or parent & child, except in case or two of grown negroes & I think they all got good homes." Toombs swore that this would be the last insolvent estate he would ever manage.[21]

Toombs and Julia traveled back to Washington, D.C., in mid–December, a week after the start of the Second Session of the Thirty-Third Congress. He was now on the Judiciary Committee, but his first effort was to protest a bill expanding pensions to widows of naval officers. "I am opposed to extending the system, because it was a vicious one in the beginning," he declared. Toombs also objected to a bill expanding bounty lands to veterans of the Mexican War, but advocated a scheme to pay federal judges the same amount that state supreme court judges made.[22]

It looked like it was going to be a run-of-the-mill session when Toombs and Julia were called back to Georgia in mid–January. Louisa's health had deteriorated badly. Lou did not have chronic health problems, although Toombs sometimes expressed concern about her well being. But a year earlier, a guest at her wedding described her as being "too fair and frail ... for much of the wear and tear of life." Still, her condition must have been a shock because Julia would not have traveled to Washington, D.C., if Louisa had been sick.[23]

Louisa's condition improved towards the end of February so Toombs headed back to Washington. He was in the midst of a fight over per diem payments to senators and the usual internal improvement bills when he got the news that Louisa was close to death. "[I] am hourly looking for the confirmation of my worst fears," he wrote to his wife from Washington. "I have mourned for my poor child as dead, tho' I can't realize it, it has weighed upon me for more than a year & I have prayed God ferverently [sic] to take me & restore her to life." As any loving father would in the same situation, he desperately shook his fist at the fates. "I can not feel in this matter 'God's will be done.'" Toombs frantically tried to clear up his affairs in Washington and get back to Georgia.[24]

The end came on Sunday, March 4, 1855. James Alexander wrote that Toombs was with his daughter when she died, but Alexander Stephens reported to his half-brother, Linton, that Toombs had not arrived home as late as Tuesday morning. "It is most probable therefore that he will never lay eyes on her form again," Stephens sobbed. Lousia's death filled Linton Stephens with grief, but it was not unexpected. "I almost loved her as a sister," he wrote to Alexander. "She was so good, so intelligent, so artless, so innocently gay and cheerful of spirit, that it was impossible to know her well without being touched with a tender and a most kindly regard for he."[25]

Louisa's death was a shattering blow. Toombs longed to toss his responsibilities aside and get away from public attention. To alleviate his family's grief, he started planning for a long-delayed vacation in Europe. He was more and more anxious to get out of the country and to "be relieved of the thousands of harassments of business, and look for a great deal of pleasure in our quiet and uninterupted strolling over the hills and plains of Europe, where nobody knows us and nobody can harass me with business or their troubles," he wrote to Julia from his plantation, Roanoke. "I wish I could be like our lost darling child [because] through God there is rest in Heaven.'"[26]

He hurriedly wrapped up his legal cases and business affairs. His lawyer friends "very kindly gave way & allowed my cases to come on this week." Toombs spent his time "pretty much speaking all day & studying all night & that too without the benefit of my specks which I begin to need." As for political news, he gave Julia his candid opinion as only he could: "All the old Whigs here have joined the Knownothings [sic] & keep very shy of me & I have spoken softly of the miserable wretches who expect to govern [a] great country like this with imbecility." His remaining political allies had begged him to stay home and help fight in Georgia's gubernatorial campaign, but he was determined to get away to some foreign countries where he could spend some leisure time with his family "which I seem to be totally incapable of getting at home."[27]

On June 6, Toombs, Julia, their daughter Sallie, Louisa's widower, Felix Alexander, and a family friend named George H. Shorter sailed from Boston. After eight beautiful sailing days, they hit rough weather before landing in Liverpool. From there they journeyed to London. The planter in Toombs was disappointed in the grassy English countryside. It was not as "striking" as "Culpepper county, Virginia," he wrote to Stephens, "and gives you no idea of its great value. The whole country seemed covered with sheep, a few cattle (all good) and a little (not much) wheat." But he was quite impressed with London: "It is much greater than I had ever pictured to my imagination, and one is bewildered with the wealth, the magnificence, the beauty and the thousand objects of grandeur and interest which arrest him at every turn."

The tourists went to Westminster Abbey and the Tower of London. In the Tower, Toombs found "objects enough for a week's examination." He also visited Parliament where he heard Prime Minister Palmerston, Fred Peel, "and a score of others of lesser note." Toombs, who could hold his own with any nineteenth century orator, complained the speaking was "very poor, the matter commonplace, and the style perfectly genteel but perfectly insipid. You could not have stood it half an hour," he teased Stephens. "I braced myself up to listen to them three mortal hours." Yet he said he was determined to go again.

Toombs mentioned that Martin Van Buren, Millard Fillmore, and Abbot Lawrence happened to be in London "lionizing themselves." Though he made a few unofficial visits to U.S. officials and may have carried some letters of introduction, Toombs preferred to stay to himself. "I avoid all social intercourse and decline all invitations and am trying to turn my trip to advantage."[28]

From London, the Toombs party traveled to France. This time, the waters were rough and one poor steward had to bring Toombs "basin after basin." Like any tourist, he bragged about the good food he found at cheap prices and he bought some souvenirs — two shirts that "fitted [me] up for a month." Then they toured Italy, Amsterdam, and Brussels. Toombs returned to England by himself for a brief jaunt through Scotland and Ireland before joining his family again. He made it a point to sample as many cigars as possible and — characteristically — tested the cigars of every country he visited.[29]

The travelers arrived in New York in mid–September. The vacation must have reinvigorated Toombs' spirits. It may have also helped him settle some important political convictions. When he got back to Georgia, he found the political scene in even more disarray than usual. Not only had the Whig Party collapsed, but the Know-Nothing movement — or Sam as it was called in Georgia — was gaining strength. The secretive Know-Nothings filled part of the political vacuum left by the Whig Party's death. The Know-Nothings built their coalition on anti–Catholicism, nativism, and against other wicked foreign influences. Former Whigs, with no other place to go, rushed to take the secret oath.

Toombs had little regard for Know-Nothings as a political party, but he was sympathetic to some of their principles. At the gubernatorial convention in June of 1853, he brayed against the "Red Republicans, Germans, Jews," who deserved, in the words of the Milledgeville *Federal Union*, the "halter rather than the blessings of Liberty." With this kind of claptrap and claims that foreigners were rampant in the Pierce administration, the influential Toombs may have inadvertently helped open the door for Know-Nothing success in Georgia.[30]

A new Southern rights movement was also taking shape in the state. Led by James N. Bethune, editor of the *Corner Stone*, a newspaper out of Columbus, Georgia, the Southern Union Movement called for outright secession. While Toombs constantly urged Southerners to exhibit more political unity, he was no more enthused about this interest group than he had been about Calhoun's a few years earlier. But he saved most of his contempt for the Know-Nothings.[31]

In a letter to the editor of the Georgia *Times and Sentinel* just before he left for his European vacation, Toombs explained his misgivings about the Know-Nothings. "Publicity is the lifeblood of a representative Republic," he wrote, and "secrecy is the natural covering of fraud, the natural ally of eror [sic] and the enemy of truth." While Toombs was an enthusiastic anti–Catholic, he objected to state-sanctioned religious bigotry. "Our constitution protects us against the putting of such tests upon the statute book," he wrote in the editorial, "but the principle is founded on truth and justice and ought to be the rule of the individual action as well as of the public conduct of every citizen." Toombs also objected to Know-Nothings' proposal that immigrants reside in the country for twenty-one years before being granted citizenship. While the naturalization laws were not perfect, granting citizenship to foreigners "is a great benefit to the State as well as to the individual who receives the high privilege."

For Toombs, the Know-Nothings were too divisive for the Southern cause. Just as many Northern Whigs had done, Northern Know-Nothings had demonstrated hostility towards the Compromise of 1850 and the Kansas-Nebraska Act. He believed the only way to guarantee the nation's peace and safety was to maintain both acts. But "the American Party in the north whenever it has had power has shown the most vigorous hostility to this legislation." In short, "political association with these men is moral complicity with their crimes."

Toombs called for the South to lay aside party divisions and unite for their own interests. Whigs, Democrats and Know-Nothings should come together and combine for the good of the South. "If we are wise enough to do this, to present one unbroken column of fifteen states united for the preservation of their own rights, the Constitution and the Union ... we shall succeed. We shall then have conquered a peace which will be enduring, and by means which will not invite further aggression."[32]

By the time Toombs got back from vacation, the campaign in Georgia was well under way. The Know-Nothings nominated Garnett Andrews, Basil H. Overby was on a third-party Temperance ticket, and the Democrats' man was Herschel V. Johnson. Toombs supported Johnson and the slate of Democratic candidates for the legislature. But besides exchanging nasty letters with the editor of the Augusta *Chronicle,* Toombs stayed out of the battle. On October 1, Johnson beat his opponents by ten thousand votes.

Two weeks later, Governor Johnson called for Toombs and Stephens and other prominent anti–Know-Nothing politicos to come to Milledgeville for a fusion party meeting. Perhaps Toombs had wearied of being politically marooned. Or maybe he believed the only way to win political battles in the future against the Know-Nothings and the alarming new Republican Party was to ally with his old enemies. Or perhaps he believed Democrats were finally on the right side of the issues. For whatever reason, Toombs announced to the Georgia legislature in November that he was joining the Democratic Party. The Democrats had stood faithfully by the South during the Kansas-Nebraska fight and he was convinced they were the South's salvation. He could not fight against the Democratic Party after the developments of 1854, he said.[33]

Toombs' suffered a bad cough and another spell of "rheumatism," before his return to Congress in late December. He was reluctant to travel to Washington because of his health but did not feel he was missing much anyway. He did not care "the snap of my fingers for the course of events."[34]

In January, Toombs was well enough to journey to abolitionist Boston where he participated in a popular lecture series about all facets of slavery. On January 24, he walked onto the stage of the Tremont Temple without an introduction. A single hiss went up from someone in the audience, but cheers and applause drowned out the heckler. Toombs took his place at the stand and made his usual pitch: Congress had no authority to restrict slavery in the territories and slavery was the most favorable condition for black people.[35]

He opened with a brief review of the debates in the Constitutional Convention. Many members of the convention, both from slaveholding and non-slaveholding states, had anti-slavery sentiments, he reminded his New England audience. "Artful and unscrupulous men have made much of it to deceive the North." But no constitutional clause gave the federal government the power to "abolish, limit, or restrain" slavery anywhere, he said. On the other hand, the clauses that mentioned slavery were intended to either to "*increase* it, to *strengthen* it, or to *protect* it." These clauses were not afterthoughts. They were each debated, referred to committees, reported upon and adopted."

"Monstrosities" like the Missouri Compromise and the Wilmot Proviso were nothing more than "a novel and extraordinary pretension" that violated a fundamental condition of the Union. All the states were political equals—"no more, no less"—he proclaimed. The South was simply asking the federal government to protect its "persons and property" until a new state could determine whether it wanted slavery within its borders. All the anti-slavery agitation accomplished "loosens the bonds of union ... disturbs domestic tranquility, weakens the common defense, and endangers the general welfare by sowing hatreds and discords among our people."

The nastiest pillar of Toombs' argument was that black people were unfit to have political power and incapable of living as freemen. The black man had been in bondage since the dawn of recorded history, he said. The African had made no steps toward "civilization." "Annihilate his race to-day," Toombs declared, "and you will find no trace of his existence within half a score of years; and he would not leave behind him a single discovery, invention, or thought worthy of remembrance by the human family." Toombs pointed to Haiti and Jamaica to prove blacks were unfit for citizenship. "Denied social equality by an irreversible law of nature and political rights ... incapable of maintaining the unequal struggle with the superior race; the melancholy history of his career of freedom is here most usually found in the records of criminal courts, jails, poor-houses, and penitentiaries."

If the American slave was subordinated to the master in the South, he was still happier and more comfortable than he would be anywhere else, Toombs claimed. A Southern slave had "a marked advantage" over English laborers and was "often equal to the free laborer of the North." Slaves were protected from abuse by Southern law, were allowed to attend church services, and masters were legally obliged to provide for his slaves in old age and disease, "whether capable of labor or not, from the cradle to the grave."

Yet Toombs conceded the American slavery system had its faults. The picture Toombs painted was not without "shade as well as light; evils and imperfections cling to man and all his works," he said, "and [slavery] is not exempt from them." He admitted that slaves were frequently abused. Still, he pleaded with his audience to let Southerners handle the course of slavery. He even hinted that the peculiar institution's fate could one day "find its euthanasia" as it had in England.

Finally, Toombs touched on the role slavery played in the Southern economy. Slavery was an economical and profitable system, at least in agriculture. He cited Cuba, Jamaica, Brazil and Haiti as the best examples. "The opponents of slavery, passing by the question of material interests, insist its effects on society ... is to demoralize and enervate it and render it incapable of advancement and high civilization." But despite twenty years of anti-slavery agitation, the Union was still strong. "Stability, progress, order, peace, content, prosperity, reign through out our borders."

While Toombs had not come to tell his audience what they wanted to hear, they were for the most part polite, applauding and hissing intermittently. Yet at the end of his speech, the Bostonians gave him three cheers.[36]

If slavery was the hot topic in Boston, Kansas was the dominant theme in the Thirty-Fourth Congress. Threats, intimidation, and sporadic violence had broken out in the territory since the spring of 1855 when a group of "border ruffians" from Missouri rode across the state line and elected a pro-slavery territorial legislature. Over six thousand votes were cast, but there were only about fifteen hundred legal voters in the entire territory. In retaliation, a group of Free-Soil Kansans held a convention of their own at Topeka that winter and, without the consent of Congress, adopted a constitution that prohibited slavery.

On January 24, President Pierce sent a special message to Congress recognizing the pro-slavery legislature. Then, on February 11, Pierce demanded a cease-fire in Kansas and stationed federal troops at Fort Riley and Fort Leavenworth. Southerners and a sprinkling of Northern Democrats commended the move. In Congress, most legislative business was set aside and the debate was on.

On February 28, Toombs said his piece. He praised Pierce for sending troops into the Kansas territory and cited a litany of laws and precedents justifying the use of federal power to quell uprisings. "It would be difficult to imagine a case calling more loudly for the interposition of the Federal power, or a case which would afford fewer points of criticism for its application," he said. Yet some were denouncing the president "for usurpation, and taking sides against the Abolitionists." Toombs laid the blame for the violence in Kansas on the inaction of the ex-governor of the territory, Andrew H. Reeder. He questioned the claim that Missouri "border ruffians" had crossed into Kansas and voted for a pro-slavery legislature, saying the accusation was a "fraudulent after-thought" gotten up by abolitionists.

"Friends of the Constitution, justice, and equality" would happily invite every American from the North and South "with property of every sort" to come to Kansas. He cheered Kansans for exercising their right to legislate a pro-slavery constitution and promised the federal government would protect them "against all who attempt to disturb you in the exercise of these invaluable rights." And when they had become powerful and strong enough, Kansas would be admitted into the nation "without reference to your opinions and your action upon American Slavery.... This is the policy of the Kansas bill; it wrongs no man — no section of our common country."

The last half of Toombs' speech was a rebuttal to John P. Hale of New Hampshire who made a scathing attack on Missourians that had crossed into Kansas and voted for the pro-slavery legislature. Speaking directly to Senator Hale, Toombs condemned New Englanders for stirring the pot in far away Kansas. "You may preach in your pulpits in favor of sending Sharpe's rifles to Kansas, and you may succeed in getting courageous men to go there to use them," he said, but those calling for violence could not be found within shooting distance of one single bullet. "One of his powerful blasts brought down the galleries," Stephens whooped to Thomas W. Thomas a day later. "He is unquestionably the ablest debater and most eloquent man now in that body."[37]

Toombs left Washington to tend some legal cases and see his family. While at home, he asked his wife to help him keep up with the latest news. "I got the *Union* you sent me on the day you wrote," he penned to Julia, "I should like to have them every day as they will post me on what is doing in Washington in the way of politics and you must write me every day about anything else." He was back in the Senate in April. He took up his duties on the Judiciary Committee and, as usual, objected to anything that opened the Treasury's purse unnecessarily. He opposed a bill to grant the daughter of a Revolutionary soldier three thousand dollars, the equivalent to five years of her father's pay. "If you now establish the principle that revolutionary services of a parent shall entitle his child to a donation of $3000," Toombs groused, "it will impoverish the nation."[38]

Meanwhile, bickering over Kansas dragged on and on. "All are busy about Kansas affairs,

Navy Board, and squandering money generally," Toombs wrote to George Crawford. Then on May 19, Massachusetts senator Charles Sumner made his famous "Crimes Against Kansas" speech. Kansas had been raped, Sumner claimed, "compelling it to the hateful embrace of slavery." During his speech, Sumner called Andrew P. Butler of South Carolina the Sancho Panza to Stephen Douglas' Don Quixote. Butler was servile to "the harlot, Slavery," Sumner said, an "uncompromising, unblushing representative on this floor of a flagrant sectionalism ... and yet with a ludicrous ignorance of his own position unable to see himself as others see him," and that he was one of "maddest zealots" for sectionalism in the Senate.[39]

Three days later, Congressman Preston Brooks — a cousin of Butler's — avenged his kinsman's honor by beating Sumner almost to death with a gutta percha cane. He hit Sumner so hard and so many times that the cane broke in half. Brooks continued beating Sumner with the hilt anyway. The Senate had adjourned, but several legislators still lingered on the floor. New York congressman Ambrose S. Murray grabbed Brooks by the arm while Edwin B. Morgan helped Sumner to his feet. Feeble old John J. Crittenden tottered down the aisle yelling, "Don't kill him!" For some reason, Lawrence M. Keitt of South Carolina advanced on Crittenden with *his* cane raised as if to strike. "Let him alone, God damn you," Keitt yelled at Crittenden. By this time, Toombs was on the scene and told Keitt to back off.[40]

"The Yankees seem greatly excited about Sumner's flogging," Toombs brayed to George Crawford a week after the incident. "They are afraid the practice may become general and many of [their] heads already feel sore." Toombs added snidely: "Sumner takes a beating badly." He did not believe the senator from Massachusetts was seriously injured, although Sumner did not return to the Senate until 1859. Toombs also claimed that he did not help Sumner because he approved of the thrashing. Toombs' reaction seemed crude and mean to many Northerners, but given some of the South's violent values, it was not unique. Preston Brooks was praised by the Southern press and received a woodlot of canes from Southern admirers, some inscribed with the words "Hit him again!"[41]

Congress' attention quickly turned from Sumner's beating to the race for president and it adjourned to attend the conventions. Stephen Douglas and James Buchanan were the favorites for the Democratic nomination. Buchanan had a long and distinguished resume, but most importantly for the Democrats, he was minister to the Court of St. James's under Pierce and had been able to avoid taking a position on the Kansas-Nebraska Act while in far-away England. Toombs had met with Buchanan while vacationing in London and talked with him "very satisfactorily on the slavery question." In February, Toombs was inclined to think "we cannot do much better than to run him." But Douglas was canvassing hard for the nomination and Toombs feared that "Buck" and Douglas would "beat each other and give place to some incompetent outsider." On June 2, the Democrats held their convention in Cincinnati and bypassed Pierce for Buchanan.[42]

On June 17, the Republicans held their first national convention in Philadelphia. They nominated John C. Fremont for president. Fremont was an adventurer, an explorer, a military hero in the war with Mexico and had briefly been a senator from California. While the Democrats' platform endorsed popular sovereignty and promised to resist every attempt to agitate the slavery question, the Republicans swore to admit Kansas as a free state. This was "the most effectual way of securing to her citizens the enjoyment of the rights and privileges to which they are entitled, and of ending the civil strife now raging in her territory." The Republican platform also opposed extending slavery into the territories. The Know-Nothings held their convention the same month and gave the nod to the former Whig president Millard Fillmore.[43]

When Congress reconvened, the first order of business was Kansas. A few days after Preston Brooks administered his justice to Charles Sumner, news came to Washington that Lawrence, Kansas, had been sacked by a proslavery mob. Homes of antislavery sympathizers were burned to the ground, antislavery presses were destroyed, and the Lawrence hotel had been shelled with a cannon. On May 24, John Brown sought vengeance by forming a ragtag band he called the Army of the North. This army did battle by hacking to death five proslavery men in the Pottawatomie Massacre. The raiding and looting truly caused bleeding in Kansas.

Toombs proposed legislation on June 24 that he thought would be the "final and complete" solution for the "difficulties" in Kansas. The bill called for a thorough census in the Kansas territory and required the president to appoint a five-man commission to assure its validity. A slate of delegates would be elected to draw up a legitimate constitution for Kansas. Finally, the bill urged Congress to bring Kansas into the Union immediately, whether it was slave or free. Toombs knew this last proposition was unusual because Kansas did not have enough population for statehood, but he felt there was a "higher expediency" in this case, "in consequence of the troubles, the commotions, the civil broils, the discord, growing out of the existing state of things there."[44]

By any standards, Toombs' bill was a pragmatic effort to bring peace to the Kansas frontier. Even though he and Stephens suspected there were enough proslavery residents in Kansas to set up a proslavery constitution, the bill was generous to the North in both symbolism and substance. Over the next few days, Toombs' bill was debated and amended. On July 2, Toombs thanked the Senate for considering his measure then launched into an attack on Northern extremists who were out to sabotage it, namely William Henry Seward. Despite accusations by Northerners that border ruffians had invaded Kansas and stuffed and seized ballot boxes, Seward too had asked that Kansas be free to decide on the slavery question. Toombs saw "a basis for speedy and satisfactory adjustment of this question.... There was a common point of agreement between us."[45]

While Seward believed the non-slave Topeka Constitution was the legitimate choice of the residents of Kansas, Toombs thought enough slaveholders were in the territory to make sure the pro-slavery Lecompton Constitution was valid. Now Toombs was offering a chance to let the people truly decide. This main principle of the Kansas-Nebraska Act was the one he was standing upon "in no fraudulent or double sense, but as an honest man ready to maintain it in the Senate and before the country at any time and all times," he said. "I determined to give peace to the country if this would do it."

As for New Hampshire senator Jacob Collamer's accusation that "real Settlers" in Kansas had been "invaded, overridden, trampled underfoot, ravished, plundered, imprisoned, [and] murdered," this hypothesis could be tested by Toombs' bill. "I offer you a pure and undefiled ballot-box," Toombs declared. Instead, the likes of Seward, Sumner and Collamer "tender me a cartridge-box." But these "Black Republicans" and "Abolition Senators" were an extremist Northern minority. "I see around me able, patriotic and venerable statesmen — some of whom have for fifty years, in peace and in war, been honored and trusted by the North, by the South, by mankind," he said. "They give me a different account of the North."

Toombs said he was weary of the South getting blamed for the violence in Kansas. "If two men fight over a squatter's claim, and one is killed, it is forthwith heralded over the country as a southern aggression," he complained. "If a foul-mouthed Senator gets a caning for an insulting, vulgar speech this is the last extremity of southern aggression." Then turning directly to Seward, Toombs told him: "You will abuse your own countrymen as long as they stand out against your treasonable and wicked schemes for overturning the liberties of the country. As long as they are patriots, they will get your abuse. As soon as they qualify themselves for treason — as soon as they unite with you in your sectional schemes, they will get your plaudits." But, said Toombs, "as long as they will stand up for the country, they will have the honor of your condemnation — an honor to be coveted."

Toombs tempered his thrusts at Republicans and abolitionists with reassurances to the moderates in his audience. His bill was simply a fair way to determine the will of the majority. "If you, a majority, wish to exclude slavery, do so; I offer you the right, if you have the power." Toombs reminded his listeners that his bill would protect Kansas voters with the military and a presidential commission. "No minority ever received such assurances of the integrity and fair dealing of any measure, in the history of this Government."[46]

Debates and amendments went late into the night. Then the Senate finally passed Toombs' bill by a vote of thirty-three to twelve. The next day, the Republican majority in the House killed it and a similar bill introduced by Stephens a week earlier. Instead, the House voted to admit Kansas under the Topeka Constitution. "All these gentlemen want is to get up murder and bloodshed in Kansas for political effect," Stephen A Douglas growled.[47]

But the Senate still debated several variations of the Toombs bill. On July 9, Senator William Pitt Fessenden of Maine called it a "fraud and a cheat ... apparently designed for the purpose of pacificating Kansas, but bringing with it the purpose of making Kansas a slave state." "The bill has but a single object," Toombs bristled in an unprepared speech on the floor. "It simply proposes to enable *bona fide* inhabitants of Kansas to make a State constitution, in order to [bring] its immediate admission into the Union.... The primary purpose is to leave the people of Kansas free to make what form of constitution they please."[48]

Fessenden objected to the bill, he said, because it provided no protection to the people of Kansas before the election. But Toombs reminded Fessenden the proposed presidential commission would have the military to enforce the law. What better way was there to bring peace to Kansas honestly, fairly, legally, and constitutionally? Toombs asked. The law would be backed up by military force. "Show me any other agency by which to accomplish these ends." Opponents of the bill knew it did justice to Kansas. But "they know justice and peace are fatal to their schemes."

While Fessenden blamed the "pro-slavery powers" for the war in Kansas, Toombs had his own theory: "You may say that if the pro-slavery men had not gone into Kansas, there would have been no trouble. Very well: and so if the emigrant aid society men had not gone there, this difficulty would not have taken place." Toombs pointed out that Free Soilers had a prominent hand in arousing violence in Kansas. "These pious imposters keep at a safe distance from the disorders they foment. They do not go to Kansas, but stand in their pulpits and say to the people, 'Go, take these rifles; if you kill anybody, it is self-defense; if anybody kills you, it is murder.'"

Toombs once again reminded the Senate that Kansas had a right to choose or reject slavery. Toombs swore to stand by whatever decision the people of Kansas made about slavery. But he closed with a dire warning: A fair election was "the only road to success." If Kansas was taken by a "cartridge box" instead of a "ballot box," it would lead to war.[49]

For all the debate, Kansas was left unsettled. The session wound down with Toombs conducting his never-ending battle against congressional pork. He voted against federal funds for harbor improvements, Indian spoilage claims, and bounty payments to Revolutionary War veterans and their descendants. "Some of those men who are now calling for this money never struck one lick, never fired a gun, and probably some of them never remained in the service after the resolution of 1780 [that granted officers half pay for life] was passed."[50]

Toombs also managed to get some politicking done for James Buchanan and the Democrats. On August 2, the New York *Times* published a letter Toombs sent to a friend in Athens, Georgia. Electing Fremont would be "the end of the Union, and ought to be," Toombs wrote. "The object of Fremont's friends is the conquest of the South. I am content that they shall own us when they conquer us, but not before." Toombs knew better than that. But it was what his Southern Democratic base wanted to hear and it riled Republicans. Toombs had made declarations like this before, noted the *Times*. "Mr. Toombs occupies an easy chair in the Federal Senate, as if the contingencies upon which he predicted dissolution has not occurred.... Men like Toombs have little or no weight with the public opinion of the South."[51]

Toombs went back to Georgia when Congress adjourned and wasted no time getting on the stump for the Democrats. Although he took potshots at Republicans whenever he could, he knew Fremont had no prospects in the South. Southern Democrats' real enemies were the Know-Nothings. "Have spoken in Hancock, Taliferro, Columbia and at Bulah," he wrote hurriedly to Stephens. "The K[now] N[othings] are active and violent and were making some impression in the 8th Dist." Toombs was discouraged by the local political situation, but "the tide is turning very perceptibly and many are coming back." The Know Nothings were "vigilant" and "untiring" and "fighting for their necks,—in truth many of them deserve to lose them."[52]

One of the highlights of the campaign was a debate in October between Toombs and Benjamin H. Hill. Hill was a young Know-Nothing who had served only one term in the Georgia legislature but had a reputation as a fierce debater. He had bested Alexander Stephens in a debate the day before and was ready to show the old dogs some new political tricks. Hill made the usual accusations: Toombs was a political opportunist who had switched between Whigs, Constitutional Unionists, and Democrats; he was a turncoat who refused to support Southern rights when he voted for the Compromise of 1850 and the Kansas-Nebraska Act; his Kansas bill was a cheat and a swindle that would deprive the South of a first-rate slave state.

Toombs replied that the Kansas-Nebraska Act simply reinforced the non-intervention principles of the Compromise of 1850 since it did not legislate for or against slavery. His votes were also consistent with the Georgia Platform. The North had tried to legislate the South out of the right of equal enjoyment of the territories with the Wilmot Proviso, Toombs reminded his audience and young Hill. "The South had endeavored to take the question of these rights out of Congress, to establish the doctrine of non-intervention."

When Hill accused Toombs of being a secessionist, he replied that if Fremont were elected, "I will not stand and wait for fire, but will call upon my countrymen to take to that which they will be driven — the sword. If that be disunion, I am a disunionist." Then quoting Patrick Henry: "If that be treason, make the most of it. You see a traitor before you."[53]

It may have been during this period that a quote was attributed to Toombs that inflamed the North more than anything he ever said. It would be hard to exaggerate the anger it provoked. It was said that Toombs swore he would "*call the roll of his slaves at the foot of Bunker Hill.*" Northerners could not believe their ears. The Reverend Theodore Parker wrote to Senator John P. Hale of New Hampshire just to make sure Toombs had actually said it. Hale responded that Toombs had said something like to him personally, and although he could not remember the exact words, recalled Toombs saying: "I should see the slave-holder and his slaves on Bunker Hill." But Northern writers used the more incendiary version of the phrase to demonize Toombs into a whip-wielding, slave driving, fire-eater and used the remark to incite anger and rage against the South generally.[54]

The quote made Toombs one of the most hated men in Free Soil, abolitionist, and Republican circles. Abolitionist Wendell Phillips suggested Toombs, along with Jefferson Davis, Lawrence Keitt and others should be hanged as traitors. British novelist Anthony Trollope noted that Toombs' name was "mentioned with execration" by even the children in the North.[55]

Yet Toombs may have been blamed for a statement he never made. He denied saying anything like that. Alexander Stephens wrote that there was no "particle of proof" that Toombs made the statement, that it was abolitionist propaganda. Reporter and lecturer Henry Grady, who was a friend and admirer of both Toombs and Stephens, maintained every chance he got that Toombs never said it. Whether he did or not, the statement was so outrageous, so infuriating — so Toombsesque — that it sounded like something he *might* have said. Truth or lie, the quote was harnessed to him forever and was used to inflame the slavery question before the war and the race question afterwards.[56]

On election day, Buchanan won 174 electoral votes to Fremont's 114 votes. Fillmore, on the Know-Nothing ticket, took only Maryland. The Democrats won Congress by a comfortable margin, but the Republicans made an ominous splash considering they were a new party that did not even mount a campaign in the South. "I got home Saturday night from Athens and found myself a good deal incommoded in the throat from arguing my cases in the Supreme Court, and besides took an additional cold which does not mend the matter," Toombs wrote to Stephens in December.

More importantly, Toombs had advice to offer about the administration: "If he [Buchanan] will observe two rules he will get along smoothly, and if he departs from either he will never touch bottom till he gets back to Wheatland." First, Toombs wanted Buchanan to put only those who had supported the Kansas-Nebraska Act in the cabinet: "No dodging, no compromising it." Second, he believed Buchanan should appoint men who were popular in the section and party from which they were chosen, such as Howell Cobb or Hershel Johnson for the South. "With these requisites I don't care who the men are," Toombs wrote. But "without them I should only care that no friend of mine should be buried under the ruin."[57]

Toombs did not arrive for the third session of the Thirty-Fourth Congress until December 22. Besides his usual battles against congressional pork, Toombs' attention was caught by a contested senatorial election in Iowa. James Harlan was a thirty-six-year-old former school teacher, a lawyer who had dabbled in politics, and the former president of Iowa Wesleyan University in Mount Pleasant. In 1855, he found himself appointed to the U.S. Senate as a Free Soiler before the Senate threw him out due to irregularities in Iowa's legislative process. Harlan was re-elected by the Iowa legislature, this time as a Republican. After eight fruitless ballots and several adjournments, no decision was reached. On January 7, 1855, the Iowa house convened, but the state Senate was still adjourned. The sergeant-at-arms was told to summon as many senators as could be found — mostly from the local tavern. This legislature then declared itself "in convention" and elected Harlan senator.[58]

Toombs weighed in on January 6, 1857, almost two years after the election. He dissented from the Senate Judiciary Committee's report, which concluded that Harlan was not a duly elected senator from Iowa. His argument maintained that a majority of the Iowa legislature participated, thus Harlan's election was legitimate whether there was a quorum of the state Senate or not. "The fact is, that when this election was made, a large number of Senators, although a minority, were present," he said. "The absence of those who were not present did not vitiate the election." Still, Harlan was removed from the Senate seat a few days later.[59]

Toombs had always been a maverick, but this was an especially tough and commendable position for him to take: he defied the Judiciary Committee, defied his own Democrats, and stood up for a member of a party that he despised. Despite his tough Southern partisanship and rhetoric that sometimes lapsed into demagoguery, Toombs was at heart a fair-minded man who wanted to make sure the law and the political system worked at its best.

Late January brought sad news: Alexander Stephen's sister-in-law, Emma, passed away after a difficult childbirth. Then word came that thirty-eight-year-old congressman Preston Brooks had suddenly died. "In him many of us have lost a friend, the country a patriot statesman," Toombs said of Brooks on the Senate floor. "Though quick to resent an insult, he was generous, kind, and even gentle in nature; and it gave him more pleasure to repair a wrong done by himself, than to right one inflicted on him by another." Toombs was reportedly in tears while he spoke. He did not know Brooks very well but his death and the death of Emma Stephens hit him hard. Alex Stephens said that it was the only time he had ever seen Toombs openly weep.[60]

There was not much in political matters to cheer Toombs either. He had grown weary and suspicious of Franklin Pierce. "I am certain Pierce for the last six months has done all he could to make Kansas a free State," he wrote to Thomas W. Thomas in February. Toombs had also become skeptical about Buchanan. Buchanan had made a trip to Washington in late January to consult with Southerners about the cabinet. Toombs figured Buchanan would follow the same policy "tho' [sic] it is due to him to say he utterly repudiates the policy," Toombs wrote, "and I do not think that he is at all solicitous that it should come in as a free state."

Toombs was unsure about who would be in the cabinet, but he thought Howell Cobb and John B. Floyd were likely picks. "At the North all is uncertainty. The scramble is not only not interesting to me but is positively loathsome, and I hardly feel the least interest in how it will terminate." Toombs had met with Buchanan and was displeased with the results. Buchanan was sympathetic to Southerners but he had denounced the Kansas-Nebraska Act and disliked Stephen A. Douglas. More ominously for Toombs, the conservative Buchanan hated party troublemakers. "Buchanan has been [here in Washington] for a week, until yesterday; he talked a great deal to every body but *said nothing*," Toombs grumbled. "I supposed he had his program in his pockett [sic] and therefore he got as little out of me as I did out of him."[61]

By the end of February, Buchanan's cabinet was taking shape. "Lewis Cass and [Howell] Cobb have been definitely appointed," Toombs reported to Stephens. Besides the gossip about who else would or would not be in the cabinet, "things go off here calmly but without enthusiasm, indeed rather with indifference." Toombs' one complaint was the bane of nineteenth century politicians: the patronage. "We have lots of office seekers here who are a great pest to those of us who are compelled to stay here."[62]

On March 4, James Buchanan was sworn in as the fifteenth president of the United States. During his inaugural address, he promised to serve only one term, condemned the violence in Kansas, and bragged about the large surplus in the federal treasury. Buchanan also imprudently hinted that the Supreme Court was about to permanently settle the slavery question. The argument over when a territory could vote for or against slavery was now a matter of little practical importance. "The whole Territorial question thus being settled upon the principle of popular sovereignty.... Everything of a practical nature has been decided."[63]

Two days later, the Supreme Court handed down its verdict on *Dred Scott v. Sanford.* The decree found the Missouri Compromise unconstitutional and Congress could not prohibit slavery in any territory. Southerners like Toombs thought the Supreme Court had vindicated what they had been saying all along: the Constitution protected slavery and Congress had no right to interfere with it. Talk of a conspiracy between Chief Justice Roger Taney and President Buchanan was flung about and Republicans encouraged the rumors. But Buchanan and most Southerners believed the Supreme Court had ended the quarrel.

Before Toombs wrapped up his business in Washington, a reconciliation with an old enemy was arranged. Back in late 1853, Toombs had gotten into an ill-tempered public argument with V.A. Gaskill over the men in Pierce's administration that had not supported the Compromise of 1850. Then Gaskill accused Toombs of calling Secretary of War Jefferson Davis a disunionist who was "sitting in the councils of the nation." In a harsh response that was widely published in the South, Davis admitted that he believed a state had a right to withdraw from the Union, but only as "a last remedy." Davis closed by noting that anyone who would make such charges was "radically false and corrupt." Toombs replied that Davis was worthy of the "swaggering braggarts and cunning poltroons" who followed him. Many saw the exchange as a prelude to a duel, but nothing ever came of the matter except hard feelings.[64]

Senators John J. Crittenden of Kentucky, Andrew P. Butler of South Carolina, James Mason of Virginia and John Rusk of Texas arranged for letters to be delivered to each man asking that "all past controversy shall be no more regarded by either of you — that when you meet, you shall receive, speak to, and treat each other as is common among gentlemen." Toombs and Davis agreed in writing to bury the hatchet. The reconciliation "was sincere, integral, and ended with a treaty of alliance, offensive and defensive, in behalf of fire-eaterism and extreme sectional views," the New York *Times* wailed.[65]

Despite Toombs' sour impression of Buchanan at the beginning of February, he was an important advisor to the new president. "I had a very long and satisfactory interview with Buchanan about our Mexican policy, in which I was happy to find he generally concurred," Toombs wrote to W.W. Burwell. He advised Buchanan that England, Spain and Mexico were his three important missions, "the others were mere feathers for peacocks and genteel ... friends." Toombs also wished to buy Cuba by purchasing Spanish debts owed to British subjects. He had been asked to go to England to see the deal through, "but I do not like to leave the Senate.... It is my decided strong conviction that I ought to be on this side of the water."[66]

The only trip Toombs was interested in taking was to Texas. Before the war with Mexico, the Mexican government had granted large tracts of land to individuals to encourage settlement. W.S. Peters and Associates had received a large allotment of land but had mismanaged their investments into financial and legal trouble. Toombs had bought some 90,000 acres from the "Peters' Colony" and he speculated in Texas land off and on for the rest of his life.[67]

Toombs wanted to check out his extensive land holdings near the Ft. Worth area. In the late spring, he began his travels with a small entourage, including his brother Gabriel, Felix Alexander, and several slaves. Toombs was greatly impressed with the fertile country in lower Arkansas and upper Louisiana and Mississippi. "The country from this to Vickburg is a perfect garden," he wrote to Julia from New Orleans, "splendidly improved & well cultivated. We have seen nothing to compare with it even in Europe. It is as fertile as Old Egypt."[68]

From Galveston Island, they traveled across the piney woods of southeastern Texas to Austin and then to Waco. Again he found the country "exceedingly beautifull" [sic] and was "greatly surprised at the numbers, civility & even the refinement of the people, Gentlemen [sic], ladies." He met many old friends on his trip "& am everywhere treated with the greatest kindness & hospitality." His only regret was that he would miss Julia's birthday. "How much I should like to celebrate it with you at home!" he wrote, "but I shall be wending my way on the broad prairies of Texas while I suppose you will be with old and well friends in Carolina."[69]

When Toombs arrived at Fort Worth, he confronted a mob of squatters who had settled on his land. He offered to pay for any improvements that had been made or to sell the land to any that wanted to buy. But he managed to evict the squatters who were not willing to pay.[70]

Toombs had heard all sorts of stories about wild and rowdy Texans, but it was a spooked horse that gave him the worst of it during his trip. On a buggy ride with a friend the horse shied and they were thrown to the ground. Toombs sprained an ankle severely and had to hobble around on crutches until he returned to Georgia in mid–June. "I am now improving and doing pretty well with a walking cane for short distances," he wrote to W.W. Burwell.[71]

At home in Washington, Georgia, Toombs occupied himself by recuperating from his trip, ginning up for the state elections, and preparing for his own reelection to the Senate. Although he had not taken his seat in the Senate until 1853, he had been elected in 1851 and his six-year term had passed. As Toombs prepared his speeches and got ready to take the stump for Georgia candidates, affairs in Kansas intruded. The pro-slavery legislature in Lecompton had passed a bill calling for an election of delegates to a constitutional convention. The bill banned from the polls residents who had moved to Kansas after March 15, 1857, and made no provision for submitting the constitution to the voters.

On May 27, Buchanan's handpicked governor of Kansas, Robert J. Walker, said in his inaugural address that the convention, after framing a state constitution, should submit it to the voters of "actual bona fide resident settlers" of Kansas for ratification. If the convention failed to do that, then perhaps Congress should refuse to admit Kansas. Governor Walker also ruffled Southern feathers when he suggested Kansas had been rendered unsuitable for slavery by an "isothermal" line that restricted labor, production, and profit and loss.[72]

"Was there ever such folly as this Walker has been playing in Kansas?" Toombs snorted to W.W. Burwell. "Everything was quiet, going on smoothly, to some decision and determination, and the country was quite indifferent what that should be, when [Walker] puts in, and merely to give himself consequence and to seem to settle what was rapidly settling itself, raises the devil all over the South. Worst of all," Toombs went on, "Buchanan intends to sustain him, and thereby ruin himself and this administration."

The Kansas Constitution was the people's business, not Walker's. Walker had not been called upon even for advice, was arrogant and insolent. Toombs believed the Kansas constitutional convention should ignore the governor's suggestions and submit the constitution to all the people who "happen to be in Kansas when the ratification takes place.... His 'isothermal' and 'thermometrical' arguments and follies I suppose simply means that Kansas is too cold for 'niggers,'" Toombs raged. It was the people of Kansas who ought to decide the fate of slavery in their state, not Walker. "The condemnation of him is universal as just."[73]

Like most Southerners, Toombs was outraged at Walker's pronouncements. He chaffed at Governor Walker's suggesting who could and could not vote in Kansas. However, Walker was not that far removed from Toombs' earlier position. Toombs had admitted several times, both publicly and privately, his doubts that Kansas would be a slave state. And he had fought hard for a popular vote on a state constitution in the Thirty-Fourth Congress. But Toombs loudly denounced Walker and found himself allied with anti–Cobb, anti–Buchanan factions and other Democratic extremists that were popping up in Georgia. But Toombs was doing some groping to get the kind of political leverage he had had in the early fifties.

At any rate, Buchanan's operatives rushed to soothe Toombs' bruised feelings and to try to shut him up. Thomas R.R. "Tom" Cobb alerted his brother Howell that Toombs had been loudly denouncing the administration. Tom Cobb had warned Toombs that his anti–Buchanan rhetoric would split the Democratic Party. But Toombs "professes great concern that the Administration should do something to manifest its disapprobation of the objectionable features in Walker's inaugural," Tom Cobb wrote to his brother. Toombs was complaining publicly about Walker's "Isothermal line" and the "dictation" of who should vote when the Kansas Constitution was submitted for ratification. "We have disputed as to Walker's position, he [Toombs] insisting that Walker *dictates* that they shall submit it to a vote, of all the persons in the Territory at the date of the voting, and that he says that Mr. Buchanan stands on the same position."[74]

Howell Cobb also reassured Alexander Stephens, knowing word would get back to Toombs. "I have never heard the President or a member of his cabinet express a wish that the question in Kansas should be decided one way or the other," Cobb wrote, "except the southern men who desired Kansas to be a slave state and one of them from the North who expressed the same opinion and wish." Despite Toombs' carping, Howell Cobb knew Toombs was valuable to the administration when he played on the team. "I am glad to hear that Toombs is in good spirits, for the late issues [Kansas] may endanger his election," Cobb wrote again to Stephens a few days later. Cobb cautioned that Toombs would not find success by competing for extremists in the Democratic Party. "His reliance is and should be upon the main body of the party, composed of the most conservative and national men."[75]

But Toombs was as self-confident as a cat in a canary house. "I hear from different quarters some 'better Democrats' than I am are after me," he wrote to Stephens. "Bah! what fools! If they succeed and shall labour half as hard as I have and succeed no better I pitty [sic] them from the bottom of my soul."[76]

Toombs spent the rest of the summer putting his political house in order and watching events in Georgia. In June, Democrats retaliated against the Buchanan administration — and Howell Cobb in particular — by nominating for governor a little-known former state senator named Joe Brown. Brown was a poor boy who had worked his way into the legal profession, into the state legislature, and was serving as a circuit judge when he seized the Democratic nomination. "Who in the devil is Joe Brown?" Toombs is purported to have asked when he heard of the nomination.[77]

The Know-Nothings gave their nomination to Benjamin H. Hill in July. The campaign in Georgia centered on which party most vigorously denounced Governor Walker of Kansas. The Know-Nothings took great pleasure by insulting Buchanan while the Democrats balanced denouncing their president's Democratic appointment without denouncing their president. "The K[now] N[othings] here open vigorously with a very reputable ticket and are quite fierce against both you and me," Toombs wrote to Stephens in late mid–August. But Toombs thought if Democrats could stay with the strategy, their "firm" would not be defeated. His message was simple: "I condemn Walker, disapprove the retaining of him by the administration, but advise a strong and active adherence to the Democratic organization, and show the utter untrustworthiness of the American party on any question."[78]

When the state elections rolled around in October, Joe Brown beat Benjamin Hill by a whopping eleven thousand votes. The Democrats took six out of Georgia's eight congressional seats and the state legislature kept a healthy Democratic majority. Toombs faced a brief challenge for his senate seat from former governor Charles J. McDonald and Benjamin Hill. But on November 7, he won 169 votes in the Georgia legislature to beat the Know-Nothing candidate, Eli Baxter, who got only seventy-four votes. "I find my win gratifying," Toombs wrote to Julia nonchalantly, although he admitted he was tired of "wandering about in extra crowds." He suggested mirthfully that he should be exempt from future campaigns and be "entitled to spend [the next six years] at home with you."[79]

Toombs stayed in Milledgeville a few extra days to attend Georgia's Democratic convention. He and Stephens were on the Resolutions Committee and helped draw up declarations that condemned Robert Walker, proclaimed Congress had no authority to meddle in Kansas' preparations for statehood, and called upon Northern Democrats to join them to maintain these objectives. Then he retired to Roanoke for a little R and R. He spent a month (except for a few days in Milledgeville) on his plantation enjoying himself with "farming operations, hunting, etc., etc., and regret that my vacation is running rapidly to a close," he wrote to W.W. Burwell. But Toombs was determined to return to Washington to defeat Walker's Kansas policy "and those who *palliate, justify or support it.*" He had been "warmly and cordially supported by the great mass of the party," he boasted, but "the few 'King's men' who dissented were not strong enough to raise the standard of rebellion and therefore quite gracefully acquiesced; I determined that my future should be untrammelled, and I was much gratified to find the great majority of the Democrats of Geo. fully up to the same mark."[80]

On December 15, Robert Walker resigned as governor of Kansas. Still, Kansas dominated the Thirty-Fifth Congress like no other subject. December 21 saw Kansans vote on a pro-slavery provision of their constitution that had been drawn up at Lecompton. This dubious document passed 6,134 to 569 because members of Kansas' Free State Party stayed home on election day. The pro-slavery minority declared the constitution ratified and immediately sent it to Washington. Two weeks later, the entire constitution was submitted to the people of Kansas. It was rejected by over ten thousand votes. The legalistic and provincial Buchanan decided to support the Lecompton Constitution anyway. It was an immense political blunder. Southern Democrats were delighted; Northern Democrats were livid. Buchanan had split the party.

Buchanan sent a special message to Congress on February 2, urging admission of Kansas under the Lecompton Constitution. Despite the rejection of the Lecompton Constitution by Kansas voters, Toombs agreed with Buchanan's decision and spoke in the Senate the same day. He said admitting Kansas was desirable. The only hitch was how the territory should be admitted. The state ought to be admitted under the Lecompton Constitution "because it comes with legality; it comes clothed with the dignity of representing the will of the majority, legally expressed." Toombs dismissed the "pretended government" that had drawn up a constitution at Topeka. The Lecompton Constitution had been recognized by every political party, every department of government, and all the party organizations. For those who said admitting Kansas under the Lecompton Constitution violated the Kansas-Nebraska Act, Toombs replied the South was simply asking for "no prohibition on us, or our institutions, or property [during the territorial stage].... We did not want new lessons on popular sovereignty in 1854. We had no new theory on that subject."

The second part of Toombs' speech was a weak argument contending the vote for the slavery provision of the Lecompton Constitution was legitimate while votes for the entire constitution were not. He admitted there was a right to submit the entire constitution to a vote, but there had been no provision in the law for that. As far as Toombs was concerned, the Lecompton Constitution was entirely legitimate. The convention had been called for by the people, elected delegates had framed a constitution, and they submitted legitimate portions of it for a vote. "It stands on every form of legality. The law, the peace of the country, the right, demand that the policy of the President shall be sternly upheld by the representatives of the States and of the people."[81]

Buchanan's special message to Congress caused strife in the Senate, but it caused a brawl in the House. On February 5, Galusha Grow, a Republican from Pennsylvania, and Laurence Keitt of South Carolina traded insults on the House floor. Keitt lost his temper and tried to throttle Grow. That started a near riot involving nearly fifty representatives. "Such a row you never saw," Alexander Stephens wrote to his half-brother, Linton. But Stephens recognized that the incident foreshadowed what was to come. "All things here are tending to bring my mind to the conclusion that this Govmt. [sic] can not or will not last long."[82]

In between battles over Kansas, Toombs fought skirmishes over the Naval Board of Inquiry and he tangled with Jefferson Davis over increasing the size of the army—Toombs, of course, was against it. As the debate dragged on and on, his patience grew short. "This [Kansas] question has been discussed since the session commenced," he complained on the Senate floor. "We have continued from time to time, probably every week, when any gentleman desired it, to argue the question up to this [fifteenth] day of March." Toombs believed Republicans were delaying the proceedings because the Lecompton Constitution had a good chance of passing. "The country has rights," Toombs seethed. "The majority have rights, and they have duties; and one of the duties is that the business of the country shall be done decently, and in order and in due time." When Toombs said he hoped the Senate had enough fidelity to its principles and to the country to "crush" the disruptive factions, the galleries burst into applause.[83]

"I do not know that it will be quite so easy a matter to crush us," William Pitt Fessenden, the junior senator from Maine, said.

"I did not say it was easy," Toombs growled.[84]

As the debate in the Senate inched into the long night, Toombs' crankiness subsided. When a motion to adjourn was made, Toombs objected because there was no quorum. "All we can now do is wait for those members who are absent, and let those who are here speak if they choose."

"Suppose we do not want to speak?" Fessenden asked.

"We can sit quietly and take a doze," Toombs said.

"I think that is the best thing we can do," Fessenden replied.[85]

A few days later, Toombs delivered another long set-piece in which he once again maintained Congress had no authority to determine a state's form of government. The question, he said, rose far above a mere sectional issue. In his judgment, the rights, honor and "safety" of the South were at stake and "the principle involved in this question is worth more to them than the union of these States." The question, he said was a constitutional one, not a "sectional one." He was outraged by the hypocrisy he found in the North. When the Supreme Court supported restrictions on slavery, it was cheered; now it was condemned.

"This tribunal ceased to be the proper arbiter of constitutional questions when it decided this constitutional point against the fanaticism of the North!" Toombs cried.[86]

In the House, Stephens struggled to push the Lecompton bill through, but it stayed tied up in debate and parliamentary snarls. To make things worse, a cabal of Southern Know-Nothings voted with Republicans on some procedural issues that stalled the bill even longer. Stephens resigned himself to waiting for the Senate to untangle the mess. "Alas for my country," Stephens wrote to Linton. "How shamefully she is represented."[87]

Despite Stephens' despair, Toombs had no doubt about the Lecompton Constitution's fate. "I was well aware from the beginning, that these gentlemen [of the North] had no other idea except to amuse the country," he told his Senate colleagues. "There was no real opposition to this measure." The senators from New England had only been making it an issue for the sake of the "tender-hearted women who are in favor of progress — spinsters who are left in that country. I apprehend that the whole purpose is accomplished."[88]

On March 22, the floor and galleries in the Senate were packed with unruly spectators as the ailing Stephen Douglas denounced the Lecompton Constitution. It was "a void, rejected, repudiated" document "brought into existence not only by fraudulent voting, but forged returns, [and] sustained by perjury."[89]

After Douglas finished, Toombs lambasted him for criticizing supporters of the Lecompton Constitution and the administration. But Toombs saved his best venom for those who had supported congressional nonintervention during the debates over the Compromise of 1850 and the Kansas-Nebraska Act and now were trying to meddle in the constitutional proceedings of Kansas. "I say that all these men who to-day declare that Congress has no right to cram constitutions down the throats of a majority, deny every act of their public life, for they have held it to be right to cram free constitutions down anybody's throat." It was contemptible and hypocritical. Apparently, "you can cram freedom whether the people want it or not, but take care how you cram slavery."

The Lecompton Constitution had been approved in a legal election, the question had been legally submitted to the people, a majority of legal voters had affirmed it. Yet the North was trying to prevent Kansas from coming into the Union with slaves. "I tell you that when the laws can take away our rights, they are not worth maintaining," Toombs raged. "I scorn any man who tells me that the great right to two thousand million dollars worth of property depends on legislation, on Senate votes or House votes."

If it came to that, the South would "stand by the Constitution" and if Northerners chose to separate, "I will bid you an affectionate farewell.... Whenever you think it is more to your advantage and mine to quit, I will bid you good morning with a great deal of pleasure." Toombs wanted no sectional strife, but he warned Northerners not to try to take away the South's property. "You will be entitled to it when you win it, and not till then."

Toombs was "amazed," he said, at those who stood for prohibiting slavery in Kansas, especially John J. Crittenden and Stephen Douglas. Refusing to admit Kansas was an "enormous outrage" that Republicans, Northern Democrats, and their Know-Nothing allies were perpetrating to confuse the American people. But Toombs thought the voters had "wisdom enough, judgment enough, honesty enough to protect themselves against false friends and against open enemies."[90]

The next day, Toombs paced back and forth nervously in the Senate chamber as the bill to admit Kansas under the Lecompton Constitution passed thirty-three to twenty-five. A few days later, Toombs went home. "All well in Geo.," he reported to Stephens who was stuck in Washington. "The weather is delightfull [sic], trees and flowers in full bloom and nature looks charming." Except for the "sad recollection of public events at Washington I should almost feel as tho' I were transferred to a new and fairer land." He was tending his law practice and avoiding the stump, but those he had talked to had nothing but criticism for Crittenden "I must [do] the K[now] N[othings] the justice to say that none, seem more earnest or decided in their condemnation of them than they do." His informants also "seem better informed of the real state of the case and the treachery of these men than I had any idea of and condemn them I think with real earnestness."[91]

Despite the bill's success in the Senate it remained bogged down in the House. On April 1, the House rejected the bill and substituted a measure that called for another vote on the entire Lecompton Constitution. The Senate, in turn, rejected the measure the next day. Finally, a special conference committee with four Democrats and two Republicans was appointed. The committee churned out the so-called English Bill that allowed Kansans to vote for the Lecompton Constitution but reduced their land by almost twenty million acres. As an incentive, the English Bill promised to pay a grant (Republicans called it a bribe) from the proceeds of the sale of twenty million acres of federal land. If the voters rejected Lecompton, then Kansas would have to wait until the territory had the usual ninety thousand residents.

Stephens was the real author of the bill and worked tirelessly to push it through the House. Toombs, on the other hand, kept a low profile. He had little doubt the English Bill would get through the Senate. "I think it is a wise measure — a good measure," he told his colleagues the day before the final vote. "I like it because it settles this question upon a principle, and not a concession." The bill ended the clamor about "cramming" a constitution down free people's throats.[92]

On April 30, the English Bill passed in the House 112–103; in the Senate, it won by nine votes. Although bloodshed subsided in Kansas, the deal was rejected in August when Kansans voted against the Lecompton Constitution. Kansas had to wait to until 1861 to be added to what was left of the Union.

As the turbulent session limped to an end, Toombs fought the usual battles against spending federal money on internal improvements, pensions, and other appropriations he saw as overly charitable. When a bill requesting a pension for an army widow named Gaines came up, Toombs sneered that senators' heads could easily be turned by fascinating ladies. "I am told that attachment to the ladies, when it gets in the head, is worse than anywhere else." The chamber burst into laughter.[93]

The only other issue that riled him involved British ships boarding and searching American ships suspected of carrying slaves in the Gulf of Mexico. Tensions escalated until British warships were actually firing at American vessels. "England is kicking you all over your own neighborhood," Toombs intemperately railed at his colleagues in the Senate. "It is our sea, and that ought to be a sufficient right to keep her out of it." He did not want raise a false cry of war, but "the Government ought to send a force to the Gulf, and seize the vessels committing these outrages, and either sink them or bring them to our ports and hang the officers." Toombs was ready to vote for resolutions to send the American navy to the Gulf to "prevent the continuance of this war upon our commerce." Great Britain "claims the right of disgracing our flag, and searching our vessels in the Gulf of Mexico at our own doors."[94]

"Mr. Toombs knows perfectly well that we would never think of such a thing as hanging the British officers as pirates, and that they could not be convicted of piracy under any known code of law" a New York *Times* editorial said. "Threats of this kind are only worthy of a debating club or a tavern." Another editorial had some fun at Toombs' expense. "Our government will naturally rejoice that Mr. T. has declared war" and that "if nobody else should be prepared for war, *he* is ready." Despite Toombs' declaration of war, the conflict was resolved through diplomatic channels in June when the British renounced the rights of seizure.[95]

Toombs hung around Washington just long enough for the special session then hurried home to Georgia. He spent the interim between sessions fretting about his crops, his business deals, and putting in long hours at his law practice. "I am in the court house from morning until near 7 o'clock in the evening & have to listen to all the speakers as I am to conclude the argument on my side," he lamented to Julia from Marietta, "so that in truth I have not had a moment of daylight for visiting since I got here and need every night for consultation with appropriate counsel & preparation."[96]

The second session of the Thirty-Fifth Congress was a mundane session with more partisan debating than governing. "We are doing no better in politics, I fear a good deal worse," Toombs wrote to Julia from Washington, D.C. "The joining of factions prevents anything from being done." However, there were a few issues that aroused him. In his State of the Union address, Buchanan mentioned the possibility of buying Cuba from Spain. Toombs was enthused by Louisiana Senator John Slidell's bill to appropriate the funds for the purchase. Although he was well known for being stingy with the government purse, Toombs thought Cuba was one bauble worth the price.[97]

When his colleagues — led by Senator Seward — expressed doubts about appropriating money to buy a foreign land, Toombs reminded them that millions in public money had been used to purchase peace with Mexico, "connected, as the proposition undoubtedly was, and as it was understood by all parties, with the acquisition of territory." The rub was the island's 450,000 slaves. While this specific bill did not address the matter, Toombs was content to leave the issue to the voters in Cuba. Despite the recent brawl over Kansas, he believed the island would be opened to "all the people of the Republic, North and South, East and West, with ample constitutional protection to all property held in any of the States." But whether it was Cuba, Canada, or parts of Central America, Toombs said he would accept any countries advantageous to the United States.

Seward had cautioned that the U.S. could not absorb Cuba because of the differences in language, race, manners, custom, and religion. Toombs answered that this had not been a problem when Florida was bought from Spain or when Louisiana was purchased from France. "At every acquisition of territory made by the Republic, we have had exactly the same difficulties of race, of language, and of conditions of people different from our own, all of them different possibly from the people of any State of the Union; but we have molded them into one American people." With one exception: "I do not count the Mexican purchase, because I admit that was rather a forced sale."

As for the economic benefits, Cuba would enrich the whole country. The North could buy coffee, sugar, and exotic fruits while selling grain, produce, and manufactured goods. "It will be nature's commerce; beneficent, prosperous, beneficial to all engaged."

But Toombs ended on a disingenuous note when he claimed that obtaining another potential slave state did not motivate him. "The idea of getting one slave State would have no effect on me," he assured the Senate. His only motive was Cuba's "fine ports," securing the Gulf of Mexico and the rest of the Caribbean sea. "Probably younger men than you or I will live to see the day when no flag shall float there except by permission of the United States of America. That is my policy."[98]

To no one's surprise, the debate over Cuba turned nasty a few weeks later.

On February 14, the Senate got around to presenting Toombs' credentials. The forty-nine-year-old Senator had "partially grey, but thick hair" that hung "bushily upon his head." And he still had a powerful voice that "filled the hall, every nook and corner completely," wrote the Washington correspondent for the Milledgeville *Federal Union*. "Toombs is built for an orator, tapering like a wedge from his shoulders, which support a round, well developed head, to his feet," the profile continued, "with arms and hands moving gracefully in gesticulation, his oratory and its accompaniments attract a stranger so much that often the depth to which he is diving is unnoticed. It is best for him not to have exceeded ten minutes in preparation before he speaks, for then the glow and fire of his nature arises in him."[99]

On February 25, the Cuba issue flared up again. When the Senate resumed consideration of the Cuba Bill, the debate once again turned into a vicious argument over slavery. It degenerated from there when James Doolittle of Wisconsin tried to take up the Homestead Bill. In the wrestling match over parliamentary procedure, Seward proclaimed the Homestead Bill was a question of "lands for the landless freemen" while the Cuba Bill was a "question of slaves for the slaveholders." When the chair decided not to restrict debate, Toombs blew his top.

He was outraged at the "little, paltry tricks, of two-penny demagogues, to prevent coming to a vote on this question." According to Toombs, demagogues in the Senate were playing games with the legislative process. A demagogue might be "a dirty dog," in Toombs' description, "but he has got a principle; he appeals to the people; he rouses the masses; he speaks home to the prejudices, to the passions, and sometimes to the vile prejudices and vile passions of the masses," Toombs said. "But the man he drives is worse than he is; and that is the way with 'land to the landless.'"

Cuba was a question of national, not sectional, policy. But Republicans were trying to obfuscate the issue with diversions and scare tactics. "If you do not want to give $30,000,000, say so like men," Toombs urged. "What are you afraid of? Are you afraid of lacklanders? They will not object to getting more land. The more we have, the better chance for them." Except for Republican delaying tactics, the Cuba issue could be settled in ten minutes and "the land for the landless in ten minutes more."

Ben Wade of Ohio interrupted to tell Toombs that the South "may have occasion to shiver on [the Cuba] question." The galleries broke into applause when Wade posed his famous question: "Shall we have niggers for the niggerless, or land for the landless?" William Pitt Fessenden of Maine and Seward made similar attacks on the Cuba Bill. "The Senator from Maine is for appropriations bills," Toombs sneered when he gained the floor a few hours later. "Give land to the landless, says the gentleman to my left, [Mr. Wade]; ... give us liberty, says the gentleman from New York. Take any form but Cuba; that I cannot stand."

Still, Toombs claimed that attacks from the likes of Wade and Seward meant nothing. "If I wanted a man to benefit slavery I would take the Senator from New York," Toombs said snidely. Men like Seward and Wade had freed not one single slave "unless he has done it clandestinely." Seward "may go and tell foolish old men and spinsters and old maids in New York that he has done a thriving business on freeing negroes, but he has never freed a one."[100]

But for all Toombs' excitement and bluster, the Cuba Bill came to nothing.

Buchanan had called for an extra session of Congress, but Toombs had no intention of attending. He had had enough of Washington "as I am compelled to sit here in the senate [sic] 12 or 14 hours per day ... when I get home I am ready enough to get to bed." But

Toombs had another reason to get out of town. He had recently become a grandfather. "I am very anxious to see Sallie & the baby and will take the first few days I possibly can to go with them," he wrote again to Julia.[101]

Toombs went home to take it easy for a few weeks before resuming his law practice and setting up for the next political battles. But the relaxation he was looking forward to so much a week earlier got on his nerves in a hurry. Toombs was not a homebody. "There is no news here of any sort," the bored Toombs wrote to Julia in March. "The town seems duller than ever; indeed it seems to be going to decay about as fast as those things can be done." Travel was barely an option: "The roads have not been so bad here for twenty years, it is hardly safe to ride in the streets of the town, they are cut up & the mud holes are too deep."[102]

Toombs' concerns about the roads were warranted. Julia broke her leg in a carriage accident a few weeks later. He did his best to stay out of politics and occupied most of his time taking care of her and being a grandfather to his grandson, little Robert. But by the end of the summer, he found it necessary to "put in" at the request of William Crawford. He set his law practice aside and accepted speaking engagements all over Georgia, even though his September cases had to "go to the Devil."[103]

Georgia Democrats were split between followers of Buchanan and Stephen A. Douglas. Even though Georgia's Know-Nothing Party had formally dissolved and renamed itself simply the Opposition it was still able to effectively accuse both Buchanan and Douglas Democrats of sacrificing slavery and Southern rights during the fight over Kansas. Toombs campaigned hard for both Democratic factions throughout Georgia. While he favored the Buchananites, he campaigned as a moderate determined to keep both sides and the Union together. On September 8, in a speech at Augusta, he explained the position he had taken the year before. He said that Congress had excluded Southern institutions from the territories for thirty years, so he thought it "wise, prudent and politic to settle the question against our common enemy, Congress." The Kansas bill left the people free to form and regulate their domestic institutions as they wished. Even the Supreme Court had decided in favor of the policy.

Toombs assured his audience that he was a "steady and uncompromising adversary" against Douglas' squatter's sovereignty policy. "Yet I do not belong to those who denounce him," Toombs said. "Mr. Douglas is at full liberty to take either side he may choose, and if he maintains his ancient ground of neither making nor accepting new tests of political soundness I shall consider him a political friend and will accept him as the representative of the party whenever it may tender him." Even if he wandered "after strange gods," Toombs still preferred him and "would support him tomorrow against any opposition man in America."

But Toombs did not believe the issue should be used as a test for party fealty, especially for his Northern Democratic friends. Appealing directly to the voters, he promised if they voted for the Buchananites, factions in the North and South would be conquered and the country would be saved "from the curse of being ruled by the combination now calling itself the opposition. We shall leave this country to our children as we found it united, strong, prosperous and happy." This was one of the last times Toombs urged keeping the Union together.[104]

The Opposition tried to drive the Democrats to secessionist extremes on national issues, but the Democrats won the September elections by focusing on state matters and riding the popular Joe Brown's gubernatorial coattails. Still, Georgia Democrats were missing a valuable partner: Stephens had retired from Congress and did not run for reelection.[105]

On October 16, a more infamous Brown raided the federal arsenal at Harper's Ferry. John Brown led nineteen followers on a raid at the Harper's Ferry Armory. The idea was to somehow spark a slave revolt throughout the South. When it was discovered that Brown had received encouragement and financial support from some prominent Republicans, it confirmed in the Southern political mind that Republicans were devils in swallowtail coats. Toombs made no public comment until later, but like most Southerners, he blamed the Republicans for the words, if not the deeds. "We know they have received indirect encouragement from William H. Seward, Joshua Giddings, Horace Greely, and other Republican leaders, who, by their speeches and writings, have encouraged fanatics to such deeds as this," the Milledgeville *Federal Union* wrote. Cobb summed up the South's feeling concisely when he called Brown's raid a practical result of Republican abuse of the South.[106]

Toombs did not inflame the situation publicly. Instead, he campaigned with his usual stump speeches. "I went to Sparta to make my great agricultural speech, which the world has already forgotten without being at [all] conscious of the magnitude of its loss," Toombs kidded Thomas W. Thomas. Despite his levity, he was not encouraged by the prospects for the next congressional session. The recent elections gave Democrats the majority in the Senate, but the House had fallen to Republicans. He certainly did not like the way things were shaping up. "Old Buck is determined to rule or ruin us," he wrote. "I think he means to continue his own dynasty or destroy the party, and the times are at least favourable to his accomplishing the latter result and the country with it." Electing a Southern Democrat as president was crucial. "If we can beat the Black Republicans next year with [R.M.T.] Hunter or as wise a man as he is, I think the North will put down Republicanism itself," Toombs predicted. "If they beat us I see no safety for us, our property and our firesides, except in breaking up the concern."

John Brown's raid galvanized Toombs' hostility toward Republicans. He was beginning to sound like a man ready to go to war. He thought the South should do whatever it could to defeat Republicans "whose principles and whose leaders are so openly hostile not only to her equality but to her safety in the Union," he wrote to Thomas. It would be a "calamity" if Republicans ever became the dominant party, and if it ever happened, "we should prefer to defend ourselves at the doorsill rather than await the attack at our hearthstone." It was madness to wait for an overt act. "They have already declared war, and if the North elect them it is endorsing the declaration, and we ought to meet it with promptness and decisions."[107]

Washington had seldom seen more animosity and partisanship than in the Thirty-Sixth Congress. The House nearly ignited when Republicans nominated Ohio's John Sherman as speaker. Sherman had endorsed Hinton Helper's book, *The Impending Crisis*. Helper's book was a sharp criticism of slavery, slaveholders and the Southern economy. Sherman was untenable and many Southern members were "willing to fight the question out, and to settle it right there," one correspondent wrote to Stephens.[108]

Toombs tried to keep the retired Stephens informed about the political situation in Washington with a flurry of letters. "We are all at sea here; no organization of the House and no appreciation of the real state of the times by our friends in either house," he wrote. "It is a mere Gallipago's [sic] turtle business with them." Ignoring Southern Democrats' previous willingness to obstruct legislation, Toombs called the Republicans "stern, confident, and defiant. They manage their side of the house with ten times the skill of ours." As for the "old fogies" in the Senate, they were "all candidates for the Presidency from highest to lowest, and are as silent, sanctimonious and demure as a wh[or]e at a christening." Buchanan and his cabinet were "as rabid and imbecile as ever and much more profligate; they hesitate at no abuse of patronage to compass their petty party ends. God almighty have mercy on these poor people!"

Toombs was in a gloomy mood and sure that Sherman would be elected speaker. But his sights were set past congressional bickering and on the presidential election. He thought Douglas would be a strong candidate at the Charleston convention. "He cannot possibly be elected, but I think will nominate whom he pleases," Toombs wrote. He very badly wanted to see his friend Stephens run. Stephens had a lot of support and Toombs regretted very much that Stephens had retired. "I think [it] very unwise in you and hurtfull [sic] to the country. I think you could be nominated, especially after the old fogies are done fighting their battle of weakness, for none of them have any strength."[109]

Even the holiday season could not lighten Toombs' spirits. "Everything has been dull and stagnant during the Christmas," he wrote again to Stephens a few days later. "Even negroes cease to excite on either side. The social intercourse between North and South or rather between Dems. and Reps. seems almost wholly to have ceased, and all sides seem sullen and ill-natured."[110]

January found Toombs still sizing up the prospects for the presidential election. He wrote to Stephens that no one could get the nomination without Douglas' support and Douglas's supporters and even Douglas himself were talking about Stephens's possible prospects. "This may be because you are not in the ring by your own act of exclusion," Toombs wrote. Toombs was intending to give a major speech in the Senate although his throat was sore and he had a bad cold. But "I think I shall speak early next week. I shall give a very thorough review of the present and urge the union of all sound elements to drive out the Black Republicans next fall as the only mode, of giving peace and security to the country."[111]

On January 24, Toombs gave the speech that put him firmly in the procession of radical fire-eaters. Until now, he said, the government had been able to surmount every foreign and domestic threat. But now hostility reigned in the country, in the Senate Chamber, the House, state legislatures, "from the pulpit and the press, and from popular assemblies throughout the length and breadth of this broad land." The country was "virtually in civil war." Some senators "thundered their denunciations against slavery and slaveholders, against confederates and their institutions, and thus seek to apply the torch to our homesteads, and to desolate our land with servile and internecine war." This was no longer acceptable. The South wanted peace, and "though the road to it shall lead through war, we intend to have it." The real troublemakers were abolitionists who "formed a coalition with all the waifs and strays — deserters of all former political parties" and called itself the Republican Party. This coalition was trying to limit, restrain, and restrict slavery by refusing to enforce the Fugitive Slave Act. Toombs went into a long litany to show slavery was imbedded in the Constitution and that Republicans — "these hypocrites" — tried to ignore that inconvenient fact. He accused them of hypocrisy, theft, and murder. "They have showed themselves capable of any violation of the Constitution of their country, and they have shown that no oaths can bind them to maintain the compact."

Toombs' railed against abolitionists, Republican hypocrisy, and other opponents of slavery. These groups were "kind enough to ask us 'let us be brothers or we will cut your throats;' that is, if we can get your negroes to do it." Then Toombs extended an invitation: "When they get ready for this brotherly work, in the name and behalf of my constituents I extend to them a cordial invitation to come down to see us." Republicans, he said, were trying to spark a war with propaganda. Almost daily, Northern governors and state legislatures denounced the South, Southerners, and slavery. "The pulpit, the press and the lecture room, join in this crusade against the people of the South, and counsel the adoption of all means to harass, endanger and destroy us.... Is this peace? If it is, I prefer war." Take John Brown. The only people Toombs knew who approved of the raid on Harper's Ferry were Republicans. He conceded that some Republicans denounced Brown's actions. But thousands approved it. "They tell us they condemn his acts, but admire his heroism," Toombs said. "I think the Republican party must be pressed for a hero."

He urged his Southern colleagues not to let the government fall into the "traitorous hands of the Black Republican party." Every day, Republicans declared war against the South and its institutions. "Listen to 'no vain babblings,' to no treacherous jargon about "overt acts ... they had already been committed," Toombs declared. "Defend yourselves, the enemy is at your door; wait not to meet him at the hearthstone — meet him at the doorsill, and drive him from the temple of liberty, or pull down its pillars and involve him in common ruin."[112]

Toombs' Doorsill speech was a combination of stump oratory for the folks back in Georgia, a sincere and deeply felt statement of Southern grievances, and an ominous warning to Republicans to cool the rhetoric. Reaction to the speech was predictable. The New York *Tribune* called it "Bombast" and "volcanic oratory." The New York *Times* thought it "a cool, calculated, pre-determined menace" and "the studied rhetorical display of one who has his assigned part to fill." The *Times'* editorial was the mirror image of some of Toombs' speech. "Mr. Toombs makes a grave mistake in counting upon the passive cowardice of millions of Northerner freemen," the *Times* warned, and the editorial writer wondered where Toombs got the notion that "Northern men are slow to defend their honor. True courage, the Senator has seemingly yet to learn, does not consist in bluster and braggadocio."[113]

But Toombs took the criticism in stride because his Doorsill speech helped defeat John Sherman as speaker of the House. On January 30, Sherman withdrew and Republican William Pennington — more acceptable to the South because he had supported the Fugitive Slave Law — was elected the next day. "We have whipped out Sherman and the Helperites," Toombs crowed in a letter to Stephens. He thought Pennington would be a good choice because "he professes to be only a New Jersey opposition man." Toombs was proud that his speech helped defeat John Sherman and the Sewardites. His speech brought the South together and "every Southern vote stood together solidly for two days and every Northern Democrat but two stood with them."[114]

Stephens was extremely impressed and pleased with his friend's effort: "It is exactly on the right line. It is in better tone, temper, and shows more real statesmanship with less impulse of [bare?] passion than any speech I have ever seen from him," he wrote to J. Henly Smith. If every Southerner could see the speech's "deep truths," the "profound philosophy," and the "true national patriotism it breathes throughout," then Democrats would not only carry the next elections, "but the country would be [safe?] just so long as they would maintain sternly that line."[115]

Toombs was elated with Pennington's victory and the Republicans' disarray. It was "gall and wormwood" to the Republicans, he wrote to Stephens. His speech "brought them into national discredit and strengthened the opposition to Seward inside his party. The party are dumfounded here.... The Northern members are circulating it largely and say that it has and is producing a very healthy reaction against the Blacks."

Other political news concerned legislation by Senators Albert G. Brown and Jefferson

Davis of Mississippi who were proposing elaborate protections of slavery in the territories. Toombs thought it was "foolishness of folly to raise and make prominent such *issues now*" [italics in the original]. The Kansas-Nebraska Act had settled the question by repealing the Missouri Compromise and the Supreme Court had declared Congress could not legislate against slavery in the territories. Toombs thought hostility to Douglas was the only reason for the mischief. "I wish Douglas defeated at Charleston, but I do not want him and his friends crippled or driven off." Alienating Douglas men would be suicide in the next election and Toombs was going to "resist it to the last extremity" in the Democratic caucus.

Finally, Toombs confided to Stephens his worries about the political future in the South. The election of Pennington brought a "brood of abolitionists into this district" and he feared Washington would soon be completely overrun with them. Toombs predicted further Republican victories would abolitionize the border states and raise similar movements throughout the South within a few years. "Thus the strife will be transferred from the North to our own friends. Then security and peace in our borders is gone forever." It would be a mistake to wait for some "overt act" by Republicans, Toombs wrote. It would be a disaster if the Republicans won control of the government. Toombs himself would "raise an insurrection, if I could not carry a revolution, to save my countrymen, and endeavor to save them in spite of themselves." He did not mention how far he had moved towards secession to protect the Northern senators who were trying to compromise with him. He was working on his next speech that would be a "defence [sic] of the 'slave power.' The "denunciations of us everywhere in the North under this name is doing us much harm.... I am now gathering up and analyzing facts for this purpose."[116]

On February 27, Toombs used the debate over the Brown and Davis resolutions to criticize the North for systematically subverting the Constitution. Armed to the teeth with court cases and legal precedents, Toombs demonstrated that Republican states like Wisconsin were violating the law when they tried to get around slavery provisions in the Constitution using state legislation and state court rulings. These antics made the Republican Party unconstitutional, in Toombs' view. Republicans could not carry out their platform "without trampling under foot one of the great coordinate branches of this Government. Are you ready to do this?" he asked his Republican colleagues. "March on, then, to the unholy work."[117]

Toombs elaborated on his crusade against Republicans a week later when Benjamin Wade of Ohio attacked his speech. "The fact that the Black Republicans have attempted, and are now endeavoring, to perpetrate these wrongs, proves them unfit to be rulers of a free people," Toombs declared. Republicans had passed "personal liberty acts," granted runaway slaves bail and jury trials, and enacted other legislative devices to flaunt the Fugitive Slave Act. "This dark catalogue is unequaled in the history of national bad faith," Toombs said. "Yet in the face of these atrocities, we are told these States have not violated the Constitution."

As a senator and citizen, Toombs said he was bound to support the Constitution. "But when the revolution begins, constitutions end. My first, my only allegiance, is due to Georgia." Toombs said if Georgia left the Union, then he would vacate his senate seat "and shall no longer be bound by a compact which your party has annulled and disregarded, even when acting under its obligations." Toombs assured the Senate that he was not "educated in the school of passive obedience" and he would not "maintain the Union when the Constitution is overthrown. "The cry of Union by those who subvert the Constitution is simply adding hypocrisy to treachery."

Abolitionists had been trying to cause a slave rebellion for twenty years, Toombs said.

John Brown even attempted an invasion. Now Republicans were trying to "effect their diabolical purposes" by elevating their party to power. Republicans could not keep trying to practice their "crude and reckless theories which have produced nothing but discord in the past and promise nothing but ruin in the future." Who demanded the Wilmot Proviso? Who asked for slavery to be kept out of new territories? Who wanted to revive the Missouri Compromise? "Not the South. Not Democrats. But abolitionists."

Toombs again asked Republicans to stop passing anti-slavery laws and to adhere to the Constitution. Or, if the Republicans hated slavery so much, why not let the South go? But by now, Toombs seemed resigned to secession. "There is no harmony between their professions and their conduct; this argues hypocrisy, not sincerity," Toombs said. "If you honestly wish to relieve your souls from the guilt of complicity with slaveholding," he told Republicans, "say so with manly firmness. We will give you a discharge whenever you want it."[118]

Toombs was down in the dumps about presidential prospects as well. The strife was "fast and furious between the friends of the different candidates," he wrote to Stephens. It was like the "officers of ships being engaged in cheating one another at 'three up' in the forecastle while the vessel is labouring among the breakers." It meant a sure defeat for Douglas who was weak in the Northeast and in large pockets of the South. Nor was Douglas likely to step off the stage for a more electable candidate. "I fear he is not patriot enough [to] struggle for the country with the banner in any other hand than his own."[119]

The Senate adjourned briefly in April so Democrats could attend the party convention in Charleston, South Carolina. Washington was pretty well vacated, Toombs wrote to Stephens sourly. "All the scheming active politicians have 'hied away' to Charleston to select an almoner for the Great Democratic party." No prominent Democrat had enough clout to get the nomination. R.M.T. Hunter of Virginia was "an honest man and they want no such a person to guard the exchequer." Vice President Breckenridge could carry Pennsylvania easily, but New York "will not touch him, his character is too good for them." And Douglas "will be beaten, I think, with absolute certainty. He will get as good as no support in the North but of the Northwest, and his enemies are numerous, vindictive and remorseless." Douglas had made too many enemies with his aggressive policies, "and nothing but a large break in the South in his behalf can possibly elect him." Toombs was not anticipating a lot of support for Douglas in the South, "altho' I am quite sure he is stronger in the South than he will be with her representatives at Charleston; but I suppose speculations will be of no use now as the end is near."[120]

When the Democratic convention convened, a dispute immediately broke out over the platform. Southerners insisted on inserting a plank that protected slavery in the territories. They delivered an ultimatum during the hostile floor debate: the plank would be adopted or they would walk out. When William L. Yancy of Alabama proclaimed "we yield no position here until we are convinced we are wrong," the excited Southern spectators in the galleries went wild. Ohio's George Pugh told Yancy that Northerners were not children to be told what to do. Then the crowd began to turn nasty. "Gentlemen of the South," Pugh said, "you mistake us — you mistake us! *We will not do it!*"[121]

The convention was in such an uproar that it was impossible to vote. The proceedings adjourned for the day, but neither side was willing to compromise. On April 30, Douglas's backers pushed through a popular sovereignty plank. The convention went into pandemonium. The Alabama delegation left. As they walked out, delegates from six other states — including Georgia — marched out with them. With Southerners gone and the traditional two-thirds rule in place, Democrats could not choose a nominee. Even Douglas, who had led on fifty-seven ballots, could not clinch the victory. On May 3, the convention adjourned. The remaining Democrats agreed to reconvene in June at Baltimore and try again. The Southern delegations that had walked out decided to meet in Richmond. There was no nominee, but there were lots of agitated and frustrated Democrats.

"We have been all excitement here until yesterday when we heard of the final break up at Charleston, and things are now so complicated that it is difficult to tell what is best to be done," Toombs wrote to Stephens. He thought Douglas' men erred by voting for the platform before nominating their candidate. Toombs was still willing to compromise, if only to get a strong nominee. He telegraphed the Georgia delegation to participate in building the platform, whether it was the radical document with the plank to protect slavery or the so-called Tennessee Platform which was a compromise between the factions. A rupture then became inevitable. "But he [Douglas] and his friends expected to profit by the secession of two or three states and therefore urged it in common with the various elements of combustion in the So. West."

Toombs realized the nomination of Douglas was now impossible, "and if it were possible to nominate him he cannot be elected," Toombs wrote. Toombs predicted that Douglas could not carry the free states and he could not win the election if the entire South voted for him. The rivalry and rancor was so great that Toombs did not see how things could be reconciled unless both sides called a truce, "which I think none of them have patriotism enough to do." The only chance was for some arrangement to be made before reconvening in Baltimore. "If this cannot be done I shall stand by the bolters and let things rock on." The real difficulty was that Douglas had too many Democratic enemies in both the North and South and the delegates had "committed themselves so far against Douglas that they were lost if he was nominated, and they therefore preferred ruining the party with themselves than ruining themselves without the party."[122]

A few days later, Toombs changed his mind about the platform. He endorsed a scheme in which Virginia, Kentucky and Tennessee would join the other bolters if the slavery plank were not included when the Democrats reconvened in Baltimore. He was also alarmed to hear that Georgia was trying to raise another delegation to send to the convention. "A bogus delegation would only complete the demoralization and ruin of the party in Georgia, and would certainly be fatal to Douglas even if he should carry the nomination at Charleston," Toombs wrote to Stephens. "Douglas has pressed his name upon us until I shall accept it and resist him to the bitter end, tho' I see nothing but disaster and defeat in the future." Toombs hoped Douglas would simply withdraw. "That I am now satisfied he never intended to do in any event whatever."[123]

Publicly, Toombs urged compromise. He wanted the seceding delegates to attend the convention in Baltimore to renegotiate the platform. If a platform still could not be agreed upon, Toombs thought a state convention should be called to settle it. He urged Democrats to unite. But no party would ever induce him "to give my assent to any declaration of principles which affirms or admits, directly or by necessary implication, that there is any rightful power anywhere to exclude slave property from any portion of the public domain."

Truth was "often slaughtered in the house and by the hands of its own friends," Toombs wrote in an open letter. "It is sometimes wise to accept a part of our just rights, if we can have the residue unimpaired and uncompromitted by the partial installment." But in Toombs' opinion, the South was surrounded by danger and being asked to sacrifice too much. "I do not concur in the opinion that the danger to the Union is even one of our greatest perils," he railed. "Our greatest danger today is that the Union will survive the

Constitution." The North hated the Constitution and daily trampled it underfoot. He warned his readers not to mistake the nature of the peril. "Look to the preservation of your rights. The Union has more friends than you have, and will last at least as long as its continuance will be compatible with your safety."[124]

Since the beginning of his national political career, Toombs tried to strike down laws prohibiting slavery from the territories. He had fought the Wilmot Proviso with iron fists in the late forties and had argued endlessly with the North during the fifties to stop anti-slavery legislation. But this was the first time he had endorsed any scheme to protect slavery in federal territory. This more radical Toombs also found himself at odds with some important political friends in Georgia: Governor Joe Brown, Howell Cobb, and most importantly, Alex Stephens. "I was satisfied with the Cincinnati enumeration of principles and I think it was all that ought to be asked," Stephens had written.[125]

"I do not concur with you as to the extent of our obligation to maintain nonintervention," Toombs shot back at Stephens, "and if I did I certainly do not feel bound to surrender the judicial question when it has been determined in principle in my favour." He had fought slavery restrictions for years and was not about to change his position now, "and recent events do not at all incline me to modify my hostility." Toombs was even more adamant that the Georgia delegation should back the slavery protection plank when the Democrats reconvened in Baltimore. "Without that I can see nothing but turmoil and disaster; but I shall abide the fortunes of those who will struggle for our equal rights in the territories."[126]

A few days later, Toombs conceded to Stephens that while they may have agreed in principle about slavery in the territories, they differed widely on action. "I agree with you that [what] we ought to demand is to call upon our Northern allies to stand by their bargain; but I complain of them that they will not do it." Toombs took his extreme position in part because Douglas was trying to reinterpret the Supreme Court's ruling in the Dred Scott case. Douglas had said that a territory could legislate against slavery before it became a state; he had also published an article in *Harper's Weekly* questioning whether the Supreme Court was correct when it ruled that slavery was legal in the territories. It had decided this in the Dred Scott decision. "But Mr. Douglas will not stand to it. The Illinois resolutions passed 4th Jany. by his friends expressly declare that it cannot go into the territories without positive legislation."

Toombs did not want to see this become a test of party loyalty, but "I must stand upon the true intent and meaning of our present declaration of principles." Nor was he willing to let the powerful, popular, and highly respected Douglas — who could well be the next president — assail the Supreme Court's ruling without protecting slavery, even in a Democratic platform. Toombs did not understand Stephen's inflexibility either. "These are in brief the reasons upon which my late action been based," Toombs wrote in dismay, "and it does seem to me they are so exactly your own that I am at a loss to discover why our action should not be the same."[127]

On the very day that Toombs was explaining himself to Stephens, Republicans were gathering in Chicago to select their nominee. Republicans were positively giddy as the noisy convention was called to order. They possessed a splendid roster of talent won from the ruins of the Democratic and Whig parties and had a dozen issues they could run away with. The platform endorsed internal improvements, a protective tariff, a homestead bill, and a Pacific railroad bill. It also promised not to attack slavery where it already existed but, ominously, would prevent its expansion into the territories. On the third ballot, an unknown corporate lawyer from Illinois named Abraham Lincoln won the nomination.

On May 21, Toombs made a two-hour speech in the Senate to publicly explain his position. Nominally, he was defending the seven resolutions submitted by Jefferson Davis and Albert G. Brown that called for protection of slavery in the territories. Toombs condemned the resolutions when they were introduced in February. But now "they announced principles so just and so proper, of such universal acceptance, that they needed no support from anything I might be able to say in their favor."[128]

Government's first duty was to protect the rights of its citizens, Toombs said. He had nothing but criticism for those who would not protect slavery in the territories. It was the South's constitutional right to carry slavery into a new state. But according to the Republicans' "new theory," territorial governments had no right to legislate on their own domestic institutions. He was simply asking Congress to stop meddling in the South's domestic institutions. The Kansas-Nebraska bill would have passed Congress "as easily as a bad pension [bill]" if not for the question of congressional intervention.

Still, Toombs did not think protecting slavery would split the Union. But if that was what it came to, if dissolution of the Union was the cost of protecting slavery, "I say, let it come, and the sooner the better." He would support no government that did not protect his constitutional rights. "That is the price of my allegiance; and when it ceases to perform that duty, I will do what I can to build up new systems, better suited to perform the great ends of all human government, the protection of life, liberty and property."[129]

"You will see from my speech fully where we differ, tho' I am perfectly prepared to accommodate the party difficulty when you [think] proper," Toombs wrote to Stephens. He swore that he "never, never did and never will, surrender the constitutional right of protection." However, the resolution passed in the Senate forty-two to two (only Hannibal Hamlin of Maine and Lyman Trumbull of Illinois voted against it, Toombs pointed out), despite Douglas' "clamour" against it.[130]

On June 4, Georgia Democrats gathered in Milledgeville to nominate their slate of candidates for state elections. They endorsed the bolt at the Charleston convention and authorized the same men to do the same thing if the slavery protection plank was not approved when the Democrats reconvened in Baltimore. The convention in Milledgeville reflected the national split in the party when moderate Democrats protested the instructions to the delegation and followed Herschel V. Johnson in a walkout of their own. "I do not see but that both wings passed substantially the same resolutions," Toombs sighed from Washington, D.C., "and why they split I can not tell except under it lies more personal preferences for the Presidency." Toombs believed there was no compromise to be found between the Douglas and anti–Douglas factions of the Democrats and that "personal hostilities and personal advantages" caused much of the strife. He was still out there fighting, but he despaired for the condition of the party and thought no Democrat would stand a chance in November. "I have ceased to interest myself further than to give my decided opinions to all who ask for them."[131]

The Democrats reconvened in Baltimore on June 18 and the arguments began almost immediately. Toombs watched as a fight broke out about readmitting the delegates who had bolted at Charleston. The debate was academic because the Douglas men forced a resolution through to replace the original delegates. So the Southerners walked out again. What was left of the convention put a popular sovereignty plank into the platform and nominated Stephen A. Douglas for president and Herschel V. Johnson, former governor of Georgia, for vice president.

A few days later, the original delegates rented a different hall in Baltimore and nominated

Vice President John C. Breckenridge of Kentucky and Joseph Lane of Oregon on the Southern ticket. The platform demanded federal protection of slavery in the territories. For what it was worth, this was the ticket that received the endorsement from President Buchanan.

Yet another group, the Constitutional Union Party, put up a candidate as well. They too met in Baltimore, and nominated former speaker of the House John Bell, a Whig from Tennessee, for the presidency and Edward Everett for the vice presidency. Their platform simply endorsed the principles of the Constitution, the Union, and law and order. This faction was made up of remnants of Whigs and Know-Nothings from border states and was scoffed at by political sophisticates as the "Old Gentlemen's party" or the "Do-Nothing party."

Congress adjourned on June 28 and Toombs headed to Georgia to campaign for Breckenridge. By now, he had made up his mind that the crisis could not be resolved and publicly advocated secession in his stump speeches. Stephens was more circumspect and had even been chosen as an elector for Douglas. While there was dissention in the political partnership, Toombs and Stephens were not willing to spoil a good friendship. "I saw Mr. Toombs," Stephens wrote to J. Henley Smith in July. "Did not talk politicks [sic] with him except in a very general way. We differ widely and radically on present issues; but as I do not intend to take any active part again in public matters, I have made up my mind never to let such things interfere with my private relations.[132]

But the mood in Georgia favored Toombs' scorched earth style of politicking. The state was anticipating the "downfall" of the government, and "I hope they will continue in that temper until the time for action comes," Toombs wrote to J. Henley Smith. At Georgia's Democratic Convention in August, Toombs inflamed Democrats when he gave essentially the same speech he had made in the Senate on May 21. They applauded wildly when he characterized the presidential election as a mandate on the rights of slave owners. Toombs confirmed that he was a disunionist, although a "conditional" one. If he could not get equal rights for Southerners, he said, then he was "for the South taking care of herself." "The speech of Mr. Toombs was much more national, than partisan, in its character," wrote the Milledgeville *Federal Union,* "and deserves the attention of all parties."[133]

Senator Toombs in 1860. Courtesy of the Georgia Historical Society, Savannah, Georgia.

In October, Toombs traveled to Montgomery, Alabama, and dared the nation to elect a Repbulican: "Let the night which decides the election of Lincoln be ushered in by the booming of hostile cannon of the South," he roared to the cheering crowd. In Atlanta, one witness said that Toombs "spoke like a madman and acted like a fanatic." But the nation answered right back on November 6 when Abraham Lincoln and Hannibal Hamlin won the presidential ticket. They carried less than 40 percent of the popular vote but they took 180 electoral votes. Douglas won 29 percent of the popular vote but carried only Missouri and New Jersey. Breckenridge got 18 percent of the popular vote and seventy-two electoral votes, including Georgia's. Bell finished with a paltry 13 percent of the popular vote (588,879) and 39 electoral votes. More conspicuously, Lincoln and Hamlin carried 18 free states, Breckenridge 11 slave states, and Bell took three border states.[134]

Election results boomed like a volley of cannon fire across Georgia. While few questioned whether the Union would end, there were differences over how to bring Georgia's separation about. Privately, Stephens urged caution; Governor Joe Brown recommended the legislature convene a special secession convention. Toombs believed the most effective tool to pull the state out of the Union was for the legislature to call for a special election to see if Georgians were willing to stay in the Union under a Republican president.[135]

The Georgia legislature, which had been in session since the beginning of November, invited some of the state's brightest political minds to come before them and formally make their views known. On November 13, Toombs addressed the lawmakers. He brought them no encouraging news. "The stern, steady march of events has brought us in conflict with our non-slaveholding confederates upon the fundamental principles of our compact of Union." Although the South had tried to avoid this conflict, Toombs said, "the door of conciliation and compromise is finally closed by our adversaries."

Toombs gave the legislators a litany of "crimes" against the South: the North had refused to protect slavery in a territory until statehood. Northern politicians were "perverting" the government for their own economic, political, and sectional advantages. Abolitionists and Republicans were conspiring to incite insurrection, discontent, and lawbreaking against the South. Lincoln had been elected "by the perpetrators of these wrongs with the purpose and intent to aid and support them in wrongdoing." This left the South without protection. Lincoln's and the Republicans' main purpose was the "final and total abolition" of slavery. The inauguration of Lincoln would give Republicans vast powers and patronage in the executive and judicial branch.

"Will you let him have it?" Toombs roared to the Georgia assembly.

"No, no. Never!" they cried.

"Then strike while it is yet today!" he urged. "Withdraw your sons from the army, from the navy, and every department of the Federal public service. Keep your own taxes in your own coffers — buy arms with them and throw the bloody spear into this den of incendiaries and assassins, and let God defend the right."

Toombs concluded with one last detail. "If you desire a Senator after the fourth of March, you must elect one in my place," he told the Georgia lawmakers. He had served the state in one capacity or another for twenty-five years, and he was still willing to serve Georgia, but he would resign from the Senate. "Make my name infamous forever, if you will, but save Georgia," he cried. "I have pointed out your wrongs, your danger, your duty. You have claimed nothing but that rights be respected and that justice be done. Emblazon it on your banner —fight for it, win it, or perish in the effort."[136]

This was Toombs at his demagogic best — or worst. He had probably heard from Stephens numerous times that Lincoln was no abolitionist. Toombs knew the Republicans could not strike slavery down with the stroke of a quill pen. So whether he actually believed his own rhetoric is doubtful, but it was the message his Southern audience and the Georgia legislature wanted to hear. Sober deliberation, earnest reflection, and common sense had no place in the South in the autumn of 1860.

Yet this was exactly what Alexander Stephens wanted to talk about the next night. On November 14, he addressed the legislature. Toombs sat on the speaker's platform, arms folded and glowering at his friend.

Stephens tried to appeal to the audience with reason, questioning whether the South was truly a blameless victim of Northern perfidy. "I give it to you as my opinion," he said, "that but for the policy the Southern people pursued, this fearful result would not have occurred." Georgia did not have to secede because of the election of one man. Stephens ticked off the reasons Lincoln was no threat to the South: he was put into office with a minority mandate; the second session of the Thirty-Sixth Congress would be dominated by Democrats; and Lincoln would need Senate consent for his appointments. "No man can be appointed without the consent of the Senate." Stephens said.

"If the Senate was Democratic, it was for Breckenridge," Toombs interrupted.

Stephens drew a round of applause when he told Toombs that Georgia would be safe, then, if a Breckenridge Senate approved Lincoln's appointments. "I trust, my countrymen, you will be still and silent," Stephens admonished the audience (and Toombs). "I am addressing your good sense."

Answering Toombs' accusation of the night before that those who were cautious about secession were "misleading, not enlightening," Stephens said he would never submit to aggression against the South's constitutional rights. Yet, "this Government ... with all its defects, comes nearer the objects of all good Governments than any other on the face of the earth, is my settled conviction. Contrast it now with any on the face of the earth."

Toombs life-long friend, Alexander Stephens (1812–1883). Courtesy of the Hargrett Rare Book and Manuscript Library, University of Georgia Libraries.

"England," Toombs bellowed.

"England, my friend says. Well, that is the next best, I grant; but I think we have improved upon England."

Stephens refuted Toombs' complaints about the North one by one: even the tariff had been passed almost unanimously in the House and Senate and Stephens pointed out that Toombs himself had voted for it.

"That tariff lessened the duties," Toombs replied.

"Yes, and Massachusetts, with unanimity, voted with the South to lessen them," Stephens said, "and they were made just as low as Southern men asked them to be, and those are the rates they are now at."

Navigation laws had been passed to expand and protect American shipping and had benefitted both North and South. Even with the "evils in the system," Stephens said, did they outweigh the advantages the government afforded its citizens? "Have we not at the South, as well as the North, grown great, prosperous and happy under its operation? Has any part of the world ever shown such rapid progress in the development of wealth, and all the material resources of national power and greatness, as the Southern States have under the general government, notwithstanding all its defects?"

"In spite of it," Toombs snorted.

"Without [the government's policies] I suppose he thinks we might have done as well, or perhaps better than we have done," Stephens said, pointing to his friend. "This grand result is in spite of the Government? That may be, and it may not be; but the great fact that we have grown great and powerful under the government, as it exists, is admitted. There is no conjecture or speculation about that."

Stephens' remedy for Georgia was to call a convention and let the people vote for or against secession. Then Stephens took a jab at Toombs' scheme to let the Georgia legislature frame the question for the special election: "I have no hesitancy in saying that the Legislature is not the proper body to sever our Federal relations, if that necessity should arise."

"I am afraid of conventions," Toombs said.

"I am not afraid of any convention legally chosen by the people," Stephens answered. He pointed out that the Constitution and Georgia's constitution had been written by conventions with representatives chosen at the ballot box. Hold a state convention, Stephens urged. "But do not let the question which comes before the people be put to them in the language of my honorable friend who addressed you last night: 'Will you submit to abolition rule or resist?'"

"I do not wish the people to be cheated," Toombs chimed in.

"How are we going to cheat the people by calling on them to elect delegates to a convention to decide all these questions without any dictation or direction?" an exasperated Stephens asked. "Who proposes to cheat the people by letting them speak their own untrammelled views in the choice of their ablest and best men, to determine upon all these matters involving their peace?"

Stephens called Toombs' scheme unfair. If Toombs had his way, the legislature would frame the question as a choice between submission to abolition rule or resistance. "Now, who in Georgia would vote 'submission to abolition rule?'"

"The convention will," Toombs cried.

"No, my friend, Georgia will not do it," Stephens replied. Stephens was positive the convention would stand by the Georgia Platform. "Under that there can be no abolition rule in the General Government. I am not afraid to trust the people in convention upon this and all other questions." Besides, said Stephens, the Legislature was not elected to decide secession. They were there to legislate. "They have sworn to support the Constitution of the United States. They did not come here to disrupt this Government."

Stephens believed calling a convention was the only way to preserve peace and harmony in Georgia. The last thing Stephens wanted to see was insurrection or war, at least "without the authority or law." Turning to Toombs, he said "My honorable friend said last night 'I ask you to give me the sword; for if you do not give it to me, as God lives, I will take it myself.'"

"I will," Toombs cried.

"I have no doubt that my honorable friend feels as he says," Stephens said. "It is only his excessive ardor that makes him use such an expression; but this will pass off with the excitement of the hour. When the people shall speak, I have no doubt he will bow to their will, whatever it may be, upon the 'sober second thought.'"

Stephens' vision for the convention was a coming together of men to rationally consider the secession question. He hoped the convention would conclude that there was no reason to break up the Union at least until Lincoln committed some unconstitutional act.

"Commit some overt act?" Toombs scoffed.

Stephens replied with a legalistic answer about the meaning of "overt," but he still thought Lincoln should have his chance. "As long as he conforms to the Constitution he should be left to exercise the duties of his office."

Toombs let Stephens get through the rest of his speech without interruption. Stephens assured the audience that he was for preserving the honor of his state and the South. War was a last resort. But if all failed, "we shall at least have the satisfaction of knowing that we have done our duty, and all that patriotism could require."[137]

After Stephens concluded, Toombs shouted for three cheers. "We have just listened to one of the brightest intellects and purest patriots that lives," he roared. When someone commented on Toombs' good sportsmanship, he replied "I always try to behave myself at a funereal [sic]."[138]

Toombs' rude and boorish behavior is difficult to explain. He may have been drunk; it was no secret that a few spirits took Toombs a long way. Or he could have been shilling for Stephens, acting as a sort of Greek chorus to highlight his friend's moderate political views; Toombs probably knew or suspected the legislature was going to vote in favor of Stephens' convention anyway. Or he maybe he was being obnoxious just to get under Stephens' skin. Whatever the reason, that day he wired one of South Carolina's most ardent fire-eaters, Lawrence Keitt: "I will sustain South Carolina in secession. I have announced to the legislature that I will not serve under Lincoln. If you have power to act, act at once. We have bright prospects here."[139]

After hearing the debate between Toombs and Stephens, the Georgia legislature moved quickly. On November 16, it authorized one million dollars to place Georgia "in a condition of defense." On the twenty-first, the legislature instructed Governor Joe Brown to call an election to choose delegates to a convention that would meet on January 16 to determine Georgia's fate.[140]

Toombs stayed in Georgia when the Second Session of the Thirty-Sixth Congress convened on December fifth. He was preparing to leave and had to decline an invitation to speak in Danbury because "my public duties deprive me of the pleasure of accepting your kind invitation." However, he used this refusal to dispense some advice. While he still saw separating from the "wrong doers as the ultimate remedy," he was willing to give the Union one last chance. Toombs believed the only hope was if a series of constitutional amendments were adopted that repealed the North's personal liberty laws and gave protections for Southern rights. "If the Black Republican party will vote for the amendments, or even a majority of them in good faith," he advised, "they can be easily carried through Congress; then I think it would be reasonable and fair to postpone final action until the legislatures of the northern States could be conveniently called together for definite action on the amendments." If Republicans were sincere about finding a way out of the crisis, Toombs believed, they would adopt the amendments at once. "If they will not do this, you ought not to delay an hour after the fourth of March to secede from the Union."[141]

Toombs was pilloried for his retreat to moderation — or what passed for moderation in that political climate. "Some of the Taliaferro boys have been to Augusta this week," Stephens wrote to his half-brother, Linton, on December 22. "The minute-men down there are in a rage at Toombs's letter. They say that he has backed down, that they intend to vote him a tin sword. They call him a traitor." Toombs' new fire-eater friends were claiming they never had any confidence in him.[142]

A few days later, they were still calling Toombs names. But Stephens saw Toombs' scheme as "a master-stroke to effect his object. He has more sense than any man in this movement." Stephens believed Toombs was trying to seduce moderates into the new Confederate government that was about to be formed, perhaps with Toombs as president. There may have been something to this theory: if anyone knew how cagey Toombs could be, it was Stephens.

Toombs arrived in Washington, D.C., in mid–December to a government that was incapable of dealing with a national emergency. Radical Republicans were demanding an end to slavery as loudly as secessionist Democrats demanded an end to the Union. Buchanan said his prayers and waited for Lincoln to be inaugurated.

On December 18, in a last ditch effort to prevent dismemberment, seventy-four-year-old Senator John Jordan Crittenden of Kentucky proposed six constitutional amendments to quell the agitation. The first amendment proposed extending the Missouri Compromise to California to protect slavery during the territorial phase. Next was a ban on abolishing slavery on government property. Third, slavery would stay in the District of Columbia as long as it existed in Maryland or Virginia. Fourth, Congress would not be allowed to interfere with interstate transportation of slaves. Slaveholders would also be compensated for fugitive slaves rescued by abolitionist mobs. Finally, the Constitution could not be amended to reduce the three-fifths representation of slaves and Congress would be forbidden to alter the slave clauses in the Constitution or to interfere with slavery.[143]

Toombs may have gotten a whiff of Crittenden's proposals in advance. That would explain his suggestion about the pro-Southern Constitutional amendments to the people of Danbury. Perhaps Stephens had been wrong and Toombs was sampling public opinion to test support for the kind of package Crittenden proposed. When Crittenden asked Toombs if the compromises were acceptable to Georgia, Toombs replied: "Not by a good deal; but my State will accept it, and I will follow my State to [Hell]." Stephen A. Douglas also stated that Toombs would have agreed to the compromise. Despite the abuse Toombs took from the press, he was prepared to support the measures.[144]

Although Crittenden's compromises had wide public approval, South Carolina voted itself out of the Union on December 20. The same day, Vice President Breckenridge appointed a special Senate committee. Its mission was to forge a legislative compromise to stop the disunion crisis. The committee was as carefully balanced as a tightrope walker carrying stacks of dishes on each end of a balancing pole: R.M.T. Hunter of Virginia, Lazarus Powell and John Crittenden of Kentucky represented the border states. Stephen A. Douglas of Illinois, William Bigler of Pennsylvania and Henry Rice of Minnesota represented Northern Democrats. There were five Republicans: William Henry Seward of New York, Jacob Collarmer of Vermont, Ben Wade of Ohio, James R. Doolittle of Wisconsin, and James Grimes of Iowa. Jefferson Davis and Toombs spoke for the lower South. The House set up a corresponding body called the Committee of Thirty-Three that had one representative from each state.

Contention broke out immediately in the Committee of Thirteen. On December 22, Toombs proposed his own resolutions. They still sought compromise, but were harsher than Crittenden's. The first resolution asked for a guarantee that settlers could immigrate to a territory "with whatever property they may possess, (including slaves,) and be securely protected in its peaceable enjoyment," until the territory was admitted as a state.

The second resolution called for protection of slavery everywhere the Constitution had jurisdiction and with no restraint on states "to prohibit, abolish, or establish and protect slavery." The next three resolutions asked that people harboring fugitive slaves be prosecuted as aiding and abetting a crime; that runaway slaves be denied habeas corpus, trial by jury, or "other similar obstructions of legislation" in accordance with the Fugitive Slave Law of 1850; and that federal laws be passed for the punishment of those who aided and abetted "invasion or insurrection in any other State."

Finally, Toombs proposed no slavery laws be passed in Congress "without the consent of a majority of the senators and representatives of the slaveholding States." Nor should any constitutional provisions about slavery (except the African slave trade) "ever be altered except by the consent of each and all of the States in which slavery exists."[145]

All of Toombs' resolutions were voted down. The border states reported favorably for the Crittenden compromise and the spokesmen from the lower South gave their conditional support. But the Republicans defeated the proposals when William Henry Seward cast the deciding negative vote. Toombs was livid. "I came here to secure your constitutional rights or to demonstrate to you that you can get no guarantees for these rights from your Northern confederates," he wired to his constituents in Georgia. His propositions were all treated with either "derision or contempt" by the Republican Party.

According to Toombs, the Republicans on the committee were not interested in compromising or promising anything to the South. They were nothing but stooges for their party and controlled the thirty-three members of the House committee. The Black Republicans, "your enemies, who only seek to amuse you with delusive hope until your election, in order that you may defeat the friends of secession." If the people of Georgia were willing to let Republicans control them, "it shall not be my fault. I have put the test and frankly." Georgians could have no more faith in Northerners, Toombs said. Trusting them was fraught with "nothing but ruin to your prosperity." He advised the January convention to vote for secession. "Such a voice will be your best guarantee for security, tranquility, and glory." Toombs' rhetoric was calculated to stoke Georgia's secessionist fire, but his anger was genuine.[146]

Still smarting from the failure of the Crittenden Compromises, Toombs granted an interview to a student from Yale in the last week of December. He lavished the student with his usual Southern hospitality and charm. When the student asked about the current crisis, Toombs nonchalantly replied that the "crisis" had passed and that fifteen Southern states would soon secede to form a new nation.

Toombs rehashed his arguments that slaves were property protected by the Constitution but the North refused to see that. "You Northerners wish to make a new Constitution, or rather to give such an interpretation to the old one as to make it virtually a new document," he told the interviewer. "How can society be kept together," he asked, "if men will not keep their compacts?" Toombs said the South would be happy to remain in the Union if it was treated as an equal part of the country. But the North "tax us and will not protect us. D[am]n it, we will meet you on the border with the bayonet.... *What you tax you must protect.*"

Toombs complained that he could travel through foreign countries such as England and France with his property and was safe. "But if I happen to lose my servant up in *Vermont—*" the writer noted that Toombs spat out the word with derision—"and undertake to recover him, I get jugged." Toombs also pointed out that Northern politicians such as "Billy" Seward took an oath to uphold the Constitution, even though it protected slavery. "This inconsistency runs through most of the Northern platforms. How can we live with men like that?" Much more to his liking were abolitionists like Wendell Phillips, who renounced the Constitution and his citizenship. "This is logical and consistent," Toombs told the student. "I can respect such a position as that" he said, then he spat a "competent" amount of tobacco juice into the fireplace.

The interviewer commented that if war came, it would be an "ugly" time.

"Ugly time? *Oh, no*!" Toombs scoffed. "War is nothing." Men would die, property would be destroyed, fences overturned, and in Toombs' phrase, "the Devil raised generally." But it would all have a good effect. "Only yaller-covered literature men and editors make a noise about war. Wars are to history what storms are to the atmosphere,— purifiers."

Toombs then said to the student haughtily "We are the gentlemen of this land, and gentlemen always make revolutions in history."

The interviewer was appalled by Toombs' political views. But he liked Toombs in spite of his politics. Toombs was courteous, sincere, a warm-hearted man who was known to hold children in his arms in the Senate Chamber and was "one of the kindest of the noblemen ... in the sphere of his unpolitical sympathies."[147]

On December 30, after a week of bickering, Crittenden's committee reported that it could not come up with a two-thirds majority. Crittenden said it was the darkest day of his life. Toombs told Stephen Douglas that the fate of Georgia was staked on the Committee of Thirteen. If Crittenden's package had passed, he would have complied with Stephens' wishes and secession may have been prevented. But Toombs knew now the Union was finished. He and Julia started making arrangements to leave the capital permanently. "I write a few lines to you this morning to ask you what I shall do with your furniture that is in our house," Julia wrote to Alexander Stephens on the first day of the new year. "I have given up the ship ... I shall go home with Mr. Toombs when he goes to the convention."[148]

On January 3, 1861, Crittenden offered an extraordinary resolution in the Senate. He suggested his constitutional amendments be submitted to the public in a national referendum to attempt to settle the conflict once and for all. It would be "an open shame," Crittenden declared, "if, under such circumstances as now exist, this great Government is allowed to fall in ruins."

Crittenden's plan was again hailed as the one that might save the Union. The idea was praised widely. "A fair, just, and honorable compromise," Stephen Douglas called it. Even the temperamental Republican Horace Greeley admitted that if put to a vote, the compromise would pass by "an overwhelming majority."[149]

Still, extremists in both parties denounced the measure. On January 7, Crittenden made a long and impassioned plea for his compromises in the Senate. These measures were required for the security of the country. The politicians were incapable of finding a solution, so Crittenden was ready to "resort to the great source of all political authority — the people themselves. This is their Government; this is their Union; we are but representatives."

Crittenden scolded Congress for being unable to compromise on a solution, he criticized the North for trying to exclude slaveholders from the territories, and the South for acting too rashly. He was confident that if his measures passed, it would heal the chasm that was beginning to engulf the country. If his amendments passed, it would mean peace and the Republicans could get on with governing the country. "Let them commence now by this first glorious act of pacification. It will be a noble starting point."[150]

The floor belonged to Toombs immediately after Crittenden sat down. If Crittenden had offered doves to the country, Toombs loosed the hawks of war. This day, he took his final step in severing his connection with the Union. More senators were present in the chamber than usual and the galleries were crowded to capacity. Many were anxious to hear what the senator from Georgia had to say.

He plunged right in to attack the Committee of Thirteen and the Republican Party. "The success of the Abolitionists and their allies, under the name of the Republican party," he said, "has produced its logical results already. They have for years been sowing dragons' teeth, and have finally gotten a crop of armed men. The Union, sir, is dissolved."

While Congress debated the South was girding for revolution. Toombs assured the Senate that Southerners sought only a new government, not a new constitution. Again, he reminded his colleagues the South had demanded nothing from the North except protection of slavery, which was imbedded in the Constitution. Yet Republicans had tried to outlaw Southern "property" from the territories, had "aided and abetted" insurrection, and tried to subvert Southern institutions. The South was demanding "nothing more than their constitutional rights.... Give us these, and peace restores itself. Refuse them, and take what you can get."

Toombs went through the resolutions he had proposed earlier and gave explanations for them one by one. The South had a right to secede because the compact of the Constitution had been broken. The Supreme Court itself had decided Southerners had the right to take their slaves into the territories, yet Republicans not only discarded the decision, but tried to drive Southerners out of the territories. But the South was not going to submit to Republican will. In Toombs' view, Republicans were cynically turning a blind eye to the South's constitutional rights.

Even on the Committee of Thirteen, where Toombs had been led to believe some Republicans "were the moderate men who were among, and not of the organization," they had repudiated a decent compromise. At the very least, he was willing to settle for an extension of the Missouri Compromise line. But he would take nothing less. "I will not buy a shameful peace. I will have equality or war."

Toombs refused to stay in a country that "gives me less rights than it gives a foreign nation." But he offered one last, faded olive branch: "We have appealed time and time again, for these constitutional rights," he told the Senate. "You have refused them. We appeal again. Restore us these rights as we had them ... and it will restore fraternity, and peace, and unity, to all of us. Refuse them, and what then? We shall then ask you 'Let us depart in peace.' Refuse that, and you present war."[151]

With that, Robert Toombs ended his career on the national political stage. He had tried to find a way to keep the Union from tearing itself apart. But incremental political missteps — zealous, self-righteous rhetoric, flagrant provocations by the North and witless fantasies spouted by loud-mouthed Southern fire-eaters — led Toombs to tear his country apart.

The fights, the arguments, the camaraderie, the great debates, and sorry rhetoric over the Mexican War, the Wilmot Proviso, the Compromise of 1850, Kansas-Nebraska, John Brown's raid, statehood for Kansas, and Lincoln's election nourished Robert Toombs. But what he said also cornered him. In the end, the fights over slavery in the territories and the North's refusal to consider the South's point of view radicalized him. So Toombs was impelled to follow the course of other secessionists and lead Georgia into the bloodbath that was to come.

5

Dixie

"The [Buchanan] administration is dead broken down," Robert Toombs wrote to former South Carolina congressman Lawrence M. Keitt. "The old gentleman is alternately wreaking, wracking, cursing and railing. At one moment he exacts pity and anon contempt." Toombs fully expected Georgia to leave the Union and was "extremely anxious that we should meet and make a common country [at] the earliest possible day." Toombs believed secession was only days away. "We shall soon by your side to share your evils and dangers at home."[1]

Governor Joe Brown had called for a state convention to determine Georgia's fate and Toombs had, of course, been elected as one of the representatives from Wilkes County. Toombs had only a day or two at home before he left for the convention that met on January 16 in Milledgeville. The assembly was a who's who of Georgia's political elite: Toombs, Howell Cobb, Tom Cobb, Alexander Stephens and his younger half-brother, Linton, George W. Crawford and almost three hundred other political celebrities were there. Secessionists, who wanted to take Georgia out of the Union immediately, had a small majority over the so-called Cooperationists. The Cooperationists were split: they either wanted to give what was left of the Union one last chance or secede, then negotiate a better deal for the South before rejoining.[2]

The convention gaveled to order on January 16. After the rules were established and various committees organized, the delegates closed the doors to the public and threw out the press to mask the dissention between Secessionists and Cooperationists. It did not take long for the disagreements to surface. Secessionist Eugenius Nisbet submitted a resolution declaring it was Georgia's "right and duty" to secede and join other states to form "a Southern Confederacy upon the basis of the Constitution of the United States." Cooperationist Herschel V. Johnson immediately countered with a resolution of his own: "The State of Georgia is attached to the Union, and desires to preserve it, if it can be done consistent with her rights and safety." The resolution acknowledged Georgia's grievances but called for a congress of Southern states to meet and consider what should be done next.[3]

After an "elaborate debate," Toombs voted for Nisbet's plan. It passed 166 to 130. Toombs was then assigned to the seventeen-member committee to write the ordinance of secession. Next, the convention read a resolution from the New York legislature that condemned South Carolina and pledged aid and money to uphold the authority of the federal government. Toombs' shot back with a resolution of his own praising Governor Joe Brown's "energetic and patriotic conduct" in seizing Fort Pulaski on the Savannah River.[4]

The next day, the Ordinance of Secession was presented to the convention. "The Union now subsisting between the State of Georgia and other States, under the name of the 'United States of America,'" the ordinance declared, "is hereby dissolved, and that the State of Georgia is in the full possession and exercise of all those rights of sovereignty which belong and appertain to a free and independent State." Cooperationists tried to rally support or at least delay the vote to stall for time and recruit vacillating Secessionists. But the secession ordinance passed with 208 yeas and 89 nays. Toombs voted yea. Most of the Cooperationists had folded and went with the Secessionists. At 2:00 P.M., convention president George W. Crawford tottered to the podium and declared Georgia "free, sovereign, and independent."[5]

Parades, cannon blasts, bonfires, speeches, brass bands and other celebrations commenced throughout Georgia. The Cooperationists could not believe what had just happened. Stephens blamed secession on Tom Cobb's address to the Georgia legislature several months before. Cobb had told Georgians they could make better terms out of the Union than in it. "This one idea did more, in my opinion, in carrying the State out," Stephens wrote, "than all the arguments and eloquence of all others combined."[6]

In addition to his duties at the convention, Toombs also concerned himself with arming the newly sovereign Georgia. On January 24, New York City police seized the schooner *Montgomery* in the East River. On board were six cases of muskets, small arms, and ammunition bound for Savannah. "Is it true that any arms intended and consigned to the State of Georgia have been seized by public authorities in New York?" an outraged Toombs demanded in a telegram to New York City mayor Fernando Wood. The pro–South, pro-secession Mayor Wood had his own political grudges against state authorities in Albany and its control over New York City's police force. Wood replied that officers had indeed impounded the arms. He apologized but made clear that he had no authority over the police. "If I had the power, I should summarily punish the authors of this illegal and unjustifiable seizure of property." Despite Toombs displeasure and Mayor Wood's political posturing, the arms stayed put.[7]

Meanwhile, the convention dragged on for several more days and wrestled with turning Georgia into an independent state. Converting federal courts and federal property into state property, applying state and federal laws to Georgia's new status, a new bill of rights and other matters extraordinary and mundane, had to be addressed. Perhaps because of the secessionist majority, Toombs believed the convention was the supreme manifestation of the will of the people of Georgia. When an argument broke out over changing the state seal, the whole meaning of the convention came into question. As small matters do in the hands of politicians, it became a subject of importance. "These three hundred gentlemen who surround me are the people in their sovereign capacity," he said. The delegates at the convention *were* the one and a half million people of Georgia. "The power of the people is unlimited," said Toombs. "Our power as their representatives is the same as theirs. Where can it be limited?" Since the Constitution had been disposed of, they now had to answer only to a constitution of their own making. "We are the people," he said, "owing no allegiance to any Prince, Potentate, Power, or any thing under Heaven but ourselves and Society." Toombs acknowledged the matter at hand seemed trivial, but the principle was fundamental. When asked where the delegates derived this power from, Toombs answered that his "certificate" came from the people of Wilkes County and his majority "of their votes to represent them in a sovereign Convention, by which they placed no limit on my power." In the end, a committee of inquiry was appointed to change Georgia's seal.[8]

Toombs was also made chairman of the Committee of Foreign Relations. The committee was responsible for appointing commissioners to other Southern states as well as giving instructions to the delegates going to the provisional congress that would meet in Montgomery, Alabama, in February. The next day, to no one's surprise, Toombs and Howell Cobb were chosen as delegates-at-large. Alex Stephens, Tom Cobb, Eugenius Nisbet, and several others were also delegates.[9]

On January 29, Toombs submitted the report of the Ordinance of Secession to the convention. The document was an elaborate justification of the convention's actions. As Toombs explained it, the non-slaveholding states had over the years tried to weaken the South's security, disturbed its peace, refused to comply with constitutional obligations to protect "property, and by the use of their power in the Federal Government, have striven to deprive us of an equal enjoyment of the common Territories of the Republic." This constant hostility put the sections in a "virtual civil war." The South had hoped wisdom and debate would correct the "insults, injuries and dangers" inflicted by the North. Yet "after a full and calm hearing of all the facts, after a fair warning of our purpose not to submit to the rule of the authors of all these wrongs and injuries, have, by a large majority, committed the Government of the United States into their hands." Thus the people of Georgia, "have declared with equal firmness, that they shall not rule over them."

Toombs proceeded with the usual litany of complaints: anti-slavery laws, abolitionists, Republicans. In the end, the federal government had been incapable of protecting the South from these offenses. Thus Georgia refused to submit to a government that had fallen into the hands of Republicans because the federal government had outlawed Southern property in the territories. Republicans were trying to ban slavery where it should rightfully exist, refused to recognize slavery's protection by Federal law, and gave "sanctuary to thieves and incendiaries who assail it to the whole extent of their power, in spite of their most solemn obligations and covenants." Republicans' avowed purpose was "to subvert our society, and subject us, not only to the loss of our property but the destruction of ourselves, our wives and our children, and the desolation of our homes, our altars, and our firesides." To avoid these evils, Georgians sought "new safeguards for our liberty, equality, security and tranquility."[10]

His work done at Milledgeville, Toombs took the train to Montgomery with his friend Stephens to attend the Southern Convention to set up a new country. It was widely believed that whatever happened at Montgomery, Stephens would likely be the first president of the Confederate States of America. Other names were floating around — William Yancy, Jefferson Davis, Howell Cobb, and even Toombs — but Stephens was touted as the best candidate because of his moderate course throughout the crisis. On the other hand, Stephens thought Toombs the best candidate for the job, that he had "superior qualifications for the Presidency to those of any other man." Whatever the outcome, both men probably expected to fight political battles standing back to back as they had for the last twenty-five years.[11]

The delegations from Georgia and South Carolina happened to be on the same train. Former senator James Chesnut and his wife, Mary, joined Toombs and Stephens in their coach to discuss the new nation. When the conversation turned to the presidency, Chesnut said the South Carolina delegation was looking to Georgia to choose the first president. Stephens replied that his friend Toombs, Howell Cobb, George W. Crawford or Herschel V. Johnson would "suit very well." Chesnut told Stephens that the South Carolina delegation favored either him or Toombs for president. Stephens answered flatly that he was not interested in the job.[12]

Matters were left there for the time being. Three miles from Montgomery, the train derailed. The train was going twenty miles an hour when the engine and every car except the last one with Toombs and Stephens left the track. It was "a bad smash-up," Tom Cobb wrote to his wife. James Chesnut commented, "This comes of Sunday traveling." Two hours later, the delegations made it into Montgomery, shaken but no worse for the ordeal. Montgomery was quickly filling with politicians, newspaper reporters, hopeful office seekers, opportunists, and the merely curious. The city's two hotels promptly reached their capacity. Still, Toombs, a servant he brought with him and most of the others took rooms at the Exchange Hotel while Stephens rented a room in a boardinghouse a few blocks away.[13]

After everyone settled in, Lawrence Kiett paid Stephens a visit. Kiett told him again that South Carolina preferred him for president. "I told him that I would not say in advance whether I would or would not accept," Stephens wrote later. Stephens must have realized that as president, he would give the new nation a legitimacy that uncompromising secessionists like Toombs or Howell Cobb lacked. Stephens was still a Unionist who had little enthusiasm for the proceedings at Montgomery and he hoped there might yet be a chance the South could come to terms with the North. Even if the convention chose him unanimously, he said, "I would first consider whether or not I could organize a Cabinet with such concert of ideas and ability as to justify hopes of success on such lines of policy as I should pursue."[14]

In short, Stephens was still not interested.

This opened the way for Toombs. Unlike Stephens, Toombs may have been intrigued at the thought of leading a new nation. Although they had disagreed with each other over the years, they had never competed for a political office. Toombs may or may not have campaigned among the Southern delegates for the presidency. He knew a veneer of moderation and unanimity was vital for the new Southern nation. He also knew that he had made too many firebrand speeches along the way, despite all his efforts to compromise with the North. He had also made too many political enemies to cakewalk into the office. Besides, Toombs had worries at home. His daughter, Sallie, was having serious complications with her pregnancy.[15]

On February 4, the convention was called to order. Howell Cobb was elected president and rules and procedures written by Stephens were adopted. The next day, the convention got down to the business of drafting a provisional constitution for the temporary government of the new confederacy of states. The new constitution was based on the United States Constitution with a few minor changes made mostly by Stephens. For instance, the provisional constitution allowed cabinet members to also be members of the Confederate Congress, and the Confederate Congress could not appropriate additional revenue unless asked by the Confederate president or the head of an executive department.[16]

Toombs did not serve on the Constitutional Committee. Instead, he was on an inconsequential committee that invited the commissioners from North Carolina to occupy seats on the floor when the provisional congress was in open session. Toombs may have been lying low, waiting to see what was going to happen. If he was going to be the first president of the new nation, it would not do for him to have a profile that was too high.

The constitution was adopted after only four days of deliberation. Then it was time to elect the president. Before the convention, Robert Toombs was one of the front-runners. But besides his reputation for blistering orations, Toombs was also known as a hard drinker, or at least someone who was unable to hold his liquor. By most accounts, Toombs was sloshed after only two drinks. "He was easily affected by the smallest indulgence," according to one biographer who knew him personally. "When he measured himself with others, glass for glass, the result was distressing, disastrous." Another friend said that Toombs never had an "insane thirst" that "impels one to delirium tremens." Toombs himself knew he was incapable of hard drinking and it was said he never asked anyone into a bar to have a drink. While his political chums were knocking them back at the tavern he nursed only a drink or two most of the evening. "He always disappointed his adversaries at the bar calculating that drink would disable him at an important part of the conduct." In the male world of nineteenth century politics saturated with tobacco, cigars, snuff, and alcohol, an incapacity to drink was a severe handicap. This may also explain why Toombs was apt to talk big but act moderately.[17]

But Toombs overindulged while he was in Montgomery on several occasions. He could often be found in the Exchange Hotel bar making wisecracks, telling stories, joking with whoever came by. Stephens, who sipped spoonfuls of whiskey all day long for medicinal reasons, believed Toombs blew the presidency because he drank too much. "He was in the habit of getting tight every day at dinner," Stephens wrote bluntly to his half-brother, Linton. A day or two before the election, Toombs drank more than was good for him at an important banquet. Then he went to a late party, got even drunker, and made a spectacle of himself. Stephens reported that Toombs was "*tighter* than I ever saw him, too tight for his character and reputation by far." Stephens believed this incident doomed his friend's chances at the presidency. "I think that evening's exhibition settled the Presidency where it fell," Stephens wrote.[18]

If so, no one told Toombs. The selection for the president and vice president of the Confederacy was scheduled for February 7 at noon. The Georgia delegation met that morning to see what was what. Stephens proposed Toombs for president right away. When Stephens asked him if he would accept the office, Toombs replied yes, if it were "cordially offered [to] him." Stephens believed all the delegations were unanimous behind Toombs. But Tom Cobb, who detested Robert Toombs and had no affection for Stephens, claimed that he and his brother Howell Cobb conducted a "counting of noses" and "heard" the delegations from Alabama, Mississippi and Florida favored Jefferson Davis. South Carolina, he said, was divided between Davis and Howell Cobb. Tom Cobb even claimed that some of the Georgia delegates favored his brother. Howell Cobb then chivalrously offered to withdraw on the spot so that Davis could be unanimously elected. Tom Cobb's claim could not be verified because Georgia delegates Benjamin H. Hill and Augustus R. Wright were conveniently absent from the meeting.[19]

"*Toombs was much mortified*, though he said he did not want the place," Tom Cobb wrote to his wife. "His manner indicated some surprise," Stephens reported. Whatever Toombs' reaction, the delegation agreed to withdraw his name if there was a split. Another member of the Georgia delegation, Augustus H. Kenan, said that if the rumor were true, then Stephens should be nominated for the vice presidency.

"I second that, heartily," cried Eugenius Nisbet.

Toombs, unperturbed by the turn in his fortunes, said "I do, too; what do you say, Aleck?"

The stunned delegation was silent. Howell Cobb, miffed that he was not going to be nominated by his own delegation, got up and left. Francis Bartow and Tom Cobb followed a few minutes later.[20]

Stephens said he would accept the vice presidency if the nomination was unanimous. Unenthusiastic about the convention in Milledgeville, not wanting to be in Montgomery, and against secession in general, he wanted no office in the new government. But he took the vice presidency "for the sake of harmony." He also may have accepted because vice presidents had so little to do.[21]

The delegation sent Martin J. Crawford to find out who the other states were supporting. He was also asked to find out if the states would unanimously stand behind Stephens for vice president. At noon, Crawford met the Georgia delegation at the capitol. Toombs did not have the full support of the other states but they would all line up behind Stephens, he said. So however unenthusiastically, Toombs threw his support behind Davis.[22]

When the convention reconvened, Davis and Stephens were unanimously elected. Stephens did not attend the session. Instead, he may have started asking around to find out why Jefferson Davis was elected president instead of his friend Toombs. He soon learned that the delegations from Florida, South Carolina and Alabama would have indeed voted for Toombs. Even Mississippi might have gone for Toombs instead of Davis. But someone — probably Tom Cobb — had been spreading rumors that Georgia was going to propose Howell Cobb. Cobb had been in and out of the favor with Democrats too many times to be fully trusted so the delegations settled on Jefferson Davis as a compromise candidate. "Jefferson Davis is elected President and A. H. Stephens Vice-President," Tom Cobb snarled. "The latter is a bitter pill to some of us, but we have swallowed it with as good a grace as we could."[23]

Stephens wrote years later that there was no canvassing or electioneering in Montgomery. But Tom Cobb politicked hard for his brother. "We saw they had us," he wrote when Stephens was nominated. Cobb saw the convention through the eyes of a campaign manager: *everyone* in Montgomery was competing for the first office, he claimed. "The crowd of presidents in embryo was very large," he wrote to his wife. "I believe the Government could be stocked with offices from among them."[24]

No record of Toombs' feelings about being set aside survives. His friends — and his enemies — left no account of his reaction. Toombs himself was uncharacteristically quiet. But he seems to have taken his defeat in stride. He continued his work in the provisional congress and hurled his usual barbed comments and anecdotes at whoever would listen. Mary Chesnut recounted in her diary one of Toombs' stories about a dinner that he had had in Washington with General Winfield Scott. Whenever a glass of wine was brought to the old general, he would lift it and say: "Save the Union; the Union must be preserved."

Toombs, fed up with the general's patriotic demonstrations, said he knew why the old general held the Union so dear. Then he told a story about a steamboat explosion. While the passengers were flailing in the water, an old woman ran up and down the bank crying "Oh, save the red-headed man!"

When the hapless redhead was pulled out of the water, the rescuer was puzzled about the old woman's sudden indifference to the victim. "Why did you make that pathetic outcry?" he asked her.

"Oh," the old woman said, "he owes me ten thousand dollars."

"Now, general," Toombs said, turning to Scott. "The Union owes you seventeen thousand dollars a year!"[25]

Toombs did not reserve his arrows for Yankees. He could not let Howell Cobb pass "without giving him a lick," as Stephens put it. At one banquet, Toombs gleefully turned to Cobb and toasted him for doing more for secession "than any other man." As Cobb's chest swelled with pride, Toombs, referring to Cobb's tenure as Buchanan's Treasury secretary, said Cobb had left the North "without a dollar in the treasury. He did not even leave old 'Buck' with two quarters to put on his eyes when he dies." Stephens chuckled that "this is a sore point with Cobb; but Toombs seems disposed to rub in the salt."[26]

The Confederate Congress put Toombs on a committee to inform Jefferson Davis that he had been elected to an office he had not run for and did not want. Toombs was also put on the committee to draft a permanent constitution for the new Confederacy. Everyone knew the new constitution would closely resemble the old one with a few significant changes. One of Toombs' and Stephens' pet provisions was to keep the section allowing cabinet members to hold seats in the Confederate Congress as well. Toombs had been impressed with this practice when he visited the English Parliament in 1855.

Toombs was also chairman of the Finance Committee and helped craft significant bills that molded the shape of the new nation. The bills from his committee ranged from instructing collectors in the ports of seceded states to keep enforcing revenue laws against all foreign countries "except the State of Texas" to putting through legislation that created a clerical force for Confederate executive departments. There were also bills authorizing issuance of treasury notes and establishing the Confederate Post Office Department.[27]

Jefferson Davis arrived in Montgomery late on February 15. Toombs, Crawford, and Stephens tried to pay a courtesy call to him at ten in the morning "but he was not up," Stephens wrote to his brother. Inauguration Day started off cold and cloudy. But the crowd was still thrilled by the militia companies, fancy horses and buggies carrying dignitaries, and the brass bands that played favorites like " La Marseillaise," "The Yellow Rose of Texas," and a popular tune written a few years before by the famous Northern minstrel show performer Dan Emmett. The song was called "Dixie."[28]

At noon, the clouds parted and the warm sun beamed down on the officials seated on the inauguration platform. During the ceremonies, the thin, sickly Davis twiddled with his cane. Toombs looked out over the crowd with an "imperious expression which had become habitual," according to one Northern reporter. When the time came, Davis walked to the podium. He struck the perfect chord by proclaiming that it was "joyous, in the midst of perilous times, to look around upon a people united in heart, where one purpose of high resolve animates and actuates the whole." It was a sentiment that would not last long in the new Confederacy.[29]

Toombs no doubt planned to attend inauguration events and rounds of lavish parties and dinners. But he received a telegram urging him to hurry home. Sallie had given birth, but she was in dire straits and the family was afraid she would not survive. Toombs was "completely unnerved" and left Montgomery immediately.[30]

It was widely assumed that Toombs would be appointed secretary of state, although Davis initially wanted to make Toombs the secretary of the treasury. He knew from their Senate days that Toombs was an expert on public finance and had a well-deserved reputation for being tight with government purse strings. At first, he offered the State Department to South Carolina's Robert W. Barnwell, but Barnwell declined. Instead, South Carolina was promoting Christopher Memmiger for the Treasury. Davis owed favors to South Carolina and complied. But he asked Stephens where Toombs should be placed in the cabinet. Stephens suggested letting Toombs have his pick. Instead, Davis offered the state portfolio to Toombs.[31]

Toombs might have gotten the Treasury Department if he had been able to stay in Montgomery. But he stayed by his sick daughter's side in Augusta, Georgia. When he received Davis' telegram offering him the State Department, he declined. "I cannot," he wired back. "Confident I can serve the country better where I am." Davis asked him to reconsider. Toombs wired back again that he could not because his daughter was sick. Look to North Carolina or Virginia for a secretary of state, he suggested. Toombs said he might accept a temporary position, but if Davis was thinking of a permanent place in the cabinet, "omit me."[32]

Toombs really wanted a seat in the Confederate Senate when the permanent government was established. He knew he was not Executive Office material. "I have spent twenty two [sic] of the last twenty three [sic] years of my life in the legislative compartments of the late government," he wrote to Davis in a followup letter, "and therefore have more experience in that than any other branch of the public service." But Sallie was getting stronger and Stephens was pressuring him to take the position. So on February 20, Toombs accepted. He wired Davis that he would take the department, but only temporarily.[33]

If Davis had followed his initial desire and put Toombs in the Treasury, it would have been a perfect fit. But giving Toombs the State Department was a disaster. Toombs was no diplomat and had a well-known tendency to be undiplomatic. His grasp of foreign affairs was shaky at best. And he did not care for Jefferson Davis. Toombs himself realized he would be a lousy administrative executive. Still, on February 21 his name was submitted to the Confederate Congress. Sallie was now out of danger and Toombs was back in Montgomery on February 24. He took the oath of office three days later.[34]

Toombs moved into a cramped office in a warehouse that had been converted into the Confederate government's headquarters and renamed the Government House. He gave the plumb position of chief clerk to his son-in-law, William Felix Alexander, and left the day-to-day chores of the office to him and clerk William Browne. It was said that Toombs would ally the Confederacy with the devil himself if it helped the cause. But he laid out a more practical foreign policy in an interview to a reporter from the New York *Times* a few months later. He was a firm believer in the carrot-and-stick approach of King Cotton. Toombs believed if the South stopped exporting cotton to England and France, then those countries would have to recognize the Confederate States of America as an independent nation in order to maintain their textile industries.[35]

Toombs possibly in 1861. Courtesy of the Hargrett Rare Book and Manuscript Library, University of Georgia Libraries.

Toombs was particularly interested in drawing France into a political alliance. With France on her side, the Confederacy would have the "means of overtaking and outstripping England in the race to industry." Toombs also thought

France might look the other way while the Confederacy extended a new empire into the tropics. "With Europe thus comfortably secured," the reporter wrote, "the Southern Secretary was quite at ease in regard to the pending war with the North."[36]

Privately, Toombs had doubts about the King Cotton policy. After the war, he said if he had been president, he would have "mortgaged every pound of cotton to France and England at a price that would have remunerated the planters, and in consideration of which he would have secured the aid of the armies and navies of both countries." And during a debate in the Confederate Congress, Toombs criticized a "cotton loan" bill that allowed the government to borrow cotton, sell it to Europe, and issue bonds to back the planters. Cotton may be king, Toombs said, "and yet, before the first autumnal frost has blighted a leaf upon his coronet, he comes to this hall a trembling medicant, and says 'Give me drink, Titinus, or I shall perish.'"[37]

If Toombs expressed his reservations to Jefferson Davis, it did no good. On paper, the secretary of state was responsible for the Confederacy's foreign affairs. His office also reviewed applications for letters of marque and reprisal, preserved congressional bills and resolutions signed by the Confederate president, kept one copy of every book printed in the Confederacy and put the Confederate seal on civil commissions. In reality, Toombs' primary duties consisted of relaying messages back and forth between the ministers Jefferson Davis had appointed and dispatched to other parts of the world. Toombs had little influence in foreign affairs, in the cabinet, or anywhere else. His post was so inconsequential that he claimed to carry the business of the State Department around in his hat. He left much of the operation to his clerks and found himself with nothing to do except, as one visitor put it, "talk politics, tell stories and say some very clever things." Secretary of State Toombs was little more than another clerk with a fancy title.[38]

Once, a hopeful office seeker approached Toombs and pulled out a fist full of recommendation letters.

"Perfectly useless, sir," Toombs said, along with a few expletives.

He asked Toombs to just take a look at them and...

Toombs took off his hat and pointed into it. "Can you get in here, sir? That's the Department of State, sir!"[39]

But Toombs still had influence in the Provisional Congress. That was where he was happiest anyway. As chairman of the Finance Committee he sponsored bills that looked after his own department such as when he offered resolutions urging Jefferson Davis to send commissioners to Arkansas and the Indian Territories to investigate the possibilities of new allies for the new nation.[40]

Toombs was also still on the committee to draft a permanent Confederate Constitution. He and Stephens and other members labored vigorously on the document. The Confederate Constitution was like a fraternal twin of its older sibling. Yet it differed by emphasizing states rights, protections for slavery, and limited the president to one six year term. Toombs lost his favorite provision to allow cabinet members to also hold seats in Congress. He backed the policy "with great force," as Stephens put it, but it was voted down in committee. He fought hard for it when it came to the floor but lost there too. However, the final document had a provision allowing cabinet members to sit in the House or Senate and discuss measures that affected their departments.[41]

He did get several pet stipulations passed on public spending. He inserted a clause forbidding the Treasury Department from paying bounties. It was also his idea to forbid Congress from appropriating any money for internal improvements except for maritime purposes.

His work also prohibited Congress from paying extra compensation to government contractors after a service was performed. Toombs may have also been responsible for requiring the postal service to become financially independent by March 1, 1863. On March 11, the permanent Constitution of the Confederate States of America was unanimously adopted.[42]

His work done in Congress, Toombs turned his attention back to the State Department. President Davis selected Martin J. Crawford, Andre B. Roman of Louisiana and John Forsyth of Alabama as official commissioners to Washington. Their mission was to ferret out how the Lincoln administration planned to deal with the new nation. Davis was typically high-handed in appointing his diplomats. Crawford "knew not one thing about it until Mr. Toombs told him about an hour before his name was sent in," Stephens wrote to Linton.[43]

When Toombs' cut their orders, he instructed them to try to get an official reception; if they could not, accept an unofficial interview. Toombs also told them to try to get their mission recognized by the Senate. Crawford reluctantly arrived in Washington on March 3, the day before Lincoln's inauguration. He attempted to get an interview with the Buchanan administration but realized he was wasting his time. Buchanan was too worried about his personal safety and his personal property to be effective. All that, "together with the cares of state and his advanced age, render him wholly disqualified for his present position," Crawford grumbled. "He is as incapable now of purpose as a child."[44]

The commissioners were optimistic at first. Seward had said publicly that the Union should pursue a peace policy. Better still, most of Lincoln's cabinet favored abandoning Fort Sumter. While the new administration dithered, the commissioners gathered bits of information and gossip that hinted Lincoln was planning to desert southern fortifications. "Things look better here than believed," they wired to Toombs. "The impression prevails in administration circles that Fort Sumter will be evacuated within ten days."[45]

"Can't bind our hands a day without evacuation of Sumter and Pickens," Toombs wired back. It was "idle to talk" of a peaceful negotiation until Sumter was handed over to the Confederacy, Toombs told them. The commissioners were to "pertinaciously demand" federal troops withdraw from Forts Pickens and Pensacola in Florida as well.[46]

Crawford, Roman, and Forsyth tried in vain to get an interview with Seward. When they received no reply, they asked Senator R.M.T. Hunter of Virginia to intervene with the State Department. Seward promised Hunter that he would check with Lincoln. Hunter passed on Seward's polite but curt reply the next day: "It will not be in my power to receive the gentlemen of whom we conversed yesterday." Toombs exploded when he received the news: "You have shown to the Government of the United States with commendable promptness and becoming dignity that you were not supplicants for its grace and favor, and willing to loiter in the antechambers of officials to patiently await their answer to your petition," he assured his commissioners, "but that you are envoys of a powerful confederate of sovereignties, instructed to present and demand their rights."[47]

Instead of returning home, Forsyth, Crawford, and Roman decided to stay in Washington and play for time. They had been assured through Supreme Court Justice John A. Campbell that Seward was positive Lincoln would abandon Fort Sumter. "There is a terrific fight in [Lincoln's] cabinet," Forsyth wrote to Confederate secretary of war Leroy P. Walker. "Our policy is to encourage the peace element in the fight and, and at least blow up the Cabinet on the question."[48]

Lincoln was also stalling for time. He held a cabinet meeting on March 15 and asked each secretary for an opinion of sending provisions to Fort Sumter. The majority thought replenishing the fort was a bad idea. The Confederate diplomats were flushed with victory.

They were positive that Fort Sumter would be evacuated within five days. "We are sure that no steps will be taken to change the military status," they telegrammed to the Confederate State Department. "With a few days' delay a favorable answer may be had.... What shall we do?"

"Wait a reasonable time and then ask for instructions," Toombs wired back.[49]

So they waited. "You have not heard from us because there is no change," Roman and Crawford wired Toombs five days later. "In the present posture of affairs precipitation is war." In another dispatch, they wondered if they should "dally longer with a Government hesitating and doubting as to its own course, or shall we demand our answer at once?"[50]

Lincoln held another cabinet meeting on March 29. He told his secretaries that conceding Fort Sumter would not be enough to keep the upper South in the Union. A second vote was taken. This time, the majority sustained Lincoln's determination to resupply the fort in Charleston Harbor. "The war wing presses on the President; he vibrates to that side," the shaken Crawford and Roman wrote to Toombs. They knew that something was up because Lincoln had also conferred with naval officers and engineers. "Their form of notice may be that of the coward, who gives notice when he strikes," the commissioners wrote. "Watch at all points."[51]

The commissioners sent daily updates to Toombs to warn him of the escalating military buildup. Seward had stopped talking to Justice Campbell and the commissioners were in the dark. All they could tell Toombs was to make sure Mississippi River defenses were strengthened. A large military movement was at hand. "Having no confidence in the administration, we say, be ever on your guard," they wrote to Toombs. "We have assurances from our officials at Washington that the govt. is pledged to no hostile movement (reinforcements, etc.) without notice," a suspicious Toombs wrote to Stephens. "But their activity in naval and army preparations for the last few days indicate a hostile purpose, which a few days will develop."[52]

The commissioners suspected Lincoln's true intentions. On April 7, they wrote to Toombs that they would present their official request for a formal meeting to negotiate the separation of the sections and demand an official response. "We believe a hostile movement is on foot and part of it sailed against the Confederate States," they wrote. "If Seward's reply is not satisfactory we shall consider the gauntlet of war thrown down and close our mission."[53]

They received a polite refusal the next day and decided to leave Washington. As Crawford, Roman, and Forsyth were packing, Lincoln informed Governor Francis W. Pickens of South Carolina that Fort Sumter would be re-provisioned "peaceably, otherwise by force." "Under no circumstances are you to allow provisions to be sent to Fort Sumter," Secretary of War Walker wired to General P.G.T. Beauregard who had been dispatched to Charleston Harbor to defend the fort. When the Confederate State Department received the news, Toombs wired back bleakly: "We have no further instructions to send you."[54]

On April 9, Davis held a cabinet meeting to decide how to respond to Lincoln's act of aggression. Toombs paced the floor with his hands behind his back as he listened to the discussion. The majority of the cabinet favored starting the long-anticipated war for the South's independence. Finally, Toombs turned to Davis. "Mr. President, at this time, it is suicide, murder, and will lose us every friend at the North," he said. He told Davis the South was about to wantonly strike a hornet's nest that would swarm and sting them to death. "It is unnecessary; it puts us in the wrong; it is fatal." Toombs' reasoning was the mirror image of Lincoln's position in the North. "So long as the United States neither declares war nor establishes peace," Toombs told the other cabinet members, "the Confederate States have the advantage of both conditions." Toombs bleakly wired a simple message to his commissioners a few days later: "You had better leave Washington immediately — make no delay."[55]

The shelling began at 4:30 the morning of Friday, April 12. Charleston cheered and Lincoln's fleet watched helplessly as Fort Sumter was bombarded with shot, shells, and cannonballs for a day and a half before Major Robert Anderson surrendered. The joyous tidings arrived in Montgomery just after noon on Saturday. The entire city was "frantic with celebration" one reporter wrote. Huge bonfires were built while people shouted and roared and danced and darted wildly from one place to the other as cannons and shotguns were fired all night long. If an observer had not known it was a celebration, he might have mistaken it for a riot.[56]

Toombs and Stephens went to a dinner party hosted by Jefferson Davis and his family the next evening. All seemed well until a telegram arrived saying Lincoln had called for 75,000 militia volunteers to put down the Southern insurrection. So Davis issued his own proclamation calling for Confederate privateers to resist "this wanton and wicked aggressiveness." Lincoln's proclamation also pushed Virginia into the arms of the Confederacy. The Virginia secession convention sent a telegram to Toombs to announce they were leaving the Union. Virginia seceded on April 17.[57]

Governor John Letcher of Virginia immediately requested a commissioner come to his state and discuss an alliance. Davis asked Alexander Stephens if he would go. "I was strongly inclined not to accept the position, owing to my health and the apprehension that night travel might make me sick," Stephens grumbled, but Davis and Toombs insisted. Davis issued Stephens' commission and Toombs gave Stephens his orders. "Congratulate the governor and people of Virginia for seceding and establish friendly relations with the newest seceded state." Stephens was also instructed to conclude an offensive and defensive alliance "on terms mutually advantageous to both the contracting parties, and looking to their long union under a common government."[58]

Stephens addressed the Virginia secession convention and urged the state to join the Confederacy. He had doubts about the mission, but on April 25, Virginia signed a military and economic alliance with the Confederacy. "Of the importance of this arrangement at this particular juncture I need not speak," Stephens wrote in his official report to Toombs.[59]

Now that diplomatic efforts in Washington had failed, war had started, and Virginia was safely in the Confederate column, Toombs was again able to focus on his European diplomats. One of the first acts Jefferson Davis performed as president was appointing William L. Yancy of Alabama, Pierre A. Rost of Louisiana, and A. Dudley Mann of Virginia as ambassadors to Europe. Toombs instructed them to seek interviews with Queen Victoria's principal secretary for Foreign Affairs in London. They were to explain why the Confederacy was established, discuss why it was a viable nation, and to disabuse any European notions that the situation was temporary. If Washington gave Parliament the impression that the Confederacy could be induced back into the Union, "you will leave no exertions unemployed for its definitive removal," Toombs informed his commissioners. They were also to let the British know that upon recognition, the Confederacy was willing to impose import duties "so moderate as to closely approximate free trade." These arguments were also to be made in Paris, Brussels, St. Petersburg, and other European capitals.[60]

Toombs wrote a long dispatch to Yancy, Rost, and Mann in late April explaining the South's version of events. The commissioners in Washington, aware of the "embarrassments" in the split Lincoln cabinet, graciously "did not demand a formal reception or recognition of the independence of the Confederate States," Toombs wrote. But while the Lincoln government was plying the Confederacy with "words of conciliation and promises of peace a large naval and military expedition was being fitted out ... for the purpose of invading our soil and imposing on us an authority which we have ever repudiated." Toombs directed the commissioners to read his disingenuous report to any foreign affairs ministers that would listen.[61]

On May 17, President Davis commissioned John Pickett as a special agent to Mexico. Pickett had good connections there and had served as United States consul in Vera Cruz since 1853. Toombs wrote Pickett's orders, but they were based on Pickett's analysis of the situation in Mexico. Pickett was to go to Vera Cruz to explore the possibilities of forming an alliance with the Mexican government. Pickett was instructed to emphasize several features the two countries had in common: both nations had primarily agricultural economies; slavery and Mexican peonage were practically twin labor systems; and as neighbors, they could buy and sell cheaply to each other. It was only natural the two countries would have trade relations and "cordial diplomatic cooperation."[62]

The Confederate government was not ready to ask the Mexican government for recognition. Pickett was ordered not to demand a formal reception but only to size up the situation. "You should also feel the pulse of the merchants and shipowners on the subject of privateering," Toombs wrote. Toombs' orders also directed Pickett to remind Mexican authorities that Southern statesmen and diplomats "from the days of Henry Clay to the present time have always been the fast friends of Mexico, and that she may always confidently rely upon the good will and friendly intervention of the Confederate States to aid her in maintaining those principles of constitutional liberty which she has successfully asserted."[63]

Other diplomats were also dispatched. Albert Pike was sent to Indian Territory to negotiate with Cherokees, Creeks, Choctaws, and other Indian nations to determine if any alliances could be made. Pike badgered the State Department for money, ammunition, and rifles. "An Indian would not pick up a musket if it lay in the road," Pike instructed Toombs. Charles J. Helm was also selected as a special agent to be sent to Cuba and the Caribbean Islands. Helm was to play up the favorable trade aspects between the Confederacy and the islands. The Confederacy could give great rates on cotton, lumber, and tar in return for fruit, molasses, and tobacco. Helm was specifically instructed to relieve Cubans of any suspicions they might have that the Confederacy would try to "acquisition" the island. "You will leave no efforts untried to remove such erroneous belief," Toombs wrote. Cuba would remain a colony of Spain. "It is true that, during the existence of the late Federal Union, there were persons in the Southern States who favored the acquisition of that island as a means of rendering their political power more nearly equal to that of the United States," Toombs wrote without mentioning that it was a measure he had backed loudly and firmly just three years before. But the new Confederacy hoped that, "politically, the two countries may exist separately but bound together in the firmest manner by the most friendly and unlimited commercial intercourse."[64]

A special session of the Confederate congress reconvened on the twenty-ninth of April. Toombs was still a member and his first act was to offer a resolution for a bill that backed Jefferson Davis's call for privateers. As secretary of state, of course, Toombs reviewed and signed letters of marque and reprisal. Five days later, Toombs voted for a formal declaration of war against the United States. Then Toombs delved into the arcane world of government finance. He was still chairman of the Finance Committee and he was back in his element. Congress complied with most of the amendments he attached to financial bills. He recommended compensation for Executive Department officials who spent their own or others' money on official business. He approved of money for contracts to remodel and provide furniture for government buildings and the Confederate Executive Mansion. And he recommended bills for additional regiments of Marines, including clothing and musicians. Finally, he endorsed funding to move the capital from Montgomery to Richmond.[65]

Between his duties in the State Department and the Confederate Congress, Toombs found time to be the go-between with Governor Joe Brown and the Confederate government in military matters. He also followed news about the boys in Georgia regiments closely. "The troops of Geo. were sent to assist in taking Norfolk's navy yard at the request of the govr. and convention of Va.," Toombs informed Howell Cobb. At Gosport Naval Yard, "the Govt. succeeded in sinking 8 or 10 public vessels and doing other great injuries to the fixtures and other property establishment; but we secured between 1,000 and 2,000 cannon of the best description, a considerable amount of small arms, three thousand barrels of powder, and a vast supply of shot, shell and other munitions of war." Toombs was also pleased that Colonel Robert E. Lee—"who is considered the best officer in the army"—would be leading soldiers from Georgia and other southern states in the defense of Virginia and Maryland.[66]

Toombs spent most of his time signing letters of marque and reprisal and growing weary of being a messenger between Davis and his diplomats. It did not take long for him to become disillusioned with the government's war effort. Davis' military strategy was retreating or counter-maneuvering and waiting for an opportunity to strike. Toombs had been reluctant to start the war. But when the shooting started he could hardly wait to shoot back.

Confederate clerk John B. Jones recorded in his diary that Toombs was outraged at the Confederacy's delays. Toombs wanted to seize the initiative and take the war to the enemy. "He was most emphatic in the advocacy of his policy, and bold almost to rashness in his denunciations of the merely defensive idea," Jones wrote. Toombs opposed all delays, said they were "fraught with danger." The enemy was in the field, their purposes were well-known. "Why wait to see what they meant to do? If we did that, they would not only invade us, but get a permanent foothold on our soil."

It was invade or be invaded, Toombs complained. He knew war was terrible, that it was not child's play. But he was infuriated that Alexandria and Arlington Heights in Virginia had been occupied by the federals without a fight. "The enemy should not have been permitted to cross the Potomac," he railed to the cabinet. "During the month which had elapsed since the passage of the ordinance in Virginia, nothing had been done, nothing attempted." True, Virginia had not officially joined the Confederacy. The state had telegraphed Davis daily for help and Toombs was livid because nothing had been done! If he had been in Davis's place, he declared, he would have "taken the responsibility."

When Toombs confronted Secretary of War Leroy Walker, Walker claimed that all he could do was organize and arm troops as authorized by Congress. Thirty thousand had been mustered already and at least five thousand volunteers were joining daily. Toombs harrumphed that five *hundred* thousand volunteers ought to be accepted for the duration of the war, not just five thousand for six or twelve months. Walker replied that Davis could not transcend the limits proscribed by Congress.[67]

Despite his growing disillusionment, Toombs rode to the new capital city of Richmond with Jefferson Davis and former Texas senator Louis T. Wigfall. The vast crowds along the route wanted to see Davis and hear what he had to say. But Davis was too ill for very many public appearances. He made a few short speeches but tried to avoid the crowds as much as he could. All along the route, the crowds chanted "Toombs! Toombs!" Toombs would come out, say a few words, and the train would pull away from the noisy station with cheers and band music fading in the distance.[68]

The indispensable clerk John B. Jones had been sent to Richmond beforehand and secured offices for the cabinet departments in the blocky new customhouse. Jones got the best suites for the War Department. Offices for Treasury, Justice, and Navy as well as the Cabinet Room and other executive departments were located on the upper floors. Other government offices were placed in Mechanics Hall. Toombs protested as soon as he saw the arrangement. The War Department could have been located anywhere, he complained. Treasury should have been put in the customhouse because it was fireproof. As for the State Department, his hat could apparently no longer contain it; he requested "a room or two anywhere." Jones evidently told Toombs in so many words that if he did not like the accommodations to go see Jefferson Davis. Toombs may or may not have taken it up with Davis, but Jones noted that the office arrangement was not countermanded.[69]

Toombs was peeved. He made no further effort to hide his contempt for Davis and the rest of the cabinet. At one point, Toombs told Davis that he should ask all the cabinet officers to resign so they could be replaced with representatives from states that had joined the Confederacy after the move from Montgomery. When Davis told Toombs he disliked asking for resignations, Toombs volunteered to do the dirty deed. "It was a bombshell in the ranks," Toombs recalled years later. When the cabinet asked if this request was coming directly from President Davis, Toombs told them exactly what had happened, "but they declined to give up their places."[70]

Arguments frequently broke out when he was in cabinet meetings. "Virginia was in a terrible condition when we got here," Toombs groused to Stephens. "I think [Commanding General of the Union Army Winfield] Scott could have come to Richmond as easily as he could go to Baltimore." There was a serious lack of weaponry in Virginia and the militias were providing their own arms. Still, Toombs wanted to get on with the fighting as soon as possible. "I do not think the present status can be maintained until Congress meets nor do I believe that Lincoln intends to maintain it until then." He believed Lincoln would wait to strike a decisive blow until just before the Confederate Congress convened. Yet the Davis government was doing little to help. "The prospect ahead looks very gloomy," he wrote to Stephens. "It will take courage and energy to avert great disaster and we have far too little of the latter for the crisis. I fear the trouble is getting too big for the grasp of some of our most reliable people." Despite his growing pessimism, he still had high hopes for his new country and was able to put a barb right where he wanted it. When he heard General Winfield Scott's claim that the Union blockade would starve the Confederacy into submission, Toombs wrapped an ear of corn and mailed it to the old general with a calling card that simply said "R. Toombs."[71]

By July, the frustrated Toombs turned his venom on the whole cabinet. Davis worked "too slowly for the crisis," he railed. Treasury Secretary Memminger was mishandling the Treasury Department and was "misled by every little newspaper paragraff [sic] that the thing is going swimmingly." Secretary of the Navy Stephen R. Mallory was "good for nothing but to squander public money." As for being secretary of state, Toombs hated it. "I have place without power, & [am] responsible for nothing I disapprove." Toombs wanted to leave the cabinet "as quietly and inoffensively as possible." He had already tendered his resignation to Davis, but Davis apparently asked him to stay on longer. "I am sure I am of no use [in the cabinet]," he told Stephens, "but to divide the responsibility of measures I do not approve."[72]

On July 24, Toombs put on his best public voice and again submitted his resignation. "I resign because in my judgment duty calls me to the battle-field," he politely wrote to Davis. Toombs said he regretted leaving his position "which you have rendered so entirely pleasant to me and in the administration of which I am not aware that we ever had a single difference of opinion to any degree affecting the public interest."[73]

"I received with great regret your resignation as Secretary of State," Davis wrote back. "But [I] cannot complain that the same patriotism which induced your entrance into my cabinet in that position now prompts your withdrawal for another field where you believe your services to be more useful to the country." Publicly, it was a sorrowful parting of two patriots, both called to separate duties. Privately, each man could hardly wait to get away from the other. Davis had a grudging respect for Toombs and never criticized him publicly. But when he was imprisoned in Fort Monroe, Davis let it slip to one of the guards that he thought Toombs was a man of "great natural force and capacity, but a destroyer, not a builder up; [he was] a man of restless nature, a born Jacobian, though with honest intentions."[74]

Toombs attended the short session of the Confederate Congress after he resigned from the State Department. But he had gotten it in his head that he could serve the Confederate cause better in the army than in the cabinet. Davis must have winced when Toombs began lobbying for a generalship. Toombs was insubordinate even when he was in a *good* mood. He had no military experience except the short stint in a ragtag Georgia militia some thirty years before, and he was vulnerable to drink and prone to rash talk. But Toombs was still a powerhouse in Georgia and Davis wanted to preserve harmony with Governor Joe Brown and Alexander Stephens. So Davis sighed and signed orders to make Toombs a brigadier general. On August 2, Toombs' appointment was just one of many Davis submitted to the Confederate Congress. For whatever reason, Toombs' appointment was backdated to July 19 and he was confirmed on August 29.[75]

Toombs' family and friends did not share his enthusiasm for this new career. Julia hated the idea and wept when she talked about it with Tom Cobb. But at a dinner with friends she put on a brave face as Toombs joked that she had failed to give him a son for war. Thus he was "compelled" to go himself, he said. Gabriel Toombs begged Alexander Stephens to talk some sense into his hardheaded little brother. "I write you as a *friend* to aid me in a matter of the *greatest* consequence to me personally, and if I am not mistaken of importance to our Confederate States," Gabriel wrote to Stephens. "It is to ask you cooperation with me in trying to induce my brother to resign the office of General in the army."[76]

Gabriel was sure that his brother's zeal had blinded his judgment. "He has never been educated in the science of war and has no experience in the business, and besides is physically unfit for camp life," Gabriel wrote. Since his last severe attack of rheumatism he has but little use of his arms, and his throat and lungs have been so much affected this winter and spring as to give his friends great solicitude for him. Without naming other private and personal reasons these are sufficient to decide the case against him." Gabriel knew that if anyone could sway Robert Toombs, it was Stephens. If that did not work, Gabe suggested an appeal to Jefferson Davis might change things. "While I am entirely independent of my brother in the sense the world calls independent, no mortal perhaps was ever more dependent upon another for happiness, than I am upon him," Gabriel wrote. "So you can imagine what my feelings must be when I tell you I look upon his going into the army as an unnecessary sacrifice of his life."[77]

Toombs got caught up in military pomp and pageantry right away. On August 1, he attended a muster at the Richmond fairgrounds. The fifty-one-year-old brigadier general was enthusiastically galloping about when his horse threw him. His foot was caught in the stirrup and he hung onto the bridle of his prancing and stamping horse as he landed dangerously close to the wheels of Mary Chesnut's carriage. "Down there among the horses' hoofs was a face turned up towards us, purple with rage," she wrote in her diary. The horse was quickly brought under control. Toombs was apparently still a good horseman. He remounted, "tousled and tumbled, dusty, rumpled, and flushed, with redder face and wilder hair than ever, he rode off gallantly, having to our admiration bravely remounted the recalcitrant charger."[78]

Brigadier General Toombs was assigned command of the 1st, 12th, 15th and 17th Georgia Regiments and encamped at Manassas, Virginia, in mid–August. He was playing soldier and having the time of his life. "I have been a fortnight in camp & find the change very gratefull to me," he wrote to Jefferson Davis. "It is next to repose itself in comparison with the last six months." He had busied himself studying battle tactics, drilling, and viewing his regiments that kept him "agreeably employed without addling the brain."

Perhaps Toombs felt Davis would listen to his advice now that he was out of the cabinet and in the field. If his troops were allowed to enter Maryland and cut telegraph lines, then Washington would be with little or no resistance, he wrote to Davis. He believed George McClellan's army must be in terrible shape or he would have attacked. "I do not see why he allows the present state of things to exist one hour without assaulting unless he is even worse off than we suppose."[79]

But it did not take long for Brigadier General Toombs to become as frustrated as he was when he was secretary of state. He was painfully eager to follow up the South's recent victory at Manassas and the Confederate generals were just sitting there! They had his men throwing up lines of sand for defenses instead of forming lines of battle, he complained. "The army is dying," he lamented to Stephens from camp near Fairfax, Virginia. "I don't mean the poor fellows who go under the soil on the roadside, but the army as an army is dying, and it will not survive the winter. Set this down in your book, and set down opposite to it its epitaph, '*died of West Point.*'" Replacing Secretary of War Leroy Walker with Judah P. Benjamin was not going to do any good either. "We have patched a new government with old cloth," Toombs sniffed. "We have tied the living to the dead."[80]

The inactivity was driving Toombs crazy. His men were "chained to the rock of immobility" just to linger and "complain and wear ourselves away until spring comes to our relief," he wrote to Stephens a few days later. "Davis is here. His generals are fooling [him] about the strength of our force in order to shield their inactivity. He talks of activity on the Potomac but I fear he does not feel it strong enough to move this inert mass."[81]

When he was not complaining, Toombs kept himself occupied by entertaining Confederate dignitaries from the political and military worlds, reviewing his troops, and grumbling about the paralysis of the war effort. He even found time to write a letter recommending eyeglasses made by a Washington optometrist named D. Woolfson that was included in advertisements in the Augusta *Chronicle*. Toombs' recommendation for a Doctor Sclossor, who removed several corns from his feet "without any pain and it seems to be effectual," also appeared in advertisements. By November, Toombs was already talking about resigning his commission.[82]

Toombs left his command and returned to politics in mid–November. He may have gone home to Georgia to shepherd his bid for a seat in the permanent Confederate Senate.

Toombs campaigned against cotton loans that allowed the government to borrow cotton in return for bonds, issuing valueless money, and other schemes he accurately predicted would bankrupt the Confederacy. Instead, he advocated heavy taxes and low tariffs to pay for the war.[83]

But Toombs' eat-your-peas attitudes and his boisterous reputation was too much for Georgia politicians who were more interested in putting up a united front for Davis and the war effort. The permanent Confederate Constitution divided senators into three classes. Those elected in the first class served a two-year term. The second class served four years and the third class served six years. Toombs lost the first election to President Davis's friend Benjamin H. Hill. An informal roll call for the second senate seat put Toombs behind Alfred Iverson by thirty-six votes. But a recess was called and the second round of elections commenced at 3:30. Toombs' forces caucused and lobbied effectively. Toombs squeaked by Iverson with only nine votes. Toombs was elected as a first class senator, thus he would only serve two years.

"The election of Mr. Hill and Gen. Tombs [sic], while it will doubtless disappoint some," opined the reporter for the Augusta *Chronicle*, "will, I believe, prove generally satisfactory to the great mass of people of our State." Toombs was probably more disappointed than anyone else. He had been in his state's elite leadership clique for years. Now he was reduced to a third-rate first class senator. The rebuke by the Georgia legislature vexed him greatly.[84]

Toombs returned to Richmond to take his place in the Provisional Congress. It was a no-frills session. As usual, he kept a close eye on where his colleagues tried to spend government money. He voted against indemnifying citizens who had suffered financial losses at the hands of the federals; against special compensation for a delegate from Arizona that attended the session named G.H. Oury; and against giving members of Congress $8.00 per twenty miles traveled in lieu of their regular mileage. He also tried to kill a bill to expand the Quartermaster and Commissary departments. Toombs was as well becoming alarmed at Davis' growing authoritarian regime. He voted against an amendment that declared people "alien enemies" who had abandoned their property since the outbreak of the war and he voted for a bill preventing the sale or confiscation of their abandoned property.[85]

Congress adjourned February 17. A few weeks later, Toombs resigned from the Senate. His ego had been bruised by the snub from the Georgia legislature and he was growing to hate everything about Jefferson Davis' administration. His friend and biographer Stovall Pleasant said that Toombs resigned because he "had a different conception of his duty" and felt that he would be shirking his responsibility if he did not fight. But Toombs felt he had been treated shabbily and added that Georgia was not the only place where good men had been "so ill used." In his resignation letter to Governor Brown, Toombs whined: "The manner in which the Legislature thought proper to confer this trust upon me, relieves me from any obligation to sacrifice either my personal wishes or my conviction of public duty in order to accept it."[86]

By March 4, Toombs was back in the field with his command. But now he was unhappy that an artillery company from Wilkes County had been assigned to the infantry. He went to personally complain to Secretary of War Judah P. Benjamin. Toombs' men had enlisted as artillery and would not serve as infantry. Many were threatening to return home. "Please attend to this matter for the boys before you leave," Toombs urged Stephens. "I feel great interest in the matter because I know all the men. They are from my town mostly and I got many of them to volunteer for the war in that company as artillery which they would not have done otherwise."[87]

As usual, Toombs was also discontented with things in Richmond. His troops were in good health and good spirits, but were "hoping for some stirring events soon somewhere." Confederate senator Porcher Miles of South Carolina had recently submitted a bill to establish a War Department and Toombs disliked that idea as well. "I suppose that Miles' bill meant Lee for com[mander] in chief and Mr. [Judah] Benj[amin] for [secretary of] war [sic]," he groused to Stephens. "It is the old policy under new arrangements. The President, I thought, must have Lee about him, and they together will be Sec. at War, no matter who is in the office nominally. B[enjamin] will make them as good a head clerk as they can get."[88]

Toombs was nearly in despair by mid–March. Instead of fighting Union general McClellen, General Joseph E. Johnston ordered a retreat from Manassas to find better ground to meet up with reinforcements. The Confederates destroyed or left behind tons of supplies and this grieved Toombs tremendously. Leaving the "beautiful counties of Loudon, Fauquier, Prince William, and Fairfax, and the Lord only knows how many more" also pained him. "We have got to fight somewhere," he wrote, and "if I had my way I would fight them as long as I could rally men to defend their own homes." He did not know what was to become of the country. "Davis' incompetency is more apparent as our danger increases. Our only hope is providence."[89]

"We have finally stopped our retreat at this place, but how long I do not know, but think from appearances it may be some time," he wrote to Julia from near Orange Court House a few days later. For all his displeasure at the generals' military tactics, Toombs found the prospect of again serving in the cabinet even more distasteful. There were rumors that he might be appointed as secretary of war. Julia must have expressed some hope it would happen, but Toombs told her and his contacts in Richmond to forget it. "So far as I am concerned he [Davis] will never give me a chance for personal distinction, he Thinks I pant for it — poor fool!" There may have been something to Toombs' suspicions because John B. Jones noted in his diary that Toombs and others — "the brightest lights of the South — " had been shrouded by Davis.[90]

Toombs sincerely believed his fighting the war would help the Confederate cause. "I want nothing but the defeat of the public enemy & to retire with you for the balance of my life, in peace & quiet in any decent corner of a free country," he wrote to Julia. "We have got to win our independence in spite of the gov. of Mr. Davis & we will do it, & the war will end with him the most unpopular man in the Republic."[91]

Toombs saw his first real action in April. McClellan had slowly crept down the Virginia peninsula while the Confederates took positions between Fort Monroe and Richmond with the line secured at Yorktown. Toombs was dispatched to reinforce John B. Magruder. Then he was ordered to march into the Shenandoah Valley, Fredericksburg, and Richmond. Each order had been issued and countermanded on the same day. Toombs took it with uncharacteristic good humor: "We have got used to these things and the boys make a joke of it."[92]

As McClellan inched his army down the peninsula, Jeff Davis moved the army back to defend Richmond. On April 13, the Confederates marched right through the city. Toombs paraded his troops down Main Street "with childlike delight," one reporter wrote. Toombs, soaking up the cheers and hurrahs, rode at the head of one of his regiments. He marched it down the street and out of sight of the crowd. Then galloped back to ride at the head of another regiment. "It was somewhat amusing," an observer wrote, " but a harmless entertainment for the brilliant orator and statesman."[93]

By now, Toombs had his Georgia brigade and General David Rose's brigade under his command as well as a Virginia and Kentucky regiment. On April 16, McClellan's forces probed Yorktown's defenses. Toombs led his troops into battle and helped repel a Yankee attack at Dam No. 1. He was praised in Major-General Magruder's official report for leading "promptly and energetically" at the end of the battle. The same could not be said for Toombs' mare, Grey Alice. She was extremely skittish in battle and Toombs had a hard time controlling her. The next day, Toombs went to Tom Cobb's headquarters and discussed the battle. Then the conversation turned to Grey Alice. "By God, Cobb," Toombs is supposed to have said, "she trembled like an aspen leaf and seemed to think all the shell were meant for her."[94]

When McClellan found no soft spot in the Confederate defenses, he settled in for a siege. On May 3, Magruder withdrew back towards Richmond. "We had a rough time in the Peninsula, & lost about ⅓ of my men by exposure mainly, having only lost some 10 or 12 killed and thirty or forty wounded," he reported to Stephens. As usual, the commanders' maneuvers were not to his liking. "We were kept in the trenches, often times a foot deep in water, for eighteen days, without any necessity or object that I could [learn, except] the stupidity and cowardice of our officers." Toombs believed McClellan's force was smaller than the Confederacy's and they could have whipped him. "But as usual we burnt up everything and fled, were attacked in the retreat, and left in the hands of the enemy some ten or twelve hundred of our killed, wounded and sick, and that after a decided victory. This is called generalship!!"[95]

Perhaps the monotony of life in camp was getting to him. "I am in despair about the present state of things," he complained to Linton Stephens. "Neither Davis or his generals have capacity or industry equal to the crisis & I fear nothing but a national convention setting him [Davis] aside prevent our ruin." Toombs hoped the army could get through the summer without a disaster. If not, he was thinking about going public with his concerns. "Davis every day more and more exhibits his want of capacity and his inability to see it." The cabinet was weak "beyond description," the generals "totally unfit to destroy and demoralize armies." Toombs was also outraged to hear that habeas corpus had been suspended. It was "the basest, falsest, most despotic measure ever put on a statute book & will do no good. I am doubly humiliated to see it is not openly resisted by the people."[96]

Toombs started drinking to relieve his frustration. Tom Cobb reported that he was drinking too much and "preaching mutiny" to his troops because Congress had passed a conscription act in April. Toombs concurred with Governor Joe Brown, who undermined the act whenever he could and as often as possible. Cobb reported that Toombs was quieter when he sobered up, but he could not keep a lid on his contempt for Davis for long. When Davis and Robert E. Lee inspected the troops, Toombs quipped that meant they would not fight "till frost if they can help it." Davis had no capacity for military leadership and "his generals but little more than he has & if it be possible to ruin our cause by imbecility they will do it." Mary Chesnut also noted that Toombs was cursing everything Confederate "from the President down to a horse boy. He thinks there is a conspiracy against him in the army.[97]

By late May, Toombs' spirits were looking up again. The Confederacy had some successes at Yorktown and Williamsburg. Longstreet was finally preparing to attack McClellan, who had moved to the outskirts of Richmond. "Now things look much more hopefull [sic] than they did a week ago," Toombs wrote to Julia. He was sure the Confederates concentrated around Richmond could "whip the Yankees out of Va [Virginia] in twenty four hours." Toombs thought the impending battle would be decisive and that there would be "a great change one way or the other within a few days, before you get this we will have fought & won or lost a great battle or the enemy will have retreated before us." On another note,

Toombs had recently seen Davis and described him as "polite & formal. So am I." Then he promsied: "I shall quit the army immediately after the battle is over if I live through [it]."[98]

But Toombs played little part in the big clash he had hoped for. On May 31, Joseph E. Johnston struck McClellan's army while it was cut in half by the swollen Chickahominy River. The Battle of Seven Pines was a Union victory that forced the Confederates to withdraw back towards Richmond. Toombs and his brigade were sent to protect the Mechanicsville Bridge, well away from combat. But instead of fighting Yankees, Toombs managed to pick a fight with the Committee of Public Safety in Randolph County, Georgia. Committees like these had formed to urge planters to grow less cotton and more food crops or to lend out their slaves to work on civic projects and fortifications. When the Randolph County committee tried to force Toombs to send some of his slaves to clear obstructions out of the Chattahoochee River, Toombs, as usual, bristled at being told what to do. He fired off a widely publicized telegram saying: "My property, as long as I shall live, shall never be subject to the orders of those cowardly miscreants, the Committees of Public Safety in Randolph County, Ga. and Eufala. You may rob me in my absence, but you cannot intimidate me."[99]

"As to what I may choose to plant on my own estate, I shall neither refer it to the newspapers nor to public meetings nor to legislatures," he fumed to Julia. "I know what sort of people compose all those classes & it is impossible to increase my contempt for them." Toombs advised the members of the committee to get their guns, shoot some Yankees, then "we will settle what sort of seeds shall be put into it."

The committee fired back that Toombs was demonstrating the "inflated ego" for which he had "acquired some notoriety" and stated that he had lost his perspective. "You are presuming too much, sir, upon the prestige of your past services, and the devotion of your party, when you conclude that either will screen you from merited condemnation, when guilty of infidelity to the interests of the country." Although Toombs publicly told the committee to go to Hell, privately he was hurt by their criticism. Tom Cobb said that Toombs had been "galled" by the committee's rebuke. Toombs also planted more corn than ever before.[100]

Toombs' drinking was also getting out of hand. "He is drunk almost every afternoon and makes himself ridiculous," Tom Cobb wrote to his wife. "He will be arrested very soon and *I think he wants to be*." Cobb also noted that Toombs' brigade was "utterly demoralized and disorganized." When a Colonel Magill sent a request to have his regiment transferred from Toombs' command, Toombs sent a note to the officers asking the reason. According to Tom Cobb, Toombs was sure they would blame Colonel Magill. To his surprise, they blamed him. "Whereupon he got drunk, rode down to the camp, cursed the officers and men as a set of disloyal cowards and ordered the regt. to the rear to guard the baggage, saying they were not fit to face the enemy." Toombs' drinking had become so bad that on the day before the Seven Days' Battle, his personal physician asked him to keep his "mind unclouded during these important operations." Toombs went on the wagon for a week.[101]

By the end of June, McClellan and the new Confederate commander, Robert E. Lee, clashed on the Virginia Peninsula in the Seven Days' Battle. On the third day of fighting, Lee prepared to throw fifty-seven thousand men at the Union right in a small village called Gaines' Mill. Lee ordered his generals to hold their positions, observe the enemy and attack only if the Federals retreated. Toombs was stationed at an out-of-the-way defense called Garnett's Farmhouse. Despite orders to hold their fire, Toombs attacked a line of Union rifle pits and lost over two hundred men. Magruder was livid when he found out that Toombs had ordered the attack. Toombs said his brigade was "brilliantly heroic."[102]

The next day, Lee wanted to play it cautious until he could determine what McClellan was going to do. Lee ordered John Magruder not to risk any attacks. But General David R. Jones ordered Toombs to occupy any vacated Federal defenses. When Confederate artillery cleared a few breastworks, Toombs ordered G.T. Anderson's troops into an assault. Toombs' brigade was advancing under murderous fire when Magruder ordered the advance to stop. The Georgians suffered heavy casualties. Toombs was blamed for the incident, but confusion and mistakes in Magruder's chain of command were also very much to blame.[103]

In his official report, Toombs claimed that he was just following General Magruder's orders. He heard heavy fighting on his right and he moved his men forward. Privately, Toombs blamed "that old ass Magruder." His men "fought like lions [in] this unnecessary battle, and the thanks we got for it was a lie sent out from Magruder's headquarters before the action was over that I had attacked without orders and was repulsed," he complained to Alexander Stephens. "The next day he ordered another attack with 7th and 8th Georgia who were roughly handled and driven back. That too I think he sought to put on D. R. Jones."[104]

A few days later, Magruder was ordered to assist Longstreet who was stationed against McClellan's left flank at Malvern Hill. By the time Toombs arrived with his twelve hundred exhausted troops, the Union Army was pounding the disorganized Confederate lines. Toombs was ordered to advance across an open clover field and take a gulch filled with entrenched Yankees called Labor-in-Vain Ravine. Toombs was stunned. He thought it was a mistake. He refused to move until he saw the order in writing. When a messenger brought the written orders, Toombs charged under heavy fire. He lost almost two hundred men in ten minutes. As retreating Confederates separated his brigade, Toombs reorganized as many men as he could. He ordered what was left of his command to take cover behind a fence. In his official report, Toombs blamed the fiasco on difficulties of the ground and the nature of the attack.[105]

Toombs' report left out a significant incident that occurred during the battle. When Major General Daniel H. Hill rode up, he reprimanded Toombs for not throwing his men into the fight. Hill yelled something implying Toombs would not or did not want to fight. Toombs heard it as "Your brigade would not fight" or that Hill "always knew [Toombs' brigade] would not fight" and that Toombs "pretended to want to fight, but would not." In a letter to Hill, Toombs demanded an explanation.

Hill replied that he recalled saying something like, "You have been wanting to fight, and now that you have one, you have got out of it." Toombs had "a thousand times" criticized the command for not fighting, Hill wrote. Toombs shot back a childish note accusing Hill of trying to "menace and intimidate" him and demanded "personal satisfaction for the insult you cast upon my command and myself on the battlefield." Toombs was challenging Hill to a duel.

It may have been at this point that Robert E. Lee got wind of what was going on. Lee brought in Toombs' friend Colonel Henry Benning to settle the feud. A few days later, Hill wrote a half-hearted apology. He conceded that Toombs was perhaps doing everything he could under the circumstances. But Hill absolutely refused to duel with Toombs. Not only was he opposed to dueling but also he had a war to fight and a duel "would be highly improper and contrary to the dictates of plain duty."[106]

Several witnesses who were there indicated that Hill may have lost his temper. R.J. Moses, who was Toombs' aide-de-camp, wrote that Toombs was doing his best to rally his troops. Even Tom Cobb said that Hill "did most wantonly charge Toombs with cowardice to his face." But Thomas Jordan, P.G.T. Beauregard's chief of staff, was also there. He recalled that Hill told Toombs to either "move up or resign his brigade into hands that had the nerve to lead it." Hill was willing to let the squabble die. But Toombs would not be mollified and made the most of the insult. He called Hill a "poltroon," "coward," and "liar" every time one of Hill's superior officers — or a reporter — was around.[107]

Whatever happened at Malvern Hill, Toombs had established a reputation for big talk and moderate action — just as he had in his political life. Lieutenant Melvin Dwinnell of the Eighth Georgia Infantry Regiment wrote that the average soldier could not comprehend some of Toombs' actions "if he was so ready to fight." While most of the rank-in-file held Toombs in high esteem, Confederate officers considered him to be a strutting, political buffoon who was only playing soldier. "Toombs has a divided judgment as to his course, and halts, as an ass between two bundles of hay," wrote General P.G.T. Beauregard's chief of staff. Toombs could not make up his mind whether to resign and "cowhide Hill," or "make some facile Georgia member of Congress resign, take his place and overturn the Government from the floor of Congress." Brigadier General Gilbert Moxley Sorrel noted sourly that Toombs "was for once and all a politician, and in the wrong shop with a sword and uniform on." General Kirby Smith claimed to see Toombs as nothing more than a "politician and demagogue." Colonel Edward Porter Alexander simply noted that Toombs was not "entirely a subordinate & respectful brigadier." Tom Cobb predicted Toombs would soon be arrested.[108]

When the Confederate Army was reorganized, Toombs' brigade was assigned to General James Longstreet's division. As McClellan dawdled, the Confederates kept busy maintaining fortifications around Richmond. At one point, Stonewall Jackson inspected the city's defenses. When he came upon Toombs' picket lines, Jackson was angry to see the fortifications disconnected from the right and left wings. Fuming, Jackson rode to Toombs' headquarters. Toombs was sprawled under the shade of a fly tent, trying to stay cool from the hot summer sun. Jackson berated Toombs for his lack of vigilance. Toombs said he had given the responsibility to one of his staff officers and the officer had given the task to one of his aides. But Toombs thought the fortifications were "all right, while General Jackson was of the decided opinion it was all wrong." Jackson ordered Toombs "with some sharpness" to go personally and make the fortifications "and then [Jackson] turned and rode away."[109]

Despite being reprimanded by Stonewall Jackson, Toombs still thought all the work on fortifications was a waste of time. "Toombs came over to see me yesterday," Tom Cobb wrote to his wife. "He is very smart and amused me much by his pungent remarks." Cobb was congratulating himself for not being bothered by an engineer in fortifying *his* position. Toombs began ranting about engineers' limitless ability to find more digging to keep the troops at work. "He finally swore he believed one engineer could find work for all the men that had been sent to hell [sic] since Adam sinned," Cobb wrote. Toombs added: "According to scripture, Tom ... that is a big pile."[110]

Cobb's earlier prediction that Toombs would be arrested came true a week or so later. Toombs continued his knack for getting into trouble. On August 13, his brigade was dispatched to Gordonsville. A few days later, Toombs rode off early in the morning to visit Jeremiah Morton, who was an old friend from his congressional days. Meanwhile, Longstreet detailed some of Toombs' brigade to guard the road to a small post on the Rapidan River called Raccoon Ford. Toombs returned after a lavish dinner and found his men on picket duty. Toombs, who never really grasped military protocol, spluttered that no one could issue orders to his men without consulting him first. So he marched his bewildered men back to camp.[111]

According to Toombs' version of the story, when he saw A.P. Hill's division between his pickets and the ford, he sent a message to Longstreet asking permission to withdraw his troops. Toombs retired them on his own authority to cook rations and be prepared to move out at any time as he had been ordered. When Longstreet found out Toombs had countermanded his orders, he was furious. "He ordered me arrested for 'usurpation of authority,' a new crime to me and to the articles of war," Toombs wrote to Stephens from Gordonsville on August 22. "This was the sole and only cause of my arrest which of course was very unexpected to me." Toombs did not mention that the morning after he withdrew his troops, Federal cavalry came down the unguarded road and surprised Jeb Stuart. Stuart barely escaped. Major Norman Fitzhugh was captured as well as orders showing some of Lee's troop locations. Stuart's coat and plumed hat were also taken prisoner.[112]

Toombs' sword was stripped away but Longstreet allowed him to ride at the rear of his brigade. Longstreet waited for Toombs to explain himself but the next thing he knew, Toombs had strapped his sword back on and was criticizing the commanders in stump speeches to the troops. Toombs was promptly confined to Gordonsville.[113]

Toombs spent his confinement writing a long letter of apology to Longstreet. He begged Longstreet to suspend his arrest so he could fight with his brigade. He had put his sword on only for convenience, he explained. Toombs believed apologizing made everything all right again. So he mounted Gray Alice and rode out to meet his men. When they saw him, his brigade raised a loud cheer "which so incensed the magnates Lee and Longstreet, &c., who were near by, that I got no reply to my request but was ordered peremptorily to this place [Gordonsville]," Toombs wrote to Stephens, "and two charges put in against me for breaking my arrest and disobeying orders not immediately coming here." Once again, Toombs failed to realize his problems were self-inflicted and he blamed "the thousand lies" of his "enemies" for his trouble.

"The whole thing was as unexpected to me as that this letter should produce a hostile meeting between you and me," he wrote in amazement to Stephens. "My zeal for the public service and desire to prepare my starving regiment for battle is my sole and only fault. I must think it a pretext."[114]

A few days later, Longstreet received Toombs' letter. He instructed Adjutant-General Gilbert Moxley Sorrel to reply that since Toombs was not an experienced military man and the violations did not appear to be intentional breaches of authority, he would be welcomed back. A courier was sent to Gordonsville to give Toombs the news, but Toombs was nowhere to be found. The perplexed messenger returned to Longstreet's headquarters. Moxley had little respect for Toombs' abilities as a soldier, but since Toombs was a fellow Georgian he decided to give him one more chance. He dispatched the messenger back to Gordonsville.

This time, Toombs got the message. He was told to waste no time if he wanted to join the fight. Toombs joyfully mounted Gray Alice and galloped as hard as he could to find the battle at Second Manassas. Toombs arrived, hat in hand, just as Longstreet was issuing a dispatch to Toombs' command.

"Let me carry it!" Toombs cried.

"With pleasure," Longstreet said and gave him the paper.[115]

Toombs galloped off, stopping just long enough to ask Sergeant William Houghton the whereabouts of his brigade. Toombs found General David Jones, who was commanding, and gave him General Longstreet's orders. It was just before dark when Toombs met his brigade at a place called the Chinn House. Toombs' 2nd, 15th, and 17th Regiments had chased the Yankees off of Chinn Ridge over "field, swamp and wood" for almost a mile.

Now there was a gap in the line. As he dashed up and down the ranks, Toombs heard a voice call out to him. He wheeled Gray Alice around. A mortally wounded Union colonel was lying on the ground. Toombs looked down and recognized Daniel Fletcher Webster, the great Daniel Webster's son. Toombs ordered a detail to stay with the dying man and do what they could to relieve his suffering. Then Toombs reformed the 17th Georgia Regiment. The regiment was out of ammunition, but Toombs ordered them to hold their position with the bayonet until ammunition wagons or reinforcements arrived.[116]

After the engagement, Toombs rallied his men. Even though he had missed most of the action, he was still as excited as a coach whose team had just won the big game. "Boys, I am proud of the report given me of you by General Jones," he exclaimed. "I could not be with you to-day, but this was owing to no fault of mine. Tomorrow I lead you."

His men yelled "Hurrah for General Toombs!"

"Go in and give the damned invaders hell!" one soldier recalled Toombs saying during the fight. Another claimed that Toombs said: "Go it, boys! I am with you again. Jeff Davis can make a general but it takes God Almighty to make a soldier."[117]

The next day, General David Jones sent Toombs' brigade to support Stonewall Jackson at Ox Hill. The Battle of Chantilly broke out on September first, although Toombs' men saw little action. As Lee crossed the Potomac and crept towards Washington, D.C., Toombs marched to Hagerstown, Maryland. Toombs' antics amused one soldier in the 8th Georgia Regiment when he saw the brigadier-general riding across the Potomac River, waving his sword menacingly at hoards of non-existent Yankees. Toombs stayed in Hagerstown until September thirteenth then received orders to march south to the small village of Sharpsburg. There, he saw his greatest and last action as a Confederate general at the Battle of Antietam.[118]

General David Jones ordered Toombs to hold a one hundred twenty-five-foot stone and wood span that crossed the Antietam River called the Rohrbach Bridge. Toombs concealed his Second, Twentieth, and Fiftieth Georgia Regiments in the woods on the slopes. His guns covered both the bridge and the road from Sharpsburg. He had taught himself enough about battle tactics to recognize "an important and commanding position" when he saw one.[119]

On the morning of September 17, the Federals opened fire on Toombs' position. Throughout the morning, General Ambrose Burnside's 13,000 soldiers tried to cross the Antietam and fight their way to Sharpsburg to wrest it from the Confederates. But Toombs' measly force of four hundred men tore several Yankee regiments to shreds as they bottlenecked at the mouth of the twelve-foot-wide bridge. By early afternoon, Toombs was running low on ammunition and he was in danger of being flanked. His men finally gave up their defenses about 1:30 and withdrew to a predetermined spot in a forty acre cornfield where the 15th, 17th, and 11th Georgia Volunteers reinforced Toombs' brigade.

It took Burnside's troops over two hours to cross the river and prepare their advance. In the meantime, Toombs men replenished their ammo and were ordered to move to higher ground close to Cemetery Hill. Toombs was dismayed to see Yankees already occupying the spot as well as parts of the cornfield all the way down to "Burnside's Bridge" across the Antietam. "Under this state of facts, I had instantly to determine either to retreat or fight," Toombs wrote coolly in his official battle report. "A retreat would have left the town of Sharpsburg and General Longstreet's rear open to the enemy, and was inadmissible. I, therefore, with less than one-fifth of the enemy's numbers, determined to give him battle, and immediately and rapidly formed my line of battle in the road within 100 paces of the enemy's lines."

Then Toombs fired on the Federal columns. The barrage threw Burnside's column into "considerable disorder," and Toombs ordered a charge, which, "being brilliantly and energetically executed by my whole line, the enemy broke in confusion and fled." Within thirty minutes, Toombs' soldiers had chased the Yankees back down the slopes, back across the bridge, and all the way back across the Antietam. Toombs wanted to pursue further, but was ordered to a new position before his artillery could be reinforced.[120]

"Toombs rides up and down the line like one frantic, telling the men to stand firm," remembered Virginia private John Dooley. According to Captain Charles W. Squires of the First Company of the Washington, Georgia, artillery, Toombs' stand at the bridge was "the talk of the army." Toombs' efforts were also highly praised by none other than General Robert E. Lee, who wrote that Toombs' brigade "maintained its position with distinguished gallantry." Despite having arrested him three weeks earlier, Longstreet also complimented Toombs for his "gallant defense of the bridge at Antietam, and in his vigorous charge against the enemy's flank."[121]

Toombs fought boldly at Antietam and was a deserving war hero. Robert E. Lee gave him a citation for distinguished gallantry. Toombs' defense of the bridge and counterattack at the outskirts of Sharpsburg delayed McClellan long enough for Lee to slip away and avoid losing the entire Army of Northern Virginia. In part, Toombs' success can be attributed to the fact that, for once, he had followed orders.

The next evening, Toombs and his aides were riding to Colonel Henry L. Benning's headquarters when they blundered into some Union cavalry. One of Toombs' aides took a shot at them and they returned fire. A ball shattered Toombs' hand. Gray Alice bolted, but he got her under control and his party made it to Colonel Benning's headquarters. Then Toombs turned over his command and went home to heal.[122]

He returned to his plantation in Washington, Georgia, to look after his crops and consider his future. Another senate election was approaching and he quietly put his name in the hopper. But the Toombs political machine had been emaciated by the war: most of his political operatives were in the field fighting Yankees or had been killed. Toombs had also made too much anti-administration noise for the tastes of the sitting Georgia legislature.

The legislators voted on November 18. On the first ballot, Toombs came out a poor third behind Herschel Johnson and James Jackson. On the second ballot, Johnson won 111 votes. Jackson got forty votes and Toombs had a dismal nineteen votes. Toombs professed indifference to losing, but he was truly and deeply hurt by the rejection. For now, he thought he could best serve the cause by staying in the army. "But I am well aware that that scoundrel Jeff Davis will avail himself of any opportunity [to] drive me from it, with dishonor if he could," he wrote to Linton Stephens.[123]

Toombs was bitter about his defeat and lashed out at anyone who disagreed with him. When the Confederacy was formed, he said, he honestly tried to bury the political hatchet and eliminate bickering and bad blood between the parties. He had made a truce with the Know-Nothings. He had united with his former enemies to get them elected and appointed to public offices. But "the scoundrels sneaked into the legislature under the cry of no party, and every act of their stupid, false and treacherous career has proven how unworthy they were of my generosity and how just was the public condemnation of them. But in spite of their villainy, I got a public good out of them."

Toombs accused those in the Confederate Congress of backing Jefferson Davis because they feared being branded traitors. "They are a terribly whipped set of scoundrels and are afraid to do right lest they may be thought to be what they really are, traitors to public liberty." Toombs swore that if he lived until the next election, he would actively campaign against Davis and his minions, "and I do not in the least doubt what will become of these treacherous cowardly impostors."

Toombs was also alarmed at some of the "very foolish" taxes Governor Joe Brown had proposed. What he had learned in twenty-five years of government could be uttered in three words: "order, security and justice." Anything less was injustice and robbery. "For ten years I have referred all my votes to these three objects. Extortion is a crime against God and man; punish that and let the production and distribution of wealth alone. Producers have nothing to do with morality. That is a question for consumers, and not then for the legislative power."[124]

Toombs rejoined his command in January 1863. He wintered near Fredericksburg, but the inactivity and his resentment drove him crazy. So he resigned. "The separation from you is deeply painful to me," he told his men. "I do not deem it proper on this occasion to enter into a detail of the causes which impose this duty upon me," he said enigmatically. "It is only necessary now for me to say, that, under existing circumstances, in my judgment, I could no longer hold my commission under President Davis with advantage to my country, or to you, or with honor to myself."

He praised his men for their bravery, sacrifices, and heroism. But their courage in the field was not their only claim to distinction. "Since I took command over you, I have not preferred a single charge against, or arraigned one of you before a court martial," he boasted proudly. "Your conduct never demanded of me such a duty. You can well appreciate the feelings with which I part from such a command." He ended with a dramatic flourish: "Nothing less potent than the requirements of a soldier's honor could, with my consent, wrench us asunder, while a single banner of the enemy floated over one foot of our country. Soldiers! comrades! friends! Farewell!"[125]

Toombs never explained publicly why he resigned, but it was an open secret that he thought he deserved a promotion for his exploits at Antietam. Confederate postmaster John H. Reagan lobbied to get Toombs a higher rank. Longstreet believed Toombs had potential as a military man, but lacked discipline. However, Jefferson Davis was not sorry to see him go and pretended he could do nothing to promote Toombs. Davis wrote that he had already given Toombs a high military grade "before his capacity to command had been tested." He claimed that since Toombs had not been recommended for promotion, he had gone as far as he could go. Furthermore, Davis hoped that Toombs would get over his irritation and "no longer attribute to unworthy motives my having selected others for the promotion to which he judged himself entitled." Robert E. Lee stated flatly "I make no objection to the resignation of Robert Toombs."[126]

If the brass was happy about Toombs' resignation, his men were not. "We can only hope to get another general who will treat us as kindly and be as respected by his command as well as General Toombs [was] respected and regarded by his," one of Toombs' soldier confided to his diary. "I hope justice will reward him yet and the day of retribution will soon return." As for Toombs, he had no regrets. "I am fully satisfied that I can not remain in the service with any advantage to the public or with honor to myself," Toombs wrote to Stephens. He believed — probably correctly — that Davis wanted him to resign. "But I waited my own time and points, and got them as well as was possible from so false and hypocrital [sic] a wretch. I simply resigned without assigning any reason, reserving to myself all the points."[127]

Political points, that is. Losing a war hero with the political prestige of someone like Toombs was a blow to the administration. John B. Jones noted that the resignation was making "some sensation in certain circles." Jones predicted Toombs was about to make a political "disturbance." Rumors were swirling that he was about to run for governor and Jones thought Toombs might try to make peace with the United States which would be "death to the government—and the destruction of Toombs." Even Governor Joe Brown had Toombs on his short list of hand-picked successors. "I have the highest confidence in his patriotism, ability, statemanship [sic], and soundness on the vital question of state sovereignty," the governor wrote to Alexander Stephens. "I should be glad to know whether he would consent to be a candidate."[128]

But Toombs had his own ideas about his future. He intended to catch up on his "neglected political studies," look after his plantations, and fret about his books. When he sent a book by French economist Claude Frederic Bastiat to Stephens, he urged Stephens to "take care of it and bring it back to me, as it is probable I shall have nothing else to do for the next year." He also asked Stephens to try to find a copy of David Ricardo's *The Principles of Political Economy and Taxation.* "My copy is missing from my library, and I fear is with the missing boxes of my congressional library," he wrote. "The last edition was published in 1821, and it is therefore rare, but apt to be found in all old bookstores."[129]

Yet Toombs was not one to spend much time reading European economic theory and browsing in old bookstores for nothing. In a letter to W.W. Burwell, he declined the governor's chair in favor of running for a congressional seat. "The necessities of war control the entire industry of the country, and I fear is greatly endangering public liberty," he told Burwell. Toombs thought that as a congressman, he would be better able to "preserve rights and check abuses." There had been talk that Davis would do everything to oppose Toombs and he was delighted with the prospect. Davis had "greatly outraged justice and the constitution," but Toombs did not think the public was ready for someone "to correct abuses when the empire is rocking to its very foundations, and would not look favourably upon a volunteer opposition." If Davis' forces declared war on Toombs, then that was fine with him. "I shall be justified in any extremity to which the public interest would allow me to go in hostility to his illegal and unconstitutional course."[130]

By June Toombs was out on the hustings. In a "State of the Country" address at the Sparta Baptist Church, he made clear that although the South was united for independence, the differences came in how to achieve the goal. Toombs attacked the conscription acts that drafted able-bodied men between the ages of eighteen and forty-five except a long list of exemptions—including planters and overseers, the hideous Tax-in-Kind act that required farmers to "donate" 10 percent of their yield to the government, Davis' declaration of martial law, and the suspension of habeas corpus. This was exactly what Lincoln was doing in the North. "Are you more jealous of the rights of Yankees than you are of your own?" asked Toombs "I cannot believe it!" Toombs urged his listeners to make their motto "independence, liberty, one and inseparable, now and forever."

This was Toombs' political comeback and he designed his performance to be composed yet argumentative. It was a major speech and was covered throughout the South, and even in the New York *Times*. The reporters noted that Toombs was "unusually calm, deliberate, and argumentative, and indulged in no invective, no passion.... He made no allusion to any private grievance ... and everyone must have been impressed with the idea that he has nothing at heart but his country's own good."[131]

It was the first time Toombs came out publicly against Jefferson Davis. But he was not alone. As the war turned against the Confederacy and its citizens suffered from inflation, privation, and other hardships, Governor Brown, Vice President Stephens, Linton Stephens in the Georgia legislature, and a host of other ambitious political strategists all began snapping at Davis' heels. Many believed he had become a dictator, a Southern version of Lincoln. At one point, the House even debated removing him. Congressman William W. Boyce of South Carolina, apparently without irony, recommended calling a convention to oust Davis and give dictatorial powers to someone like Robert Toombs.[132]

In July, Vicksburg fell and Robert E. Lee suffered an immense defeat at Gettysburg. "We are gloomy and in great trouble; North, South, East and West the clouds look dark and threatening," Toombs wrote miserably to Stephens. Events had also given Toombs second thoughts about going back into politics. "I wish to go back into the army and intend to do so in some capacity," he wrote. "If we can get up a vol[unteer] reg[iment] in this neighborhood I shall take its command if desired; and if not I shall take such other position as will enable me to do the most good with one hand." Desertion was up and recruitment was down. So Georgia had to fall back on the "melish." Although Toombs felt he owed the government no favors, he had recruited a few disappointing volunteers from Wilkes County. "They pretend to be afraid if they go in for six months the Govt. will keep them." One month later, Toombs got himself appointed colonel of the Georgia Home Guard.[133]

Toombs stayed on the campaign trail throughout the summer. In August, he published a long article in Augusta *Constitutionalist* highlighting the causes of the Confederacy's rapid economic collapse. In his view, the administration had made two grave mistakes. It tried to finance the war on credit and printed too much money. The North understood the principles of currency, Toombs pointed out, while the South's currency had depreciated until "the actual necessaries of life cannot be purchased." A restructure of the tax system and loans were the only way to correct the economy and win independence. The present system was utterly insupportable. "It is upsetting the very foundations of private rights, weakening daily public confidence in our cause at home and abroad," he said, "sowing dangerous discontents among the people, which are daily deepening and widening. Patriotism demands that all good men should unite to correct these evils."[134]

Toombs' summer reading had purpose. He was campaigning on the economy. "The real control of our affairs is narrowing down constantly into the hands of Davis and the old army, and when it gets there entirely the cause will collapse," Toombs wrote bitterly in another letter to W.W. Burwell. "They have neither the ability nor the honesty to manage the revolution." Blunders by the administration and the military had gotten some of the South's best men killed. What was not the fault of incompetent leadership was the fault of the conscription laws. "There were thousands outside who wanted to take the places of those inside," Toombs lamented. It was clear to Toombs why the army's morale was so low. "When we began to hunt up men with dogs like the Mexicans, they necessarily became as worthless as Mexicans, and every day has seen the deterioration of the troops brought in as conscripts."

As for government and politics, "I do not see how anything else is left to me or anybody else except the entire surrender of the country, executive, legislative and judicial departments to Mr. Davis." Toombs felt sure that Davis would ruin any chance for Southern independence. "Unless we change our policy the currency will collapse within ninety days. But govt. seems determined to rely upon force and fraud to sustain the army. Those means have always failed and always will. No power but God's can prevent it and therefore if we fold our arms we must be speedily overthrown."

Toombs had also been giving some thought to slavery. "I am fully persuaded that the road to liberty for the white man does not lie through slavery," he wrote. For instance, down in Vicksburg, he believed the vast number of slaves could not "be left there with safety and cannot be carried away without the ruin of the owners of them." The fields had been devastated and that part of the South would still have to support refugees, two armies, and the people. "The country should arouse itself and be heard," he wrote dismally, "but I have but little hope that it will."[135]

The Davis forces were not about to take Toombs' threat lightly. "Our community has been exercised to some extent lately, in order to defeat Genl. Toombs from Representing [sic] this Congressional dist.," George W. Lamar wrote to Davis. "A Candidate was *found and announced* who can defeat him, but I am happy to say that it is reported and *believed* that he [Toombs] has withdrawn."[136]

Toombs did no such thing. He campaigned gamely, but had little hope of getting elected. He also joined his ragtag home guard at Camp Fair Grounds near Athens in September and marched to Atlanta in October. The New York *Times* had some fun at Toombs' expense when he announced his intention of uniting "with the thousands of his countrymen who have found honorable deaths, if not graves, on the battle-field." The paper invited him to "expose his person to our fire at once.... Little as we value him, we should surely prefer hearing of his having fallen on the battle-field, to hearing that he had been reduced to the painful necessity of making away with himself after the fighting was all over."[137]

"I shall leave here Wednesday morning for Milledgeville with the purpose, if I can be elected, to run for the Senate," he wrote to Stephens in November. Even if he had no chance of winning, Toombs was determined to run as an opposition candidate "to offer whatever resistance I can to the ruin of the revolution and the destruction of public liberty." Toombs was not optimistic about his chances but felt Davis had to be stopped. "Mr. Davis's present policy will overthrow the revolution in six months if the enemy only [give] him time enough to stand still and do nothing," he said. "I shall do what I can to avert so dire a calamity." Toombs was realistic enough to know that the Georgia legislature was too conservative to elect a malcontent as noisy as himself to the Confederate Senate.[138]

In Milledgeville, Toombs was given a seat on the Senate floor when he arrived. A week later, he addressed a joint session of the legislature. "I wish I could tell you the sky is bright," he told the legislators, but he was there to tell them "rather truthful things." Toombs harped on his themes of the evils of impressments, Davis' economic policies, and conscription. These policies and more had "sown the seeds of discontent broadcast over the land, and is generating hostilities to the Government itself."

Toombs conceded the government and president should have extraordinary powers during war, but he cautioned the legislature to guard against encroachments upon liberty. The president right down to the local magistrate were "but servants of the people, and not their master; and therefore a check should be imposed on all unconstitutional measures." As for himself, he would take the censure, detraction, and malice that would come by saying these things. "Make my name forever infamous," he said, "if you can but save my country."[139]

Toombs' speech was interrupted by laughter and several outbursts of loud applause. Despite the warm reception, the election on November 25 turned out as he had expected. He consistently ran a distant second to the more moderate Herschel Johnson. On the third ballot, Johnson beat Toombs by sixty votes. It was the third time in as many years that Toombs had lost an election for an office he wanted. "Genl. Toombs did not have as much strength as I supposed with the members," Governor Brown commented to Alexander Stephens.[140]

After his defeat, Toombs bivouacked with his militia around Savannah. A few weeks later, as he rode the train with his men to Augusta, a cold snap dropped the temperatures. Some of Toombs' men built a fire on the wood floors of the boxcars to warm themselves. When a hapless railroad agent told them they were not going anywhere until they put the fire out, Toombs came upon the scene "cursing and using much bitter language," arrested the agent and threatened to have him cut up and thrown into the tinderbox for fuel. The first chance he got, the railroad agent reported Toombs' threats to the authorities.

Then on January 23, still smarting from his loss, Toombs made an ill-tempered speech to the militia troops. He invoked the Magna Carta, the beheading of Charles I of England and France's Louis XVI as examples of what happens to tyrants, hinting that President Davis might deserve the same fate. "There is no concord where there is no liberty," Toombs bellowed. "*And let discord reign until liberty is restored.*" Some of his listeners thought he was calling for the overthrow of the government. As Toombs gave his speech, several officers from the adjutant general's office mounted their horses and rode away to Savannah.[141]

Toombs was arrested a few days later. The charges were unclear, but he was court-martialed. Rumors flew that he was going to be hanged for treason. But the Central Railroad and Banking Company brought the charges, perhaps because Toombs refused to procure a passport or maybe because he allowed his men to set fires in the railroad cars a few weeks earlier.

Whatever the reason, the court-martial took place in early February. But Toombs was not one to trifle with in a courtroom and he defended himself during the proceeding. First, he contended the court had no authority over his case because his military hitch had expired a few days before the proceeding began, thus he was not answerable to any military tribunal. Toombs also pointed out that the court was biased because one of the judges, Colonel George A. Gordon, was the nephew of the president of the railroad. A few weeks later, P.G.T. Beauregard quietly dropped the charges.[142]

Toombs returned home and got into yet another controversy over both Georgia and Confederate regulations. When Governor Brown recommended planting grains instead of cotton, Toombs was, as usual, outraged. "As to what I shall choose to plant on my own estates, I shall neither refer it to the newspapers, nor to public meetings, nor to legislatures," he fumed to his brother Gabriel. "Let them take up arms and come with me to drive the intruders away from our soil, then we will settle what sort of seed we will put into it." Toombs was also fighting a court case over impressment of his slaves. Some of his slaves had been commandeered to work on the fortifications around Stewart County. The slaves had been confiscated by the Stewart County sheriff but were returned in March.[143]

Toombs spent most of the spring at home dispensing political advice. He was particularly pleased that the Stephens brothers were fighting another round of conscription laws. He was also outraged that the Confederate Congress had suspended habeas corpus. The Habeas Corpus Act authorized Davis to arrest and imprison anyone that openly defied the government. "Govr. Brown should avail himself of the first opportunity to test the legality of this proceeding," Toombs wrote. As if he had not been in enough trouble, he added mischievously that he would "give Mr. Davis an early opportunity to make me a victim by advising resistance, resistance to the death, to his law."[144]

By the summer of 1864, Georgia was beginning to howl thanks to Sherman's army. Governor Brown was forced to call out the state militia. General Gustavus W. Smith, who had just taken command of the Georgia militia, requested Toombs as his chief of staff.

Toombs once again took his place in the militia and was stationed around Atlanta. But by July, Union forces were driving the Confederates back towards the city. When Davis replaced Joe Johnston, who had lost more than twenty thousand men and more than half of northern Georgia, with General John Bell Hood, Toombs was delighted. "The tone of the army is greatly improved," he wrote. "General Hood is displaying great energy and using his best exertions for the effort."[145]

Toombs was doing his best to train and organize his troops. But "Poor fellows! They are green and raw, undisciplined and badly officered." Toombs did not mention they were probably old men and boys since the South's manpower was so badly depleted by death, war wounds, and desertion. "They march right into the trenches, and are immediately under the enemy's fire all day.... The pressure is so great that we are compelled to put them to the work of veterans without an hour's preparation." Toombs coveted every man fit for battle. He despised deserters—"Poor creatures! What do they want to live for?" He even rebuked his beloved Julia when she asked him to release a favored doctor. "I can not get Dr. Bob home, that is, I will not try," he said. "Every able bodied man in Georgia should be here. Bob can doctor, the rest of us can fight."[146]

Around the middle of July, Toombs realized that Atlanta would fall. On July 20, Hood attacked Sherman at Peachtree Creek but was forced back to his original positions. "Before you receive this letter, the struggle for Georgia will have begun & perhaps ended on the battlefield of Peachtree Creek," Toombs wrote to Julia during the battle. The army was in bad condition, much disheartened and "badly officered but I still think they will fight with firmness proportioned to the magnitude of the interests involved." Two days later, Hood was again defeated and lost thousands more men during the Battle of Atlanta. "The militia have behaved with great gallantry," he wrote to Julia. "This is sincerely true. They have far exceeded my expectations, and in the fight on Thursday equaled any troops in the line of battle."[147]

Hood fought one more disastrous battle at Ezra Church. Finally, he withdrew back to Atlanta and waited to see what Sherman was going to do. Instead of trying to beat the city into submission, Sherman decided to choke it to death with a siege. Toombs did what he could as Sherman tightened his grip. "Finally the Yankees began an attack on a part of our line & Genl [sic] Hood came by & I was obliged to ride with him to look at a portion of our defences [sic] & prepare to resist an assault," he wrote to Julia. "But as usual it passed off with only a demonstration." However, the siege quickly began to wear on Toombs' nerves. The Union was shelling the town furiously "and we lose from three to twelve of our poor milish every day."[148]

By the end of the month it was obvious that Atlanta was doomed. "We have a question of famine upon us," Toombs wrote to Stephens. The army was in a "deplorable" condition and Toombs, as usual, blamed the West Point generals and Jefferson Davis. "Hood I think the very best of the generals of his school, but like all the rest of them he knows no more of business than a ten-year-old boy, and don't know who does know anything about it [sic]." Toombs was appalled at the waste of war and thought the Confederacy needed to husband its resources. "But ours are wasted with a wild recklessness that would disgrace the Choctaw Indians."[149]

Atlanta fell in early September. Governor Brown dismissed the militia and sent them home for the fall harvest. Toombs also returned home to wait for events to unfold. Sherman captured Georgia county by county and tried to capitalize on the political quarrels within the Confederacy. He proposed to spare Georgians the wrath of his army if they would help him fight John Bell Hood. Sherman publicly invited Stephens and Governor Brown to a conference in Atlanta to talk about a separate peace for the state. "The people do not hesitate to say that Mr. Stephens was, and is, a Union man at heart," Sherman wrote to General Henry Halleck, "and they feel that Jeff. Davis will not trust him, or let him have a share in his government."[150]

Toombs was appalled at the idea. "Do not by any means go to see Sherman," he advised Stephens, "whatever may be the form of his invitation. It will place you in a wrong, *very wrong* position." Toombs realized that Sherman wanted to detach Georgia from the Confederacy. "Better any fate than that." Toombs reminded Stephens that, constitutionally, Davis was the only official that could make peace. "Nothing could be of more evil tendency than for other officers of the Confederacy, or state governments, to meet any person, and much less a general of an army, to discuss the question."[151]

Sherman's invitation set off a furor. John B. Jones noted rumors that Jeff Davis himself was going to Georgia to head off Governor Brown, Stephens, and Toombs from negotiating with Sherman. But Sherman's offer came to nothing. Governor Brown publicly refused Sherman's proposal. Stephens liked the idea, but also refused on the basis of "the entire absence of power on my part."[152]

On October 12, Major General Gustavus Smith was ordered to reassemble the militia at Lovejoy's Station just outside of Atlanta. But the Federals continued to push the militia southeast. Toombs was called back to his old command. When he tried to join his troops at Macon, the train he was on made too many stops for his liking. Exasperated by the delays, the fifty-four-year-old Toombs leapt from one of the cars "with the agility of a boy," one soldier recalled. Pulling two navy pistols from his coat, Toombs ran up to the locomotive, and "using the most forceful English, of which he was master," cussed the engineers until the train was moving again.[153]

By the time Toombs arrived in Macon, the situation was dire. Union forces skirmished with the militia but made no decisive moves. Still, it was obvious that Macon could be taken at the enemy's whim. "Things are very bad here," Toombs wrote to Governor Brown. "Sherman in person is leading, say, 30,000 men against us. We are retreating as rapidly as possible, consistent with good order and efficiency." The legislature would grant Brown "large and liberal powers," Toombs believed. "Tell them the country is in danger. Let all of her sons come to her rescue."[154]

But it was too late. Sherman had already started his march to the sea. The militia took heavy losses in a battle at Griswoldville, Milledgeville was cut off, and Macon could no longer be defended. On November 22, Governor Brown, General Gustavus Smith, Howell Cobb, and General Richard Taylor met. They decided to abandon Macon and move to the remnants of the militia toward Savannah. The militia swung south first to Albany and then marched east to Thomasville. Toombs rode ahead of his troops and arrived in Thomasville the middle of the night only to find that no transportation had been arranged and that General Taylor was stranded. Toombs dragged the local railroad agents out of bed, bawled them out, and then sent a telegram to Savannah threatening "dire vengeance" if he found the same situation there. Taylor's engine appeared in short order.[155]

The militia was able to stay in Savannah for less than a month before the city fell and was evacuated. General Smith's command retreated through South Carolina to Augusta. But Toombs stayed in winter camp only a short time before he came down with asthma and went on sick leave.[156]

Toombs recuperated at home and kept a low profile. He probably paid very close attention to a meeting that Alexander Stephens attended at Hampton Roads, Virginia, with Confederate senator R.M.T. Hunter, Secretary of War John A. Campbell, U.S. secretary of state William Seward and Abraham Lincoln. Lincoln and Stephens had been friends in their old Congressional Taylor Club days. Stephens asked how Truman Smith of Connecticut was doing. Lincoln asked about Thomas S. Flournoy of Virginia, William Ballard Preston, and how was Robert Toombs?

Stephens urged the two sides declare a truce, but Lincoln was firm: he would only accept reunion. The talk turned to slavery, emancipation, restitution for property that had been seized or destroyed, the recently passed Thirteenth Amendment. Lincoln suggested that Stephens go back to Georgia, get the legislature to call off the militia, and pass the Thirteenth Amendment "prospectively," to take effect in, say, five years. After four hours Stephens rose to leave. He tried once again to get Lincoln to consider an armistice. Lincoln said he would consider it but did not think he would change his mind. Everyone shook hands and the conference ended there. Toombs read the result of the conference as Lincoln saying, in effect, "we have settled your rights of property, and are ready to receive your submission."[157]

Toombs spoke briefly in Augusta two weeks later. He had not recovered from his time in the army and seemed to have given up to the South's inevitable defeat. His speech was a half-hearted effort that listed the blunders and errors of the Confederacy. Bad management, bad legislation, the conscript laws, and fiscal policy beset the Confederacy. "The greatest cause of desertion, and discontent," he said, "are the oppressive and unconstitutional exactions of the government."[158]

Toombs resumed the remnants of his law practice and kept track of the situation as best he could from his plantation in Washington, Georgia. It irritated him that he had no reliable news from Richmond. And he could no longer get the newspapers from Macon. When Senator Augustus Hill Garland stayed overnight at the Toombs plantation, "they represented a great despondency in govt. officials and people about Richmond and they seemed to suppose that Richmond would have to be evacuated long before this," he wrote to Stephens. "I suppose they will remain there until it will be too late to remain with safety or fight with success."[159]

But a few weeks later he had recovered his fighting spirit. "My health is again good, having wholly recovered from chills, fever and jaundice and I am again ready to take the field," he wrote to Stephens. He had no hope for solutions from Richmond, though. "They will swear all is right until Lee's defeat or evacuation, and then — chaos. I fear the congress has not nerve enough to see and appreciate the evil and the remedy." Toombs' remedy: "It is begone Davis." Toombs hoped the militia might be able to recapture Savannah and Dalton while the Federals were occupied in North Carolina, Virginia and the Gulf. "I think there is an opening either way & I should like to get in before them, especially in Savannah." But Jefferson Davis was leading the remnants of the Confederacy to ruin. "Nothing can save us but the overthrow of Davis & that must come quickly to be of any service," Toombs wrote to General Gustavus Smith.[160]

But Toombs' hopes were for naught. He was having dinner with Governor Brown on April 8 when news reached them that Lee had surrendered his army to Grant. The two men looked at each other. What could be said? It was over. In Crawfordville, Alexander Stephens gathered his family at his plantation, Liberty Hall. Joe Brown went to Augusta to learn what he could about the terms of the surrender. Toombs went back home to Washington. On May 4, the remains of the Confederate administration clattered into town hoping to rally the citizens and to withdraw some treasury funds that had been deposited in the local bank. The entourage consisted of Davis, his wife, Varina, John C. Breckenridge, who was Davis' sixth secretary of war, Secretary of the Navy Stephen Mallory, Postmaster General John H. Reagan, a few aides, and a small contingent of soldiers.[161]

Most of the cabinet stayed in town at the Heard House, but John Reagan stayed with his old friend Toombs. That evening, Toombs asked Reagan if everyone had enough money, if they had good horses, and if Davis needed an escort for his travels. Reagan told Toombs that everyone was all right considering the circumstances. They bid farewell. Later, Reagan told Davis about Toombs' offer. "That is like Toombs. He was always a whole-souled man," Davis said. Davis and Toombs had had their differences, but at a time like this both men were willing to temporarily bury the hatchet.[162]

The next day, the Confederate cabinet was officially disbanded. Some of the group went home, others stuck with Davis as he fled south into territory still unoccupied by federal troops. One of Davis' aides saw Toombs as they rode out of town. Toombs was wearing his old Websterian frock coat and shabby, broad brimmed hat. He was preparing an old buggy "drawn by two ancient gray horses." When someone asked him where he was going, he replied he was going to see Alex Stephens then cussed a few blue streaks about the Yankees. Before the Davis party left town, someone hid five thousand dollars from the Confederate Treasury on the Toombs property. Toombs turned the money over to Union authorities a few days later.[163]

A day or so afterwards, Toombs was sitting on his veranda talking to a few friends when a young lieutenant named Lot D. Young limped by on crutches. He was looking for change for two forty dollar gold pieces to pay the remaining soldiers of his company. Toombs did not have change, but said one of his friends, a Confederate major, was in charge of some Confederate funds that happened to be in house. Toombs invited the lieutenant to sit on the porch. When the major returned with the change, Lieutenant Young thanked them. Toombs walked the young soldier through the yard and to the gate, still talking, still asking questions. As he said goodbye, Toombs pulled a twenty dollar gold piece from his vest pocket and put it in Lieutenant Young's hand.

"Here, Lieutenant, take this from me. You will doubtless need it."

When Lieutenant Young politely declined, Toombs replied, "Here, take it, sir; you are a d[am]n long way from home and you will need it before you get there."

The thrilled lieutenant shook Toombs' hand and hobbled on his way.[164]

By now, federal authorities were trying to round up the leaders of the rebellion. Howell Cobb had been in custody for a few weeks. Patrols were frantically looking for Jeff Davis. Stephens was arrested on May 11 and imprisoned in Fort Warren on Boston Harbor. But Toombs made no effort to hide. On May 12, the 4th Iowa Cavalry rode up to Toombs' plantation to arrest him. He had just walked out of his study to see what was going on. "By God, the bluecoats!" he said and disappeared into the house.

Julia met them at the front door.

"Where is General Toombs?" an officer asked.

"He is not here," she replied.

"Unless General Toombs is produced, I shall burn the house," the officer said.

"Then burn it," she said.

The troops gave Julia and her family some time to move furniture and other valuable possessions into the yard. They searched the house thoroughly, even between the mattresses and under bureaus "as if a man of Gen. Toombs' size could be hid like a paper doll!" a friend of the family wrote in her diary. The soldiers then ate the dinner that had been set for the Toombs family.[165]

But Toombs had slipped out the back door. He had been tipped off that the Federals were on their way and he had probably prepared an escape plan. As he told it years later: "I didn't like the idea of staying in Boston harbor and Fort Warren [Prison], even in the company of Mr. Stephens. I preferred Paris, so I took my horse and scooted."[166]

6

Un-Reconstructed

Robert Toombs was on the lam. His fortune was in peril. His slaves were gone. His way of life had disappeared in the noise and smoke and blood of the Civil War. In 1860 he had slaves. When he returned from exile in 1867, he had employees.

By most accounts, Toombs was considered a "good" slave owner, if such a thing ever existed. One of Toombs' slaves, Alonza Fantroy Toombs, recalled that his father was a slave preacher and the senator's carriage driver. Senator Toombs "learnt" his father how to read and write. According to Alonza, Toombs was a good provider who gave his slaves good clothes, good food, "an' we was treated fair. Dere warn't no mean peoples on our plantation." Alonza also recalled that not one slave left Toombs' plantations after the South surrendered. He also said that Toombs gave every one of his former slaves a mule, some land, and a house to get them started when the war ended.[1]

Alonza was interviewed in June of 1937, more than seventy years after the Civil War. His story may have been true. On the other hand, the eighty-six-year-old former slave may have been remembering with advantage. Or he may have been saying what he thought a white interviewer wanted to hear about slavery. Whatever the case, many of Toombs' slaves liberated themselves when they had the chance. In 1857, a slave named Pierce planned to run away with another slave named Felix. Toombs offered Pierce's services to Howell Cobb, but Cobb refused and claimed that Pierce was "becoming lazy and worthless." The slaves tried to flee but were caught. Felix was taken to the Richmond auctions. But Pierce was taken back to Toombs' house in Washington, D.C. As he was preparing to leave for Georgia, Toombs wanted to take Pierce with him "if he wants to come," he wrote to Stephens. "If not [I] shall let him run at large as you requested me."[2]

Then there was the remarkable story of Garland White. White belonged to Toombs and, like Alonza's father, was taught to read. He studied for the ministry and received his certification to preach the gospel on September 10, 1859. In 1860, Toombs took White with him to Washington, D.C. where he was a house servant. In Washington, White struck up a friendship with Senator William Henry Seward and at some point escaped to Canada.[3]

White made it to London, Ontario, and was assigned to a local mission by the Black Methodist Episcopal Conference. When the war broke out, White recruited throughout the North for the newly established United States Colored Troops and signed up most of the men in the 28th United States Colored Infantry. In 1864, he wrote to Seward requesting a commission as chaplain to the unit. Secretary of War Edwin Stanton formally assigned him to the post a few months later.[4]

But in the summer of 1865 Toombs was a fugitive, roving the mountains and back roads of Georgia on his own underground railroad, doing his best to hide from those who were searching for him. He did not fear prison, a trial, or even execution. But he dreaded being a trophy. He did not want to be paraded through the streets like a carnival exhibit or an exotic prize by his "beloved brethren of the North." He was willing to sell his life dearly to prevent that.[5]

The day the Federals came to his front door, Julia was "was taking account of what had been left us." As the soldiers rode into the front yard, Toombs slipped out the back and hid in the woods. At two o'clock in the morning, a twenty-year-old former Confederate lieutenant named Charles Irvin, whose family happened to live across the street from Toombs, got word to bring Toombs' horse, Grey Alice, to John Chenault's place. The Chenaults lived about eighteen miles from Washington. Irvin met Toombs there and they rode north to an isolated island in the Savannah River called Harrison Landing. They stayed a week or so. But they had to flee when they found out that someone had alerted the federal authorities.[6]

Despite his fame and the substantial reward offered by the federal government, Toombs was able to hide in the homes of both friends and political enemies throughout the state as frustrated Union soldiers combed the countryside. Sometimes he traveled disguised in a checked suit, sack coat, and slouch hat under the name Luther Martin. Sometimes he traveled openly. Toombs and Irvin never stopped at a house where Toombs did not know the people, Irvin recalled, "though the people did not always know them." Yet there was always the danger of capture. One night, Toombs and Irvin were leaving a friend's house. As they walked through the door, a black servant said, "Good-bye, Mas Robert." Toombs ignored him, but muttered to Irvin when they were outside: "What must I do if I can't disguise myself?"

From Harrison Landing, Toombs and Irvin traveled to the mountain country in north Georgia around Tallulah Falls. Toombs stayed with friends while Irvin attempted to make arrangements to smuggle him to Savannah. From there Toombs hoped to get out of the country. Irvin spent a great deal of time on the road between Talluah Falls, Savannah, and Washington, passing messages back and forth between Toombs and Julia, trying to get forged papers and securing funds for a stay abroad. But the plan fell through when a squad of soldiers arrested Irvin in Savannah for wearing brass buttons. Obviously, passing through that city would be too dangerous.

In the meantime, wild rumors began to fly. The New York *Tribune* reported that Toombs had committed suicide. "Can't give my assent to the truth of that," Stephens wrote in his diary from his cell at Fort Warren. Toombs' friends also spread rumors that he had already left the country and was in Cuba or Mexico or some other safe location. "I have been trying to arrest Toombs for two weeks," the baffled General James Harrison Wilson wired to Secretary of War Edwin Stanton, "but he has so far succeeded in eluding my men."[7]

Toombs shaved the tuft of beard that usually hung from his chin and cut his hair short to keep from being recognized. The simple disguise worked when he stayed with a friend who ran a county post office. Every day local men gathered there to read the papers. When the talk turned to Toombs, one old man said, "I knew Toombs was too sharp to stay here and let the Yankees catch him." Toombs was in the room and this perked up his ears when his name was mentioned. "He is gone now, but I tell you, boys, he was one of the smartest men we ever had in this country."

"Yes," Toombs chimed in, "he was a pretty smart man; I knew him very well. He was a little peculiar sometimes, but as big a hearted fellow as ever raised a boll of cotton."[8]

Toombs passed his days in northern Georgia hunting and fishing. But by the end of June it was time to move on. The plan now was to get Toombs out of the country through Florida. Toombs and Irvin rode south again and passed close to home through Elbert, Oglethrope and Wilkes counties. Toombs must have ached to see Julia, but he did not dare try. While staying close by at Henry P. Mattox's plantation, he had actually set up a meeting with her but abandoned the reunion when he was told Yankee soldiers were on the prowl.

It may have been too late anyway. His house had been spared from burning a few months earlier. But on July 30, General Edward Augustus Wild ordered Julia to leave. She was allowed to take only her clothes and a few mementos. The authorities installed a school for blacks in the basement and General Wild set up his quarters in the living room. Julia begged military authorities to parole her husband if he surrendered. But Secretary of War Stanton refused. "If Mr. Toombs comes within reach of the U.S. forces," Stanton ordered, "he [should] be immediately arrested and sent in close custody to Fort Warren."[9]

In the meantime, Toombs and Irvin separated. Toombs dispatched his friend to give Julia some letters and to tell her that he was going abroad and would send for her when things were settled down. Then Toombs hid out with Linton Stephens at Sparta. He took cover so well that Irvin rode hundreds of miles back and forth across central Georgia trying to track him down. Irvin finally found him by accident when he looked through the window at the home of Colonel Jack Smith. Colonel Smith took them across the Oconee River where they stayed with a family named Deas. Mr. Deas apparently did not recognize Toombs, even after an evening of talking politics. Finally, Deas' sister said: "Joe Deas, are you a fool? Don't you know that is General Toombs?" She and one of the household's former slaves had heard him make a speech seventeen years before at Toomsboro and both remembered his voice.

"Good Lord!" Toombs told Irvin when the former slave recognized the former senator, "go give that negro some money."

Deas escorted Toombs and Irvin to Colonel David Hughes' farm in Twiggs County. Toombs stayed at the Hughes place while Irvin made his way to Macon to talk with General Gustavus Smith. General Smith told Irvin that the ferries across the Ocmulgee River were crawling with Yankees who were looking specifically for Robert Toombs. General Smith advised Irvin to take Toombs back to the mountains and wait until the heat was off. Besides, a local doctor had recognized Toombs and was threatening to squeal to the authorities.

So Toombs and Irvin rode back the way they came. By October, rumors that Toombs had fled the country were generally accepted and the Federals were less vigilant in searching for their prey. Toombs and Irvin retraced their steps once again, this time getting as far south and west as Houston County. Toombs stayed with a friend named Brown. He requested an ambulance to ride in for the rest of the journey. Toombs may have been having health problems or perhaps he was just tired of being in the saddle. Whatever the case, as Mr. Brown went off to secure an ambulance, Brown's younger brother came along and recognized Irvin. As Brown, Irvin, and Toombs talked together, the conversation turned to the fate of various Confederate leaders. The younger Brown asked Irvin what had happened to General Toombs.

"Gone to Cuba," Irvin replied tersely.

Mr. Brown could not get an ambulance, so Toombs and Irvin rode west to Alabama. At Tazewell, they encountered a squad of occupying Yankees. Irvin told Toombs to keep quiet, not to say anything, while he had a look around. They rode through town as casually as they could, but the Yankee soldiers eyed them suspiciously. The Federals may have suspected something, but let them pass. As soon as they were out of view, Toombs and Irvin spurred their horses and put a safe distance between themselves and Tazewell.

Finally, Toombs made it to Roanoke, his plantation in Stewart County in western Georgia. He told his overseer to get him an ambulance. Then he and Irvin rode to the ferry and crossed the Chattahoochee River into Alabama. Sadly, Toombs had to leave his favorite horse behind. Gray Alice neighed and whinnied and pawed at the riverbank as she watched him cross to the other side of the river. Toombs always got emotional when he told the story, even years later.

In Alabama, Toombs and Irvin boarded the train to Evergreen. Several passengers recognized him but fortunately kept his identity to themselves. However, General Joseph Wheeler was also onboard and kept a suspicious eye on Luther Martin. Toombs did his best to hide behind a newspaper. From Evergreen, they took a steamer into Mobile. The steamer was filled with Yankee soldiers who were nosing around and questioning everybody on board. Irvin recalled this was the only time when he saw Toombs get nervous.

Apparently, the suspicious soldiers could find no reason to arrest Toombs and the fugitives made it to Mobile where they checked into a hotel. Toombs avoided the dining room and used room service while Irvin made arrangements to stay with the famous writer Augusta Evans. While Irvin and Toombs were at the Evans' home, General Joseph Wheeler paid a visit. Toombs and Irvin probably hid while Wheeler was there. He mentioned that he was sure he had seen Robert Toombs on the train. Mrs. Evans changed the subject.

Another engraving from a Daguerreotype, probably around 1860. Courtesy of the Hargrett Rare Book and Manuscript Library, University of Georgia Libraries.

Irvin and Toombs stayed at the Evans house for a week then made their way to New Orleans. There they stayed with friends until a steamer was ready to depart. Irvin met with P.G.T. Beauregard and somehow secured for Toombs a passport to Cuba from the Spanish embassy. On November 4, Toombs boarded the steamship *Alabama.* Irvin had left a new suit in Toombs' stateroom. As soon as Toombs changed clothes, he was on deck, mingling, greeting friends who happened to be on board, and working the crowd. A throng had assembled at the docks to see the boat off and Irvin cautioned Toombs to remain discreet. But the gregarious Toombs would have none of it.

"No, I want fresh air and I will die

right here," he told his companion. "I am impatient to get into neutral waters, when I can talk. I have not had a square, honest talk in six months." It did not take long before anybody who was interested knew that Bob Toombs was on board.

"I am fully satisfied that I acted prudently in avoiding an arrest and leaving the country," Toombs wrote to Stephens a few weeks later from Cuba. Stephens had been recently been released from prison and had been at home in Crawfordville only a few weeks. Toombs complained to Stephens about Andrew Johnson's Reconstruction policies such as not pardoning top Confederate officials or anyone with assets of more than $25,000. But Toombs was especially incensed at the possibility that Johnson would give former slaves the vote. He was also unhappy about Georgia's new constitution that had been hastily drawn up at Milledgeville. Toombs was grieved that the legislature had passed the Thirteenth Amendment that forever eliminated slavery. When it came to enfranchising former slaves, he said, he saw no difference between Johnson and the Radical Republicans. Whether the states or the federal government gave the vote to blacks made no difference, it was all the same to him, a "pretended quarrel ... to make the poor and unfortunate people of the South more readily subject themselves to their degredation [sic]."

But Toombs was happy to be "out of the muss." He had great sympathy for the people he had left behind but contempt for what he considered political double-crossers such as Herschel Johnson and Joe Brown who were working with the Yankees to further their own political careers. "They seem to glory in their shame, and revel in the ruin and degradation of those whom they pretend to serve," he wrote. But the political reality was that the North had won and Stephens, ever the pragmatist, was thinking about running for Toombs' old seat in the United States Senate. Stephens had said publicly that he favored some of Johnson's Reconstruction policies. Toombs hoped his friend would reconsider. "Your own action and that of the legislature will have been taken before you get this letter and therefore I can only express the hope that my opinions may be wrong and that you will be able to promote the public interest and advance your reputation as a member of the Senate."

As for his own future, he saw none in his former country. Stephens believed Toombs might be able to get a pardon. But Toombs felt no one in Washington would help and he did not think anyone who remained unreconstructed had a chance. "Nobody is strong enough to keep me out of Fort Warren except Johnson." A military court would hang him "much more rightfully than it could the poor woman (Mrs. Surratt I believe) who was hung in Washington; for I did try to take 'the life of the nation,' and sorely regret the failure to do it."

Toombs was unwilling to live in a "conquered country" like the southern United States and at the moment was very pleased with Cuba. He was also thinking of settling permanently in Mexico. "It has many advantages for people who seek to establish themselves of the better classes," he wrote, although "I do not care for its disorders." He believed the "Spanish element" would be kicked out soon and the country would be taken over by European or Anglo-Saxon elements. "It will be mixed and I shall stand a better chance than in an old established society. So will my family."[10]

But for now it was Cuba. Toombs and Julia were reunited in October and spent the winter together there. Then in May of 1866, Julia returned to Georgia to visit family and friends and to check on the chances for her husband's safe return. "I am anxious to know what you think in regard to civil law, & Mr. Toombs' return," she wrote to Alexander Stephens. As yet, Toombs was unsure of his destination. He was giving Halifax serious consideration, but there was an outbreak of cholera there so he stayed put.[11]

In the end, Toombs departed for France. He spent his time nursing his asthma in the spa waters at Enghien and waiting for Julia to join him. When she arrived in July, they lived in high style, attending operas, traveling, and seeing the sights throughout Europe. However, Toombs had to fund his exile by selling Roanoke, his plantation in Stewart County, for about five dollars an acre. He liked to say that he ate about an acre of dirt a day while he was in Europe.[12]

The Toombses hobnobbed with illustrious Europeans and ran into many Confederate exiles. Toombs even befriended the ruthless Louis Adolphe Theirs who became president of France's Third Republic a few years later. They also spent time in England, Germany, and Switzerland. But they were not the average American tourists. Toombs became one of the ambassadors at large for the lost cause of the Confederacy.[13]

If some stories are true, once in a while he took it too far. One female tourist claimed that her party encountered Toombs on Rigi Mountain in Switzerland. The lady correspondent claimed that "a large, loosely, but powerfully-made man, but common looking in the extreme" started a conversation with her group. Her husband recognized him as Robert Toombs, but she did not think anyone else in the party knew who he was. She also thought he was intoxicated.

When the conversation turned to American politics, Toombs got belligerent and said something about the South not being conquered, that it would give America more trouble. When her husband politely inquired how another revolution would be fought, "the wild beast in the old man's eyes glared." Toombs cussed and said "with blood and bones, and manhood, Sir, like I've got."

When her husband pointed out that the South's resources appeared exhausted, Toombs cussed the Yankees even more.

Enough was enough. Their guide, Walter, finally said: "Mr. Toombs, this is hardly the place for such conversation — before ladies."

"You know my name!" Toombs exclaimed in shock.

"Yes, Sir I do," Walter replied. Then her husband made the mistake of telling Toombs he was no gentleman to use the language he had in front of ladies.

Toombs called the husband a liar and rushed forward to strike him. Walter restrained Toombs as the husband ignored the drunken nonsense and walked on to catch up with the ladies who had ridden ahead.

Toombs demanded the husband's card and challenged him to a duel.

The correspondent made a point of mentioning that Toombs "had an open knife in his hand, and besides being drunk was so large and strongly built that he would probably have been more than a match for both of them."[14]

It is a wild tale. Toombs *was* capable of outrageousness when he was drunk and prone to an occasional violent act — he once beaned Senator William Yancy in the forehead with an inkpot on the floor of the Confederate Congress. But Toombs was usually a tough talker who was slow to action and he was not in the habit of picking fights with strangers. If there was any truth in the tale, it was probably an exaggeration. It could have been Toombs at his inebriated worst; it could have been an imposter cashing in on Toombs' celebrity. Or it could be an outright fabrication. Whatever the case, it is the kind of story that solidified Toombs' reputation in the North as an untamed, drunken, Southern partisan barely in control of his common sense and his loud mouth.[15]

Tragedy struck in October. Sallie Toombs DuBose, their only remaining child, suddenly died. She was only thirty-one-years-old. She left behind four children. To add to the sorrow, no one in the family knew how to get the word to Toombs or Julia. Gabriel Toombs frantically wrote to Alexander Stephens asking how to contact his brother.[16]

"I was prepared for anything but that," Toombs wrote to Stephens when he received the news. "All the personnal [sic] hopes, sufferings, inconveniences, exile, and all I could bear with a spirit unbroken, indeed they weighed not a feather upon me & only tended to stimulate any purpose to a still more thorough devotion to our unhappy country, but this blow is unsupportable [and] it has crushed my heart & buried my hopes in the grave."[17]

It took over a month to make arrangements to go home. Julia seems to have been particularly anguished. Initially, Toombs wanted to stay in France while Julia returned home. Yet she was "unequal to the sepration [sic] and journey" and he decided it was best to go with her. But at the last minute there was a change of plans. Perhaps they felt it was not safe for Toombs to return home. Whatever happened, Julia left Paris and Toombs returned to his lonely hotel rooms.[18]

Toombs was alone in his grief and as he had done before, he found solace in writing to Julia. "The night you left I returned to the room & did not go to sleep until after two o'clock," he wrote to her. "I felt so sad at parting with you, and could not help thinking of what a long dreary trip you had that night." Despite his talk of resettling in another land, he was now anxious to get home and was trying to find the fastest way back to Georgia. "I shall [have] a long journey of five thousand miles from here to Havana & do not know that I shall meet a human being to whom I am known," he wrote to her. "But if I keep well I shall not mind that especially as I am homeward bound, for altho my hearth Stone is desolate, & clouds & darkness hover over the little remnant that is left of us, and upon all of our poor friends & country men, yet when you get home Washington will contain nearly all that is dear to me in this world."[19]

A few days later, he wrote to Julia about his bleak, companionless Christmas. Mostly, he longed for Georgia and to be by Julia's side. "I see no body [sic]," he wrote, "& am very much alone since you left, I shall soon start on my long & dreary voyage, with nothing pleasant in it except at the end hoping to find you to be well at our desolate home." His New Year's celebration had been no better. "In a foreign land, with all that is dear to me remaining on Earth beyond the ocean far far [sic] distant either on the road to a desolate home or around its desolate fire sides!" But things had to get better. "God knows I can not [sic] regret that 1866 is gone, & think its calamities will not enter with us into 67." He was still trying to book passage home although he was unsure of the fate awaiting him there. An acquaintance from Tennessee that was in Paris thought it would be safe for Toombs to return. Toombs thought his friend "ought to know something of Andy Johnson."[20]

A few days later, Toombs received encouraging news from General Grant's aide-de-camp about his status, but it threw him into doubt as to whether he should linger in Havana or go to Canada. President Johnson had recently dissolved the court-martials and all of Washington was distracted by his troubles with Congress. Still, he was "perplexed in the extreme," and wished Julia was with him. "If you were only with me I should know what to do," he wrote to Julia. He did not want leave Europe until spring then he would have to decide where he wanted to stay. For Toombs, exile had become just as bad as being locked up. "The worse that can happen to me is a prison & I dont [sic] see much to choose between my present position & any decent fort," he wrote to Julia. "I am now much worse than nothing, spending what little money we have left and without enjoyment & without benefit to my Self or any body [sic] else."

Finally, he decided that if the authorities were determined to lock him up, then he would set out for Canada. But he was worried about what would happen to Julia and his grandchildren if he were sentenced to prison. The thought "makes me very wretched," he wrote. "I want to be with you at least long enough for us to see what arrangements can be made for them." He was finally able to set out on January 15. "I shall have a long & lonesome voyage, with not much else to cheer me but that I shall find you & our dear little ones at the end of my journey, if I am permitted to see you & find you all well, I shall be compensated for its fatigues & dangers." He arrived in Cuba in February. Apparently the situation was still unsure, so he made his way to Canada for a short stay before traveling to Washington, D.C. Toombs managed to visit Andrew Johnson, whom he had known from his Senate days. Whatever transpired at the meeting is unknown, but Toombs returned to his home in Georgia on February 26 no longer fearing imprisonment.[21]

If he wanted to return home quietly as he said, it was a useless desire. Newspapers from Georgia to Washington, D.C. announced his arrival. "The Hon. Robert Toombs returned to his house in the village this evening," ran a dispatch from the Washington, Georgia, *Gazaette*. "Let the past be buried — childless he weeps o'er the grave of his daughter." Toombs also wanted to weep when he saw how different things were in the South. Everything was "much worse" than he expected, so much had changed so rapidly and "the spirit of the great body of the people utterly broken, bankruptcy & ruin wide spread [sic] throughout the land," he wrote to John C. Breckenridge. Freed slaves had access to the courts, property rights and education. Georgia was under military rule and was being run by Radicals with Governor Joe Brown leading a parade of "negroes, Yankees, refugees, & much other waifs & floats as can be alarmed by the cry of confiscation or bribed by the expectation of place or plunder."[22]

The whole situation offended and riled Toombs, and as far as he could see, no one was speaking for the "old, incorrigible traitors" like him who were determined to remain unreconstructed. "The Radicals thus far have had the field to themselves, the military authorities having forbidden all who hold office under the state to write or utter one word against the 'place of union' & yet their purpose has been but small & the discontent daily incendiary," Toombs yelped. He had not forgotten how to exploit a political opportunity when he saw it. He endorsed a small organization out of Cincinnati that still promoted the Kentucky Resolutions of 1798 which maintained the United States was just a compact. This was a statement that "contained the principle of my whole political life," he wrote. But before making any bold political strokes, he decided to bide his time.[23]

Instead, he concentrated on making money. Although his brother Gabriel had looked after his business affairs while he was in Europe, his finances had suffered tremendously. Toombs quickly rebuilt his lucrative law practice and took on his son-in-law, Dudley DuBose, as his law partner. Before long, Toombs was arguing cases before the Georgia supreme court, an institution he had helped establish almost thirty years before. "I will aid Linton with pleasure in your case in [the] Supreme Court, and take charge of it if he should be absent," Toombs wrote to Alexander Stephens in November of 1867. He did not mind taking on more cases since he was "at leisure" and "only" preparing a half dozen cases to argue before the court. "You know when one is engaged in that line of business," he quipped, " 'it is but little trouble to add a few more cases to the dockett.'"[24]

Toombs especially enjoyed litigating against railroads. As the railroads were rebuilt and expanded throughout Georgia, he came to believe they should be harnessed to benefit the public, not to line their corporate pockets with taxpayer money. Over the years, he sued railroads dozens of times on behalf of the State of Georgia. While he held no official state position, he acted as a sort of ad hoc solicitor general. He thought corporations, with their bottomless pockets, were too powerful and a danger to society. They absorbed everything including the treasuries of the federal and state governments. "This is all wrong, violates justice, transfers the sweat of the poor to the coffers of the rich, appropriates the public fund to private use and profit, and opens the flood gates of fraud and public demoralization."[25]

Toombs had almost as much fun as he had in the old days when he rode the circuit. "I lost today by old Beasley's getting drunk, and the court 'no go,'" he wrote to Stephens a few days later. "I am trying to get his wife to sober him by tomorrow, and have adjourned the court on my own action today." But "old Beasly makes it a point always to get drunk at the wrong time and keep perfectly sober when nobody cares a 'cuss' whether he is drunk or sober."[26]

As 1868 rolled by, Toombs thrust himself back into politics. He was beginning to enjoy his role of spokesman for the unreconstructed rebel. When a special session of "that ragamuffin band of negroes [sic] & thieves called the legislature" was called, he canceled a business trip to New York because he felt he had to be at the state capitol. "I think an *unconquered* & *unrepentant* rebel could do more for the public interest at home than abroad at this time," he wrote to a friend. When Democrats nominated former New York governor Horatio Seymour and former Union general Francis P. Blair for the presidential ticket, Toombs endorsed them at a Democratic rally in Atlanta. Yes, Blair had fought the South during the war, but he was now "an advocate of peace — peace for the whole country." Besides, they were running on an anti-Reconstruction platform. Toombs struck a moderate tone, but the audience ate it up. "We can compare the scene to nothing less than a stupendous camp meeting," the reporter from the Atlanta *Constitution* gushed, "where everybody is converted, and vieing [sic] with each other to see who can shout the loudest."[27]

On July 21, Georgia's Reconstruction legislature adopted the Fifthteenth Amendment which gave former slaves the right to vote and prevented anyone who had participated as an official in the Confederacy from holding political office. The next day, Republican banker and railroad man Rufus Bullock was inaugurated as Georgia's twenty-fifth governor.

Two days later, Toombs was the main attraction at a massive Democratic rally in Atlanta, fifteen thousand strong. Three different bands and the occasional cannon blast serenaded the crowd. The president of the proceedings, prominent physician Dr. James F. Alexander, made a few perfunctory remarks, the prayer was gotten out of the way, and the Democratic presidential ticket was quickly endorsed. The speakers, Toombs, Howell Cobb, and Benjamin Hill, were introduced. When Toombs rose first and walked to the podium, the crowd roared.

Three years of Radical peace was ten times worse than four years of war, Toombs told his audience. From there he had them in the palm of his hand. He accused the Radicals of imposing debt the South could never pay, military despotism, and thievery. "After insulting our women and stealing our spoons we expected peace, but our kind feelings were met by theft and plunder," he raged.

He railed at supposed disenfranchisement of the white man. The conquering Radicals claimed they had the right to the lives, property, and liberties of the South, he said. It was "one of the most infamous doctrines that ever was yelled from the bowels of the damned." The South was being deprived of the justice it deserved. "Had Georgia received justice, she would have been deprived of the great clemency that gave her [Governor] Bullock and a nigger government." But Democrats could rescue the South from its plight. "Good men are coming," he promised. "Old and young men are coming and all the women are with us.... United with this grand army of liberty; its banners are numberless, its hearts are one."[28]

The speech at the Bush Arbor meeting was vintage Toombs: angry, defiant, profane, spellbinding ... and the rhetoric of the past. Still, he was frequently interrupted by shouts and applause. His "truths" were widely praised in Georgia papers while the Northern press criticized him for his "denunciation of law and invocation of violence." Whatever their opinion, people talked about the speech for years afterwards. Yet Toombs, who was his own harshest critic when it came to his public performances, was not pleased with the effort. "The speech at the convention I wrote out hurriedly from rough notes (except that part prepared for another purpose last summer) and I omitted (forgot) a good deal of the best of it and was mortified that I omitted the notice I took of Seymour and Blair, by accident," he complained to Stephens.[29]

Toombs probably spent the next couple of weeks vacationing at White Sulphur Springs, West Virginia, with Stephens. They reinvigorated themselves with the mineral waters and sulfur baths and politicked with a number of Southern Democrats who had come to discuss tactics to defeat Republicans in the approaching election. After a few weeks, Toombs traveled to Augusta with politically unpredictable Benjamin Hill. Hill was making his reputation by tongue-lashing Radicals at every chance. The local Democrats gave Toombs and Hill a spontaneous welcome and called for some speeches. Toombs tore into Radicals and Southern traitors like Governor Bullock, Foster Blodgett, and especially Joe Brown, who had aligned with the Republicans. "Brown was full of blood-talk," Toombs proclaimed, "but he never killed a chicken, nor even a musketo [sp]."[30]

At fifty-eight-years-old, Bob Toombs could not run for office. He made it a point of pride — and publicity — to refuse to take the loyalty oath to the United States Constitution. But he embarked on a whirlwind political tour of the state to promote Democrats and bludgeon Radicals. Within weeks he gave major speeches in Augusta, Cedar Town, and Atlanta. Georgia Democrats carried the elections in October thanks to Toombs, Hill, and political organizations such as the Ku Klux Klan. But Ulysses S. Grant won the Electoral College in a landslide and a 310,000 majority in the popular vote and Republicans dominated Congress.[31]

So Toombs quietly went back to his law practice. He tended his business interests, gave an occasional speech to agricultural fairs, political and civic organizations, and he became increasingly interested in the affairs of several universities. For instance, he was instrumental in creating the chair of history and political science at the University of Macon and getting Alexander Stephens appointed to it. "I know that the University and the public will be great gainers by your taking upon yourself these new cares and duties," he wrote to his friend, "but I do not know whether you will find the change of life agreeable to you." And he still dabbled in politics. In January of 1870 he tried without success to prevent Governor Bullock from eradicating opponents of Radical Reconstruction from the Georgia legislature. But Julia was ill and for the most part he restricted himself to writing letters containing business or legal advice and damning Republicans.[32]

When the Democrats won control of the state legislature in December of 1870, Toombs bolstered the victory in what came to be known as his Magna Carta lecture. Much of the time, Toombs was a spontaneous orator who used only a few notes when he made his speeches. But the Magna Carta lecture was a scripted set piece. Toombs first gave the speech to a standing room only crowd on May 11 in Augusta. The lecture equated centuries of battle over the principles of the Magna Carta with current battles over the Constitution.

Since the Magna Carta's inception, it was a given that justice would be done and an individual's rights would be respected, he maintained. "These [principles] had never been denied for seven hundred years, until the present evil days," Toombs would say. The same principles had been prominent in the Constitution and society had been organized to protect them.

But Republicans had initiated a civil war and were currently bent on destroying those principles. "The assassins of liberty are now in power, but a reaction is coming," he would say. "Stand firm, make no compromise.... Push forward, and make a square fight for your liberties." Then he would bend his body slightly forward, his eyes blazing, and hold a copy of the Magna Carta in his raised hand. "When you can tear the live thunder from its home in the burning ether and bind it a captive at the footstool of tyranny," he would cry, "then, and only then will I accept the situation."[33]

The speech was targeted at the forces resisting the New South, the South that was embracing industry and technology and shedding agriculture as the engine of its economy. It hearkened back to nostalgia for issues of the past. The South, and the people in it, had been reshaped by the war. But Toombs could never bring himself to acknowledge that the old disputes about constitutional principles and the meaning of justice had been settled. He was becoming the personification of the old politics while younger politicians had already found new things to argue about.

Yet Toombs still commanded tremendous respect in certain Georgia political circles. Many people still asked him for political, legal, and business advice even though he was quickly falling into the category of elder statesman — or a relic from the wrong side of history — depending on who used the adjectives. However, his Magna Carta speech was extremely popular and he was requested to read it from Augusta to Mobile, Alabama.

Reporters also eagerly sought interviews with him. He could be counted on for salty comments and colorful anecdotes that made great copy. Toombs obliged journalists by exaggerating his political opinions and saying outrageous things. It was usually difficult to determine when he was serious and when was just saying things for effect. He talked endlessly of another revolution. "Revolution, yes; always, and ever, and from the first, revolution!" When someone asked him if he was interested in seeking political office again, he said, "No, unless there is a chance for another fight; I'm in for that now and any time." A more apocryphal story has a Northerner boast: "Well, we licked you" to which Toombs supposedly replied: "Licked us? No sir! We wore ourselves out licking you."[34]

Occasionally, he played wild pranks. When a correspondent from the New York *Tribune* named E.V. Smalley came to Washington, Georgia, for an interview, Toombs arranged for him to meet the grand cyclops of the Ku Klux Klan. The grand cyclops was actually mild mannered Dr. Henry F. Andrews, editor of the Washington *Gazette*. Toombs had apparently arranged for Dr. Andrews to tell the reporter all kinds of lurid stories about the Klan's antics, including a dozen or so murders Dr. Andrews was supposed to have committed.

The reporter, shaken by the meeting, crossed the town square and met with Toombs in his office a few hours later. Toombs did his best to live up to his unreconstructed rebel image. He blustered and fumed about Northern Democrats, Radicals, Republicans, and how the South would again make war on the North. The Republican Party was composed of "thieves, robbers, and prison convicts." The Union Army was "a horde of mercenaries, marauders, and thieves." He said most of the members of the Georgia legislature would never go back to the counties they represented because they would be hanged.

Toombs also objected to blacks having the vote. He believed since their livelihood depended on those who owned property — such as himself— their votes could be manipulated.

There was no harm in blacks voting as long as the whites all belonged to one party, he said. But he feared the time when whites would divide and blacks would be courted by "the lower classes of white men." If this coalition formed a majority it might attack the interests of the "landed proprietors"—like himself. When asked if slavery would ever return, Toombs thought not. It would have died out eventually because it would have ceased to be profitable, he said. And profit was the bottom line. "There never was any question of morals connected with slavery," he said. "It was only a matter of profit and loss."

The interview ended after an hour or so and the reporter walked into the street thinking he had met an acrimonious and insolent rebel who disdained the North and everything and everyone in it. The reporter was shocked when he ran into Toombs a little while later and Toombs invited him back to his house. Toombs introduced him to his family, his servants, and spent the next few hours charming him with tales of his travels in Europe, funny stories about his days in Washington, and his vast knowledge of history, and especially the history of the struggle for liberty. "Once at home the manner of the General changed at once and instead of the bitter political partisan he became the genial host," the reporter wrote in his story. "When I took my leave I should have concluded that the General had, in our first conversation, amused himself by astounding me with extreme views he did not entertain, had I not heard from many sources of his violent reactionary opinions."[35]

A few days later, Toombs gave a similar interview to a correspondent from the New York *Herald*. But the *Herald* reporter did not fall for Toombs' Southern charm. As he asked around, the reporter found that everyone admired Toombs for his oratory and his generosity. But Toombs was caricaturing himself by his own rhetoric. He would never again be a party leader, they said. He was "behind his time" and "too old ever again to come up with the level of the age."[36]

Scaring Northern reporters with outrageous stories, whether true or not, may have been good fun to Toombs. But Toombs indeed had close connections with the Klan. His son-in-law, Dudley DuBose, organized the first Klan cell in Wilkes County and was the grand titan in Toombs' old congressional district. John C. Reed, who became friends with Toombs when Toombs was an old man, helped establish the Klan in Oglethorpe County and became the grand giant. There is no evidence that Toombs himself ever wore a hood, rode with, or was a member of the Klan. But he certainly approved of their purposes and probably knew a great deal about their activities. Toombs told a reporter that the Klan was the "natural protest of an oppressed people against tyranny" and that the Klan "tempered" the "despotism" of the Radicals.[37]

One Radical Toombs was delighted to get rid of was Governor Rufus Bullock. Governor Bullock secretly resigned and left the state in October of 1871. Toombs had been accusing Bullock of corruption at every turn. Rumors swirled that the governor had squandered state funds, bribed favorite papers, sold pardons, and mismanaged the Western and Atlantic Railroad, which was owned by the state, into near bankruptcy. When an investigation was conducted into the administration, Toombs donated his legal services to the legislative committee. The work of the committee eventually extradited Bullock back to Georgia and Toombs personally drew up the affidavit for his arrest. Bullock was tried for embezzlement in 1876 but found not guilty.[38]

In January of 1872, Georgia Democrats put James M. Smith in the governor's chair. But Toombs was not impressed with the current crop of party leaders. "The legislature is feeble, raw, irresolute and easily led away, but I think the majority in the House is patriotic and honest," he wrote to Stephens. "I think this class has scarcely a majority in the Senate."

Toombs otherwise occupied himself by traveling, practicing law, arguing cases before the Georgia Supreme Court, and giving the occasional stump speech. When not involved in state politics, he involved himself in politics at the University of Georgia where he tried to get his friend, Charles C. Jones, appointed as a department chair. Toombs also helped Stephens out of a financial bind. Stephens had invested twenty thousand dollars into a Democratic newspaper called the Atlanta *Sun*. The paper constantly lost money and was finally bought by the Atlanta *Constitution*. Stephens was in debt up to his ears. When Toombs asked him who he owed money to, Stephens reeled off a long list of names as Toombs furiously scribbled on a piece of paper. A few hours later, Toombs returned with twenty thousand dollars worth of receipts in his hat. He had bought the outstanding debts and poured them out in Stephens' living room.[39]

But Toombs could do nothing to comfort his friend during the summer of 1872. On July 14, Linton Stephens died after a sudden illness. Toombs made the announcement the next morning in the Georgia Supreme Court. After a few opening remarks about Linton's life, "his feelings seemed to master him," one reporter wrote, "and he was obliged to take his seat." Alex Stephens was inconsolable. Linton was his half-brother, most trusted confidant and closest advisor. Stephens was so distressed that he could not even attend Linton's funereal. "My God," Toombs wrote to his friend, "what can I do but mingle my tears with yours?"[40]

In the meantime, Toombs managed to pick a nasty public fight with Joe Brown. It began in 1842 when Charles Mitchell left the city of Atlanta five acres of property to be used as a railroad station. Twenty-five years later, Joe Brown's law firm filed a suit against the state on behalf of Mitchell's heirs claiming the deed was never clear. So the family wanted to buy the property back. However, the value of the property had increased tremendously. The legislature rejected the Mitchell family's petition several times. But Governor Bullock's regime passed a bill that allowed the property to be sold back to the family for $37,000 instead of the hundreds of thousands of dollars it was reputed to be worth. Ironically, the property had been bought by one of Toombs' business partners, Hannibal Kimball.

Toombs claimed that Joe Brown had lobbied the Georgia legislature on behalf of the Mitchell family while he was in the state Senate. Toombs also claimed that during his short tenure as chief justice, Brown tried to influence the Georgia Supreme Court on a related case that would benefit the Mitchell family. It was a clear conflict of interest if not outright corruption. "It is a high crime in the highest judicial officer of the State to bring his influence to bear in any way to control the action of the Legislature," Toombs moralized.[41]

Brown did not deny the charges but responded by calling Toombs a poltroon, a liar, and publishing a stilted conversation he supposedly had with a Colonel J.C. Nicholls who was representing Toombs in the matter. Brown implied that Toombs, through Colonel Nicholls, challenged him to a duel. Then Toombs left Atlanta right away. Toombs "responds in *newspapers*," Brown sniffed. "I leave the public to judge who is the poltroon, and whether General Toombs preferred *newspaper* artillery to heavier metal."[42]

Nothing ever came of the duel between Bob Toombs and Joe Brown. There may have never been a challenge in the first place. At the time that Colonel Nicholls was supposedly in Brown's office relaying Toombs' challenge, Toombs was so sick in bed that he was barely able to sit up. He was so incapacitated that he was unable to attend to any business. Journalist Henry Grady later recalled that Toombs made no preparations for a duel. On the other hand, Brown supposedly wrote a new will, put his affairs in order, resigned from his church, and spent a lot of time target practicing. "I should not be surprised if he drew a diagram of General Toombs," Grady wrote, "and marked off with square and compass the exact spot he wanted to hit." Toombs said nothing about the affair. He simply preferred to ignore his critics. "I am rarely in the habit of paying the least attention to reports of my speeches by my opponents," he wrote. "It would be a labor compared to which that of Sysiphus was pleasant exercise."[43]

By the summer of 1872, even Republicans had grown tired of the stench of corruption in Ulysses S. Grant's administration. A group of reformers calling themselves Liberal Republicans met in Cincinnati and to everyone's surprise nominated New York *Tribune* editor Horace Greeley for president. When the Democrats met in Baltimore a few weeks later, they seconded the nomination and adjourned after only six hours. The regular Republicans, of course, renominated Grant. Stephens said choosing between Grant and Greeley was like choosing between hemlock and strychnine. Toombs did not care for hemlock or strychnine either and made only one major speech about agriculture at the Selma, Alabama, Agricultural Fair and that was after the election. He barely mentioned politics, saying only that Reconstruction had meant only protection for thieves and carpetbaggers.[44]

Grant beat Greeley in an overwhelming victory and Republicans maintained control of Congress. But Toombs was showing more interest in policy than politics. He lobbied the legislature for a bill that "harmonized" denominational colleges with the University of Georgia. He also probably lobbied to get Alexander Stephens elected to the U.S. Senate. But Stephens had sermonized too much against both Grant and Greeley through his editorials in the Atlanta *Sun* and was defeated soundly by the Confederate hero John B. Gordon. The votes were barely counted before Toombs met with state party leaders to get Stephens nominated for a vacancy in the U.S. House of Representatives. To satisfy local reporters and for the sake of his image, Toombs pretended that he hated the idea. "Let the [Goddamned] Government go to Hell," Toombs barked. "Alex Stephens is too good a man to have anything to do with it."[45]

Stephens was elected in February of 1873. Toombs was relatively quiet and stayed away from politics. Perhaps he had decided to let Stephens go his own way politically. Stephens favored working within the political system to conserve what was left of the old South. Toombs preferred to remain outside as a gadfly. Instead, he concentrated his energy on his law practice.[46]

Toombs conducted much of his law practice and business affairs from his rooms at Kimball House, an elegant 317 room luxury hotel in the heart of downtown Atlanta. The Yankee financier Hannibal I. Kimball had built the massive hotel in 1870 for $675,000. Although Kimball was the hated Governor Bullock's chief money man, was investigated numerous times, and considered in the 1870s to be the walking definition of carpetbagger, Toombs held a ninth interest in the hotel. He could usually be found in the lobby of the Kimball House holding court with a phalanx of admirers as he conducted business, gave pungent interviews to scribbling reporters, or just telling funny stories.[47]

Most mornings, he settled his bulk on a couch in the rotunda. He had grown plump, his curly gray hair long and rumpled, an unlit cigar perpetually in his mouth. People who did not know him took him for a man of means, perhaps a well-to-do farmer or a shaggy justice of the peace. He usually pulled a newspaper from his pocket and read until one of his thousands of acquaintances stopped by and said "Good morning, General" or "How are you, General?" Before long a crowd gathered, letting Bob Toombs regale them with anecdotes, witticisms, and sarcastic remarks. Toombs was in his early sixties and his athletic oratory had lost a step or two, but listeners still followed him down the streets of Atlanta waiting to hear what he would say next. "When he is in the humor," a reporter wrote, "and perhaps mellowed by a drop or two, his mind throws off the most brilliant witticisms which are duly appreciated by his convulsed audience."[48]

But there was little satisfaction in just spinning anecdotes for admirers and reporters. In September, the economy crashed when Jay Cooke's brokerage firm failed. Banks and investment houses closed and locked their doors and the stock exchange remained shut down for ten days. The Panic of 1873 plunged the nation into a deep depression. So Toombs took to the stump. In October he spoke in Warren County and endorsed the Granger movement, the loosely organized groups that lobbied for the interests of rural and agricultural communities. He urged the people to organize Grange and farmers' associations. He urged them to organize against oppressive railroad monopolies, to organize against the abuses of corporations, to organize against "the corruptions of designing politicians." He urged the people to send a message to their representatives that Georgia wanted a new constitution. "I am with you in the fight," he said, "and will not hesitate to accept the aid of the devil in the struggle against the enemies of my country!"[49]

A few weeks later, the Wilkes County Superior court adjourned early to let Toombs make a few more remarks. He lambasted the financial structure of the country. He condemned the new currency that had been put on the gold standard, the tariff, corporations, and the system that forced planters to buy their supplies at inflated prices but sell their cotton at the specie rates of European markets. He called for a return to the financial system of old: "A just and sufficient tariff for the purposes of revenue only, a repeal of the present National Bank Laws, a re-enactment of the *ante-bellum* banking privileges." Above all, Toombs called for a convention to draft a new state constitution.

Robert Toombs later in life. Taken sometime between 1870 and 1880. Library of Congress, LC-DIG-cwpbh-03981 (available online).

Whether Toombs' call to return to the good old days was realistic or not, his cries for a new constitution struck a chord. "The speech of General Toombs calling for a convention to remodel the Constitution of the State found an echo in many hearts," the Atlanta *Constitution* wrote. "The coming generation will do him justice. The annals of Georgia will bear the name of no greater or truer man."[50]

In January, Toombs addressed the Georgia legislature. He spelled out his vision for a new constitution that mandated a balanced budget — except in cases where the state had to once again defend itself— and annual elections for all state officials. "Every people have a right to their own organic law," he said. "Did you make the present Constitution? No! It is the handiwork of negroes, thieves, and Yankees," he cried. "We have government and no Constitution." The standing room only crowd frequently interrupted Toombs with cheers and applause. His vision of reviving the old antebellum constitution was as impractical as fighting the war again, but drafting a new one was a popular idea. One of the members introduced a bill calling for a constitutional convention the next day. The bill was defeated but the seed had been planted.[51]

In the meantime, Toombs inadvertently made a lot of trouble for Alexander Stephens. Once again it involved a lawsuit filed by Toombs against the state-owned Western and Atlantic Railroad and Toombs' vendetta against Joe Brown and Rufus Bullock. The details began in 1870 when the Western and Atlantic Railroad ran up a quarter million dollar deficit that left the state in debt. So the Radical legislature passed a bill to lease the road for $25,000 a month. Several of Georgia's big money men, including Joe Brown, Rufus Bullock and Benjamin Hill signed on with the company.

So did Alexander Stephens. He bought a few small shares in the company. At the time, Toombs was appalled. He did not object to his friend making a buck or two, "but I have had the most invincible repugnance to the whole scheme." Toombs believed the operation was a conspiracy designed to drive out competition and create a railroad monopoly. "Of course you knew nothing of these things," he wrote. But he chided Stephens for being associated with such a shady deal. "I must candidly say while I look upon your own conduct as perfectly honourable [sic] and free from any reproach I did regret seeing your name among the lessees." Perhaps because of Toombs' displeasure, Stephens had second thoughts and transferred his shares to the state a few days later.[52]

In March of 1874, Toombs had a conversation with Governor Smith and the matter of the bonds came up. The governor told Toombs it looked like Stephens' bonds had not been legally transferred to the state thanks to the chicanery of Bullock, Brown, and company. Brown had recently petitioned the governor to declare the bonds forfeited and urged the state to turn the profits over to his company with interest. After hearing the story, Toombs immediately filed suit in Fulton County Superior Court on behalf of Alexander Stephens to collect the money.

When Stephens read about the lawsuit in the Washington, D.C., papers, he was furious. Toombs had not only gone behind his back but made it appear that Stephens was trying to reclaim funds he had donated to the state. Any hint of a conflict of interest or hypocrisy gave ammunition to his opponents and made Stephens politically vulnerable. Stephens immediately had his nephew publicly withdraw the suit. Then Stephens fired off a dispatch to Specks, a reporter at the Atlanta *Herald*, saying Toombs had no authority to file the suit. Toombs wired back to the *Herald* implying that Specks was a liar and that Stephens had given his "express authority and consent" for the litigation.[53]

"I very deeply regret, indeed, am profoundly pained that you did not write to me, or let me know that you intended to bring the case referred to in your telegram before you brought it," Stephens wrote to Toombs in a stiff, formal letter. "If you had, I think I should have been saved that deep pang which ever with me attends the reverence of the ties of long & devoted friendship which has so deeply affected me in the last two days upon your unqualified charge of falsehood against me."

Stephens explained in excruciating detail why he had donated his investment to the state. He recalled conversations with Toombs over the matter. But they had only talked about the legal status of his bonds, not a lawsuit. "Now if you had written to me, as I think you ought to have done, what you intended to do after Gov.[sic] Smith had come to the conclusion which you say he did on the subject," Stephens lectured, "I feel assured I could have satisfied you that there was no understanding on my part in any of our conversations that in any event whatever you were to institute suit in my name for the recovery of my interest in that lease which had been absolutely relinquished by me to the state."[54]

Toombs was shocked by his friend's anger. "Your dispatch took me by surprise and gave me great pain," he wrote back. "I retained it without reply for consideration about eight hours, and after mature reflection I deemed it due to truth and my own honor to accept the issue thus tendered by you and to repeat what I [had] written." Not for one moment had Toombs expected Stephens to profit from his action. Toombs filed the suit to benefit the state and to keep the "spoliators" from getting the money. He also recalled the conversations with Stephens. But his conclusion was different. "We both agreed that if the title was not in the State, it was in you[r name], and in the latter event suit would have to be brought in your name."

Toombs admitted he should have alerted Stephens to his actions. But he did not understand Stephens' objection. There was no intention of undercutting his friend. "If I had remembered what never took place, or you had forgotten what did," he wrote, "or for any other reason desired it, a flash of lightning from you would have dismissed the bill in half an hour, without making issues of fact with me in the newspapers." But under no circumstances was he going to withdraw the suit.

"I very deeply regret that any thing should have occurred to break our long and, certainly on my part, sincere friendship; but I do not feel that it is my work," he wrote. "I have suffered numerous and great wrongs and injuries for my disinterested efforts to serve faithfully in office and out of office my day and generation." But he was sure he was doing the right thing for the state. His enemies had stung him before, "but [they] have failed thus far to relax my efforts in the cause of the right. I would rather receive and suffer the reproaches of every man in the world than deserve them from the meanest of mankind."[55]

Toombs and Stephens had had their disagreements over the years. But the disagreements were mostly political. They had argued vehemently during the secession crisis, but it had never affected their friendship. This was the only time they had ever questioned each other's integrity. It was a challenge to a deep and affectionate relationship that had lasted over forty years. They were not estranged, but it was not until July that they completely restored their good relations. Both men published a series of letters and accounts of what happened in the Augusta *Chronicle*. The matter was capped off when Stephens received a letter he had written to Toombs that may have contained an apology. Stephens had inadvertently addressed the letter to Toombs at Washington, D.C., instead of Washington, Georgia, and there it sat in the dead letter office for several months until an alert postal worker forwarded it to Stephens in Crawfordville.

Stephens promptly sent the letter to Toombs along with an invitation to Crawfordville. When Toombs read the letter, he "lost all unpleasant feeling, and went immediately to see Mr. Stephens," a reporter wrote. "Their meeting was not simply cordial, but was deeply affecting." Toombs spent most of the day with his old friend talking over the misunderstanding. Then they drafted an announcement for the newspapers assuring Georgians that the "cordial friendship which had for nearly forty years bound them together by a tie as strong as brotherly attachment, until this short interruption, is again perfectly restored."[56]

In May, Toombs traveled to Washington, D.C., During his stay, he visited with President Grant at the White House. The two men had little in common and were political opposites. Toombs supposedly told Grant that he made it a rule "when arriving in a city to call first and pay my respects to the Chief of Police." But the visit passed off well and Toombs behaved himself. This was not the case when he attended a dinner given by Senator John C. Gordon. Several Washington dignitaries attended, including Mississippi senator L.Q.C. Lamar. The month before, Senator Lamar had given a moving tribute in the Senate to Charles Sumner who had died in March. Sumner was still a hated name in the South and Toombs began provoking Senator Lamar for making the speech. Toombs kept at Lamar until it got so bad that the ladies finally excused themselves and withdrew to the parlor.[57]

Finally, Lamar had had enough. He said that Toombs' trip to the White House was "crawling to the seat of power, against his eulogy of a dead enemy." An argument broke out. One witness said that he had never seen "such a scoring from one man to another." Finally, when Lamar finished berating Toombs, Toombs simply said "Lamar, you surprise me."[58]

Toombs may have been in his cups; it may have just been a spirited argument; or perhaps a misunderstanding between the two men. Toombs and Lamar were colleagues and had known each other for years. But rumors of a fight and a possible duel circulated until Toombs let Georgia newspapers know that the whole affair had been exaggerated. It was not a quarrel, he said, just a difference of opinion between two friends. Lamar had simply asked what he thought of the eulogy to Sumner and Toombs told him. "This is the substantial molehill of fact, out of which scribblers and gossipers have made a colossal mountain of fabrication," he told the Atlanta *Herald*. "They perceived a gnat and swore it an eagle."[59]

After his return from Washington, D.C., Toombs spent a good deal of time making personal appearances. He was the featured speaker at the reunion of the 49th Georgia Regiment, he was one of the judges at the debates at the University of Georgia commencement, and he spent some time quelling rumors that he was campaigning for a political office. When he was asked to run for Congress, he refused. "I hate the Government of the United States," he told the Georgia *Herald*, "and would give my life to overthrow it." He would refuse to sit with the men in Congress and they would soon throw him out anyway "for I should rise at the first opportunity, and denounce as utterly fraudulent the infamous [Fourteenth and Fifteenth] amendments [sic]." As for his legacy, Toombs was happy with the things he had done before the war and was content "to stand on that."[60]

He kept with those themes in September when he made a speech denouncing the federal government for sending troops to Louisiana to quell political violence over the controversial Radical governor William P. Kellogg. Standing on top of a freight box, Toombs said he hoped the people of Louisiana could wrest themselves "from the tyranny of the worst government on earth, a government which had been imposed on the white people of that state by fraud and violence." As usual, he criticized the Fourteenth and Fifteenth Amendments and blamed all Southern ills on "Radicals, scalawags, and niggers." Toombs again denied he was seeking political office. He was not running for governor, he said. He had served the people of Georgia for thirty years and that was enough. Yet he felt he owed them one more duty. He again called for a constitutional convention to abolish "that spawn of reconstruction [sic] — our present Radical-Scalawag-Nigger-Constitution."[61]

Toombs had indeed had his fill of being a politician. A political office would have been his for the asking. But the role of "outlaw" and "rebel" suited him better than congressman, senator, or even governor. He was not included in the general amnesty passed by Congress in May of 1872 and he never applied for a pardon. When a Northerner asked him why not, he said: "Pardon for what? When I pardon you may be [sic] I will then ask you to pardon me." He was content to make money at his law practice, land speculation, and tend to his farms. Others could do battles on the floors of various legislative houses. Still, he watched politics closely and jeered or cheered the candidates. When Stephens gave a speech in Washington, Georgia, Toombs urged the audience to support him even though they could not vote for him (Toombs and Stephens still lived in different districts). Toombs had no faith in the government and did not believe the South could obtain "justice by peaceable means," he told the crowd. But he was more than willing "to let Mr. Stephens try." If anyone could do it, he believed, Stephens could. That was about as much enthusiasm as he could muster. Toombs was completely disillusioned with the American political system — and the nation. "Nothing can arrest the onward tide in favor of the [D]emocracy [sic] but their own folly," he yawned when the Democrats won the majority in the House of Representatives for the first time since 1860, "and I am afraid they will supply plenty of that."[62]

In March of 1875 Toombs came down with pneumonia. According to the papers, he worked late into the evening at his Washington law office and let the fire go out. He caught a chill and the next day suffered a high fever and pains in his chest. It was so severe that there were reports he was not expected to recover. But he was not too sick to read the papers and seethe from his bed. When Congress passed the Civil Rights Bill that allowed freedmen to use public facilities such as restaurants, theaters, and public transportation, he was disgusted.[63]

"As I expected, the Civil Rights bill passed," he wrote to Alexander Stephens. "It will accomplish its intended work, raise rows, and give Grant excuse for calling in troops, especially about election times." But Toombs had withdrawn from political life and had little interest "in which of the two factions of the North triumphs, except I wish the success of the one that speediest brings a change in public affairs and the government of the country," he wrote. "I have no interest in men or parties who recognize the 14th and 15th amendments to the Constitution, and I suppose when the country takes one set of them they will soon wish they had taken the other."[64]

By April, he was able to go back to work. But he kept an uncharacteristically low profile and concentrated on his legal cases. He surfaced in June to publicly refuse participating in Atlanta's first Fourth of July celebration since the war. "When the principles proclaimed by our ancestors in 1776 ... shall have been established, I will then, if on this side of the grave, rejoice with you," he grumbled. But for now, "I cannot shake hands with those who dug it, and filled it with the bloody corpses of the brave and true, over the bloody chasm which engulfs also the principles of 1776. I want no fraternity with States or people without liberty or equality." Instead, Toombs and Julia took their annual vacation in White Sulphur Springs, West Virginia.[65]

There had even been talk of another European vacation, but they were back in Atlanta in September. His only major political speech came a month later when he addressed a crowd in Warrenton. As printed in the papers, the speech was a dry dissertation on the merits of the federal government keeping the currency on a gold or silver standard instead of issuing greenbacks. To Toombs, anything but the gold or silver standard was unconstitutional. The value of something should not be a political issue. "The country does not want Republican rulers or Democratic rulers, but needs the ascendancy of Democratic principles," he said. "It must return to the old landmarks." He called for federal, state, and local governments to quit spending so much money, regulate railroads, and dismiss the standing army. "Restore the Government to the people," he pleaded. "Let the Government perform faithfully its great mission of administering justice and protecting property and let the people alone." For good measure, he once again called for a state convention to write a new constitution.[66]

The speech was the plea of an old man to return to the good old days. Toombs was out of touch with the people of Georgia and the needs of the New South. He was still a mighty voice, but if he had taken political office, he would have been, like his friend Alexander Stephens, a mere vestige of the old South, a sort of museum piece with a large following but little political influence. In Congress, Stephens continued arguing about the Constitution long after the issue had been settled. On the other hand, Toombs' issues were still relevant — federal authority versus state sovereignty, fiscal policy, regulation of public service corporations — but his political positions were as obsolete as powdered wigs and pantaloons. Ante-bellum fiscal policies were no solution for a rapidly industrializing economy obsessed with money and efficiency. Unlike Joe Brown or Herschel Johnson, Toombs never overcame his principles and did not adapt to new political realities until it was too late.

Nevertheless, he was still active behind the scenes in Georgia politics. Several bills to call a constitutional convention were floating around and Toombs took the opportunity to advance the cause. In January, he addressed the Georgia legislature. At the rostrum, Toombs told the packed galleries that he had been pondering a strange question: should state representatives, the servants of the people, give the voters a chance to change their organic laws? The politicians had always found excuses not to hold a convention. But "the greatest thing that could happen to the state of Georgia would be to have a democratic triumph by the sacrifice of democratic principles."

The present constitution was not made by Georgians, but by "poor, ignorant savages led by rogues." If you have a convention, he said, "I can make you a constitution by which the people will rule and the nigger will never be heard of!" Yankees had imposed this constitution upon the state. After the war, the Yankees "devastated, robbed, and ruined this country, but there is plenty good stealing here yet!" Thus Toombs told Georgians that they ought to abolish their constitution because they did not make it. "Who made it? Niggers and thieves! [Loud cheers]"

Toombs went on and on, condemning and attacking blacks, carpetbaggers, scalawags, Republicans, Northern Democrats, and anyone else with whom he disagreed. The question, said Toombs, was up to Georgians. "They say the people don't want it," he cried. "Who dares say so...? If the people don't want it they will vote it down. Why don't you put it to the people...? There are interests and men and corporations feeding upon the industries of the people who do not want them to say." Toombs promised that he would use his last strength to "speak for and raise the flag with the people."[67]

But Toombs' diatribe did more harm than good. The tone of the speech was a horrible miscalculation. Eighteen seventy-six was an election year and the last thing Northern or Southern Democrats needed was fiery rhetoric by an unreconstructed outlaw like Toombs. Democratic newspapers skewered him, even in the South. The Savannah *Morning News* said Toombs killed any hopes for a convention by his "imprudent utterances." The Memphis *Avalanche* called him a "hurtful political agitator." The Petersburg, Virginia, *News* said Toombs was an enemy and serious detriment to the South. The best taunt came from the New York *Times*: "One is almost inclined to wish at times that an asylum for political lunatics could be established in some unhealthy region, and we must confess that it would not be difficult to suggest at least a dozen fit and proper persons be received into it, by way of keeping Robert Toombs company." The Georgia legislature, determined to avoid controversial issues in an election year, declared their support for the Fourteenth and Fifteenth Amendments and killed every constitutional convention bill.[68]

Toombs was unfazed, at least publicly. He went about his law practice and even traveled to Washington, D.C., in April to plead a case before the Supreme Court. In *The Central Railroad and Banking Company v. State of Georgia,* the legal question concerned whether Georgia could collect more taxes than the one-half percent the legislature imposed when the Central Banking and Railroad Company was chartered in 1833. For forty years, the legislature had drawn up a series of reorganizations and new charters. When the legislature again redrew the charter in 1874, it consolidated a few smaller railroads and called for an assessment of the Central Railroad's assets. In effect, the legislation was imposing a higher tax on a powerful corporation.

The Central Railroad paid only the half percent required by the old law on grounds that the state could not preempt the old charter. The State of Georgia argued that the charter could be repealed or modified as the legislature saw fit. Toombs had worked the case on behalf of the state — often with no fee — all the way through the court system. He argued that no state would write a contract that gave away its sovereignty as the Central Railroad Company claimed that Georgia had. Even if a state willingly bound itself to such a contract "even to suicide," Georgia had not done so. Toombs claimed that when the legislature consolidated some of the smaller railroads, a new corporation had been formed and was subject to the laws established on that date. Toombs also cited a wagonload of legal precedents from the Georgia lower courts.

Justice William Strong wrote the opinion for the court. He ruled against Georgia on the grounds that the railroad still had the rights granted to it under the original charter. The legislature could not impose a tax of more than one-half percent on the company's assets. However, the opinion also stated that the Central Railroad and Banking Company could not claim exemptions on the assets of the smaller railroads that the legislature consolidated in 1874.[69]

So Toombs returned to Georgia with a partial legal victory. He worked in his law office and paid frequent visits to Alex Stephens, who was so sick that many of his friends feared for his life. But Stephens pulled through and was re-nominated for his seat in Congress. When asked, Toombs said the people would keep voting for Stephens "until he does die and then they will vote for his administrator, if he names one in his will." Toombs also supported Dr. William H. Felton, a Methodist preacher who had broken away from the Democrats and won the congressional seat in the Seventh District as an independent.[70]

As always, he was scornful of party authority. "We have tried this gang of conventions when they put Greeley on us," he fumed. "They ask us again to try them with [William] Tilden. I decline the offer now as I did then." When Tilden published a letter saying he would veto any bills to pay "rebel debt," compensate former slave owners for the loss of their slaves, or any losses they suffered during the war, Toombs felt vindicated. "Tilden's letter is infamous, and I am glad I committed myself from the day of his nomination (and as to that before his nomination) not to vote for him," Toombs bragged to Stephens. "I never hoped for anything good from an old Van Buren free-soiler trained in Tammany Hall and Wall Street." But Toombs thought the fate of the South was already sealed. "The mongrel crew who call themselves Democrats have the control of the 'organized democracy' would as [have] Be[el]zebub as God, and [prefer] Mammon to either if thereby they could perchance reach the treasury."[71]

Toombs accurately predicted that the Republicans would lose the popular vote. But he also thought they would get enough electoral votes to win the presidency "and if they do not they [will] carry the returns or count out enough Southern votes to put them in and the count[r]y will accept it as readily as the Romans did the consulship of Caligula's horse,—'All at once (says a great historian) the Romans became another people.' This is our fate."[72]

Toombs' prediction eerily foretold the future. When election day ended on November 7, Rutherford B. Hayes went to bed believing he had lost the presidency to Samuel Tilden. Tilden had received 184 electoral votes and 250,000 more popular votes than Hayes. But the electoral votes from Florida, South Carolina, and Louisiana could not be authenticated. Grant, fearing an outbreak of violence, sent federal troops into the disputed states and into the streets of Washington, D.C. Toombs claimed the Republicans were fomenting another revolution. "The Constitution was overthrown by the North before the war by their frequent violations of that instrument and their constant efforts ever since to govern the country in their own interest in defiance of its provisions," he wrote to Stephens. Democrats were simply standing by and letting the Republicans overwhelm the Constitution. But Toombs was still willing to stick with the party and was "willing to do anything I can (but wait) to restore good government." It was obvious, to Toombs at least, that Republicans were trying to maintain control of the government by force and intimidation. "A man must be as blind as a bat at noonday not to see in the military events in Louis[iana], Florida and South Carolina and the concentration of troops in Washington the whole policy and purposes of the Radicals," he wrote to Stephens. "They can have but one meaning, and that is to hold the government by force if their frauds fail to secure it to them." Hayes was appointed to office four months later when a special commission was formed and political independent David Davis voted at the last minute with the Republicans.[73]

The dire political situation and a gloomy Christmas, complete with rain, sleet, snow, and a strong northeaster got to Toombs. Julia's health had taken a turn for the worse and "all the rest of us with colds and the blues. The state is quiet and sad, money matters bad, generally apprehensive of the future and becoming daily more restless under the present." But in January, his spirits were rejuvenated when a bill to call a constitutional convention sailed through Georgia's House of Representatives. A few weeks later it slipped through the state Senate.[74]

Toombs was looking forward to the convention. Yet he was still not interested in running for office. "It is out of the question, sir, out of the question. I am out of politics," he declared when asked by a reporter if he had any desire to be in Congress again. "I have had my day. I have gotten old, and age should be respected, even in politics."

When the reporter pressed Toombs about serving Georgia's constituents, Toombs retorted, "Sir, do you expect me to fight skunks?"

"You have engaged in such battles," the reporter replied.

"Oh! That was in the old time. Give me a liberty pole, and I'll stir up the entire nestfull for you; but I am growing old. I am harassed with clients. I have to run away from boldness."

But when the conversation turned to the convention, the old fires were immediately re-lit. He had been fighting for seven long years to rewrite the constitution. "Humanity is given over to decrepitude and decay," he said, "but the fundamental law lasts forever."

The reporter asked Toombs about being a delegate at the convention.

"I can't refuse," said the old patriarch. "I am a Georgian. I have the good of my people and posterity to look after—I have grandchildren. No, sir—I can't refuse."[75]

In March, Toombs traveled to Washington, D.C., to renew a motion for the Supreme Court to again hear arguments for the *Central Railroad and Banking Company v. State of Georgia*. While he was gone, a campaign gathered momentum to elect him as a delegate to the constitutional convention slated to be held that summer. "There is no man in the state whom we should prefere [sic] to see in that convention," gushed the LaGrange *Reporter*. "If his counsels should prevail in that body, the people of Georgia may rest assured that a constitution will be framed in perfect accord with the wishes of the people."[76]

Toombs was ready. "The convention question begins to excite a good deal of public interest in this and some other portions of the State," he wrote to Stephens. "The opposition is mostly secret and is composed of those who wish to [prevent] additional safeguards against legislative burglary in the shape of bonds, state endorsement or other aid to private speculators. I have concluded to go to the convention from this 29th dist[rict]. if one is called and I am elected. It appears to be the general wish of the district...."[77]

A few days later, Toombs composed a letter for publication in which he cheerfully pointed out the flaws in Georgia's constitution. The existing charter was not the act or deed of Georgians, he complained. It had been imposed by force and fraud. "Large numbers of her most worthy, intelligent and virtuous citizens were denied the privilege of even voting for members of the convention," he wrote, "who with but few exceptions were hungry, hostile, alien enemies, domestic traitors, and ignorant, vicious, emancipated slaves." The constitution subordinated the states to the federal government, consolidated the power of the federal government, and coerced the state into allegiance with the United States. "We deny it," Toombs railed. "Let us assert the truth and maintain it when we can, or leave the truth to be defended by our children and children's children whenever opportunity offers."

The governor's term was too long. The judiciary was inadequate. The state senate was "a mockery and a nuisance." Giant corporations threatened free representative government. These corporations had harnessed steam and electric power and contributed benefits and blessings to mankind. But they also brought new dangers to good government and to society. "They first absorb individual capital — all right enough — then all they can borrow, still right enough, and next the treasuries of municipal corporations, public lands and all other public property, then the treasuries and credit of the national and state governments," he wrote. "This is all wrong, violates justice, transfers the sweat of the poor to the coffers of the rich, appropriates the public fund to private use and profit, and opens the flood gates of fraud and public demoralization."

So what was the remedy? "Let us make a new constitution," he urged, "and by that constitution make the depository of the public treasury and public credit political burglar proof and put the key in the pockets of the people by declaring that no debt shall ever be created by the legislature or binding upon the State, except for the public defense." Toombs advocated a revision of the homestead law to make estates more secure for women and children. He advocated disposing of all future bond questions. Any penal codes should be left for the legislature. Moving the capital from Atlanta back to Milledgeville or some other city was "not worth a thought."[78]

The letter "did as much to fire the heart of North Georgia as any other instrumentality," one reporter gushed. "It was a glorious letter, the very concentration of thought and argument." As for Toombs, he and Julia took their summer vacation in Hot Springs, Arkansas. The steamy mineral waters of the lower Ozark Mountains obviously agreed with him. He came back to Georgia twenty pounds lighter, in perfect health except for a cataract in his left eye. Toombs told the press this was going to be the last public service of his life. He had trimmed down as if he were an old boxer getting in shape for the last but greatest match of his career.[79]

Toombs was nominated as a delegate to the convention in May and easily won the election in June. The convention convened on July 11 in Atlanta with 194 delegates crowded into the hot Capitol Building. The convention was organized into thirteen committees each with nine members. Toombs chaired the Committee on the Legislative Department and the Final Committee of Revision. Despite the sixty-seven-year-old Toombs' earlier protests that he was through with politics, July and August of 1877 was very much like sitting in Congress or the Georgia legislature. Toombs debated, offered motions, objected to amendments, voted, argued, wrote law, and was generally in the natural environment he claimed not to miss: the clash and camaraderie of politics.

Toombs more or less accomplished the goals he spelled out in his public letter three months before. "All this convention has to do is to establish a few fundamental principles and leave the other matters to the legislature and the people," he said. The first order of business was restructuring the legislature. Toombs wanted each county to elect a senator every two years. The current senators, who were elected every four years, "now represents nobody," he complained. "They are not accountable to the people ... and there is an understanding that they are not to come back again." He wanted the representatives in the lower house to run for election every year. "In former times every man went before his constituents every year, and if he was worthy they returned him, and if he was unworthy they condemned him." In the end, both senators and representatives were elected for two-year terms.[80]

Toombs also had his say about the judiciary. He wanted the State Supreme Court to be enlarged from three to five judges. He also advocated taking the appointment of judges away from the governor and giving it to the legislature. Toombs said he would not object if some types of people in Georgia could be trusted to make wise decisions, meaning of course freedmen. Toombs' thought former slaves had to be governed as any other "inferior race." Black people had to be ruled "by the men who have the brains, the wealth, and land. In behalf of the poor African," he said, "I would save him from himself." Toombs was deservedly criticized for his elitist and racist position. When one member asked how he had the audacity to refuse the people the right to select their own judges, Toombs replied: "I dare do anything that is right. It is not a reproach to the people to say that they are not able to do all the work of a complex government." Toombs partially got his way. The Supreme Court remained with three judges, but Article VI, Section II, Part II mandated that judges would be elected by the legislature.[81]

Toombs had also declared that the Homestead Act needed to be revised. He waded in a week before the convention closed. After fixing the homestead exemption at sixteen hundred dollars, a debate broke out as to whether a wife should be allowed to consent to the waiver. Toombs maintained that it was an outrage for "an improvident man ruthlessly to tear away the protection without the consent of that wife for whom it was reared." Toombs' protections were written into the homestead clause of the constitution and specifically directed that a wife must give her consent if a husband liquidated an estate. "His speech upon the subject was one of the finest he has yet made in the Convention," the Augusta *Chronicle* wrote. "Cool and dispassionate, yet bearing upon its utterances traces of deep feeling and pardonable sentimentality, this effort made a profound impression."[82]

Another subject close to Toombs' heart was nullifying state bonds issued during the Bullock administration. Toombs stated that "no power of heaven or hell" could bind him to pay these bonds. The legislature had declared over and over the bonds were fraudulent. As far as he was concerned this was not a legitimate debt. "When they talk of 'repudiation,'" he said, "I repudiate the debt made without my authority, or that of my Government. If that be repudiation, I am one of the repudiators. What do you say to that?" The bond scheme was just a ploy by scalawags and Northern capitalists on Wall Street to rob the state.

"Those people up there have no purpose except to rob the universe," he said. "They would sell their father's sepulcher and their mother's coffin to get money."

Toombs had spent a good deal of time and legal effort in fighting these bonds over the past several years. "I have examined all the facts pertaining to these claims," he said, "and looking to nothing but the State's integrity, I affirm the matter shall go no further without my strenuous opposition.... Let the bonds die." Once again, the convention saw things Toombs' way. The debts were pronounced "illegal, null and void" in Section XI of Article VII. Toombs bragged that he had "locked the door of the treasury and put the key into the pocket of the people."[83]

Toombs as usual spoke eloquently about the issues during the convention. But he was most passionate about reigning in corporations' influence over the state government. For years railroads had avoided paying taxes, legally and otherwise. For Toombs, this was a fight to settle whether the railroads or the people were going to run the government. He took on these powerful corporations relentlessly and denounced them every chance he got. "The government of corporations is the meanest government on earth," he said. "They're enemies and deserve extirpation." "There has never been a single railroad aided by the state of Georgia which has ever paid a dividend," he insisted. "They wreck and ruin themselves and then plunder the public treasury." On making railroads concede their tax exemptions: "I say unless they surrender this unjust privilege, they should not be granted any others."[84]

Toombs faced stiff opposition from the railroad interests. His opponents accused him of shaking "the pillars upon which the property of one's country rests" and of being more willing to "pull down than build up." Toombs' proposition authorizing private individuals to revoke charters on behalf of the state was quashed. His attempts to authorize the state to amend, annul, or withdraw a corporate franchise was also defeated. But he led the fight to give Georgia the power to regulate railroad rates, to prohibit corporations from claiming immunity to taxes, and to place checks on corporate monopolies.[85]

As usual, Toombs found controversy. He fought against a provision to prevent those who had participated in duels from holding office. And he also tried to prevent the bill of rights from allowing the legislature to prescribe how and when a person could carry weapons. "Let the people bear arms for their own protection," he said, "whether in their boots or wherever they may choose." But the notoriously tight-fisted Toombs found it in his heart to support a specific provision to use taxpayer money to buy artificial limbs for soldiers who had lost arms and legs during the Civil War.[86]

If Toombs had done no more at the convention, he would have walked away a hero, the man of the hour, the man who more than any other wrested the state from the hands of carpetbaggers and corporations and gave it back to Georgia voters. But as the convention drew to a close, the $25,000 that had been appropriated by the legislature ran out. A committee was appointed to investigate how to finance the proceedings. Toombs was outraged that the convention could not authorize additional funds for itself. He said he had frequently heard of the "the Commons starving the King, but he had never heard of the King starving the Commons." If the convention voted itself the funds he claimed he would cash the check before noon that day. If the convention ordered him to pry the Treasury open with a crowbar, he said he would do that, too. "This had not taken place," the Augusta *Chronicle* noted. "The reason of his failure was probably the inability to procure a crow bar."[87]

The day the report was submitted Toombs offered to lend the convention the money from his own pocket. The hall burst into applause when the announcement was read. Then a resolution of thanks was drafted and read aloud. Toombs bowed his head, his face in his hands. The convention arose as a body to thank him. Toombs was visibly moved and tried to fight back tears. "It was a grand act of public spirit and worthy of General Toombs," the correspondent from the Atlanta *Constitution* wrote. "It was much better than 'going into the Treasury with a crow bar.'"[88]

Lending the money to the convention was a grand gesture. It started more talk about giving Toombs the governor's chair or even sending him back to Washington, D.C., as a senator. But he had no interest in public office or even stumping for the ratification of the new constitution. Instead, he went to Baltimore to have the cataract on his left eye examined. The convention had strained Toombs considerably, but he still had "the vigor and bearing of earlier manhood," one Baltimore reporter wrote. From Baltimore, Toombs traveled to New York City with Alexander Stephens where they were wined and dined by ex-mayor Fernando Wood. From there, they went to Washington, D.C. On October 9, Toombs and Stephens pulled up to the White House in their buggy to pay their respects. President Hayes came outside to meet them and briefly exchange pleasantries before Toombs and Stephens drove off.[89]

Throughout his trip, Toombs made it a point to applaud President Hayes for pulling the few remaining troops out of the South and for his conciliatory Southern policy. He called upon Democrats to support Hayes and pronounced him an "honest man and a patriot and those who oppose him were the people who wished to govern the country by sectional hate." Hayes was "a good deal better than Tilden," Toombs said and the South would be wise "to take no stock in the 'fraud cry.'"[90]

By October 13, Toombs was back in Washington, Georgia, fighting off invitations to stump for the new constitution. "It is too early to begin the campaign," he said. "Besides, the people are going to ratify the constitution without chin-music, anyhow." The convention and his trip had taken its toll and he was more interested in recuperating. "I have been much urged to speak in every part of the state on the convention question," he wrote to Stephens in November. But everything was going well so Toombs was content to let the interested parties fight over whether the capitol would be located in Atlanta or Milledgeville, a matter "about which I care but little" as long as "all sides went for the new constitution."

He was also growing more enthusiastic about President Hayes. Hayes believed his lenient Southern policy might seduce former Southern Whigs into the Republican Party, or at least soften their opposition. The strategy seemed to work on Toombs. "He is on a rock which will never fail him as long as he stays there," he wrote to Stephens. "The opposition of the Republicans is simply stupid. Their support of his principle that the army is no longer to be used to overawe or control State governments, and his civil reform policy, would do more to strengthen them, than any thing they have done since the war."[91]

Toombs made only one major speech to support ratification of the constitution. In December, the constitution won with an overwhelming majority, but Toombs was too sick to participate in the festivities. Since he returned from his long trip, he complained about a succession of colds and liver and kidney trouble and his cataract seemed no better. For the most part he stayed home in bed, "unable to attend to anything but to give directions to the most important matters of my private affairs, and turn over my professional business to other hands, except in one case which I argued in Wilkes very much to my injury."[92]

A congressional bill to put the country on the silver standard riled him. "I am against all government banking or interfering with paper money in any way," he snarled. Until there was a sound metallic standard, "we shall be floundering in a Siberian bog, and without it we can never have a free government or ever see prosperity and hopefulness again as a nation." But he realized he was only an old man shouting at mountaintops. "I must halt," he wrote to Stephens. "My back is aching and I am wearying you."[93]

Toombs tried to ignore the strong movement that was growing to make him the first governor of the state under the new constitution. Papers from all over Georgia endorsed him. Rumors spread about secret deals at the convention. One tale claimed that the delegates had prepared a resolution asking Congress to remove the restriction on Toombs that prevented him from holding national office so he could be sent back to the Senate. Toombs stopped the senatorial campaign cold. "I do not want to go to the United States Senate," he said. "I would not go if I were elected." Being governor intrigued him, though. "If I have any political ambition at all," he confessed, "it is to be the first Governor of Georgia under the rule of the new Constitution."[94]

But the new constitution declared that the next governor would not be elected until October of 1880. "The election is three years off, and no one knows the changes that will take place in that time," he told a reporter. "I will be 70-years-old, if alive, then." Any talk of a campaign was premature. National office was out of the question. He was prohibited from office under the 14th Amendment anyway. "I want to see the new generation that is coming on to take charge of matters," he said. "If I ever conclude to run the people will know it, because they will have to demand it, but I don't intend to kick before I am spurred."[95]

Toombs was serious about not seeking another public office. He also refused to become the new constitution's guru. "I have been asked a thousand questions about the constitution," he told a reporter. "Every Justice of the Peace, nearly has written to me about it. They are astonished at my ignorance and seem to think that I am feigning it." Toombs had his political opinions and was never reluctant to give them freely. But when it was a legal question he never made a judgment until he researched and investigated it.[96]

Toombs practiced law as his health allowed and gave an occasional interview to the newspapers. He observed and commented on everything. The silver question: "We ought to get back to the standard silver dollar of 412½ grains, nine-tenths fine." On Communism: "If the Government be unjust and laws oppressive, Communism may come and I say let it come," he said. "I would lead it myself to secure justice." But he drew a sharp distinction between Communism and Socialism. Toombs, the conservative constitutionalist, the man who had "locked the door of the treasury and put the key into the pocket of the people" had some sympathy for socialism. It is a movement of the cultural leaders and intellectuals of European society, he said, while Communism "begins in the lower walks, and is generally agitation among laborers and disaffected people of the poorer classes. They are both outgrowths of unjust systems of legislation and tyrannical administrations."[97]

In November, Toombs was invited to address the first legislature under the new constitution. His conscience had been lately aroused by the plight of the poor. He told the legislature that not a single sun had set since 1867 that did not find the people poorer than when it rose. He blamed the old Radicals and the new robber barons for the ills of Georgia. "When the Republican Party got through here, we were ten thousand millions in debt, everybody breaking, everybody ruined," he said, "and that is the condition today throughout the United States." People across the country worked hard and made nothing. "It becomes us, and especially our legislators, to know how this is," he said. "It is not all the fault of the Government. Our own folly has something to do with it; but the great part of it has been done by bad government."[98]

Toombs saw bad government everywhere and it was still up to its old tricks. Congress had just passed the Arrears Bill that broadened eligibility and granted lump sums to qualified veterans of the Civil War. "I am sorry to see the new pension bill pass," he wrote to Stephens. "It seems to me that the Democrats can be driven by the radicals anywhere with clamor about Union soldiers. I would prefer that the villains should remain in power forever than to aid them in such infamous measures."

For all his denials that he did not want to be in Congress, he sometimes missed leading a good legislative fight. "I wish I could have been heard in the House thirty minutes on [illegible] bill," he wrote. "I should have reviewed the infamous folly and wrong of further robbing the South to pay extra compensation to the alien and domestic hirelings for overturning the government and plundering the people. I would far rather buy rope at the public expense to hang them and to bury them alongside of comrades at Arlington, which Congress stole from an old lame woman the lineal descendant of Martha Washington."

Toombs was also more concerned with the economy and the effect it was having on the poor. "In this county more people have gone under, dead broke, this winter than in any previous one in its history," he wrote. "We have reached the point when nobody prospers and no business pays." It cost more to produce crops than to sell them. This was the government's fault and "in my opinion never can be remedied except by revolution — it may be bloodless, tho' I fear it will not be, but come it must and will." The state and national debt was greater than all the property of the country and he feared the balance would be paid "by the sweat of the poor." How much better is that than imprisonment for debt? "Well it is a great deal worse; for imprisonment for debt compels the creditor to support the debtor. Now you turn loose the debtor and make him work to support the creditor and himself too. Thousands of poor fellows are daily committing suicide notwithstanding that 'conscience makes cowards of us all,' [as] Shakespeare says."[99]

In April, he once again got into trouble when he spouted off about a bill in the Georgia legislature to ban concealed weapons. "What in the [hell] are you making such a fuss about carrying concealed weapons for?" he snorted at reporters. "Everybody is expected to lay aside his pistol and the first thing you know some [damned] coward who regards neither law nor honor, will shoot you in the back. It is wrong, sir!" It was a right to carry a pistol for self-defense, he said. "Suppose [a] man comes upon you and finds just before he gets to you that you have a derringer in your pocket," he said. "Nine chances to one he will come up smiling with a proposition to bury the hatchet." As usual, his remarks caused a stir. The Chattanooga (Tennessee) *Times* said that Toombs wanted to be governor and was appealing to "the boys" who made up the "class of habitual carriers of pistols and knives" for votes. The Monroe (Georgia) *Advertiser* said that Toombs was the only man in the state that opposed legislation that banned carrying pistols. "He wants every man to carry a pistol ... to keep cowards from shooting him in the back." The Gainesville (Georgia) *Eagle* simply said: "The general should be watched."[100]

That summer Toombs gave a remarkably candid interview to his journalist friend, Henry Grady. This interview also set off a firestorm. But Toombs wanted to set the record straight about many things. To begin with, he said he never thought the U.S. Constitution was very good. He would not have supported it had he been in Philadelphia in 1789. In his view, it was a compact that required good faith between the states and not a binding charter. The trouble came when the North betrayed the South. He said that he was never the blatant secessionist that the Northern newspapers caricatured him to be. He recounted how his first vote had been for Andrew Jackson, how he had fought for the Compromise of 1850 and then helped form the Constitutional Union Party despite the abuse he got from some political factions in Georgia. "It has never been my custom to consult my constituents on public matters," he said. "When, therefore, they became angered at my adherence to the compromise that promised to save the Union, I only stuck to it the closer."

Toombs knew there would be trouble after Lincoln was elected. "But I was still unwilling to commit myself to secession, and then, too, I was not certain that Georgia could be carried on that issue." He explained how he supported the Crittenden Compromise "heartily and sincerely although the sullen obstinacy of Seward had made it almost impossible to do anything." When it failed, he returned home and led Georgia out of the Union.

Toombs believed the majority of the delegates at Montgomery were opposed to Jefferson Davis for president. But a Davis clique dominated the convention. "If the vote had been cast by delegates rather than by States, he could never have been elected," Toombs said. Although he and Davis never liked each other, he accepted the position as secretary of state because he was afraid refusing would be perceived as a lack of harmony and confidence in the new nation. "I was never satisfied with my position in the Cabinet," he admitted. "The trouble was that too many of our leaders sought such places when they were needed in the field." Toombs was in office for less than six months, but he was proud of his record in the Confederate State Department. "I secured our [international] recognition as belligerents, established relations with the unseceded Southern States, and then insisted on retiring. By this time, other States had joined us."

When he was asked what had caused the failure of the Confederacy, Toombs did not hesitate for an answer: the Conscript Act. It demoralized the troops and the entire Confederacy. "There was no necessity for it and it sprang from Mr. Davis's desire to have the appointment of officers," Toombs said. "He was crazy over his West Point martinets, and when he could not appoint the officers for the volunteers, he went to Congress and demanded the Conscript law and got it." There were other reasons: the bureaucracy at Richmond, the economics of war, but mostly Toombs blamed Davis for the defeat. "Davis is a remarkable man," Toombs said. "He is a good writer and that is all. He was a slow man and always acted rashly at last." According to Toombs, Davis was small-minded and "jealous as a Barbary hen." Establishing a functioning government under Jefferson Davis would have been "an impossibility."

Toombs was one of about thirty Confederates who had not been granted a pardon. When Grady asked him about taking the oath of loyalty, Toombs replied: "As to the talk about the Northern people forgiving me, I have nothing to say. As I have not forgiven them, and don't expect to, I am indifferent as to the state of their feelings."

When Grady asked about the various great men he had known and worked with over the years, Toombs was chock full of one liners. Daniel Webster: "The greatest man I ever knew. Not the most eloquent, but the greatest." John C. Calhoun: "The greatest logician I ever knew." Toombs claimed that he had known every president except Washington, John Adams, and Jefferson. Millard Fillmore was "a fine scholar and an honest man." Franklin Pierce the "best gentleman of them all" without "any especial force, but was clever and correct." Martin Van Buren: "The most accomplished statesman, but he was not a broad man." John Tyler "was great at a female seminary commencement or a cattle show." James Buchanan: "A fine statesman in a small way, and an unequaled leader of small bodies of men." Remarkably, Toombs' harshest criticism was against the man that he was instrumental in getting elected, Zachary Taylor. "Taylor was the most ignorant President of them all. It was amazing how little he knew. He was a soldier and nothing else."[101]

Toombs was denounced far and wide for his comments about Jefferson Davis and especially his criticisms of the South. Yet he remained popular and addressed the legislature a few weeks later. The railroads were still in charge and were robbing the people of Georgia, he said. "A set of railroad men meet in the Fall, at the Kimball House and impose a tax on the people which you must pay." He urged the legislature to regulate railroad rates. "You must remedy this evil," he told the members. "If you can't see a way to do it, resign and go home, and let them send a nigger in your place. You are a fraud. [Laughter]." Toombs urged the legislature to appoint railroad commissioners to regulate rates "and to shut the way to oppression." European countries had regulations, sixteen states had regulations, "and there is nothing to keep you from it," he told the legislature, "but the power and bribery of railroads." The bill was soon passed. But the railroads were fed up with Toombs and retaliated by questioning how his legal battles had been financed over the years, particularly this one. Toombs had to write a public letter explaining that whatever the state had paid him in legal fees had been more than returned by the taxes he had forced the railroads to pay.[102]

As another presidential election rolled around, Toombs leaned away from the Democrats. Earlier in the year, he told Stephens that many Southern Democrats he had been corresponding with were also thinking about renouncing the party. "We have been the servile tools of the knaves and fools, mostly the former, long enough," he wrote. "And many thoughtful men would tremble to see the Democratic party as now constituted in power, even to beat Grant or the devil." In another letter to Stephens, Toombs said he could never vote for a party that endorsed the Fourteenth and Fifteenth Amendments. "I may vote for individual men simply because of personal preference, but I will never degrade my intellect, manhood and truth by vindicating in any way such a lie," he wrote. "I will acquiesce in it until I can change it or see some prospects of doing so, but will do no more." The coalition of corporations, bondholders, bankers, and protectionists had now become omnipotent because of the "imbecility and corruption of the Democratic party."[103]

By the end of the year, Toombs had publicly but reluctantly endorsed Grant for a third term. Grant had made a triumphal return to the United States after an extended world tour with dreams of once again pursuing the presidency. In November, a "reunion" of the Army of the Tennessee was held in Grant's honor at Chicago. The event was part reunion, part welcome home party, and a kickoff to another anticipated Grant-for-president campaign. Congratulatory and laudatory telegrams poured in from all over the country. Toombs could not resist giving General Grant's nose a tweak. When he was asked to convey a few words, he wired:

> I decline to answer except to present my personal congratulations to Gen. Grant on his safe arrival to this country. He fought for his country honorably and won; I fought for mine and lost. I am ready to try it over again. Death to the Union.
>
> R. Toombs

The telegram caused an uproar. Even Toombs' supporters were aghast at his impudence. Reporters at the Atlanta *Constitution* checked to make sure the telegram was authentic and had not sent by one of Toombs' enemies under his name. Toombs played innocent. He said he had merely wanted to congratulate General Grant on his return. "I then went on to say that I was ready to fight again for my cause — that of establishing the rights of the States to secede. Why shouldn't I say it? I feel it — I mean it — it is in my heart, and why should I deny it?" He said he was too old to crawl and lie and hide his feelings about the Union. "Yes, Sir, I telegraphed the Chicago man my honest views," he said defiantly. "I speak for no one but myself, and I don't care to tell a [damned] lie about it!"[104]

If Toombs was simply making a joke and trying to cover it by playing the old, obstinate rebel, it backfired. If his sentiments at that moment were sincere, it was a rare lapse of judgment in how it would be received by the Georgia audience he meant it for. Toombs was criticized from every corner. "General Toombs is given of late to saying very foolish things," one editorial in the Augusta *Chronicle* huffed. "The days of his usefulness are nearly over, and he is presuming upon and abusing his past reputation." Still, both Toombs and Stephens said they preferred Grant over Samuel Tilden in the next election.[105]

By 1880, Toombs' eyesight was failing badly. He had bragged about a remarkable improvement the year before, but by March the cataracts were taking his vision. He practiced whatever law his deteriorating eyesight would permit, but realized he would soon be facing mandatory retirement. "My eyes are fast failing me, the sight in one being entirely extinct and the other progressing with unexpected rapidity, and I have been labouring as much as possible to finish up my private business and to close my professional business which is now almost exclusively confined to the R. Road tax cases which I now feel will outlast me," he wrote to Stephens. "The courts, while generally deciding principally against the R. Roads, show an unmistakable purpose to delay them as much as possible." After six years of working in the state and federal courts against the railroads on behalf of Georgia, Toombs "despaired" of ever seeing the cases settled.

He also professed to have given up on politics. He said he could not even bring himself to write editorials he had promised to the Cincinnati *Enquirer* and the Augusta *Chronicle* about the Democratic Party. But he had no pangs about sharing his feelings with Stephens. "I think the policy of conciliation, even [to] the extent of wholly sacrificing its own principles, has pretty effectually destroyed the Democratic party," he wrote. The party had abandoned free trade, sound currency, opposition to the banking system, subsidies to railroads, and had not threatened to use force when the presidential commission selected Rutherford B. Hayes president in 1876. "Indeed it were [sic] useless to enumerate errors which have been adopted by the Democratic party under the false and cowardly pretext 'of accepting the situation,' which simply means abusing all constitutional safeguards and turning over the Federal Government to the present Republican party." The Democratic Party no longer had any principles and it panged him that John B. Gordon and Benjamin Hill represented Georgia in the Senate. "They are a reproach to the State."[106]

Despite his protests that he was no longer interested in politics, he was following the early maneuvers in presidential contest. "It appears to me at this distance from headquarters that Grant is weakening," he wrote to Stephens a month later. Toombs wanted to see Grant get the nomination for several reasons. He thought that a "true" Democrat could easily defeat Grant. But most of all, Toombs wanted to see Grant elected because if another crisis came about, "he would be more apt to destroy the Union, which I so earnestly desire." Toombs even predicted that if Samuel Tilden were re-nominated by the Democrats, Grant would carry Georgia by seventy thousand votes.[107]

On June 8, the Republicans bypassed Grant and gave the nomination to the inoffensive James Garfield of Ohio and the equally nondescript Chester A. Arthur from New York. Two weeks later, the Democrats fell back on the military-hero formula and nominated General Winfield Scott Hancock and Indiana banker William H. English. Despite his disgust with the Democratic Party, Toombs pronounced himself satisfied with the ticket and even said he might vote in the election ... if he lived. If he was disappointed, he kept quiet when Garfield won the election and the Democrats lost the House of Representatives.[108]

Toombs was more interested in spending his summers with Julia at their new home in Clarksville. Clarksville was an out-of-the-way spot in Habersham County in northern Georgia that was a popular getaway for the affluent vacationers. Their new home sat on twenty-one acres and had a variety of gardens and fruit trees. In Clarksville, Toombs could put away his cares and get away from the pressures of business, reporters, politicians, and his law office.[109]

And he was still cherished by the people of Georgia. In November, he was invited to address the legislature concerning the bitter senatorial race between Joe Brown and A.R. Lawton. By Toombs' standards, it was a mild effort. He criticized Joe Brown, the leading candidate, for his administration during the Civil War, his treachery to the Southern cause, and his business and political shenanigans during Reconstruction. "Some men have become princes, but those who produce are biting the dust of poverty," he said. "Gov. [sic] Brown is one of those rich men. In an hour he got into the Senate. After he got into the Senate he tried to get his hand in the Treasury [Applause]." Despite Toombs' denunciation, the legislature sent Joe Brown to the Senate.[110]

He was mellowing despite himself. "We have closed the old and entered upon the new era in our political history," he wrote to Charles C. Jones. "Let the past go upon the record as soon as possible. Many of the materials for its full, complete, and truthful history have already passed away. Time is still at work in the destruction of others. The present is daily making up its own record."[111]

At seventy-years-old, Toombs occupied himself with the financial affairs of the Methodist Church, hosting or appearing at dinner parties, saying outrageous things for newspaper interviews, and making an occasional speech to a political group or civic organization. These speeches were still filled with the usual anti-government, anti–Republican rhetoric, but now they were tinged more than ever with references to God, the Bible, and religious themes. When he spoke of "human rights"—the late nineteenth century Southern variety—he said: "When God declared his Ten Commandments, why he declared human rights." He did not believe the government should interfere with education. "I have never seen a word, from Genesis to Revelations where it says anything about taking a man and educating him." On his record of defending government that protected its citizens instead of a government that forced laws upon people, he said that he gloried in being an independent rebel. "When my time comes, as here I see the gate opening to me, and they call on me for my stewardship, I am ready to say to my God, I will never, never throw salt upon that altar."[112]

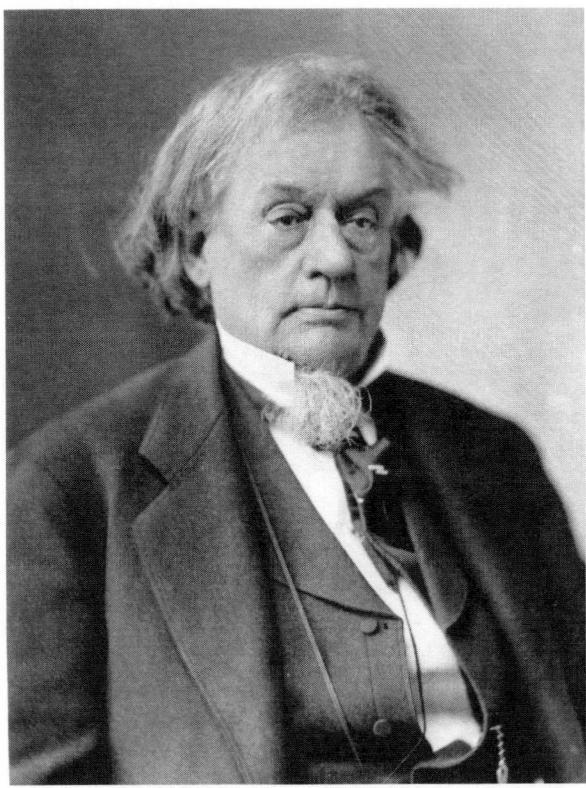

Unreconstructed. Toombs at the same photo session. Library of Congress, LC-DIG-cwpbh-03736 (available online).

By 1882, Toombs' vision was almost gone. A typical newspaper adage said that Toombs' eyesight kept failing him, "but his insight is still as keen as ever." Yet he still attended his business interests, went to his law office for three hours every day, provided legal advice (for a hefty fee), and personally worked an occasional case. That spring, he found himself in the peculiar position of being special counsel for Charles A. Phinizy, president of the Western and Atlantic Railroad, in a legal action over whether the state had the authority to compel the railroad to forfeit its charter. But his health prevented him from sustaining an argument for very long in court. "Many were disappointed who went to hear, probably for the last time, the eloquence [of] this great man," a reporter wrote from the Wilkes County Superior Court. "His physical condition was such as to prevent an elaborate argument and the tongue which always thrilled with its eloquence was now scarcely audible."[113]

During that summer, he may have been as surprised as anyone to find that Alexander Stephens was running for governor. Toombs probably encouraged his friend's campaign but the real spark behind the effort was the independent Democrat William H. Felton. Democrats in Georgia had been split for over ten years between the Bourbons who advocated the New South, accepting the Fourteenth and Fifteenth Amendments, and making all the money they could and a smaller but vocal group that wanted the Democratic Party to cling to the more traditional Democratic virtues of home rule, state and local sovereignty, and to pay homage to the common people. Stephens was always sympathetic to these independent Democrats. But he was also a pragmatic politician who, like it or not, accepted the reality of the Fourteenth and Fifteenth Amendments. He knew how to court both sides so he seemed like the perfect candidate to heal the split in the Democratic Party.[114]

At first, Stephens said he would not run. Then he allowed a statement to be released that said he would. Then he denied that he authorized the statement. Toombs was quoted in the papers as saying that Stephens "must be in his dotage" and he did not see how any Democrat could vote for him. Toombs quickly claimed that he had been misquoted. He had talked to the reporter, he said, but anything "that could be tortured into an interview is wholly untrue." Toombs insisted the article was a fabrication and since he had been at his summer home in Clarksville, knew little about the political situation. But Stephens was his candidate. "Though I differ with Mr. Stephens on the subject of internal improvements by the general government, the currency, the tariff, and taxation generally, as the question now stands if I vote I shall cast my ballot for Alexander Stephens."[115]

Despite being frail, sick, addicted to morphine and frequent sips of medicinal whiskey by the tablespoon, Stephens left the House of Representatives in Washington, D.C. and stumped throughout Georgia. He avoided issues and campaigned on his celebrity. In October he easily beat his opponent, former Confederate general Lucius Gartrell, by 60,000 votes.[116]

In December, Toombs traveled back to Washington, D.C. to argue another case before the Supreme Court. In the *State of Georgia vs. Jessup,* the legal question concerned whether the state could collect taxes from the Atlantic and Gulf Railroad, which had gone into receivership. At issue was some $66,000.00 in assets. All of the lower courts had ruled against Georgia. But Toombs and his partners hoped to get a hearing before the Supreme Court. However, the court refused to hear the case on the basis that the lower courts had the appropriate jurisdiction and had based their decisions on sound legal precedents.[117]

Defeated, Toombs headed back to Georgia and almost immediately got into another nasty public fight with Joe Brown over a donation to the University of Georgia. Brown wanted to donate fifty thousand dollars. The money was to be applied to the state debt.

The state would then issue bonds at 7 percent interest as a fund for needy students. Toombs was a member of the university board of trustees and he was wholly against the scheme. The board voted in favor of the program but the legislature took no action. "Thank God and the Georgia legislature for refusing Joe Brown's gift to the State university," Toombs wrote to one member.[118]

Joe Brown made a similar proposition the next year. Toombs objected, saying the offer was illegal because the constitution forbade the state to borrow money to give to a university. At a formal protest meeting Brown told Toombs he was a hypocrite. Toombs had endorsed a similar scheme a few years before, Brown said. When Toombs denied it, Brown pulled a letter from his pocket in which Toombs had indeed recommended such a plan. It was one of the few times Toombs was ever humiliated in public. The next day, he offered his resignation to the board of trustees. The board took no action, but Toombs attended no more meetings.[119]

Despite the fiasco, Toombs was still popular and reporters still sought him out for interviews. When asked about the current state of politics, he condemned Republicans, Democrats, and soft-money men as usual. But in one interview, he extolled the material progress that was being made in the country and the progressive political ideas that were on the horizon. Toombs was uncharacteristically enthusiastic about the likely Democratic presidential nominee Grover Cleveland. "I am pleased with the man so far," he said. "He is young and is identified with the living ideas of the day. We need such men at the head of affairs."

The reporter asked him to reflect on his long public career. Toombs said he had no regrets. "All I desire is to live like a gentleman in retirement, and serve my country by looking with pride upon its rapid strides to greater material wealth and a more perfect political freedom." This was certainly not the same Toombs who a few years before had congratulated Ulysses Grant with a telegram that said "Death to the Union" or who had claimed to earnestly desire another civil war. If the interview was accurate, either Toombs was on his best behavior for the reporter or he had mellowed as he approached his final days.[120]

Eighteen eighty-three was the worst year of Toombs' life. In February, Alexander Stephens traveled to Savannah to deliver a speech. Stephens rode from the train station to his hotel in a carriage that had a broken window. The damp, chilly air assaulted the old man's already delicate health. Stephens returned to Atlanta, but was bedridden after a few days. He grew steadily weaker and frequently lapsed in and out of consciousness. The news spread quickly throughout the state. Crowds gathered round the Governor's Mansion to wait for the latest information. In the early hours of Sunday, March 4, an announcement was made: Alexander Stephens was dead.[121]

It was a hard but not unexpected blow in Georgia. Yet no one took it harder than Robert Toombs. He hurried to Atlanta as Stephens lay in state. Thousands—young and old, rich and poor, black and white—came to pay their last respects. On Thursday morning, hundreds of mourners packed the House of Representatives chamber to attend the service. Several speakers gave eulogies. Then Senator Alfred H. Colquitt introduced Robert Toombs.

Toombs, leaning on his cane, walked to the coffin and looked upon his friend's face. After a long moment, he turned and slowly made his way to the podium. Then he began to sob. For five full minutes, he stood before the crowd and wept uncontrollably. Finally, he regained some composure. "Fellow citizens: I come to mingle my tears with all men and all women and even children of Georgia, not to make an [sic] eulogy. His acts were written in letters of gold." Toombs recounted the well-known incidents in Stephens' life: how he fought the ravages of ill health, his triumphs and defeats in state and national politics, his opposition to secession, his service as vice president in the Confederacy and subsequent imprisonment. But Toombs said his words were inadequate to depict the great events of Stephens' life "because he did nothing that was not either good and great, and often blended together. Modest, gentle, refined, and with a heart big enough to control, to take in all human wants and all human woes. His whole life was spent in the practice of virtue, the pursuit of truth, the worship of God, and doing good to mankind."[122]

Toombs was consoled by friends and gave a few interviews. Then he and Julia returned sadly to Washington, Georgia. Losing Alexander Stephens was devastating. But he could only watch as other friends and colleagues passed away. Benjamin Hill had died in 1882; Charles J. Jenkins passed in the summer of 1883. Toombs took a few final law cases, but in June he told a friend that he would probably plead his last case in Macon. He was now practically blind, his health prevented him from keeping speaking engagements, and he was constantly fretting over his beloved Julia, who had also been in poor health for several years. In July, she fell and injured herself so badly that they had to delay summering in Clarksville for several weeks.[123]

They had no more arrived to the peace and tranquility of their summer home than news arrived that the Kimball House in Atlanta had burned to the ground. The aging hotel was a well known firetrap, but fortunately no lives were lost in the blaze. However, Toombs owned a ninth share in the operation. For whatever reason, he had not insured his part of the investment. Perhaps he thought the insurance too expensive; perhaps it had just slipped his mind. It was an astounding oversight. Toombs was an excellent businessman and a meticulous investor. He lost fifteen thousand dollars instantly in the fire.[124]

When the news reached Hannibal Kimball, he raced to Atlanta from Chicago and immediately began signing up subscribers to fund a new hotel. When Kimball went to Clarksville, Toombs greeted him warmly and proclaimed that Kimball was the only man he wanted to see rebuild the hotel. Toombs agreed to lease his share of the land cheaply and took out $20,000 in stock for a new building and said he might buy more. In the end, Toombs' faith in the enterprise nearly cost him his fortune. Construction on the new hotel overran its budget by two hundred thousand dollars and it took two more years for the hotel to begin turning a profit.[125]

But the last thing on Toombs' mind was business. On August 31, Julia Toombs suffered a massive stroke. Ironically, she had told a reporter a few days before that some of the happiest days of her life had been spent in Clarksville and she would regret when "the time for her removal arrives." The family physician, Dr. H.H. Steiner, was sent for but there was little anyone could do. She lingered for three days. On September 4 she passed away.[126]

Robert Toombs was beside himself with grief. Within six months he had lost the two loves of his life, the two people who had supported him most — when he was in the right and in the wrong — the two people he had depended on for half a century. Little Alec was gone. And now Julia. When he lost Julia and Alec, he seemed to lose part of himself. It was almost as if they took the fundamental essence that made him so damn difficult and yet so damn charming — that thing that made him Robert Toombs — with them when they died. He was cursed to have outlived his children, his dearest friend, and his wife of fifty-three years. As one friend put it, he began "dying by inches."[127]

Friends and family poured into Clarksville to console and comfort him. They all rode the train together as Julia's body was shipped back home. Services were held on September 6 in the Methodist Church in Washington, Georgia. Bishop George F. Pierce, a long-time friend of the family, performed the rites. Then Julia was interred in the family cemetery five miles outside of town. "Fifty years ago I brought my wife to this house as a bride, and here we have lived all these years," Toombs told a reporter a few months earlier. "We have been blessed more than most and I thank God for it."[128]

Condolences poured in from everywhere. But Toombs was inconsolable. "I feel very gratefull [sic] for the kindness of yourself & family for me, in the unbearable loss I have sustained in the loss of dear Julia," he wrote to a relative.

> You who know her can better appreciate than the outside world, but none can appreciate my loss. We lived & loved together over the continents of the earth & the islands of the sea for nearly fifty three years, and she never gave me a moments pain from the bridal alter [sic] to the morning when I kissed away her last breath, when her quiet, gentle, loving & noble spirit, took its flight to the regions of bliss except for her sufferings & the fear of loosing [sic] her.

Toombs closed the letter in despair. "My health is poor but I care now nothing for life, have nothing to live for."[129]

After Julia's death, Toombs tried to diminish his grief by being baptized in the Methodist Church. Bishop Pierce told the papers Julia was sure that her husband would be brought into the fold. "The influence of his sainted wife," he said dramatically, "reaching from beyond the grave, has been potential in bringing about the change in the great Georgian." Toombs saw the light but that did not keep him from lapsing into frequent drinking binges.[130]

Whether due to drink, depression, or just old age, he seldom left his house anymore. But he threw it open to strangers, friends, grandchildren, a brood of nieces, nephews, in-laws, and other members of his extended family. His home became one of the social centers of Georgia. When his town broached the idea of building a fine hotel, Toombs derailed the scheme. "My home stands open, free of charge, to all strangers who are respectable, and the other kind deserve no accommodations." His spacious home may not have had all the luxuries of a first class hotel, but it was certainly comfortable. Over the years, he had made many modern improvements. His was the first home in Washington, Georgia, to have gaslight installed, the first to have running water, and at some point he attached the kitchen to the house instead of the traditional cook house. For his own convenience, he kept a law office in one corner room and had an extensive library upstairs.[131]

He also opened the doors of his sitting room to the ever-present reporters. He could still spin a good tale about senators, presidents, and other political figures he had known in his heyday. But Toombs was showing his age. The hair that was once so dark and thick and shaggy that it gave the impression of a lion's mane was thin and iron gray. He walked with a slight stoop and leaned heavily on his cane. His almost sightless eyes peered through thick cataracts and his heavy gray eyebrows sat on his thin, wrinkled face. On the few occasions he spoke in public, the powerful, eloquent voice that had stirred and impassioned so many could barely be heard. Wherever he went, he was usually aided by Billy, who had been with Toombs all of his life, first as a slave, now as a body servant. Billy was ten years older than Toombs.[132]

But Toombs was still alert, still a keen observer of politics and policy. In the 1884 presidential election, he predicted Grover Cleveland would be the Democratic nominee. He preferred others, but believed Cleveland was "the man for the Democrats to win with." During the Democratic convention in July, Toombs even telegraphed the offices of the Atlanta *Constitution* asking for special reports as they came in.[133]

In September, Toombs suffered another tragedy when his close friend Bishop Pierce

Robert Toombs' home in Washington, Georgia. He often gave speeches from the balcony to crowds that gathered in his front yard. Library of Congress, HABS, GA,159-WASH,1-.

died. Bishop Pierce had started as a Methodist circuit rider and had worked his way up through the church hierarchy to become the first president of Wesleyan College, the editor of the *Southern Ladies Book*, and president of Emory University until 1854. He was also key in establishing the Methodist Episcopal Church, South when a rift developed in the Methodist Church organization over slavery. Toombs and Bishop Pierce had been friends for years. Toombs said that Bishop Pierce fought the devil while he fought the Democrats. "We are both doing the Lord's work," he quipped. The two men had grown especially close after Julia's death and Pierce had acted as a spokesman for Toombs while he was in mourning. Bishop Pierce was seventy-three when he died.[134]

The funeral was held in Sparta. Toombs was apparently unable to attend. But he did go to the services in Washington, Georgia. When asked to speak, Toombs slowly rose from the pew. He did not have the heart or the strength to say much, but he recalled how even though they had followed different pursuits, they had never been led apart from each other. "He has been with us under various circumstances: he has been with us to the grave." Then, perhaps remembering Alex Stephens and Julia, he burst into tears. "The man who has withstood the giants of his day," the newspapers reported, "was weeping like a child."[135]

Toombs' last public speech was made on the evening of the 1884 presidential election.

New York's Democratic governor, Grover Cleveland, beat New York's perennial Republican contender, James G. Blaine. It was the first time the Democrats had held the White House in nearly a generation. In Washington, Georgia, ecstatic Democrats led a torchlight parade to Toombs' house, remembering that he had been a champion of their party years before and forgetting that he had denounced their candidates almost as severely as he had denounced Republicans. They gathered at his front porch and chanted "Toombs! Toombs! Toombs!" The old man hobbled out to his porch. His dry voice trembled with emotion: "It has been years since I have had the opportunity of rejoicing with my people in such a victory as this," he said. He thanked God he had lived to see such a day and gave his customary slam to the Republicans. "The policy of the republican [sic] party [has] been to extort enormous sums of money from the people, divert it from its natural channels in trade and pile it up in the vaults of the treasury, when the government did not need it, simply that the men in power might steal it by all manner of jobs."

Toombs spoke with great sentiment about his home in Georgia and its people. Then he told his audience that was probably the last public speech he would ever make. Then he bid them farewell.[136]

Toombs kept his word. Over the next year, he made many public appearances and granted several interviews to reporters but never made another public speech. He was even too sick to make an appearance when they re-interred Alexander Stephens and erected a monument to him at Liberty Hall in Crawfordville. If the newsmen were hoping for the Toombs of old who spouted outrageous comments and indelicate tales about politicians of the past, they were disappointed. Toombs had undergone a profound spiritual conversion and spent much of his time talking about the Bible and his Christian faith. "The greatest vice to which the human family is addicted is gambling," he told a friend, yet "there isn't a word in the Bible in condemnation of it." When another friend asked him if he thought selling liquor was sinful, he wrote back to say he did not think so. But he hoped his friend would find a different line of work. "The Lord's prayer [sic], which I have always considered the duty of every man to repeat daily ... requires us to pray to God continually to 'lead us not into temptation, but to deliver us from evil.'"[137]

In August, Toombs gave an interview to the Atlanta *Constitution*. Between interruptions by one of his great-granddaughters who crawled up in his lap and stole kisses and Toombs calling for his favorite dog, Julius, he reminisced about his family genealogy ("The earliest records show to have been opposed to kingly arrogance"), his departed wife ("my constant friend, companion and adviser") and secession ("the culmination of my political career"). The conversation turned to Ulysses Grant, who had died three weeks before. "Grant was the greatest soldier produced by the war," Toombs finally admitted. In Toombs' estimation, Grant was a simple-minded, kind-hearted soldier with no animosity towards the South. His one drawback was that he was a "West Pointer ... and with West Pointers the choice of arms is a profession into which patriotism enters but little."

Then Toombs told the story of the first time he had met Grant. The young soldier had been accused of paying out too much money when he was a captain at Fort Humboldt in California. Commanding officer Robert Buchanan demanded that Grant either resign or face a court-martial. Grant's case made it all the way to the halls of Congress. It so happened that Georgia governor George Crawford was related to Grant's wife, Julia, through marriage. Crawford appealed to Toombs on behalf of Julia's family. Toombs claimed that he helped broker a deal for Grant in which he would resign from the army immediately upon receipt of his commission. Toombs then met with Grant in the corridor of the capitol and told him the news. "True to his word he resigned," Toombs recalled, "and the next time I met him he was president."

And the Confederacy? "There was no doubt of success," Toombs said as he struggled up from the couch he was lying on. "The South could have succeeded had it not been throttled by West Point." Toombs recalled that he had been offered the presidency, but South Carolina "with singular stupidity" wrapped itself around Jefferson Davis and Mississippi had to go along. "Davis was thoroughly incompetent," Toombs said. "His forte was magazine writing. He would have been a successful magazine man, but in the bustle of practical, everyday life he was utterly lost." Toombs said that in his opinion, Albert Sidney Johnston would have been the best man to lead the Confederacy had he not been killed at Corinth in 1862. Joseph E. Johnston would have also been good but when Davis, "inspired by domestic intrigues, removed Johnston from the command of the Western army he killed the Confederacy."[138]

This was Toombs' last interview. It was as if the Toombs of old had come back to life to spark controversy one more time to thrill reporters and readers. The Augusta *Chronicle* approved of Toombs' comments about Grant. "Robert Toombs is mellowing with advancing years," an editorial noted. "His mind has been cleared of its hopeless gloom and irreconcilable animosities. He reasons now where he used to rage." But the paper bristled at his comments about Davis. Toombs was just an old man who was "left to spend a sour old age in lonely dissent from the views of his fifty-five million fellow-countrymen." The *Southern Bivouac* opined that Toombs was "merely firing off one of his too frequent phrases in which sense is much sacrificed to sound." The Dublin (Georgia) *Post* could only shake its head in amazement: "It is very humiliating for Robert Toombs to become so unbalanced as to begin abusing Jefferson Davis and praising Grant."[139]

That September, Toombs made a trip to Atlanta to consult with Governor James Boynton. When he returned home, he knew something was not right.

As he walked into his house, he told his grand-son-in-law Frank Colley, who was traveling with him, "I am going home to die — I shall never leave it again."

Colley tried to reassure him, but somehow Toombs knew the end was near. The last week of September, he had a stroke. His entire left side was paralyzed. His right leg was useless. Toombs drifted back and forth from lucidity to delirium. Sometimes he recognized friends or family who had gathered round. Sometimes he did not even know where he was. Newspapers ran reports almost daily on his condition and predicted his death at any moment. One reporter even tried to interview the dying Southern statesman, but it was no use. Toombs drifted in and out of reality. The correspondent settled for interviewing Toombs' family, his doctor, even Toombs' brother Gabriel who lived just across the street.[140]

Yet Toombs could still come up with a customary ornery remark. On October 10, he asked about the Georgia legislature. Someone told him that it was still in session. Toombs looked up at the ceiling in exasperation and shouted: "Send for Cromwell!" Another time, he was told that the prohibitionists were holding an election. He replied, "Prohibitionists are men of small pints."[141]

Around the first week of December, he seemed to rally. But he could cling to life for only so long. On December 15, at six o'clock that evening, Robert Toombs passed away.[142]

Notes

Chapter 1

1. Pleasant A. Stovall, Robert Toombs, Statesman, Speaker, Soldier, Sage (New York: Cassell, 1892), 1–2. Referred to hereafter as Stovall, Robert Toombs.

2. Robert Leckie, *The Wars of America* (New York: Harper and Row, 1968, 1981), 46.

3. Ralph Emmett Fall, *People, Postoffices and Communities in Caroline County, Virginia 1727–1969* (Roswell, GA: WH Wolfe Associates, 1989), 350; John Frederick Dorman, comp., *Caroline County, Virginia Order Book 1740–1746*, part 3 (Washington, D.C., 1970), 46; *ibid.*, *1752–1754*, part 4, 38; *ibid.*, *1764–1765*, part 1, 60; *ibid.*, part 2, *1765–1766*, 58; Stovall, *Robert Toombs*, 2; Grace Gillam Davidson, comp., *Early Records of Georgia: Wilkes County*, vol. 1 (Greenville, SC: Southern Historical Press, 1933, reprint 1968 and 1992), 67. Cited hereafter as *Early Records of Wilkes County*.

4. Godfrey Memorial Library, *The American Genealogical-Biographical Index to American Genealogical, Biographical and Local History Material*, vol. 179 (Middletown, CT: Godfrey Memorial Library, 1994), 271; Francis Heitman, *Historical Register of Officers of the Continental Army during the War of the Revolution, April 1775 to December 1783* (Baltimore: Genealogical, 1982), 545. E. Merton Coulter, *The Toombs Oak* (Athens: University of Georgia Press, 1966), 26–27. Some accounts say that Robert Toombs Sr. fought in the Battle of Kettle Creek near Savannah, Georgia, in 1779 and went back to Virginia to get his family. Atlanta *Constitution*, December 16, 1885. In most cases, the Atlanta *Constitution* was accessed from the Ancestry.com website except where noted.

5. For the 1781 legislation, see Lodowick Johnson Hill, *The Hills of Wilkes County, Georgia and Allied Families* (Atlanta, 1922), 283.

6. Toombs asserts that his father arrived in Georgia in 1784 in an application for the graduating class of 1828 from Union College, submitted April 16, 1855. Courtesy Schaffer Library, Special Collections, Union College, Schenectady, New York; Mary Bondurant Warren, *Georgia Revolutionary Bounty Land Records 1783–1785* (Athens: Heritage Papers, 1992), 182; Frank Hudson Parker, comp., *Wilkes County, Georgia Tax Records, 1785–1805*, (Atlanta: Parker, 1988), 1: 161, referred to hereafter as *Wilkes County Tax Records*. The Major never seems to have owned the three thousand acres as some biographers claim. Stovall, *Robert Toombs*, 3.

7. For the scale of Wilkes County, see "Index to Land Grants 1&2 1784–1839 Wilkes County," available at *http://files.usgwarchives.net/ga/oglethorpe/deeds/ldgrants.txt*, June 3, 2009; *Constructive Liberalism: The Role of the State in Economic Development in Georgia to 1860* (Cambridge: Harvard University Press, 1954), 71; my account of early Wilkes County relies heavily on Robert Willingham's brief but informative "An Overview of Local History," *http://www.rootsweb.ancestry.com/~gawilkes/localhst.htm*, accessed June 3, 2009.

8. Jeffrey Robert Young, *Domesticating Slavery* (Chapel Hill: University of North Carolina Press, 1999), 98; *Wilkes County Tax Records*, 1790, 205; 1793, 475; Augusta *Chronicle*, October 2, 1790; April 23, 1791.

9. Richard N. Current, ed., *Encyclopedia of the Confederacy*, (New York: Simon and Schuster, 1993), 1: 417; Eric Foner and John A. Garraty, eds., *The Reader's Companion to American History* (Boston: Houghton Mifflin, 1991), 240–241.

10. *Wilkes County Tax Records*, 1801, 1017; Stovall, *Robert Toombs*, 3; Jordon R. Dodd, *Virginia Marriages* (Bountiful, UT: Precision Indexing, 1990), 1020; Davidson, *Early Records of Wilkes County*, 2: 302.

11. Stovall, *Robert Toombs*, 3. A married man with at least one child was eligible for two draws in the Georgia land lotteries, Davidson, *Early Records of Wilkes County*, 1: 303; *Wilkes County Tax Records*, 1804, 1168.

12. *Ibid.*, 1150–1151; Avary, ed., *Recollections of Alexander H. Stephens: His Diary Kept When a Prisoner at Fort Warren, Boston Harbor, 1865; Giving Incidents and Reflections of His Prison Life and Some Letters and Reminiscences* (New York: Doubleday, Page, 1910), 425–426; Stovall, *Robert Toombs*, 4.

13. Stovall, *Robert Toombs*, 3–4. Most of what is known about Toombs' childhood comes from Stovall, who was the only biographer who had the advantage of knowing him.

14. Wilkes County Georgia Willbook, GG 1818–1819 (microform); Davidson, *Early Records of Wilkes County*, 1: 99–100. Thomas W. Cobb and Catherine Toombs were both appointed executors of the will. Thomas Cobb was a cousin to Howell Cobb. Howell Cobb was Robert

Toombs' rival and sometime political ally in later life. *Ibid.*, 100; Henry J. Pope was appointed the children's guardians. Sarah Quinn Smith, *Early Georgia Wills and Settlements of Estates, Wilkes County, Georgia* (Athens: Heritage Papers, 1959, 1994), 11.

15. Mytra Lockett Avary, ed., *Recollections of Alexander H. Stephens*, 425–426.

16. Stovall, *Robert Toombs*, 4–5. "Sporting man" was nineteenth century slang for a gambler or one who paid frequent visits to brothels.

17. Catherine Clinton, *The Plantation Mistress: Woman's World in the Old South* (New York: Pantheon, 1982), 50; Davidson, *Early Records of Wilkes County*, 2: 303; Stovall, *Robert Toombs*, 6; for a brief sketch of Wilkes County Academy, see *http://www.kudcom.com/www/mark/mark21.html*, accessed June 17, 2009; Wayne J. Urban and Jennings L. Wagner, *American Education: A History* (New York: McGraw-Hill, 1996), 119. John C. Reed contended that Toombs "never was a bookworm." But Reed befriended Toombs when Toombs was growing old. By then, Toombs's eyes were beginning to be plagued by cataracts and he was clouding his mind with alcohol. See John C. Reed, *The Brothers' War* (Boston: Little, Brown, 1905), 218; Henry Whitney Cleveland "Robert Toombs," *Southern Bivouac* 8 (January 1886): 454, reprinted by Broadfoot, 1992.

18. Tom S. Gray, Jr., "Bob Toombs," *Georgia Alumni Record*, May–June 1928, 193; E. Merton Coulter, *The Toombs Oak, The Tree That Owned Itself, and Other Chapters of Georgia* (Athens: University Press of Georgia, 1966), 23; 34–35; 49–50; Charles Morton Strahan, "The University of Georgia," *The New England Magazine*, September 1890, 56, Making of America, Cornell University website, *http://digital.library.cornell.edu/m/moa/*, June 8, 2009. Hereafter referred to as MOA Cornell.

19. E. Merton Coulter, *College Life in the Old South, as Seen at the University of Georgia* (Athens: University Press of Georgia, 1973), 86.

20. Washington (Georgia) *News*, October 16, 1824, quoted in William A. Thompson, *Robert Toombs of Georgia* (Baton Rouge: Louisiana State University Press, 1966), 7. Referred to hereafter as Thompson, *Toombs*.

21. Strahan, "The University of Georgia," 59; Thomas Brahana, "The History of Mathematics at the University of Georgia: Teaching, Research and Service," no date, available at *http://www.math.uga.edu/history/*, 2–4, accessed June 17, 2009; Paul Murray, *The Whig Party in Georgia 1825–1853* (Chapel Hill: University of North Carolina Press, 1948), 57–58.

22. Stovall, *Robert Toombs*, 7.

23. Coulter, *College Life in the Old South*, 205; Strahan, "The University of Georgia," 59–60; Davidson, *Early Records of Wilkes County*, 2: 303.

24. Information and background on the Demosthenian Society can be found at *http://www.uga.edu/demsoc/home.htm*, accessed July 4, 2009; 103–104.

25. Coulter, *College Life in the Old South*, 111–112; 114–115. The brief description of the debating societies is also taken from Chapter 6 of Coulter's *College Life in the Old South*.

26. Franklin College Faculty Minutes 1822–1836 (typescript), September 20, 1825, 69–70, courtesy of the University of Georgia Archives, Main Library.

27. Gray, "Bob Toombs," 194; Franklin College Faculty Minutes 1822–1836 (typescript), September 21, 1825, 71.

28. *Ibid.*, 70; Coulter, *College Life in the Old South*, 36, 76.

29. Franklin College Faculty Minutes 1822–1836 (typescript), 99; Coulter, *College Life in the Old South*, 77.

30. Demosthenian Society Treasurer's Book, 1825–1829, 193; Coulter, *College Life in the Old South*, 131.

31. Franklin College Faculty Minutes 1822–1836 (typescript), 101.

32. Lucian Lamar Knight, M.A., *Reminiscences of Famous Georgians Embracing Episodes and Incidents in the Lives of the Great Men of the State* (Atlanta: Franklin-Turner, 1907), 137; Stovall, *Robert Toombs*, 8–9.

33. Stovall, *Robert Toombs*, 11; Coulter, *College Life in the Old South*, 77.

34. Strahan, "The University of Georgia," 65; Coulter, *College Life in the Old South*, 135.

35. This story has been told by numerous authors but the best is probably the version in Ulrich B. Phillips, *The Life of Robert Toombs* (New York: Macmillan, 1913, 1968), 13–14. Hereafter referred to as Phillips, *Life of Toombs*. The reference to the rostrum being made of boxes comes from Knight, *Reminiscences of Famous Georgians*, 104.

36. Coulter, *College Life in the Old South*, 136. For the origins of Toombs Oak folklore, see E. Merton Coulter, *The Toombs Oak, The Tree That Owned Itself, and Other Chapters of Georgia* (Athens: University of Georgia Press, 1966) 1–8.

37. William Wells, "Union College," *Scribner's Monthly*, July 1876, 229–230, MOA Cornell, accessed July 11, 2009; for a sketch of the university's history, see *http://www.union.edu/About/history.php*, accessed July 11, 2009; correspondence with author from Julianna Spallholz, archival assistant, Schaffer Library, Special Collections, Union College, August 20, 2002.

38. For Nott's liberalization of the curriculum, see *http://www.union.edu/About/history.php*, accessed July 11, 2009; for his record on fraternities, see *http://www.assumption.edu/ahc/Theresa's%20Main%20Folder/Web%20page%20folder/Biographies/Nott%20Bio.html*, accessed July 11, 2009; the quote about discipline was found in "The Campus Business, Presented at the Lawrence University Matriculation Convocation, September 2000," available at *http://www.columbia.edu/~am875/rebell6.html*, accessed June 24, 2002.

39. "Catalogus Senatus Academici ... 1828," 25–26, Special Collections, Schaffer Library, Union College, Schenectady, NY.

40. Fred C. Cole, "Union Worthies, Number Sixteen, Robert Agustus Toombs, Class of 1828," (Schenectady, n.d.), 8; typescript from Union College Student Records, First Term 1827–1828 to Second Term 1828–1829.

41. *Catalogue of the Members of the Delphian Institute Society at Union College, Founded Feb. 22, 1819* (Schenectady, 1830), 8; Thompson, *Toombs*, 11; Cole, "Union Worthies," 9.

42. Toombs' grades from a typescript of "Union College Student Records, First Term 1827–1828 to Second Term 1828–1829"; Cole, "Union Worthies," 8. There was a request about this time for the court to remove Toombs' mother as executrix of the will because she was "totally unable to perform her duties, and since the est[ate] is going to waste, it is recommended that another be appointed." There is no date cited, but it appears that Henry J. Pope legally took over administration of the

estate on November 3, 1829, Davidson, *Early Records of Wilkes County*, 2: 303.

43. Dumas Malone, *Jefferson and His Time: The Sage of Monticello* (Boston: Little, Brown, 1977, 1981), 484–485.

44. Mary H. White and John B. Lomax, *William Lomax Family and His Descendants* (Privately printed by John Lomax, 1995), 90–91;.

45. Thomas Jefferson to John T. Lomax, April 12, 1826, Jefferson Papers, Library of Congress; Malone, *Sage of Monticello*, 485n.

46. Circular by John Tayloe Lomax quoted in W. Hamilton Bryson, ed., *Essays on Legal Education in Nineteenth Century Virginia* (Buffalo, NY: Hein, 1998), 77–79.

47. *Ibid.*, 79; "Application for the Graduating Class of 1828 from Union College," submitted April 16, 1855, Schaffer Library, Special Collections, Union College, Schenectady, NY.

48. Malone, *Sage of Monticello*, 464; 483–484.

49. University of Virginia Faculty Minutes (#2328), vols. 1 and 2, 12 April 1825 to 16 July, 1830, 233–238, Special Collections, University of Virginia Library.

50. *Ibid.*, 252–253.

51. *Ibid.*, 286–288.

52. *Ibid.*, 313.

53. Kermit L. Hall, ed., *Oxford Companion to American Law* (New York: Oxford University Press, 2002), 380; Journal of the Senate of the State of Georgia, 318–319; (Milledgeville) Georgia *Journal*, December 26, 1829; Elbert County (Georgia) Superior Court Minutes 1819 (Indexed) 1825–1831 (Microfilm).

54. Hall, *Oxford Companion to American Law*, 60; Stovall, *Robert Toombs*, 13.

55. Thomas Schott, *Alexander Stephens of Georgia: A Biography* (Baton Rouge: Louisiana State University Press, 1987), 28. Hereafter cited as Schott, *Stephens*.

56. Reed, *The Brothers' War*, 218; Stovall, *Robert Toombs*, 14–15; Hall, *The Oxford Companion to American Law*, 377. Robert Toombs does not show up in the 1830 Census, although his mother, Catherine, listed three free females, one male under five years old, and 45 slaves. See U.S. Census of 1830.

57. Reed, *The Brothers' War*, 219.

58. Atlanta *Constitution*, January 12, 1879; March 10, 1886 .

59. Avary, *Recollections of Alexander H. Stephens*, 426–427; Reed, *The Brothers' War*, 218; Rudolph Von Abele, *Alexander H. Stephens: A Biography* (New York: Knopf, 1946), 73; Stovall, *Robert Toombs*, 16–17.

60. Clifford Alexander to Edward Porter Alexander, August 4, 1853, in Edward Porter Alexander Papers, Southern Historical Collection, University of North Carolina.

61. For samples of the kinds of law cases Toombs routinely handled, see "Elbert County Superior Court Minutes, 1834–1839, indexed; 1839–1843, not indexed (microfilm); "Wilkes County Superior Court Deeds and Mortgages, vols. OOO-PPP, 1839–1846," (microfilm); Augusta *Chronicle*, November 17, 1840; Stovall, *Robert Toombs*, 18–19.

62. *Ibid.*, 19.

63. John C. Reed, *The Brothers' War*, 220.

64. Knight, *Reminiscences of Famous Georgians*, 135.

65. N. Louise Bailey, Mary L. Morgan, and Carolyn R. Taylor, *Biographical Directory of the South Carolina Senate 1776–1985*, vol. I, *Abbott-Hill* (Columbia: University of South Carolina Press, 1986), 426.

66. Dorothy Kelley MacDowell, comp., *DuBose Genealogy: Descendants of Isaac DuBose and Wife, Suzanne Couillandeau, French Huguenot Refugees Who Settled on the Santee River in South Carolina about 1689* (Louisville, KY: Gateway Press, 1981), 94–95; Stovall, *Robert Toombs*, 356; Davidson, *Early Records of Wilkes County*, 2: 357.

67. Stovall, *Robert Toombs*, 356; C. Vann Woodward and Elisabeth Muhlenfeld, *The Private Mary Chesnut: The Unpublished Civil War Diaries* (New York: Oxford University Press, 1984), 140–141; Mary Boykin Chesnut, *A Diary from Dixie* (Glouster, MA: Smith, 1961), 112.

68. Toombs to Julia Toombs, May 15, 1853, in Ralph McGill Collection, Special Collections, Robert W. Woodruff Library, Emory University. Referred to hereafter as Toombs Papers, Emory University.

69. The biographical sketch of Stephens' early life come from Schott, *Stephens*, 1–28.

70. Avary, *Recollections of Alexander Stephens*, 11–12, hereafter Avary, *Recollections*; Richard Malcolm Johnston and William Hand Brown, *Life of Alexander Stephens* (Freeport, NY: Books for Libraries Press, 1878, reprint 1971), 89.

71. Schott, *Stephens*, 9; Avary, *Recollections*, 46; Varina Howell Davis, *Jefferson Davis, Ex-President of the Confederate States of America: A Memoir by His Wife* (New York: Belford, 1890), 1: 410–11.

72. Columbus *Herald, Extra*, May 14, 1836, and Augusta *Chronicle*, May 21, 1836; Macon *Messenger*, May 12, 1836; Columbus *Enquirer*, May 13, 1836.

73. George Burns Smith, *History of the Georgia Militia, 1783–1861*, vol. 1, *Campaigns and Generals* (Milledgeville, GA: Boyd, 2000), 198; *ibid.*, 200–202.

74. See "State of Georgia," *Debow's Review* 10 (March 1851), 245–246 for a derogatory description of a Georgia muster. Available at MOA University of Michigan, accessed September 16, 2003. Referred to hereafter as "MOA UM."

75. "Results of election for officers in the Washington Guards," May 27, 1836, courtesy of the Georgia Historical Society, Washington Guards Collection, MS1099.

76. John H. Martin, comp., *Columbus, Geo., from Its Selection as a "Trading Town" in 1827 to Its Partial Destruction by Wilson's Raid in 1865* (Columbus, GA: Gilbert, 1874, reprinted, Easley, SC: Georgia Genealogical Reprints, 1972), 64–65, 71–72, cited hereafter as Martin, *Columbus Geo.*; John S.D. Eisenhower, *Agent of Destiny: The Life and Times of General Winfield Scott* (New York: The Free Press), 1997, 163–164; Martin, *Columbus, Geo.*

77. Augusta *Chronicle*, July 16, 1836.

Chapter 2

1. Anthony Gene Carey, *Parties, Slavery, and the Union in Antebellum Georgia* (Athens: University of Georgia Press, 1997), 21.

2. Robert Remini, *Andrew Jackson and the Course of American Freedom 1822–1832*, Vol. 2, (New York: Harper and Row, 1981), 361.

3. Augusta *Chronicle*, December 25, 1832; Robert Remini, *Andrew Jackson and the Course of American Freedom 1822–1832*, vol. 3 (New York: Harper and Row,) 12.

4. Carey, *Parties, Slavery, and the Union in Antebellum Georgia*, 26.

5. Stovall, *Robert Toombs*, 30; Murray, *The Whig Party in Georgia*, 60–61.

6. For profiles of the State Rights Party in Georgia see Murray, *The Whig Party in Georgia*, 2–3; Michael Holt, *The Rise and Fall of the American Whig Party* (New York: Oxford University Press, 1999), 83–84; William Freehling, *The Road to Disunion: Secessionists at Bay* (New York: Oxford University Press, 1990), 523.

7. Milledgeville *Southern Recorder*, June 9, 1835; *Georgia Messenger*, September 3, 1835; Milledgeville *Southern Recorder*, June 23, 1835; Anthony Gene Carey, *Parties, Slavery, and the Union in Antebellum Georgia*, 35.

8. Paul Boller, Jr., *Presidential Campaigns* (New York: Oxford University Press), 61; Murray, *The Whig Party in Georgia*, 64–66; Carey, *Parties, Slavery, and the Union in Antebellum Georgia*, 36–37.

9. Boller, *Presidential Campaigns*, 62; Murray, *Whig Party in Georgia*, 66; Carey, *Parties, Slavery, and the Union in Antebellum Georgia*, 37–38.

10. Milton Sydney Heath, *Constructive Liberalism: The Role of the State in Economic Development in Georgia to 1860* (Cambridge, MA: Harvard University Press, 1954), 265–266.

11. Von Able, *Alexander H. Stephens: A Biography*, 65–66; Johnston and Brown, *Life of Alexander Stephens*, 127–128; Schott, *Stephens*, 39–40; Murray, *The Whig Party in Georgia*, 77; Milledgeville *Southern Recorder*, May 8, 1838; Toombs as a commissioner of the Georgia Rail Road and Banking Company reported in the Milledgeville *Southern Recorder*, January 26, 1836; for Stephens' account of the political battle, see Henry Cleveland, *Alexander Stephens in Public and Private, with Letters and Speeches Before, During, and Since the War* (Philadelphia: National, 1866) 605–611. Toombs' slaves may have worked on the railroad. The railroad companies often compensated slave owners with shares of stock if a slave owner sent his slaves to work on the railroad. Carey, *Parties, Slavery, and the Union in Antebellum Georgia*, 136.

12. Information concerning what is now the Robert Toombs House State Historic Site in Washington, Georgia, was generously provided by Marty B. Fleming, historic site manager, and Marcia N. Campbell, interpretive specialist; purchase of the house by Toombs taken from a typescript table of "Tax Digests of Wilkes County, Georgia," 75; information on the origin of the house and previous owner Dr. Joel Abbott is in typescript of "Robert Toombs House History," no page number.

13. Milledgeville *Georgia Journal*, May 9, 1837; Milledgeville *Southern Recorder*, May 9, 1837.

14. Reginald Charles McGrane, *The Panic of 1837* (New York: Russell and Russell, 1965), 18, 43–44, 62–63, 91–93.

15. *Ibid.*, McGrane *The Panic of 1837*, 115–116.

16. Heath, *Constructive Liberalism*, 191, 195–196, 205; Murray, *The Whig Party in Georgia*, 69; McGrane, *The Panic of 1837*, 120.

17. Heath, *Constructive Liberalism*, 188, 191.

18. Biographical Directory of the United States Congress, "Berrien, John Macpherson, (1781—1856)" *http://bioguide.congress.gov/scripts/biodisplay.pl?index=B000413*; New Georgia Encyclopedia, "John Macpherson Berrien (1781–1856)," *http://www.georgiaencyclopedia.org/nge/Article.jsp?path=/TopLevel/HistoryArchaeology/AntebellumEra/People1&id=h-3239*, accessed July 4, 2009.

19. Murray, *The Whig Party in Georgia*, 69; Milledgeville *Georgia Journal*, May 9, 1837; Carey, *Parties, Slavery, and the Union in Antebellum Georgia*, 42; Milledgeville *Southern Recorder*, May 23, 1837.

20. Murray, *The Whig Party in Georgia*, 70–71; Milledgeville *Federal Union*, July 25, 1837.

21. Murray, *The Whig Party in Georgia*, 69, 72.

22. Phillips, *Life of Toombs*, 18–19; Augusta *Chronicle*, July 17, 1837.

23. Augusta *Chronicle*, October 6, 1837; October 12, 1837; November 9, 1837.

24. James C. Bonner, *Milledgeville: Georgia's Antebellum Capital* (Athens: University of Georgia Press, 1978; reprint, Milledgeville, GA: Mary Vinson Memorial Library, 1990), 93–94, 106, 109; Carey, *Parties, Slavery, and the Union in Antebellum Georgia*, 117.

25. *Journal of the House of Representatives of the State of Georgia, 1837*, 2, 32, 35, hereafter *Georgia House Journal*; Augusta *Chronicle*, November 13, 1837; Milledgeville *Southern Recorder*, November 14, 1837.

26. Heath, 211; Murray, *Whig Party in Georgia*, 21–22, 75.

27. Friends of Cemeteries of Middle Georgia, *http://www.friendsofcems.org/MemoryHill/SQLSelect2.asp?key=WE052010*, accessed July 7, 2009.

28. Murray, *Whig Party in Georgia*, 75–77; *Georgia House Journal, 1837*, 208–209, 228–229, 329.

29. *Georgia House Journal, 1837*, 177, 327–8, 373, 431, 475–476, 121, 124, 221.

30. Johnston and Brown, *Life of Alexander Stephens*, 89.

31. Cornell University, "How Stands the Case?" *The United States Democratic Review* 3, no. 9, 8, MOA Cornell, accessed July 7, 2009.

32. Carey, *Parties, Slavery, and the Union in Antebellum Georgia*, 45; Murray, *The Whig Party in Georgia*, 79–80; Milledgeville *Southern Recorder*, October 9, 1838, November 13, 1838; *Georgia House Journal*, 1838, 51, 282, 192–3, 208–209, 318, 319–320. Toombs left the session a few days before it adjourned.

33. Carey, *Parties, Slavery, and the Union in Antebellum Georgia*, 45; Murray, *The Whig Party in Georgia*, 45; Milledgeville *Southern Recorder*, May 14, 1839.

34. Milledgeville *Southern Recorder*, May 14, July 16, 1839; Murray, *Whig Party in Georgia*, 84–85; Milledgeville *Southern Recorder*, October 15, 1839.

35. Milledgeville *Southern Recorder*, November 5, 1839; *Georgia House Journal, 1839*, 215, 252–253, 322. Toombs served on the Committee for the State of the Republic, the Judiciary Committee, and the Committee for Privileges and Elections. He was also on the Select Committee for State Finances.

36. A good account of the incident can be found at *http://imaginemaine.com/Atticus.html*, accessed July 6, 2009.

37. *Georgia House Journal, 1839*, 311.

38. *Ibid.*, 88, 224, 325.

39. Georgia *Journal* (Milledgeville, GA), December 31, 1839.

40. Augusta *Chronicle*, January 7, 1840.

41. Carey, *Parties, Slavery, and the Union in Antebellum Georgia*, 47.

42. Boller, *Presidential Campaigns*, 66–67; see also Arthur M. Schlesinger, Jr., *The History of American Presidential Elections, 1789–1968* (New York: Chelsea House, 1971), 643–684.

43. Augusta *Chronicle*, May 5, 1840.

44. Augusta *Chronicle*, June 4, 6, 1840.

45. Murray, *Whig Party in Georgia*, 89; Augusta *Chronicle*, August 19, 1840.

46. Murray, *Whig Party in Georgia*, 93.

47. Augusta *Chronicle*, September 22, 1840.

48. Boller, *Presidential Campaigns*, 71; Schlesinger, *The History of American Presidential Elections, 1789–1968*, 681; Carey, *Parties, Slavery, and the Union in Antebellum Georgia*, 52.

49. Augusta *Chronicle*, October 12, 1840; *Georgia House Journal, 1840*, 35.

50. Heath, *Constructive Liberalism*, 212–214; Augusta *Chronicle*, October 1, 1840.

51. *Georgia House Journal, 1840*, 12–13, 25.

52. *Ibid.*, 191–193; Stovall, *Robert Toombs*, 33; Augusta *Chronicle*, December 28, 1840.

53. *Georgia House Journal, 1840*, 344.

54. *Ibid.*, 344.

55. *Ibid.*, 361.

56. *Ibid.*, 425–427.

57. *Ibid.*, 99–102.

58. Murray, *The Whig Party in Georgia*, 98; *Georgia House Journal, 1840*, 73, 372, 418–421.

59. Carey, *Parties, Slavery, and the Union in Antebellum Georgia*, 58; Augusta *Chronicle*, October 11, 1841.

60. Stovall, *Robert Toombs*, 37–38.

61. Paul F. Boller, Jr., *Presidential Anecdotes* (New York: Oxford University Press, 1981), 97.

62. Holt, *American Whig Party*, 129, 150; David Whitney, *The American Presidents: Biographies of the Chief Executives from Washington through Clinton* (New York: Guild America Books, 1968, 1993), 91–92.

63. Augusta *Chronicle*, June 6, 23, 1842.

64. See, for instance, Augusta *Chronicle*, September 14, 1842.

65. Augusta *Chronicle*, October 6, 1842.

66. Augusta *Chronicle*, October 8, 1842; Stovall, *Robert Toombs*, 38; *Georgia House Journal, 1842*, 46, 70, 138, 395.

67. See "Acts of the General Assembly of the State of Georgia, passed in Milledgeville at an Annual Session in November and December, 1842," *http://neptune3.galib.uga.edu/ssp/cgi-bin/legis-idx.pl?sessionid=7f000001&type=law&byte=21808738&lawcnt=137&filt=doc*, accessed July 1, 2009.

68. *Ibid.*, 276–277.

69. Augusta *Chronicle*, September 22, 1842.

70. For the Whig resolutions favoring Berrien, see Lucien LaTasle to John M. Berrien, December 23, 1842, in John McPherson Berrien Papers, Southern Historical Collection, Wilson Library, University of North Carolina, Chapel Hill, (microfilm), cited hereafter as Berrien Papers, UNC; Stovall, *Robert Toombs*, 39; *Georgia House Journal, 1842*, 441–445.

71. *Ibid.*, 446–447; Carey, *Parties, Slavery, and the Union in Antebellum Georgia*, 65; Augusta *Chronicle*, December 23, 1842. The bank both burdened and benefited Georgia's economy. The bank's opponents—Toombs among them—claimed the state frittered away revenue by investing in the Central Bank when private banks made more capital. Yet the Central Bank stabilized the Georgia's financial system during the panic as best it could by extending loans, stabilizing the currency, and keeping massive internal improvement projects such as the Western and Atlantic Railroad funded. For a brief summary of the bank's history, see Heath, *Constructive Liberalism*, 211–223.

72. Toombs to John Berrien, January 7, 1843, Berrien Papers, UNC. Locofocos were disaffected Democrats that broke off from the regular party in 1835. But Locofoco became an acrid term used by their enemies to describe any Democrat. Toombs was particularly fond of it.

73. Augusta *Chronicle*, January 4, 10, 1843.

74. Augusta *Chronicle*, June 24, 1843.

75. Augusta *Chronicle*, August 10, 1843.

76. Augusta *Chronicle*, June 29, August 15, August 16, August 17, August 29, September 2, September 14, 1843, September 16, 1843.

77. Augusta *Chronicle*, October 9, 1843; *Georgia House Journal, 1843*, 6, 192–193; Toombs to Stephens, January 1, 1844, *in The Correspondence of Robert Toombs, Alexander Stephens, and Howell Cobb*, ed. Ulrich B. Phillips (Washington, D.C.: American Historical Association, 1913), 53. Cited hereafter as Phillips, *Correspondence*.

78. For a good summary of the school system in antebellum Georgia, see Heath, *Constructive Liberalism*, 345–350.

79. *Georgia House Journal, 1843*, 70, 124, 140, 180, 182–186; Augusta *Chronicle*, December 18, 1843. The *Chronicle* reporter noted that the bill was mocked with sarcastic debates and comic amendments, much to the delight of the women in the galleries.

80. Toombs to A.L. Hillhouse, December 17, 1843, in Alexander and Hillhouse Papers contained in "Records of the Ante-Bellum Southern Plantations from Revolution through the Civil War," Series J, Part 4, Reel 12, University Publications, Bethesda, MD; Toombs to Stephens, January 1, 1844, Phillips, *Correspondence*, 53.

Chapter 3

1. Toombs to John M. Berrien, January 28, 1844, Berrien Papers, UNC.

2. Murray, *Whig Party in Georgia*, 109.

3. Stovall, *Robert Toombs*, 48; Augusta *Chronicle*, August 13, 1887.

4. Holt, *The Rise and Fall of the American Whig Party*, p. 177

5. Remini, *Henry Clay, Statesman for the Union* (New York: Norton, 1991), 660; Stovall, *Robert Toombs*, 53.

6. *Ibid.*, 47–49; New York *Times*, August 12, 1885.

7. Boller, Campaigns, 79–80; *http://www.presidency.ucsb.edu/ws/index.php?pid=25852*, accessed July 16, 2009.

8. Sarah Alexander to "My Dearest Father," January 16, 1845, Alexander and Hillhouse Papers, Southern History Collection, University of North Carolina; Toombs to Stephens, January 24, 1845, in Phillips, *Correspondence*, 60–61.

9. Toombs to Berrien, February 13, 1845, in Berrien Papers, UNC.

10. For Stephens' speech, see *Globe*, 28th Congress, 2nd Session, Appendix, 308–314, referred to hereafter as *Globe*; Holt, *American Whig Party*, 178–179; Toombs to Alexander Stephens, February 16, 1845, in Phillips, *Correspondence*, 63–64.

11. William Seale, *The President's House: A History*, Vol. I (Washington, D.C.: White House Historical Association, 1986), 278

12. George M. Towle, "Some Secession Leaders," *Harper's New Monthly Magazine* 26 (April 1863), 675, MOA Cornell, accessed July 16, 2009; Anonymous, "Recollec-

tions of an Old Stager," *Harper's New Monthly Magazine* 48 (January 1874), 254, MOA Cornell, accessed July 16, 2009; Virginia Clay-Clopton, *A Belle of the Fifties: Memoirs of Mrs. Clay, of Alabama, Covering Social and Political Life in Washington and the South, 1853–66*, 86, available at *http://docsouth.unc.edu/fpn/clay/clay.html*, accessed July 16, 2009.

13. Lauchlan Bellingham Mackinnon, *Atlantic and Transatlantic: Sketches Afloat and Ashore* (New York: Harper & Brothers, 1852), 63–65, MOA UM, accessed July 16, 2009.

14. *Globe*, 29th Congress, 1st Session, 185–186.

15. Toombs to George W. Crawford, February 6, 1846, Papers of Robert Augustus Toombs, Library of Congress. Referred to hereafter as "Toombs Papers, LOC"; Toombs to John Milledge III, February 17, 1846, John Milledge, Jr. MSS, Duke University, Rare Book, Manuscript and Special Collections Library.

16. Alexander Stephens to George W. Crawford, February 3, 1846, correspondence, in Phillips, *Correspondence*, 71–72; George D. Phillips to Howell Cobb, December 30, 1845, *ibid.*, 69–70.

17. Augusta *Chronicle*, March 24, 1846, March 10, 1846.

18. *http://mexicanamericanwar.info/*, July 16, 2009; Arthur Schlesinger, Jr., *The Almanac of American History*, 250.

19. *Globe*, 29th Congress, 1st Session, 837; Augusta *Chronicle*, May 22, 1846.

20. *Schott*, Stephens, 71; Remini, *Henry Clay, Statesman for the Union*, 693; *Globe*, 30th Congress, 1st Session, 64.

21. *Globe*, 29th Congress, 1st Session, 1217–1218.

22. For Toombs' tariff speech, see *Globe*, 29th Congress, 1st Session, Appendix, 1030–1035; Augusta *Chronicle*, August 7, 1846; *The American Whig Review* 4 (September 1846), 224–225, MOA Cornell, accessed July 16, 2009.

23. Augusta *Chronicle*, August 1, September 15, September 26, 1846.

24. *Globe*, 29th Congress, 2nd Session, 140–142. Ulrich Phillips says the last part of the speech was "an impromptu appendix" Toombs added at the last minute. Phillips, *Life of Toombs*, 42.

25. Richard Malcolm Johnston and William Hand Brown, *The Life of Alexander H. Stephens* (Philadelphia: Books for Libraries Press, 1878), 218–19. Cited hereafter as Johnston and Browne, *Life of Stephens*.

26. *Globe*, 29th Congress, 2nd Session, 240; *National Intelligencer*, January 23, 1847; *Schott*, Stephens, 76; Holt *American Whig Party*, 253; Augusta *Chronicle*, February 4, 1847.

27. For Toombs' involvement with the railroad, see Augusta *Chronicle*, June 7, 29, August 19, 23, 1847. For the Washington branch line, see Robert Willingham, *An Overview of Local History* at *http://www.rootsweb.ancestry.com/~gawilkes/localhst.htm*, accessed *June 3, 2009*.

28. Richard Harrison Shyrock, *Georgia and the Union* (New York: AMS Press, 1926, 1968), 142.

29. Murray, *Whig Party in Georgia*, 128–9.

30. *Globe*, 30th Congress, 1st Session, 61, 169.

31. For printing contracts, see *ibid.*, 481–482; for reduction of the military, see 1035; *ibid.*, 401.

32. *Ibid.*, 179, 943.

33. Eric Foner and John A. Garraty, eds., *The Reader's Companion to American History* (Boston: Houghton Mifflin, 1991), 723.

34. Holt, *American Whig Party*, 287.

35. *Ibid.*, 280–281, 309.

36. Toombs to James Thomas, April 16, 1848, Toombs Papers, LOC.

37. Augusta *Chronicle*, April 22, 1848.

38. Toombs to James Thomas, May 1, 1848 in Phillips, *Correspondence*, 104–105.

39. Augusta *Chronicle*, May 16, 24, 1848.

40. New Orleans *Picayune*, April 25, 1848; Avary, *Recollections of Alexander Stephens*, 34; Alexander Stephens to Mrs. Ann Mary Coleman, October 13, 1870, in Ann Mary Coleman, *The Life of John J. Crittenden* (Philadelphia: Lippencott, 1873), 294, available at MOA UM, accessed July 16, 2009; Toombs to John J. Crittenden, September 27, 1848, Papers of John Jordan Crittenden, Special Collections, Margaret I. King Library, University of Kentucky, cited hereafter as Crittenden Papers, UK.

41. Milledgeville *Southern Recorder*, May 2, 1848.

42. Toombs to James Thomas, May 1, 1848, Toombs Papers, LOC.

43. Boller, *Presidential Campaigns*, 85; Remini, *Henry Clay, Statesman for the Union*, 707.

44. Toombs to George W. Crawford, June 23, 1848, LOC.

45. Augusta *Chronicle*, June 21, July 15, August 12, 1848.

46. *Globe*, 30th Congress, 1st Session, Appendix, 841–842. Toombs spent the rest of his speech vilifying and insulting the Democratic platform and demanding Congress not cut Southern rights out of the Mexican Cession.

47. For Stephens' explanation for his vote, see his letter to the editor of the Milledgeville *Federal Union*, August 30, 1848, in Phillips, *Correspondence*, 117–125.

48. Phillips, *Life of Robert Toombs*, 57.

49. Augusta *Chronicle*, August 19, 1848; Holt, *American Whig Party*, 337.

50. Augusta *Chronicle*, September 6, 1848.

51. Toombs to John J. Crittenden, September 27, 1848, Crittenden Papers, UK. For the attack on Stephens, see Augusta *Chronicle*, September 6, 1848.

52. Augusta *Chronicle*, September 1, 1848.

53. Augusta *Chronicle*, September 2, 11, 15, 1848; Stephens to Julia Toombs, no date, quoted in Stovall, *Robert Toombs*, 63; Toombs to John J. Crittenden, September 27, 1848, Crittenden Papers, UK.

54. Augusta *Chronicle*, September 18, 1848.

55. Avary, *Recollections for Alexander Stephens*, 22–24.

56. Stephens won his district with 60.7 percent of the vote; Toombs carried his by 62.4 percent. *Congressional Quarterly's Guide to U.S. Elections*, 3rd ed., (Washington, D.C., 1994), 985; Toombs to John J. Crittenden, November 9, 1848, Crittenden Papers UK.

57. Augusta *Chronicle*, January 20, 22, 1849; Toombs to John J. Crittenden, December 3, 1848, Phillips, *Correspondence*, 139–140; Toombs to John J. Crittenden, January 22, 1849, Crittenden Papers UK; Nevins, *Ordeal of the Union: Fruits of Manifest Destiny, 1847–1852* (New York: Charles Scribner's Sons, 1947), 224. Toombs incorrectly dated his January 3 letter. The meeting took place January 15.

58. Toombs to John J. Crittenden, January 3, 1848, Phillips, *Correspondence*, 139–140.

59. Toombs to John J. Crittenden, January 22, 1849, Crittenden Papers UK.

60. Toombs to Crittenden, February 9, 1849, Crittenden Papers UK.

61. *Globe*, 30th Congress, 2nd Session, 609.

62. Holt, *American Whig Party*, 435–436

63. Anonymous, "Recollections of an Old Stager," *Harper's New Monthly Magazine*, 48 (January 1874), 254, MOA Cornell, accessed July 17, 2009; Toombs to Crittenden, February 9, 1849, Crittenden Papers, UK.

64. Toombs to Mrs. Chapman Coleman, June 22, 1849, Phillips, *Correspondence*, 165.

65. Holt, *American Whig Party*, 439–440; Murray, *Whig Party in Georgia*, 142.

66. Toombs to George W. Crawford, April 23, 1850, quoted in Phillips, *Toombs*, 65–66.

67. *National Intelligencer*, December 6, 1849; Augusta *Chronicle*, December 10, 1849; Nathan Appleton, *Letter to the Hon. Wm. C. Rives of Virginia on Slavery and the Union* (Boston: Eastburn, 1860), 6, MOA UM, accessed July 16, 2009; Winthrope quoted in Holt, *American Whig Party*, 468.

68. Augusta *Chronicle*, December 12, 1849.

69. Alexander A. Stephens, *A Constitutional View of the Late War Between the States: Its Causes, Character, Conduct and Results. Presented in a Series of Colloquies at Liberty Hall* (Philadelphia: National, 1868–70), 2: 178. Cited hereafter as "Stephens, "*Constitutional View*." See Holt, 469–470, for some possible political motivations on the part of Toombs and Stephens.

70. Schott, *Stephens*, 107.

71. Toombs to George W. Crawford, April 23, 1850, quoted in Phillips, *Toombs*, 65–66. The Georgia House of Representatives had armed its congressional delegation with the Wiggins Resolutions that instructed its representatives in Washington not to admit California as a free state.

72. *Globe*, 31st Congress, 1st Session, 27–28. Toombs' speech was interrupted several times by loud bursts of applause.

73. *Ibid.*, 29

74. *National Intelligencer*, December 15, 1849.

75. For Toombs' nomination see *Globe*, 34, 65. For his disruption in the House, see *ibid.*, 61–63; James Dabney McCabe, *Behind the Scenes in Washington* (New York: Continental, 1873) 193, MOA UM, accessed July 16, 2009.

76. Howell Cobb to his wife, December 22, 1849, quoted in Phillips, *Correspondence*, 180. Toombs and Stephens supported Charles S. Moorehead from Kentucky for speaker.

77. Varina Howell Davis, *Jefferson Davis: Ex-president of the Confederate States of America, A Memoir by His Wife* (New York: Belford, 1890), 411–412.

78. *Globe*, 31st Congress, 1st Session, 244–247.

79. *Schott*, Stephens, 112.

80. For the account about Hannibal Hamlin, see Charles E. Hamlin, *The Life and Times of Hannibal Hamlin* (Cambridge, MA: Riverside Press, 1899; reprint, Port Washington, NY: Kennikat Press, 1971), 202; Mark Scroggins, *Hannibal: The Life of Abraham Lincoln's First Vice President* (Lanham, MD: University Press of America, 1994,) 78–80; for Thurlow Weed's version, see Harriet A. Weed, ed., *The Autobiography of Thurlow Weed* (Boston: Houghton, Mifflin, 1883), 2: 276–177. Historians disagree on the date of the meeting. Allan Nevins places the meeting in July, *Ordeal of the Union: Fruits of Manifest Destiny, 1847–1852*, 330–331, and Holt places it in mid–April, 484–485. I think February is likely because Toombs, Stephens, and Clingman would have wanted to inform Taylor about the proposal they had forged at Howell Cobb's house as soon as possible. Henry Clay's compromises were on everybody's mind and Taylor probably misunderstood them during their early incarnation.

81. *Globe*, 31st Congress, 1st Session, Appendix 198–202.

82. Stovall, *Robert Toombs*, 78; Thompson, *Toombs*, 63.

83. For full text, see *Globe*, 31st Congress, 1st Session, 451–455. There was a rumor that Toombs visited Calhoun a few days before he died. Calhoun supposedly said to the young congressman that he had to "leave to younger men the task of carrying out my views." C.S. Moorehead to John J. Crittenden, March 30, 1850, in Coleman, *Life of John J. Crittenden*, UM MOA, July 16, 2009, 363.

84. For full text, see *Globe*, 31st Congress, 1st Session, 476–484.

85. Toombs to Linton Stephens, March 22, 1850, in Alexander Hamilton Stephens Papers, Special Collections, Robert W. Woodruff Library, Emory University.

86. For Clay's report, see *Globe*, 31st Congress, 1st Session, 944–956.

87. Toombs to Crittenden, April 25, 1850, Crittenden Papers, UK.

88. *Globe*, 31st Congress, 1st Session, 1199–1200.

89. *Ibid.*, 1216. Hamilcar Barca was a Carthaginian general during the Punic Wars and the father of Hannibal.

90. Stephens, *Constitutional View*, 2: 116.

91. Avary, ed., *Recollections of Alexander H. Stephens*, 26; Schott, *Stephens*, 119–121; Nevins, *Ordeal of the Union: Fruits of Manifest Destiny*, 327–331.

92. Augusta *Chronicle*, July 19, 1850. The Galphin claim involved money owed to the Galphin family from the sale of Indian lands during the colonial period. Secretary of War George W. Crawford happened to be the family's lawyer. Crawford did not give the case up when he came to Washington even though it appeared to be a clear conflict of interest. When Attorney General Reverdy Johnson advised the Treasury to pay the claim with accumulated interest, Crawford received a hefty fee. The newspapers picked up the story and it became enough of a scandal that Taylor considered dismissing Crawford, Johnson, and Secretary of the Treasury William Meredith from his cabinet.

93. Alexander Stephens to the Editors of the Baltimore *Clipper*, July 13, 1856, in Phillips, *Correspondence*, 195.

94. Augusta *Chronicle*, August 15, 1850.

95. Toombs to Julia Toombs, August 3, 11, 1850, Toombs Papers, Hargrett Rare Book and Manuscript Library, University of Georgia. Hereafter cited as Toombs Papers, University of Georgia.

96. Toombs to Julia Toombs, August 11, 1850, Toombs Papers, University of Georgia; Augusta *Chronicle*, December 18, 28, 1850, January 14, 1851, March 30, 1851. See also *http://www.hmdb.org/marker.asp?marker=3969*, accessed July 16, 2009.

97. Toombs to Julia Toombs, August 24, 1850, Toombs Papers, University of Georgia.

98. *Ibid.*, August 29, 1850.

99. *Globe*, 31st Congress, 1st Session, 1753.

100. *Ibid.*, 1757.

101. *Ibid.*, 1764, 1772, 1776, 1807, 1837.

102. *Ibid.*, 1775.

103. Augusta *Chronicle*, September 12, 15, October 9, 1850.

104. Holt, *American Whig Party*, 607.

105. Augusta *Chronicle*, October 9, 1850

106. *Ibid.*

107. Augusta *Chronicle*, October 9, 1850; Stovall, *Robert Toombs*, 84.

108. Augusta *Chronicle*, November 9, 1850.

109. Schott, *Stephens*, 129; Georgia *Telegraph*, December 17, 1850; Charles J. Jenkins probably wrote the platform, but Stephens, in his later years, claimed credit for it even though he did not serve on the committee that wrote it. Avary, *Recollections of A.H. Stephens*, 27.

110. Richard Harrison Shyrock, *Georgia and the Union in 1850* (New York: Ames Press, 1926, 1968), 332.

111. Augusta *Chronicle*, December 19, 1850.

112. Columbus *Times*, quoted in *Schott*, Stephens, 132.

113. Carey, *Parties, Slavery, and the Union in Antebellum Georgia*, 162.

114. Toombs to Howell Cobb, January 2, 1851, in Phillips, *Correspondence* 218–220.

115. *Globe*, 2nd Session, 588 & 764; Toombs to Julia Toombs, January 3, 1851, Toombs Papers, University of Georgia. In the letter to Julia, the irreligious Toombs says that he had no objection to Sallie, his fifteen-year-old daughter, joining a church. "I am content if she desires and you wish it. My opinion about revivals ... have been long formed & much strengthened by my experience in the world but I am not at all solicitous that they should be the rule of anybody's conduct but my own. I have therefore endeavored to stand upon the great protestant [sic] principle, in matters of religion of judging for myself and allowing all others to do the same." *Ibid.*

116. Toombs to Absalom H. Chappell and Others, February 15, 1851, in Phillips, *Correspondence*, 228.

117. Toombs to John J. Crittenden, April 25, 1851, in Crittenden Papers, UK.

118. Shyrock, 350–351.

119. Alexander Stephens to Howell Cobb, June 23, 1851, in Phillips, *Correspondence*, 238; Toombs to Howell Cobb, June 9, 1851, quoted in Thompson, *Toombs*, 79.

120. Toombs to Howell Cobb, June 19, 1851, quoted in Schott, *Stephens*, 137; Toombs to Eli Warren, August 19, 1851, quoted in Shyrock, 353.

121. Toombs to Howell Cobb, October 11, 1851, in Phillips, *Correspondence*, 261.

122. Augusta *Chronicle*, October 16, 1851. For a while, the Constitutional Union Party was a Southern phenomenon. Party members also won big in Alabama, Mississippi, and South Carolina.

123. Toombs to Julia Toombs, November 5, 1851, in Toombs Papers, University of Georgia. Toombs was always itchy to travel to some political event or the other, but he usually professed impatience and distaste for campaigning. "You can see from this letter how deeply I am immersed in this contest, yet I am getting so impatient to come home that even defeat would be better than this eternal annoyance," he wrote in the same letter to Julia.

124. Albany [Georgia] *Patriot* quoted in Augusta *Chronicle*, December 2, 1851.

125. New York *Times*, May 28, 1852.

126. New York *Times*, November 15, 1851; Athens *Southern Banner*, November 20, 1851.

127. Toombs to Julia Toombs, December 2, 1851, Toombs Papers, University of Georgia; Alexander Stephens to Linton Stephens, December 10, 1851, in Phillips, *Correspondence*, 274.

128. Holt, *American Whig Party*, 678; Alexander Stephens to Howell Cobb, December 5, 1851, in Phillips, *Correspondence*, 268; W.H. Hull to Howell Cobb, February 14, 1852, in Phillips, *Life of Toombs*, 107.

129. Anonymous, "The Presidency and the Review," *The United States Democratic Review* 30 (February 1852) 182, MOA Cornell, accessed July 16, 2009.

130. *National Intelligencer*, March 12, 1852; New York *Times*, March 17, 1852.

131. Marion Lumpkin Cobb to Callie King, March 22, 1852, Joseph Henry Lumpkin Family Papers, available at *http://dlg.galileo.usg.edu/hargrett/lumpkin/jhl0004.php*, accessed July 16, 2009; New York *Times*, April 14, 1852; Toombs to Julia Toombs, May 15, 1853, McGill Papers, Emory University; Toombs to Howell Cobb, May 27, 1852, in Phillips, *Correspondence*, 297.

132. Toombs to Howell Cobb, May 27, 1852 in Phillips, *Correspondence*, 297–298.

133. Eisenhower, *Agent of Destiny*, 328.

134. See Toombs to Howell Cobb, June 10, 1852, in John Eddins Simpson, "A Biography of Howell Cobb" (Ph.D. dissertation, University of Georgia, 1971), 174–175; Alexander Stephens to the Editor of the Augusta, Ga., *Chronicle and Sentinel*, June 28, 1852, in Phillips, *Correspondence*, 304.

135. *Globe*, 32nd Congress, 1st Session, Appendix, 816–820.

136. *National Intelligencer*, July 5, 1852; New York *Times*, July 7, 1852; Anonymous, "The Whig Convention: The Candidate and Campaign," The American Whig Review 16 (August 1852), 101, MOA Cornell, accessed July 16, 2009.

137. Boller, *Presidential Campaigns*, 88, 90. Paul F. Boller, Jr., *Presidential Anecdotes* (New York: Oxford University Press, 1981), 114.

138. Schott, *Stephens*, 151.

139. Helen Eliza Terrill, *History of Stewart County* (Columbus, GA: Columbus Office Supply, 1958), 726; John G. Winter to "Governor Johnson," October 4, 1864, quoted in "Collections of the Georgia Historical Society," *Georgia Historical Quarterly* 46 (March 1962), 48; Toombs to John J. Crittenden, December 5, 1852, Crittenden Papers, UK.

140. Alfred Hunter, comp., *The Washington and Georgetown Directory, Strangers' Guide-Book for Washington, and Congressional and Clerks' Register* (Washington: Kirkwood and McGill, 1853), 53; *Globe*, 2nd Session 32nd Congress, 262; 441; 610–615; quoted in Phillips, *Life of Toombs*, 115; *Globe*, 823. When in Washington, D.C., Toombs usually boarded, or "messed," with Alexander Stephens in one of numerous boarding houses. See Kenneth H. Thomas, *The Robert Toombs House, Washington, Georgia* (Atlanta: State of Georgia, Department of Natural Resources, 1974), 43–44.

141. The account of Louisa's marriage is taken from Thompson, *Toombs*, 89–90, and an interview with Toombs that appeared in the New York *Times*, August 12, 1885.

142. Toombs to Julia Toombs, May 9, 1853, in Toombs Papers, University of Georgia.

143. Milledgeville *Federal Union*, June 28, 1853. Stephens played little role in the convention. He was recovering from a broken arm and cuts and bruises he suffered in a train wreck. See Schott, *Stephens*, 157–158.

144. Augusta *Chronicle*, August 12, September 9, 1853.

145. Alexander Morton to Howell Cobb, July 2, 1853,

in Phillips, *Correspondence*, 330; Washington *Daily Evening Star*, June 18, 1853, *http://www.paperofrecord.com*, accessed March 3, 2003. Hereafter cited as Washington *Star* PoR; Toombs to Julia Toombs, November 9, 1853, Toombs Papers, University of Georgia.

146. Toombs to Julia Toombs, December 28, 1853, Toombs Papers, University of Georgia.

147. *Ibid.*, December 28, 1853.

Chapter 4

1. Anonymous, "Glances from the Senate Gallery," *Continental Monthly*, July 1862, 13, MOA Cornell, accessed July 17, 2009.

2. Avary, *Recollections of Alexander Stephens*, 426–428.

3. Sir William Howard Russell, *My Diary North and South* (Boston: Burnham, 1863), 181, MOA UM, accessed July 17, 2009; Anonymous, "Conversational Opinions of Leaders of Secession," *Atlantic Monthly* 10, November 1862, 613–623, MOA Cornell, accessed July 17, 2009.

4. Anonymous, "Glances from the Senate Gallery," 13 MOA Cornell, accessed July 17, 2009; Varina Howell Davis, *Jefferson Davis*, vol. 1, 411.

5. Glyndon G. Van Deusen, *Horace Greeley: Nineteenth Century Crusader* (Philadelphia: University of Pennsylvania Press, 1953, 1967), 179; Allan Nevins, *Ordeal of the Union: A House Dividing* (New York: Charles Scribner's Sons, 1947), 112.

6. Toombs to W.W. Burwell, February 3, 1854, in Phillips, *Correspondence*, 342–343.

7. Holt, *American Whig Party*, 1140.

8. Milledgeville *Federal Union*, February 23, 1854; *Globe*, 1st Session, 33rd Congress, Appendix, 755–756. Toombs recounted what happened in a bad-tempered exchange with John Bell in the Senate on May 25, 1854.

9. *Globe*, 1st Session, 33rd Congress, Appendix, 346–351.

10. Athens (Georgia) *Southern Banner*, March 9, 1854; New York *Times*, March 6, 1854.

11. Augusta *Chronicle*, March 8, 1854; *Globe*, 1st Session, 33rd Congress, 532. Toombs told John C. Reed years later that he was appalled to find the Democrats were committed to repealing the Missouri Compromise. Had he not been away on business, he claimed, he would have "crushed the scheme at its first proposal." See Reed, *The Brothers' War*, 262.

12. Toombs to George W. Crawford, April 26, 1854, Robert Toombs Papers, Duke University; Schott, *Stephens*, 173.

13. *Globe*, 1st Session, 33rd Congress, 1006, 1145.

14. *Ibid.*, 1145.

15. *Globe*, 33rd Congress, 1st Session, Appendix, 757–759. A few days later, Toombs attended a banquet. When the subject came up, he said to Lord Elgin: "My lord, we are about to relume the torch of liberty upon the altar of slavery."; Phillip R. Ammidon "An Englishman's Opinion," *New England Magazine* 5, March 1887, 478, MOA Cornell, accessed July 17, 2009.

16. Toombs to Julia Toombs, July 6, 1854, Toombs Papers, University of Georgia.

17. *Ibid.*, July 10, 1854.

18. *Globe*, 33rd Congress, 1st Session, Appendix, 1210–1212.

19. *Ibid.*, 1199.

20. Toombs to Julia Toombs, October 24, 1854, November 1, 1854, Toombs Papers, University of Georgia.

21. *Ibid.*, November 11, 1854.

22. *Globe*, 2nd Session, 33rd Congress, 94, 150–154, 267–268.

23. Thompson, *Toombs*, 90.

24. Toombs to Julia Toombs, February 26, 1855, Toombs Papers, University of Georgia.

25. James Hillhouse Alexander to Edward Alexander, February 24, 1855, Edward Porter Alexander Papers, UNC; Alexander Stephens to Linton Stephens, March 6, 1855, Alexander Stephens Collection, Manhattanville College Library Special Collections, Purchase, NY. Linton Stephens to Alexander Stephens, March 8, 1855, Alexander Stephens Collection, Manhattanville College Library Special Collections, Purchase, NY.

26. Toombs to Julia Toombs, April 28, 1855, Toombs Papers, University of Georgia.

27. *Ibid.*, May 18, 1855.

28. Toombs to Alexander Stephens, June 21, 1855, in Phillips, *Correspondence*, 353–354; Stovall, *Robert Toombs*, 126. Toombs boasted that he had not been presented to "a crowned head or a lord" while he was in Europe. Avary, *Recollections of Alexander Stephens*, 422.

29. Toombs to Julia Toombs, June 28 (misdated, possibly July 28), 1855, Toombs Papers, University of Georgia; Stovall, *Robert Toombs*, 360–361.

30. Milledgeville *Federal Union*, August 2, 1853; Montgomery, *Cracker Parties*, 126–127.

31. Montgomery, *Cracker Parties*, 143–144.

32. Toombs to T. Lomax, June 6, 1855, in Phillips, *Correspondence*, 351–353.

33. Milledgeville *Federal Union*, November 13, 1855.

34. *Globe*, 73; Toombs to Thomas W. Thomas, December 17, 1855, Robert Toombs Papers, Duke University.

35. Milledgeville *Federal Union*, February 5, 1856.

36. *Ibid.* For the full text of Toombs' speech, see Stephens' *Constitutional History of the United States*, 1: 625–647. Toombs' speech was published a few months later in *Debow's Review*. See Robert Toombs, "Slavery: Its Constitutional Status, and its Influence on Society and the Colored Race," *Debow's Review* 20, May 1856, 581–605, MOA UM, accessed July 17, 2009.

37. *Globe*, 34th Congress, 1st Session, Appendix, 115–118; Alexander Stephens to Thomas W. Thomas, February 29, 1856, quoted in Thompson, *Toombs*, 109.

38. Toombs to Julia Toombs, March 7, 1856, Toombs Papers; *Globe*, 34th Congress, 1st Session, 1022.

39. Toombs to George W. Crawford, May 17, 1856, in Toombs, LOC; *Globe*, 1st Session, 34th Congress, Appendix, 544.

40. David Herbert Donald, *Charles Sumner* (New York: Da Capo Press, 1960, 1970, 1996), 295–296. See also testimony of House Committee (Reports, I, No. 182).

41. Toombs to George W. Crawford, May 30, 1856, Toombs LOC; *Globe*, 34th Congress, 1st Session, 1305; Boller, *Presidential Campaigns*, 95.

42. Toombs to Thomas W. Thomas, February 9, 1856, in Phillips, *Correspondence*, 361; Toombs to George W. Crawford, in Phillips, *Correspondence*, 364. Instead of attending the convention, Toombs went on a business trip to New York City. Toombs to George W. Crawford, May 30, 1856, in Phillips, *Correspondence*, 365.

43. Boller, *Presidential Campaign*, 92–93; Donald Bruce Johnson, ed., *National Party Platforms*, vol. I, *1840–1956* (Urbana: University of Illinois Press, 1978), 27–28.

44. *Globe*, 34th Congress, 1st Session, 1439.

45. Schott, *Stephens*, 206; *Globe*, 34th Congress, 1st Session, Appendix, 769.

46. For Toombs' entire speech, see *Globe*, 34th Congress, 1st Session, Appendix, 769–772.

47. Allan Nevins, *Ordeal of the Union*, vol. 2, *A House Dividing*, 472.

48. *Globe*, 34th Congress, 1st Session, Appendix, 852, 869.

49. *Ibid.*, 869–872.

50. *Globe*, 34th Congress, 1st Session. See 1042, for example, and 1887–1882, 1953.

51. New York *Times*, August 2, 1856.

52. Toombs to Alexander Stephens, September 3, 1856, in Phillips, *Correspondence*, 380.

53. Stovall, *Robert Toombs*, 149–151. Some of Stovall's account sounds fanciful, but the quoted passages ring true. For a partisan Whig account, see Augusta *Chronicle*, October 29, 1856.

54. John Weise, *Life and Correspondence of Theodore Parker, Minister to the Twenty-Eighth Congregational Society, Boston* (New York: Appleton, 1864), 223–224, MOA UM, accessed July 17, 2009; for examples, see also "The Constitution and Slavery," *Continental Monthly* 1, June 1862, 624, MOA Cornell, accessed July 17, 2009; William Ellery Channing, *Thoughts Selected from the Writings of the Rev. William E. Channing* (Boston: Ticknor and Fields, 1859), 2: 172, MOA UM, accessed July 17, 2009; New York *Tribune*, March 11, 1857. The Reverend Parker attributed the quote to Toombs in a sermon in Boston as early as 1854. See Theodore Parker, "The New Crime Against Humanity: A Sermon Preached at the Music Hall, in Boston on Sunday, June 4, 1854," MOA UM, accessed July 17, 2009.

55. Wendell Phillips, *Speeches, Lectures, and Letters* (Boston: Lee and Shepard, 1872), 424–425, MOA UM, accessed July 17, 2009; Anthony Trollope, *North America* (Philadelphia: Lippencott, 1863), 169, MOA UM, accessed July 17, 2009.

56. Stephens, *Constitutional View*, 217; Henry W. Grady, "The New South," *The New England Magazine* 8, March 1890, 88, MOA Cornell, accessed July 17, 2009. Toombs was also widely quoted as saying that he would drink every drop of Yankee blood shed during the war. See, for instance, Lilla Mills Hawes, "Collections of the Georgia Historical Quarterly, Other Documents and Notes, A Description of Whitefield's Bethesda: Samuel Fayrweather to Thomas Prince and Thomas Foxcraft," *Georgia Historical Quarterly* 45, December 1961, 379.

57. Robert Toombs to Alexander Stephens, December 1, 1856, in Phillips, *Correspondence*, 383–384.

58. *Globe*, Third Session, 34th Congress, 173, 239.

59. *Ibid.*, 243, 299.

60. *Globe*, 34th Congress, 3rd Session, 500; Johnston and Browne, *Life of Stephens*, 325.

61. Toombs to Thomas W. Thomas, February 5, 1857, Robert Toombs Papers, Duke University. "Stephens left yesterday in great distress about Linton and his domestic misfortunes," Toombs added in the same letter. "He left it doubtful whether he would return again this session."

62. Toombs to Alexander Stephens, March 10, 1857, in Phillips, *Correspondence*, 398.

63.James M. McPhereson, ed., *To the Best of My Ability: The American Presidents* (New York: Agincourt Press, 2000), 361.

64. Milledgeville *Federal Union*, November 1, 1853; Augusta *Chronicle*, November 4, 1853.

65. Milledgeville *Federal Union*, March 24, 1857; New York *Times*, March 18, 1857.

66. Toombs to W.W. Burwell, March 30, 1857, in Phillips, *Correspondence*, 399–400.

67. Derrel C. Roberts, "Toombs' Texas Land," *Georgia Historical Quarterly* 55, Winter 1971, 540.

68. On Texas land deals, see, for instance, Toombs to William Crawford, April 15, 1854, in Alexander Hamilton Stephens Papers, Emory University; Toombs to Julia Toombs, May 3, 1857, Toombs Papers, University of Georgia.

69. Toombs to Julia Toombs, May 14, 1857, Toombs Papers, University of Georgia.

70. Stovall, *Robert Toombs*, 153–154.

71. Toombs to Julia Toombs, June 20, 1857, Toombs Papers, University of Georgia; Toombs to W.W. Burwell, July 11, 1857, Phillips, *Correspondence*, 403.

72. Inaugural Address of Robert J. Walker, quoted in John H. Gihon, M.D., *Governor Geary's Administration in Kansas* (Philadelphia: Rhodes, 1857), Appendix B. Available at Google Books, *http://books.google.com/books?id=w3kUAAAAYAAJ&dq=Governor+Geary%E2%80%99s+Administration+in+Kansas&printsec=frontcover&source=bl&ots=VB2PiTo7w0&sig=z6YrRzN0aUFIMIeyIo6KLbsPelM&hl=en&ei=VoNvSqT3CYXusQOG_JDoAg&sa=X&oi=book_result&ct=result&resnum=2*, accessed July 17, 2009.

73. Toombs to W.W. Burwell, July 11, 1857, in Phillips, *Correspondence*, 403–404.

74. *Ibid.*, Thomas R.R. Cobb to Howell Cobb, July 15, 1857, 404.

75. *Ibid.*, Howell Cobb to Alexander Stephens, July 21, July 23, 1857, 407–408.

76. *Ibid.*, Robert Toombs to Alexander Stephens, August 3, 1857.

77. Stovall, *Robert Toombs*, 154.

78. *Ibid.*, Robert Toombs to Alexander Stephens, August 15, 1857, 420–421. A few days earlier, Stephens and his half-brother, Linton, had been in a buggy accident. Stephens was unhurt, but Linton severely sprained his knee. "Julia says she is certain you were not born to be killed by a casualty. I hope it will not keep Linton long out of the canvass. Tell him if he has any engagements on hand or if I can serve him in any other way that I will do it with pleasure."

79. Montgomery, *Cracker Parties*, 202–203; Toombs to Julia Toombs, November 7, 1857, in Toombs Papers, University of Georgia.

80. Toombs to W.W. Burwell, November 20, 1857, in Phillips, *Correspondence*, 425–426.

81. *Globe*, 35th Congress, 1st Session, 521–527.

82. Schott, *Stephens*, 245–246.

83. For Toombs' remarks on the Naval Court of Inquiry, see *Globe*, 1st Session, 35th Congress, 240–245. For his arguments against increasing the size of the army, see *ibid.*, 674–676. For his scolding of the Republicans, see *ibid.*, Appendix, 100.

84. *Ibid.*, 100–101.

85. *Ibid.*, 116.

86. *Ibid.*, 214–219.

87. Schott, *Stephens*, 248.
88. *Globe*, 1st Session, 35th Congress, Appendix, 166.
89. *Ibid.*, 195, 198.
90. *Ibid.*, 201–204.
91. Elizabeth Fries Ellet, *The Court Circles of the Republic* (Hartford, CT: Hartford, 1869), 496, MOA UM, accessed July 17, 2009; Toombs to Alexander Stephens, March 28, 1858, in Phillips, *Correspondence*, 433.
92. William C. Davis, *The Union That Shaped the Confederacy: Robert Toombs and Alexander Stephens* (Lawrence: University Press of Kansas, 2001), 73–74; *Globe*, 1st Session, 35th Congress, 1872–1874.
93. *Globe*, 1st Session, 35th Congress, 2777–2778.
94. *Ibid.*, Appendix, 447, 2495. For examples of the British harassing American ships, see, for instance, New York *Times*, July 8, July 15, 1857, March 29, May 8, May 27, 1858.
95. New York *Times*, May 27, 1858.
96. Toombs to Julia Toombs, September 18, 1858, Toombs Papers, University of Georgia.
97. *Ibid.*, February 18, 1859; *Globe*, 35th Congress, 2nd Session, Appendix, 5.
98. *Globe*, 35th Congress, 2nd Session, 541–543. Buchanan's recommendation can be found in *Globe*, 35th Congress, 2nd Session, Appendix, 4.
99. The writer concluded that Toombs was "not so good and entertaining in advancing a scheme, as in defending an established one when assaulted." Milledgeville *Federal Union*, March 1, 1859.
100. *Globe*, 35th Congress, 2nd Session, 1351–1356.
101. Toombs to Julia Toombs, February 28, March 2, 1859, Toombs Papers, University of Georgia.
102. *Ibid.*, March 12, 1859.
103. Toombs to Alexander Stephens, August 27, 1859, in Phillips, *Correspondence*, 447.
104. Phillips, *Life of Toombs*, 177–178.
105. Montgomery, *Cracker Parties*, 233–235.
106. Milledgeville, Georgia, *Federal Union*, November 1, 1859; Nevins, *Emergence of Lincoln: Prologue to the Civil War*, 104.
107. Toombs to Thomas W. Thomas, December 4, 1859, in Phillips, *Correspondence*, 449–450.
108. Nevins, *Emergence of Lincoln: Prologue to the Civil War*, 121–122.
109. Toombs to Alexander Stephens, December 26, 1859, in Phillips, *Correspondence*, 452–453.
110. *Ibid.*, December 28, 1859, 452–453.
111. *Ibid.*, January 11, 1860, 455–456.
112. *Globe*, 36th Congress, 1st Session, Appendix, 88–93.
113. New York *Tribune*, February 2, 1860; New York *Times*, January 26, 1860. Toombs called the *Tribune* "the general receptacle of all falsehoods." *Globe*, 1st Session, 36th Congress, 838.
114. Toombs to Alexander Stephens, January 31, 1860, in Phillips, *Correspondence*, 458–459.
115. *Ibid.*, Alexander Stephens to J. Henly Smith, February 4, 1860, 460.
116. For Brown and Davis' proposals, see Nevins, *Emergence of Lincoln: Prologue to the Civil War*, 179; Toombs to Alexander Stephens, February 10, 1860, in Phillips, *Correspondence*, 461–462.
117. *Globe*, 1st Session, 36th Congress, 888–894.
118. *Ibid.*, Appendix, 155–157.
119. Toombs to Alexander Stephens, March 16, 1860, in Phillips, *Correspondence*, 464–465. Toombs reported that Julia's broken leg was improving slowly and she had "thrown away her stick."
120. *Ibid.*, April 20, 1860, 467–468.
121. Nevins, *Emergence of Lincoln: Prologue to the Civil War*, 216–217.
122. Toombs to Alexander Stephens, May 5, 1860, in *Correspondence*, 468–469.
123. *Ibid.*, Toombs to Alexander Stephens, May 7, 1860, 469–470. "I am sick of the very contemplation of such a lot of rogues as those Northern delegates proved themselves to be, and I now see that the contest is to be transferred to the South, which is the greatest calamity that could befall us."
124. *Ibid.*, Toombs to Robert Collins and Others, May 10, 1860, 476–477.
125. *Ibid.*, Alexander Stephens to J. Henly Smith, May 8, 1860, 470.
126. *Ibid.*, Toombs to Alexander Stephens, May 12, 1860, 477–478.
127. *Ibid.*, Toombs to Alexander Stephens, May 16, 1860, 478–479. Schott, 289, attributes Toombs' move to radicalism to Stephens' not being in Washington, D.C., "to moderate him."
128. "You have doubtless seen that Brown, Davis and Pugh have all introduced resolutions concerning slavery in the territories. Davis's are those approved by the President and are in the main good; but I think all of them are wrong." Toombs to Alexander Stephens, February 10, 1860, in Phillips, *Correspondence*, 161.
129. *Globe*, 36th Congress, 2nd Session, Appendix, 338–345.
130. Toombs to Alexander Stephens, May 26, 1860, in Phillips, *Correspondence*, 480–481.
131. *Ibid.*, Toombs to Alexander Stephens, June 9, 1860, 481.
132. *Ibid.*, Alexander Stephens to J. Henley Smith, July 24, 1860, 489.
133. Toombs to J. Henley Smith, August 5, 1860, quoted in Schott, *Stephens*, 297; Milledgeville *Federal Union*, August 14, 1860.
134. "Montgomery in Secession Time," *Continental Monthly* 3, March 1863, 355, MOA Cornell, accessed July 17, 2009; Avary, *Recollections of Alexander Stephens*, 55; Boller, *Presidential Campaigns*, 102.
135. Phillips, *Life of Toombs*, 197–198.
136. For the full text of Toombs' speech, see William M. Freehling and Craig M. Simpson, eds., *Secession Debated* (New York: Oxford University Press, 1992), 31–50. Stephens said that the accounts of Toombs' speech before the Georgia legislature were written after the fact and his presentation was much more "eloquent, animated, and soul-stirring" than the written version; Avary, *Recollections of Stephens*, 337.
137. For the full text of Stephens' speech, see William M. Freehling and Craig M. Simpson, eds., *Secession Debated* (New York: Oxford University Press, 1992), 51–79.
138. Avary, *Recollections of A.H. Stephens*, 58.
139. Phillips, *Life of Toombs*, 203.
140. "Appropriating Money for Georgia's Defense," Act No. 54 of Georgia Legislature, November 16, 1860, http://georgiainfo.galileo.usg.edu/1860act2.htm, accessed July 17, 2009; "Georgia Secession Convention Authorized," Act No. 14 of Georgia Legislature, November 22, 1860, available at http://georgiainfo.galileo.usg.edu/1860act.htm, accessed July 17, 2009.

141. Toombs to E.B. Pullin and Others, December 13, 1860, in Phillips, *Correspondence*, 519–522.

142. Alexander Stephens to Linton Stephens, December 22, 1860, in Johnston and Browne, *Life of Stephens*, 370.

143. *Globe*, 36th Congress, Second Session, 112; 114.

144. Samuel S. Cox, *Eight Years in Congress, from 1857 to 1865: Memoir and Speeches* (New York: Appleton, 1865), 27, MOA UM, accessed July 17, 2009; "The Republican A Disunion Party," *The Old Guard* 3, June 1865), 275, MOA Cornell, accessed July 17, 2009.

145. "Journal of the Committee of Thirteen," Senate Reports, 36th Congress, 2nd Session, No. 288, 2–3.

146. Robert Toombs to the People of Georgia (telegram), December 23, 1860, in Phillips, *Correspondence*, 525; see also Milledgeville *Federal Union*, December 25, 1860.

147. Anonymous, "Conversational Opinions of Leaders of Secession," *Atlantic Monthly* 10, November 1862, 613–623, available at MOA Cornell, accessed July 17, 2009. Some of this interview may have been remembered with advantage by the writer, but the portrayal of Toombs rings true.

148. Cox, *Eight Years in Congress*, 29; Julia Toombs to Alexander Stephens, January 1, 1861, in Phillips, *Correspondence*, 528.

149. *Globe*, 36th Congress, Second Session, 237, Appendix, 42; Greeley quoted in Alan Nevins, *The Emergence of Lincoln*, vol. 2, *Prologue to the Civil War*, 395.

150. *Globe*, 36th Congress, Second Session, 264–267.

151. *Ibid.*, 267–271.

Chapter 5

1. Toombs to Lawarence M. Keitt, January 11, 1861, Francis W. Pickens Papers, Duke University.

2. Augusta *Chronicle*, January 7, 1861; Journal of the Public and Secret Proceedings of the Convention of the People of Georgia, Held in Milledgeville and Savannah in 1861, Together with the Ordinances Adopted, Electronic Edition, available at *http://docsouth.unc.edu/imls/georgia/menu.html*, 3–7, July 17, 2009. Cited hereafter as Convention Proceedings. For an analysis of the convention's participants, see Ralph Wooster, "The Georgia Session Convention," *Georgia Historical Quarterly* 40 (March 1956): 21–56.

3. Convention Proceedings, 15–19; for the desire for the appearance of unanimity, see Linton Stephens to Eli H. Baxter, November 29, 1860, in Stephens, *Constitutional View*, 317.

4. Convention Proceedings, 20–23, 24–26.

5. Convention Proceedings, 31–32, 35, 39; Stephens, *Constitutional View*, 315.

6. Stephens, *Constitutional View*, 321.

7. New York *Times*, January 24, 25, 26, 1861.

8. Augusta *Chronicle*, January 27, 1861.

9. Convention Proceedings, 55, 64–65.

10. *Ibid.*, 104–113. Toombs apparently submitted a partial report or first draft to the convention. The report was leaked to several newspapers before it was ready. Toombs revised the version that appears in the proceedings while he was in Montgomery. See Augusta *Chronicle*, February 2, 7, 1861.

11. Augusta *Chronicle*, February 5, 1861; Alexander Stephens to Linton Stephens February 23, 1861 (typescript copy) in Stephens Papers, Manhattanville College Library Special Collections, Purchase, NY.

12. Johnston and Browne, *Life of Stephens*, 389–390.

13. Davis, *The Union That Shaped the Confederacy*, 86; T.R.R. Cobb to his wife, February 3, 1861, in Southern Historical Society Papers, vol. 28, Richmond, VA, January–December, 1900, CD ROM version by Guild Press of Indiana, 1998; William C. Davis, *A Government of Our Own: The Making of the Confederacy* (New York: The Free Press, 1994), 74; Schott, *Stephens*, 325.

14. Johnston and Browne, *Life of Stephens*, 390.

15. Alexander Stephens to Linton Stephens, February 23, 1861, (typescript copy) in Stephens Papers, UNC. If Toombs was actively soliciting political deals in Montgomery, no one at the convention ever mentioned it then or later. William Davis in *The Union That Shaped the Confederacy* portrays Toombs as ravenous for the office, but there is little evidence for this.

16. Johnston and Browne, *Life of Stephens*, 385; *Journal of the Confederate States of America 1861–1865* (Washington: Government Printing Office, 1904), 1:19, hereafter referred to as *Confederate Journal*.

17. Stovall, *Robert Toombs*, 365; Augusta *Chronicle*, July 15, 1879; Reed, *The Brothers' War*, 279–280.

18. Davis, *A Government of Our Own*, 91; Alexander Stephens to Linton Stephens, February 23, 1861, (typescript copy) in Stephens Papers, UNC. Stovall also alludes to this incident in his biography of Toombs on page 162. T.R.R. Cobb noted that Toombs was "high on wine" when he shot his mouth off to a reporter that the Confederacy would have "free trade with all the world." See T.R.R. Cobb to Marion Cobb, February 16, 1861, in Colyer Meriwether, ed., *Publications of the Southern History Association* 11 (May 1907), 179, hereafter cited as Cobb Correspondence, Southern History Association.

19. Stephens, *Constitutional View*, 329–330; Cobb Correspondence, *Southern History Association*, 282.

20. Cobb Correspondence, *Southern History Association*, 282.

21. T.R.R. Cobb to Marion Cobb, February 11, 1861, in Cobb Correspondence, *Southern History Association*, 172; Johnston and Browne, *Life of Stephens*, 390; Stephens, *Constitutional View*, 330.

22. Stephens, *Constitutional View*, 330; Stephens, *Constitutional View*, 331; Stovall, *Robert Toombs*, 217; Johnston and Browne, *Life of Stephens*, 390. In the letter to Linton published in Johnston and Browne, Stephens says that the delegation decided not to nominate Toombs, but in *Constitutional View*, he claims that Toombs withdrew his own name. I used Stephens' account to Linton since the letter was written a few days after the events and his book was written a decade later.

23. *Confederate Journal* 1, 40; *Constitutional View*, 331; Cobb Correspondence. *Southern History Association*, 282.

24. Stephens, *Constitutional View*, 333; Cobb Correspondence, *Southern History Association*, 282. John J. Nicolay quipped years later that there were more "candidates for President than states in the Confederacy." John J. Nicolay, "Abraham Lincoln: A History. The President Elect at Springfield," *The Century* 35 (November 1887), 66, MOA Cornell, accessed July 17, 2009 .

25. Isabella D. Martin and Myrta Lockett Avary, eds., *A Diary from Dixie, as Written by Mary Boykin Chesnut* (Gloucester, MA: Appleton, 1961), 7.

26. Johnston and Browne, *Life of Stephens*, 386.

27. *Confederate Journal* 1, 40, 42, 59, 98, 110, 120; Johnston and Browne, *Life of Stephens*, 386.

28. Johnston and Browne, *Life of Stephens*, 386.

29. "Montgomery in Secession Time," *Continental Monthly* 3 (March 1863), 361, MOA Cornell, accessed July 17, 2009; *Confederate Journal* 1, 66.

30. Cobb Correspondence, *Southern History Association*, 183–184.

31. Lynda Lasswell Crist and Mary Seaton Dix, eds., *The Papers of Jefferson Davis* (Baton Rouge: Louisiana State University Press, 1992), 7:56 (summary); Jefferson Davis, *The Rise and Fall of the Confederate Government* (New York: Appleton, 1881), 242; R. Barnwell Rhett, "The Confederate Government at Montgomery," in *Battles and Leaders of the Civil War* (reprint, Secaucus, NJ: Castle Books, 1983), 1:104.

32. Toombs to Jefferson Davis, February 19, 1861, February 20, 1861, both from Jefferson Davis Papers, Manuscripts Collection 55-D, Louisiana Research Collections, Tulane University.

33. Toombs to Jefferson Davis, February 20, 1861, in Charles C. Jones Jr. Autograph Files, Duke University; Stovall, *Robert Toombs*, 221; Johnston and Browne, *Life of Stephens*, 387.

34. *Confederate Journal* 1, 73; Alexander Stephens to Linton Stephens, February 23, 1861, Stephens Papers, UNC; Confederate States of America Papers, February 27, 1861, Vol. 22, hereafter cited as Pickett Papers.

35. Pickett Papers, Vol. 47; Thomas Cooper DeLeon, *Four Years in Rebel Capitals* (Mobile, AL: Gossip, 1890; reprint, Alexandria, VA: Time-Life Books, 1983), 37; John B. Jones, *A Rebel War Clerk's Diary at the Confederate States Capital* [sic], Vol. 1 (Philadelphia: Lippincott, 1866, reprint, New York: Time-Life Books, 1982), 43; Davis, *A Government of Our Own*, 301; John S. Abbott, *The History of the Civil War in America Comprising a Full and Impartial Account of the Origin and Progress of the Rebellion, of the Various Naval and Military Engagements, of the Heroic Deeds Performed by Armies and Individuals* (N.p.: 1864–1866) 297n, MOA UM, accessed July 17, 2009.

36. John S. Abbott, *The History of the Civil War in America Comprising a Full and Impartial Account of the Origin and Progress of the Rebellion, of the Various Naval and Military Engagements, of the Heroic Deeds Performed by Armies and Individuals* (N.p.: 1864–1866) 297n, MOA UM, accessed July 17, 2009. The reporter also wrote that Toombs expressed "profoundest indifference to the sentiments of the civilized world on the subject of slavery and its extension."

37. Stovall, *Robert Toombs*, 234–235, 236–237.

38. James M. Matthews, ed., The Statutes at Large of the Provisional Government of the Confederate States of America (Richmond: Smith), 1864, available at *http://docsouth.unc.edu/imls/19conf/menu.html*, 29–30, 42, 52, 158, accessed July 17, 2009; *Southern Historical Society Papers* (Richmond, 1876–1910), 29: 346, Reissued by Guild Press of Indiana (CD ROM version), 1996.

39. DeLeon, *Four Years in Rebel Capitals*, 33.

40. *Confederate Journal*, Vol. 1, 105.

41. Johnston and Browne, *Life of Stephens*, 386; *Confederate Journal*, Vol. 1, 853.

42. *Confederate Journal*, Vol. 1, 913, 915, 924; Phillips, *Life of Toombs*, 229; Stephens, *Constitutional View*, 338.

43. "Jefferson Davis ... to All Whom These Presents Shall Concern..." *Official Records of the Union and Confederate Navies in the War of the Rebellion*, Series II, Vol. 3 (CD ROM version published by Guild Press, 1999), cited hereafter as Navy O.R. II; Johnston and Browne, *Life of Stephens*, 391.

44. John J. Nicolay and John Hay, "Abraham Lincoln: A History — Premier or President?" *The Century* 35 (February 1888), 599, MOA Cornell, accessed July 17, 2009.

45. John Forsyth to Gov. F.W. Pickens, March 14, 1861, *The War of the Rebellion: A Compilation of the Official Records of the Union and Confederate Armies* (Washington: 1880–1901, CD ROM version published by Guild Press, 1996), Vol. 3, Series I, Vol. 1. Hereafter cited as O. R.; Nicolay, "Abraham Lincoln: A History — Premier or President?" 600.

46. Nicolay, "Abraham Lincoln: A History — Premier or President?" 600.

47. William Henry Seward to R.M.T. Hunter, March 12, 1861 (copy); Toombs to Confederate Commissioners, March 20, 1861, Reel 1, Pickett Papers.

48. J. Forsyth to L. Walker, March 14, 1861, O.R., Series IV, Vol. 1, 275. Peace element or not, talk of war had everybody on edge. One man said loud enough for Toombs to hear: "This war talk is nothing. It will soon blow over. Only a fuss gotten up by that Charleston clique." Secretary of State Toombs demanded to see the man's passport on the basis that anyone who said that kind of thing was "a suspicious character." Chesnut, *A Diary from Dixie*, 20. When a reporter for the New York *Herald* asked Toombs for safe passage out of Montgomery a few months later, Toombs replied that the "*Herald* man may go to hell." Davis, *A Government of Our Own*, 386.

49. John Forsyth and Martin J. Crawford to Toombs, March 15, 1861; Toombs to Martin J. Crawford, March 16, 1861, Reel 1, Pickett Papers.

50. Roman and Crawford to Hon. R. Toombs, March 20, 1861, O.R., Series I, Vol. 1 (S#1), 277; Nicolay, 604.

51. David Herbert Donald, *Lincoln* (New York: Simon and Schuster, 1995), 288; Martin J. Crawford and A.B. Roman to Hon. Robert Toombs, April 2, 1861, in O.R. Series I, Vol. 1 (S#1), 284.

52. Crawford, Roman and Forsyth to Hon. R. Toombs, April 4, 1861, O.R. Series I, Vol. 4 [S#4], 257; Crawford, Roman and Forsyth to Hon. R. Toombs, April 5, 1861, O.R. Series I, Vol. 1 [S#1], 286; Toombs to Stephens, April 6, 1861 in Phillips, *Correspondence*, 558.

53. Davis, *Rise and Fall of the Confederate Government*, Vol. 1, 681; Crawford, Roman and Forsyth to Hon. R. Toombs, April 7, 1861, O.R. Series I, Vol. 4 [S#4], 258; *ibid.*, April 8, 1861, O.R. Series I, Vol. 4 [S#4], 329.

54. L. Walker to G.T. Beauregard, April 8, 1861, O.R., Series I, Vol. 1 [S#1] Chapter 1, 289; Toombs to Forsyth, Crawford, and Roman, April 8, 1861, Pickett Papers.

55. Stovall, *Robert Toombs*, 226. There are several versions of what Toombs actually said in this meeting, but all agree he advised caution and patience. For other versions, see Davis, *A Government of Our Own*, 310; Toombs to Crawford and Forsyth, April 11, 1861, Pickett Papers.

56. Barnwell, "Montgomery in Secession Time," 364, accessed July 17, 2009.

57. Davis, *The Union That Shaped the Confederacy*, 124; "By the President of the Confederate States, A Proclamation," April 17, 1861, Navy O.R., Series II, Vol. 3; Davis, *A Government of Our Own*, 324;

58. Robert Toombs to Alexander Stephens, April 19, 1861, O.R., Series I, Vol. LI/Part 2 [S#108], 18.

59. Johnston and Browne, *Life of Stephens,* 399–400; Alexander Stephens to Toombs, no date, O.R., Series IV, Vol. I [S#127], 242.

60. James D. Richardson, *A Compilation of the Messages and Papers of the Confederacy Including the Diplomatic Correspondence 1861–1865* (Nashville: United States, 1905, CD ROM Version by H-Bar Enterprises, 1995), 57, hereafter cited as *Messages and Papers of the Confederacy*; Navy O.R., Series II, Vol. 3, 191–195.

61. Toombs to Yancy, Rost and Mann, April 24, 1861, *Messages and Papers of the Confederacy*, Vol. 2, 15–18.

62. Current, ed., *Encyclopedia of the Confederacy*, Vol. 3, 1209; Navy O.R., Series II, Vol. 3, 99–100.

63. Toombs to John Pickett, May 17, 1861; Navy O.R., Series II, Vol. 3, 99–100, 203–207.

64. Albert Pike to Toombs, May 29, 1861, O.R., Series IV, Vol. 1, 360; Toombs to Charles J. Helm, July 22, 1861, *Messages and Papers of the Confederacy*, Vol. 2, 48.

65. *Confederate Journal*, Vol. 1, 169, 181, 207, 220, 226, 259, 264.

66. See, for instance, L. Walker to Toombs, March 21, 1861, O.R., Series I, Vol. 1, 181; 184; John H. Crozier to Toombs, April 22, 1861, O.R., Series I—Vol. 1, LII/2, 64; Toombs to Howell Cobb, April 23, 1861 in Phillips, Correspondence, 562–563.

67. Jones, *A Rebel War Clerk's Diary*, 39–40.

68. *Daily Richmond Enquirer*, May 30, 1861, quoted in Dunbar Rowland, LL.D., ed., *Jefferson Davis, Constitutionalist: His Letters, Papers, and Speeches* (Jackson: Mississippi Department of Archives and History, 1923), Vol. 5, 102–103.

69. Jones, *A Rebel War Clerk's Diary*, 46–47.

70. New York *Times*, July 18, 1879.

71. Jones, *A Rebel War Clerk's Diary*, 40; Toombs to Alexander Stephens, June 8, 1861, in Phillips, *Correspondence*, 569; Davis, *A Government of Our Own*, 377.

72. Avary, *Recollections of Stephens*, 67; Toombs to Alexander Stephens, July 5, 1861, Robert Toombs Papers, Duke University.

73. Toombs to His Excellency Jefferson Davis, July 24, 1861, in Pickett Papers, Reel 22. "I will also avail myself of this occasion to express to you my admiration of the ability, integrity, patriotism, and unwearied devotion with which you discharged the great trusts which the wisdom of the people have committed to your care," Toombs wrote.

74. Jefferson Davis to Hon. R. Toombs, July 24, 1861, *ibid.*, Reel 47; Bvt. Lieut.-Col. John J. Craven, M.D., *Prison Life of Jefferson Davis* (New York: Carleton, 1866), 172, MOA UM, accessed July 17, 2009.

75. *Confederate Journal* 1, 307; "Confederate Roster Generals Confederate States Army," Southern Historical Society Papers, SHSP Roster, 8–9; S. Cooper to P.G.T. Beauregard, July 26, 1861, O.R., Series I, Vol. LI/2.

76. Thompson, *Toombs*, 175; Gabriel Toombs to Alexander Stephens, July 31, 1861, in Phillips, *Correspondence*, 573.

77. Gabriel Toombs to Alexander Stephens, July 31, 1861, in Phillips, *Correspondence*, 573.

78. Chesnut, *Diary of Dixie*, 97; C. Vann Woodward and Elisabeth Muhlenfeld, *The Private Mary Chesnut: The Unpublished Civil War Diaries* (New York: Oxford University Press, 1984), 111. The story varies slightly in each version of her diary, but the account is the same.

79. Toombs to Jefferson Davis, September 1, 1861, Robert Toombs Papers, Duke University.

80. James Longstreet, "From Manassas to Appomattox," in *Confederate Generals Speak* (CD ROM Version by Guild Press of Indiana, 1997), 113. Toombs to Alexander Stephens September [30?], 1861, Phillips, *Correspondence*, 577–578. Phillips states this letter is dated incorrectly.

81. Toombs to Alexander Stephens, October 3, 1861, Phillips, *Correspondence*, 578–579.

82. Augusta *Chronicle*, October 12, 1861; Washington *Star* PoR, February 6, 1861, March 3, 2008; Davis, *The Union That Shaped the Confederacy*, 146.

83. Phillips, *Toombs*, 240.

84. Augusta *Chronicle*, November 22, 1861.

85. *Confederate Journal* 1, 754, 190, 799, 812, 813, 834–835. Toombs took time out from the session to be a pallbearer at former president John Tyler's funeral. See Richmond *Enquirer*, January 20,1862.

86. *Confederate Journal* 2, 13; Stovall, *Robert Toombs*, 241; Chesnut, *A Diary of Dixie*, 132; Atlanta *Southern Confederacy*, March 6, 1862.

87. Toombs to Alexander Stephens, March 4, 1862, in Phillips, *Correspondence*, 589–590.

88. *Confederate Journal* 2, 31; Toombs to Alexander Stephens, March 4, 1862, in Phillips, *Correspondence*, 589–590.

89. Toombs to Julia Toombs, March 13, 1862, quoted in Stovall, *Robert Toombs*, 240; Toombs to Julia Toombs, March 19, 1862, in *ibid.*, 241; Joseph E. Johnston, "Responsibilities of the First Bull Run," *Battles and Leaders of the Civil War*, Vol. 1, 257.

90. Stovall, *Robert Toombs*, 241–242; Toombs to Julia Toombs, March 22, 1862, Toombs Papers, University of Georgia; Jones, *A Rebel War Clerk's Diary*, 116.

91. Toombs to Julia Toombs, March 22, 1862, *http://dlg.galileo.usg.edu/hargrett/toombs/rat016.php*, accessed July 17, 2009.

92. O.R. Series I, Vol. XI, Part 1, 405–411; Toombs to Alexander Stephens, March 28, 1862, in Phillips, *Correspondence*, 593.

93. Gilbert Moxley Sorrel, *Recollections of a Confederate Staff Officer* (*Confederate Generals Speak*, CD ROM Version by Guild Press of Indiana, 1997,) 60.

94. O.R. Series II, Part 1, 480; Douglas Southall Freeman, *Lee's Lieutenants, a Study in Command* (New York: Scribner and Sons, 1946), Vol. 1, n. 22, 624–625.

95. Toombs to Alexander Stephens, May 17, 1862, Stephens Papers, Emory University.

96. Toombs to Linton Stephens, May 19, 1862, in Stephens Papers, Emory University.

97. Thompson, *Toombs*, 183; Current, *Encyclopedia of the Confederacy*, Vol. 1, 396–397; Chesnut, *A Diary from Dixie*, 171.

98. Toombs to Julia Toombs, May 30, 1862, Toombs Papers, University of Georgia.

99. O.R., Series I, Vol. 14, 565; Augusta *Chronicle*, June 16, 1862.

100. Thompson, *Toombs*, 186–187.

101. Stovall, *Robert Toombs*, 250–251; Thompson, *Toombs*, 187; T.R.R. Cobb to his wife, June 15, 1862, quoted in Harold Davis, "The Civil War Career of Robert Toombs" (master's thesis, University of Georgia, 1950), 54.

102. O.R., Series I, Vol. 11/2, 661; 690; General Clement A. Evans, ed., *Confederate Military History*, Vol. 6, 173 (CD ROM Version by Guild Press of Indiana, 1997).

103. O.R., Series I, Vol. 11/2, 706.

104. O.R., Series I, Vol. XI/2, 695–696; Toombs to Alexander Stephens, July 14, 1862, in Phillips, *Correspondence*, 599–601.

105. Stovall, *Robert Toombs*, 251; O.R., Series I, Vol. XI/2, 696–698.

106. Gilbert Moxley Sorrel, *Recollections of a Confederate Staff Officer* in *Confederate Generals Speak* (CD ROM Version by Guild Press of Indiana, 1997), 87. Most of the correspondence between Hill and Toombs is in Stovall, *Robert Toombs*, 254–257.

107. Stovall, *Robert Toombs*, 257; Cobb to his wife, July 16, 1862, in *Southern Historical Society Papers* (Richmond, 1876–1910), vol. 28, 294; O.R., Series I—Vol. 42/2, 670; Augusta *Chronicle*, September 9, 1862.

108. Warren Wilkenson and Steven E. Woodworth, *A Scythe of Fire: A Civil War Story of the Eighth Georgia Infantry Regiment* (New York: William Morrow, 2002), 154; O.R., Series I, Vol. 42/2, 670; Sorrel, *Recollections of a Confederate Staff Officer*, 59; Joseph Howard Parks, *General Edmund Kirby Smith, C.S.A.* (Baton Rouge: Louisiana State University Press, 1954) 147; Gary W. Gallagher, ed., *Fighting for the Confederacy: The Personal Recollections of General Edward Alexander Porter* (Chapel Hill: University of North Carolina Press, 1989), 73; Tom Cobb to his wife, July 16, 1862 in *Southern Historical Society Papers* (Richmond, 1876–1910), vol. 28, 294.

109. O.R., Ser.1, Vol. XI, Pt 3, 649–650; Henry Kyd Douglas, *I Rode with Stonewall* (Chapel Hill: University of North Carolina Press, 1940), 114.

110. T.R.R Cobb to his wife, August 10, 1862 in *Southern Historical Society Papers*, vol. 28, 295.

111. O.R. Series I, Vol. 12/3 Series 18, 928–929; James Longstreet, *From Manassas to Appomattox* (in *Confederate Generals Speak*, CD ROM), 161.

112. James Longstreet, *From Manassas to Appomattox* (in *Confederate Generals Speak*, CD ROM), 161; Toombs to Alexander Stephens, August 22, 1862, in Phillips, *Correspondence*, 603–04; Douglas Southall Freeman, *R.E. Lee: A Biography* (New York, 1934–35) 2: 284–285.

113. Sorrel, *Recollections of a Confederate Staff Officer*, 100.

114. Toombs to Alexander Stephens, August 22, 1862, in Phillips, *Correspondence*, 603–604.

115. Sorrel, *Recollections of a Confederate Staff Officer*, 101; James Longstreet, "Our March Against Pope," in Johnson and Buel, *Battles and Leaders of the Civil War* 2, 525–526.

116. William Robert Houghton, *Two Boys in the Civil War and After* (Montgomery, AL: Paragon Press, 1912), electronic edition from *docsouth.unc.edu/fpn/houghton/menu.html*, accessed July 17, 2009; James Longstreet, *From Manassas to Appomattox*, 166; O.R., Series I, Vol. 16, 580; O.R., Series I, Vol. 16, 587; Frances Letcher Mitchell, *Georgia Land and People*, 291–292, *http://www.archive.org/details/georgialandpeopl00mitc*, accessed July 17, 2009; O.R., Series I, Vol. 16 [S# 16], 342. General David Jones says in his report that Toombs accompanied his men into battle. However, Captain Hiram L French, who was commanding the 17th Georgia Regiment, quoted Toombs' greeting in his official report, but makes no mention of Toombs leading the men into battle.

117. Vol. 12, Pt. 2, 591; Phillip Thomas Tucker, *Burnside's Bridge: The Climactic Struggle of the 2nd and 20th Georgia at Antietam Creek* (Mechanicsburg, PA: Stackpole Books, 2000), 38.

118. Wilkenson and Woodworth, *A Scythe of Fire*, 180; O.R., Series I, Vol. 16, 580.

119. O.R, Series I, Vol. XIX/1, 886, 889.

120. O.R., Series I, Vol. XIX/1, 891.

121. Tucker, *Burnside's Bridge*, 125, 148; O.R., Series I, Vol. XIX/1, 150; 841; Gamaliel Bradford, *Confederate Portraits* (Boston: Houghton Mifflin, 1914), 209.

122. Stovall, *Robert Toombs*, 268–269. Although Toombs was shot after the battle, he was officially recorded as being wounded at Antietam. *Medical and Surgical History of the Civil War* (Wilmington, NC: Broadfoot, 1991), Vol. 7, 58.

123. Journal of the Senate of the State of Georgia, at the Annual Session of the General Assembly, Begun and Held in Milledgeville, 1862 (Milledgeville, GA: Boughton, Nisbet & Barnes, 1862), 112, *http://docsouth.unc.edu/imls/gasen62/menu.html*, accessed July 17, 2009.

124. Toombs to Linton Stephens, December 1, 1862, in Phillips, *Correspondence*, 608.

125. Toombs to His Brigade in the Army of Northern Virginia, March 5, 1863, *ibid.*, 612.

126. Stovall, *Robert Toombs*, 106, 270–271; Rowland, *Jefferson Davis, Constitutionalist*, Vol. 6, 44; Robert Toombs' Military Service File, National Archives, Washington, D.C. Hereafter cited as Service File.

127. Janet B. Hewett, *Supplement to the Official Records of the Union and Confederate Armies* (Wilmington, NC: Broadfoot, 2001), Ser. 18, 410; Toombs to Stephens, March 2, 1863, in Phillips, *Correspondence*, 611–612.

128. Jones, *Rebel War Clerk's Diary*, 273; Governor Joe Brown to Alexander Stephens, February 16, 1863, in Phillips, *Correspondence*, 611.

129. Toombs to Alexander H. Stephens, April 21, 1863, in Phillips, *Correspondence*, 615–616.

130. Toombs to W.W. Burwell, June 10, 1863, in Phillips, *Correspondence*, 619–620. Toombs reported his health was good, but he was afraid that he had lost the use of his hand due to his wound.

131. Augusta *Chronicle*, June 25, 1863; New York *Times*, July 10, 1863.

132. Schott, *Stephens*, 352; George C. Rable, *The Confederate Republic: A Revolution Against Politics* (Chapel Hill: University of North Carolina Press, 1994), 134.

133. Toombs to Alexander Stephens, July 14, 1863, in Phillips, *Correspondence*, 621. Toombs urged Stephens to send a telegram as soon as he heard anything about his son-in-law Colonel Dudley Dubose, who had seen heavy fighting at Gettysburg. Toombs' daughter was extremely worried about her husband.

134. Toombs to the Editor of the Augusta *Constitutionalist*, August 12, 1863; *Correspondence*, 622–627.

135. Toombs to W.W. Burwell, August 29, 1863; *Correspondence*, 628–629. Toombs saw injustice wherever he looked. General Joseph E. Johnston was facing a court of inquiry about the losses of Vicksburg and Port Hudson. Despite his tirades about career generals from West Point, Toombs offered to represent Johnston at the court. Toombs to General Joseph E. Johnston, August 27, 1863, in Joseph E. Johnston Papers, Special Collection Research Center, Earl Gregg Swem Library, College of William and Mary.

136. George W. Lamar to Jefferson Davis, August 16, 1863, in Rowland, *Jefferson Davis, Constitutionalist*, Vol. 5, 594.

137. Harold Davis "The Civil War Career of Robert Toombs," 80; New York *Times*, December 18,1863.

138. Toombs to Alexander Stephens, November 2, 1863, in Phillips, *Correspondence*, 630.

139. New York *Times*, December 3, 1863; Augusta *Chronicle*, November 13, 1863.

140. Journal of the Senate of the State of Georgia, 1863, 42, 1109–1111, *http://docsouth.unc.edu/imls/gasen63/menu.html*, accessed July 17, 2009; Joseph E. Brown to Alexander Stephens, November 27, 1863, Phillips, *Correspondence*, 630.

141. Henry Cleveland, "Robert Toombs," *The Southern Bivouac* (Louisville, KY: 1882–1887; reprint, Wilmington, NC: Broadfoot, 1992–1993), 4: 455–457. Stephens did not think Toombs was advocating a counterrevolution, but was blustering as usual.

142. Jones, *A Rebel War Clerk's Diary*, 142; Davis, "The Civil War Career of Robert Toombs," 83, n.31; Toombs to General Thomas Jordon, February 26, 1864; Toombs to G.T. Beauregard, July 13, 1864, Service File, National Archives. Toombs and Beauregard admired each other. For instance, Toombs advised Beauregard to resist transfer from the Confederate Army of the Potomac to Kentucky to shore up Albert Sidney Johnston, Toombs to P.G.T. Beauregard, January 23, 1862 (original misdated December 23, 1862), Tulane University. In turn, Beauregard recommended Davis not accept Toombs' resignation when Toombs resigned his commission, O.R., Ser. I, Vol. 14, 826.

143. Stovall, *Robert Toombs*, 275; Augusta *Chronicle*, March 17, 1864.

144. Robert Toombs to Alexander H. Stephens, April 1, 1864, in Phillips, *Correspondence*, 638–639. The act "expressly permits men to be seized and imprisoned for innocent acts, for acts that Congress *does not, has not, dares not make criminal*," he continued. "Where is [the] law that punishes me for advising or inciting men to abandon the Confederate cause? To do this thing is a perfectly innocent action which Congress has never made criminal. Yet it allows the President to imprison me for it."

145. Joseph E. Brown to Alexander H. Stephens, June 6, 1864, in Phillips, *Correspondence*, 644; *Battles and Leaders of the Civil War*, Vol. IV, 333; Stovall, *Robert Toombs*, 277.

146. Stovall, *Robert Toombs*, 277; Toombs to Julia Toombs, no date, in Davis, "Civil War Career of Robert Toombs," 85.

147. Toombs to Julia Toombs, July 20, 1864, in Davis, "Civil War Career of Robert Toombs, 86; Stovall, *Robert Toombs*, 278.

148. Toombs to Julia Toombs, August 15, 1864, in Robert Toombs, Toombs Papers, University of Georgia; Thompson, *Toombs*, 212–213.

149. Robert Toombs to Alexander H. Stephens, August 30, 1864, in Phillips, *Correspondence*, 651–652.

150. O.R., Ser. I, Vol. 39/2, 381.

151. Toombs to Alexander H. Stephens, September 23, 1864, in Phillips, *Correspondence*, 652–653.

152. Jones, *A Rebel War Clerk's Diary*, 290; Schott, *Stephens*, 427; Johnston and Browne, *Life of Stephens*, 472.

153. "Gustavus Smith," in Johnston and Buel, *Battles and Leaders of the Civil War*, vol. 4, 667; *Confederate Veteran* 18, no. 6 (June 1910), 275.

154. O.R., Ser. I, Vol. 44, 862.

155. Richard Taylor, *Destruction and Reconstruction: Personal Experiences of the Late War*, edited by Richard B. Harwell (New York: Longmans, Green, 1955), 259–261. Richard Taylor was the son of Zachary Taylor.

156. "Gustavus Smith," in Johnston and Buel, *Battles and Leaders of the Civil War*, vol. 4, 669; Davis, "Civil War Career of Robert Toombs," 91.

157. Stephens' account of the conference is in his *Constitutional View*, 599–620; Augusta *Chronicle*, February 17, 1865.

158. Augusta *Chronicle*, February 17, 1865.

159. Robert Toombs to Alexander H. Stephens, March 16, 1865, in Phillips, *Correspondence*, 660.

160. Robert Toombs to Alexander H. Stephens, March 23, 1865; Robert Toombs to Alexander H. Stephens, March 16, 1865, in Phillips, *Correspondence*, 661; Toombs to Gustavus W. Smith, March 25, 1865, Toombs Papers, University of Georgia.

161. Schott, *Stephens*, 450; Joseph E. Brown to Alexander Stephens, April 25, 1865, in Phillips, *Correspondence*, 662; Stovall, *Robert Toombs*, 281; Davis, *Rise and Fall of the Confederate Government*, vol. 2, 694–695;

162. Stovall, *Robert Toombs*, 283–284.

163. Burton N. Harrison, "The Capture of Jefferson Davis," *The Century* 27 (November 1883), 139, Cornell MOA, accessed July 17, 2009; Mary Bondurant Warren, ed., *The Chronicles of Wilkes County* (Danielsville, GA: Heritage Papers, 1978), 316; Davis, *Rise and Fall of the Confederate Government*, 695. There is a legend that a squad of Union cavalry galloped onto Toombs' plantation and threw the money into his yard and hurried off with no explanations. But Toombs told the commander of the occupying troops in Washington, Georgia, Captain Lot Abraham, that Breckinridge had left the money "without permission." Davis also explained that General Upton's forces were around and Davis did not want to take a chance with the money. It is conceivable that someone in Davis' party ditched the money on Toombs' property hoping to send for it later.

164. Lot D. Young, "Personal Experience with Robert Toombs," *Confederate Veteran* 18 (May 1910), 275. This story is also told in Young's *Reminiscences of a Soldier of the Orphan Brigade* (Louisville, KY: Courier Journal, 1918), 20–21, also available at *http://docsouth.unc.edu/fpn/young/menu.html*, accessed July 17, 2009.

165. Stovall, *Robert Toombs*, 286–287; Eliza Frances Andrews, *The War-Time Journal of a Georgia Girl, 1864–1865* (New York: Appleton, 1908,) 242; O.R., Ser. I, Vol. 44, Pt. 2, 750. In some versions, the squad that arrested Toombs was made up mostly of African Americans with Toombs' photograph pierced on a bayonet. See Knight, *Reminiscences of Famous Georgians*, 114–115.

166. Atlanta *Constitution*, August 29, 1877.

Chapter 6

1. Born in Slavery: Slave Narratives from the Federal Writers' Project, 1936–1938, Library of Congress, at *http://memory.loc.gov/ammem/snhtml/snhome.html*, accessed July 17, 2009.

2. Toombs to Stephens, February 24, 1857, Toombs to Stephens, March 10, 1857, in Phillips, *Correspondence*, 397–398.

3. "To All Whom It May Concern," September 27, 1859, in Garland White file, National Archives, Washington, D.C., hereafter cited as Garland White File.

4. "Pastoral Credentials of the B.M.E. Church," dated October 23, 1861, Garland White File; Garland

White to William Henry Seward, May 18, 1864, *ibid.*; Budge Weidman, "Preserving the Legacy of the United States Colored Troops," no date, available at *http://www.archives.gov/education/lessons/blacks-civil-war/article.html*, accessed July 17, 2009. Special thanks to Budge White at the Civil War Conservation Corps at the National Archives for copies of the Garland White File.

5. Stovall, *Robert Toombs*, 306; Toombs to Alexander Stephens, December 15, 1865, in Phillips, *Correspondence*, 673.

6. Atlanta *Constitution*, August 29, 1877; Toombs' flight comes mostly from Stovall, *Robert Toombs*, 287–305, and an article in the Atlanta *Constitution*, July 31, 1887.

7. Avary, *Recollections of Alexander H. Stephens*, 186; Atlanta *Constitution*, July 13, 1865; O.R., Ser. 1, Vol. 44, Part 2, 860. Stanton was said to have a particular dislike for Robert Toombs. Charles F. Benjamin, "Recollections of Secretary Edwin M. Stanton," *The Century* 33 (March 1877), 765, Cornell MOA, accessed July 17, 2009.

8. Atlanta *Constitution*, March 2, 1873.

9. Andrews, *The War-Time Journal of a Georgia Girl*, 354–355, 358; O.R. Ser. 2, Vol. 8, 714, 716.

10. Toombs to Alexander Stephens, December 15, 1865, in Phillips, *Correspondence*, 673–676.

11. Julia Toombs to Alexander Stephens, May 16, 1866, Emory University.

12. Terrill, *History of Stewart County*, 726; Stovall, *Robert Toombs*, 308–309.

13. Stovall, *Robert Toombs*, 310; Washington *Evening Star*, October 22, 1866; New York *Times*, December 16, 1877.

14. New York *Times*, November 1, 1866

15. For the story of Toombs throwing an inkpot at Senator Yancy, see Atlanta *Constitution*, March 3, 1888.

16. Gabriel Toombs to Alexander Stephens, October 29, 1866, Emory University.

17. Toombs to Alexander Stephens, December 9, 1866, Emory University.

18. *Ibid.*; Toombs to C.C. Jones, Jr., December 7, 1866, C.C. Jones Jr., Georgia Portfolio, Duke University.

19. Toombs to Julia Toombs, December 23, 1866, Toombs Papers, University of Georgia.

20. Toombs to Julia Toombs, December 26, 1866, January 1, 1867, *ibid.*

21. Toombs to Julia Toombs, January 12, January 14, January 15, 1867, *ibid.*; Stovall, *Robert Toombs*, 313.

22. Petersburg (Virginia) *Index*, March 11, 1867; Washington *Evening Star*, March 2, 1867. Toombs was also horrified to discover that volumes of his personal papers had been removed and sent to Washington. He tried to recover them a few years later, but without success. New York *Times*, January 8, 1884.

23. Toombs to John C. Breckenridge, April 30, 1867, Toombs Papers, University of Georgia; New York *Times*, July 10, 1867.

24. Toombs to Stephens, November 14, 1867, Phillips, *Correspondence*, 689–690.

25. Toombs to L.N. Trammell, April 26, 1877, in Phillips, *Correspondence*, 729. For a good account of Toombs' battles with railroads in Georgia, see William Thompson, "Robert Toombs and the Georgia Railroads," *Georgia Historical Quarterly* 40 (March 1956): 56–64.

26. Toombs to Stephens, December 2, 1867, in Phillips, *Correspondence*, 690.

27. Toombs to C.C. Jones, June 30, 1868, C.C. Jones, Jr., Georgia Portfolio Duke University; Atlanta *Constitution*, July 10, 1868.

28. Atlanta *Constitution*, July 24, 1868. This account differs widely from the official version published a month later. Toombs heavily revised the published version. For the official version, see Atlanta *Constitution*, August 23, 1868.

29. For commentaries on the speech, see Atlanta *Constitution*, August 5, 7, 1868; Toombs to Alexander Stephens, August 9, 1868, in Phillips, *Correspondence*, 702.

30. Schott, 479; Atlanta *Constitution*, August 25, 1868; New York *Times*, August 24, 1868.

31. Schott, 480; Boller, *Presidential Campaign*, 125.

32. Toombs to Alexander Stephens, December 11, 1868, January 24, 1870, in Phillips, *Correspondence*, 706, 707. During their summer vacation, Toombs and Julia ran into Jefferson and Varina Howell Davis. The meeting between Toombs and Davis was cordial enough, but Davis was fond of Toombs' daughter Sallie and was quite moved when he heard of her death. Warren, ed., *The Chronicles of Wilkes County*, 201.

33. Stovall, *Robert Toombs*, 327–329; Atlanta *Constitution*, May 23, 1871.

34. Charles J. Woodbury, "Toombs" *Overland Monthly and Out West Magazine* 7 (February 1886), 125, MOA UM, accessed July 17, 2009; James U. Vincent, *A Pen Picture of General Robert Toombs with a Glimpse of the Mental Characteristics of Alexander Stephens and Benj. H. Hill* (Louisville, KY: Courier Journal, 1887), 10.

35. Atlanta *Constitution*, June 14, 1871. The tale of Smalley's interview with Toombs got wilder and wilder over the years. See Atlanta *Constitution*, May 6, 1877.

36. Atlanta *Constitution*, June 18, 1871. The *Constitution* also believed Toombs was probably pulling reporters' legs but chided him for harming the Democrats' chances in the next election. Atlanta *Constitution*, June 23, 1871.

37. Allen W. Trelease, *White Terror: The Ku Klux Klan Conspiracy and Southern Reconstruction* (New York: Harper Torchbooks, 1971), 74–75; Atlanta *Constitution*, June 14, 1871.

38. Atlanta *Constitution*, January 11, April 16, 1872.

39. Toombs to Alexander Stephens, January 21, 1872, in Phillips, *Correspondence*, 716; Toombs to Charles C. Jones, March 30, 1872, C.C. Jones, Jr., Georgia Portfolio Duke University; Atlanta *Constitution*, August 5, 1884.

40. Augusta *Chronicle*, July 18, 1872; Schott, *Stephens*, 491.

41. Augusta *Chronicle*, July 19, 1872; Willard Range, "Hannibal I. Kimball," *Georgia Historical Quarterly* 29 (June 1945): 53.

42. Augusta *Chronicle*, July 19, 1872.

43. Atlanta (Georgia) *Sun*, July 5, 1872, quoted in New York *Times*, July 9, 1872; Atlanta *Constitution*, August 29, 1880; Toombs to C.E. Merril, July 6, 1872, quoted in Augusta *Chronicle*, July 19, 1872.

44. Schott, *Stephens*, 490; Atlanta *Constitution*, November 21, 1872.

45. Atlanta *Constitution*, January 23, 27, 1873; Stovall, *Robert Toombs*, 333; Schott, *Stephens*, 495.

46. Atlanta *Constitution*, February 27, 1873.

47. Range, "Hannibal I. Kimball," 53.

48. Atlanta *Constitution*, August 22, 1873; Augusta *Chronicle*, May 2, 1874.

49. New York *Times*, October 17, 1873.

50. New York *Times*, November 17, 1873; Atlanta *Constitution*, November 13, 1873.
51. Atlanta *Constitution*, January 15, 1874; Augusta *Chronicle*, January 15, 1874.
52. Toombs to Alexander Stephens, December 30, 1870, in Phillips, *Correspondence*, 711–712; Augusta *Chronicle*, July 7, 1874; Johnston and Browne, *Life of Stephens*, 501–502.
53. Augusta *Chronicle*, April 1, 1874, July 7, 1874.
54. Alexander Stephens to Toombs, March 8, 1874, Emory University.
55. Toombs to Stephens, March 14, 1874, in Phillips, *Correspondence*, 718–720.
56. Augusta *Chronicle*, July 30, 1874; New York *Times*, July 23, 1874.
57. Henry Watterson, *Marse Henry: An Autobiography* (New York: Doran, 1919), Vol. 1, 65; Atlanta *Constitution*, May 14, 1874.
58. Watterson, *Marse Henry*, 65–66.
59. Quoted in the New York *Times*, May 25, 1874; Augusta *Chronicle*, May 26, 1874.
60. Augusta *Chronicle*, September 9, 1874, August 7, 1874; New York *Times*, August 17, 1874.
61. Augusta *Chronicle*, September 17, 1874.
62. Knight, "Reminiscences of Famous Georgians," 135; New York *Times*, October 13, 1874; Toombs to Alexander Stephens, November 6, 1874, in Phillips, *Correspondence*, 721.
63. Washington *Gazette*, quoted in the New York *Times*, March 15, 1875; Augusta *Chronicle*, April 21, 1875.
64. Toombs to Alexander Stephens, in Phillips, *Correspondence*, 721–722.
65. Augusta *Chronicle*, April 21, 1875; New York *Times*, July 5, 1875; Atlanta *Constitution*, July 2, 1875.
66. Augusta *Chronicle*, October 14, 1875.
67. Atlanta *Constitution*, January 26, 1876.
68. William Brandon, "Calling the Georgia Constitutional Convention of 1877," *Georgia Historical Quarterly* 17 (September 1933), 193; Memphis *Avalanche* and Petersburg, Virginia, *News* quoted in Atlanta *Constitution*, February 6, 1876; New York *Times*, January 29, 1876.
69. Stephen K. Williams, LL.D., ed., *Cases Argued and Decided in the Supreme Court of the United States*, Book 23 (Rochester, NY: Lawyers Co-operative, 1885, reprint 1963), 757–762. Northern newspapers had some fun when they claimed Toombs had to take an oath to support the Constitution before pleading in the Supreme Court. But Georgia papers assured their readers that the rumors were false. See Atlanta *Constitution*, April 19, 25, 1876.
70. Atlanta *Constitution*, April 29, 25, August 29, 1876; Toombs to Alexander Stephens, October 30, 1876, in Phillips, *Correspondence*, 722–723; Schott, Stephens, 504.
71. New York *Times*, November 17, 1876; Roy Morris, Jr., *Fraud of the Century* (New York: Simon and Schuster, 2003), 161. Toombs' sudden fondness for biblical allusions probably stemmed from his conversion to religion. The papers reported that he had recently professed his sins and joined The Methodist Church. Atlanta *Constitution*, October 7, 1876.
72. Toombs to Alexander Stephens, October 30, 1876, in Phillips, *Correspondence*, 722–723.
73. Boller, *Presidential Campaigns*, 134–135; Toombs to Alexander Stephens, December 17, 1876, in Phillips, *Correspondence*, 732–734.
74. Toombs to Alexander Stephens, December 28, 1876, in *ibid.*, 726; Brandon, "Georgia Constitutional Convention," 202.
75. Atlanta *Constitution*, March 14, 1877.
76. Toombs to Alexander Stephens, December 28, 1876, in Phillips, *Correspondence*, 726; Atlanta *Constitution*, March 16, 17, 1877.
77. Toombs to Alexander Stephens, April 24, 1877, in Phillips, *Correspondence*, 727.
78. Toombs to L. N. Trammell, April 26, 1877, in Phillips, *Correspondence*, 728–731.
79. Augusta *Chronicle*, June 29, 1877; Atlanta *Constitution*, May 15, 1877. Toombs did not realize anything was wrong with his vision until he tried to look at a picture in church. When he looked through the circle of his thumb and index finger, he discovered he could barely see out of his left eye. New York *Times*, June 24, 1877.
80. Stovall, *Robert Toombs*, 339; Atlanta *Constitution*, August 14, 1877.
81. New York *Times*, August 7, 1877; Stovall, *Robert Toombs*, 341.
82. Augusta *Chronicle*, August 25, 1877.
83. New York *Times*, September 2, 1877; Stovall, *Robert Toombs*, 343–344.
84. Atlanta *Constitution*, August 18, 1877; Augusta *Chronicle*, August 19, 1877; William Thompson, "Robert Toombs and the Railroads," *Georgia Historical Quarterly* 40 (March 1956): 61; Atlanta *Constitution*, September 1, 1877.
85. Augusta *Chronicle*, August 18, 1877; Atlanta *Constitution*, August 19, 1877.
86. Stovall, *Robert Toombs*, 340, 342.
87. Augusta *Chronicle*, August 19, 1877.
88. Atlanta *Constitution*, August 22; Samuel L. Small, *A Stenographic Report of the Proceedings of the Constitutional Convention Held in Atlanta, Georgia, 1877* (Atlanta: Constitution, 1877), 422.
89. Atlanta *Constitution*, September 13, 1877; Augusta *Chronicle*, September 15, October 2, October 10, 1877; New York *Times*, October 10, 1877.
90. Augusta *Chronicle*, October 4, 1877. In this interview, Toombs claimed to have lost a million dollars and three or four hundred slaves during the war, but said he would not restore slavery, even if he could. Atlanta *Constitution*, October 7, 1877.
91. Atlanta *Constitution*, October 3, 1877; Toombs to Stephens, November 2, 1877, Phillips, *Correspondence*, 731.
92. Atlanta *Constitution*, November 22, 1877; Toombs to Stephens, January 25, 1878, Phillips, *Correspondence*, 732–733.
93. Toombs to Stephens, January 25, 1878, Phillips, *Correspondence*, 732–733; see also New York *Times*, February 17, 1878.
94. Augusta *Chronicle*, February 28, April 17, 1878; New York *Times*, February 24, 1878. There had also been talk of sending Toombs to the Paris Exposition as the delegate from Georgia, but nothing came of it. See Atlanta *Constitution*, December 12, 1877; New York *Times*, December 23, 1877.
95. New York *Times*, March 18, 1878.
96. Augusta *Chronicle*, March 28, 1878.
97. New York *Times*, February 17, June 17, 1878.
98. Dublin (Georgia) *Post*, November 20, 1878; New York *Times*, November 18, 1878.

99. Toombs to Stephens, January 25, 1878, Phillips, *Correspondence*, 735–736. In this letter, Toombs referred to a book he had been contemplating. "I am only giving the headings of a few chapters in my forthcoming book on the true science of government," he wrote to Stephens. "It will give you something to think about and 'inwardly to digest' and apply in the execution of your public trust." He apparently abandoned the effort before it was ever really started.

100. Atlanta *Constitution*, April 22, 27, 29, 30, 1879.

101. New York *Times*, July 7, July 13, 1879. The interview appeared in the newspapers in several installments, but according to Grady, it was conducted in one sitting.

102. For instance, see Augusta *Chronicle*, July 12, 1879, and Galveston (Texas) *News*, July 12, 1879; Atlanta *Constitution*, July 16, 28, 1879.

103. Toombs to Alexander Stephens, March 10, 1879, in Phillips, *Correspondence*, 736; *ibid.*, April 1, 1879, 738.

104. Atlanta *Constitution*, November 13, 1879.

105. Augusta *Chronicle*, November 20, December 12, 1879.

106. Toombs to Alexander Stephens, March 25, 1880, in Phillips, *Correspondence*, 739–740.

107. Toombs to Alexander Stephens, April 25, 1880, in Phillips, *Correspondence*, 742; Dublin (Georgia) *Post*, May 5, 1880.

108. Dublin (Georgia) *Post*, July 28, 1880.

109. Atlanta *Constitution*, July 22, 1883.

110. Stovall, *Robert Toombs*, 369; Toombs to Alexander Stephens, March 10, 1879, in Phillips, *Correspondence*, 736; Augusta *Chronicle*, June 18, 1880; New York *Times*, November 16, 1880.

111. Toombs to Charles C. Jones, February 4, 1881, quoted from "*Memorial of Charles C. Jones, jr., L.L.D.: with regard to a subscription on the part of the state to his History of Georgia*," at *http://dlg.galileo.usg.edu/meta/html/dlg/zlgb/meta_dlg_zlgb_gb0428.html?Welcome*, accessed July 17, 2009.

112. Toombs to Indecipherable, May 2, 1881, Emory University; Atlanta *Constitution*, November 11, 1881; New York *Times*, June 11, 1881.

113. Atlanta *Constitution*, May 14, August 25, 1882; Augusta *Chronicle*, May 17, June 8, 1882.

114. Schott, *Stephens*, 505–506, 510–512.

115. Schott, *Stephens*, 513; Atlanta *Constitution*, August 24, 1882.

116. Schott, *Stephens*, 513, 517.

117. Atlanta *Constitution*, December 6, 1882; Williams, ed., *Cases Argued and Decided in the Supreme Court*, Book 27, 217–219.

118. Atlanta *Constitution*, December 23, 1882.

119. Augusta *Chronicle*, April 1, 1883; Thompson, *Toombs*, 254–255. The Augusta *Chronicle* suggested that if Toombs wanted to get the better of Joe Brown, then he should donate $50,000 of his own money to the university.

120. Atlanta *Constitution*, December 28, 1882.

121. Schott, *Stephens*, 519–520.

122. Charles J. Woodbury, "Toombs," 127; Augusta *Chronicle*, March 9, 1883; Atlanta *Constitution*, March 9, 1883.

123. Atlanta *Constitution*, June 3, July 8, 1883.

124. Atlanta *Constitution*, August 13, 1883.

125. Atlanta *Constitution*, August 15, 24, 1883; Willard Range, "Hannibal I. Kimball," 68.

126. Atlanta *Constitution*, September 1, 1883.

127. Reed, *The Brothers' War*, 280.

128. Atlanta *Constitution*, September 6, 7, 1883, December 28, 1882.

129. Toombs to Hilly Alexander, October 19, 1883, A.L. Alexander MSS, Duke University.

130. Atlanta *Constitution*, October 31, 1883; Reed, *The Brothers' War*, 280.

131. James U. Vincent, "A Pen Picture of General Robert Toombs," 10; Marty Fleming, Toombs House Historic Site Manager, interview with the author, October 31, 2003, Washington, Georgia.

132. New York *Times*, June 20, 1884; Atlanta *Constitution*, July 8, 9,1884; Reed, *The Brother's War*, 280. Billy died in 1887. Atlanta *Constitution*, August 23, 1887.

133. New York *Times*, June 20, 1884; Atlanta *Constitution*, July 9, 1884.

134. Knight, *Reminiscences of Famous Georgians*, 134.

135. Atlanta *Constitution*, September 14, 1884.

136. Atlanta *Constitution*, November 15, 1884.

137. Atlanta *Constitution*, April 12, May 31, June 11, 1885. Toombs helpfully included a religious tract that removed "all mysteries from the true road of regeneration and has given me more light and consolation than anything I have ever read—not even excepting the Bible itself."

138. New York *Times*, August 12, 1885.

139. Augusta *Chronicle*, August 14, 1885; *The Southern Bivouac*, vol. 4, 254; Dublin *Post*, August 19, 1885.

140. See, for example, Atlanta *Constitution*, October 1, 8, November 13, 1885; Dublin *Post*, October 14, 1885; Atlanta *Constitution*, October 4, 1885.

141. Atlanta *Constitution*, October 4, 1885; Stovall, *Robert Toombs*, 374.

142. Atlanta *Constitution*, December 7, 1885.

Bibliography

Books

Andrews, Eliza Frances. *The War-Time Journal of a Georgia Girl, 1864–1865.* New York: Appleton, 1908.

Avary, Mytra Lockett, ed. *Recollections of Alexander H. Stephens: His Diary Kept When a Prisoner at Fort Warren, Boston Harbor, 1865; Giving Incidents and Reflections of His Prison Life and Some Letters and Reminiscences.* New York: Doubleday, Page, 1910.

Boller, Paul F. Jr. *Presidential Anecdotes.* New York: Oxford University Press, 1981.

_____. *Presidential Campaigns.* New York: Oxford University Press, 1984.

Bonner, James C. *Milledgeville: Georgia's Antebellum Capital.* Athens: University of Georgia Press, 1978; reprint, Milledgeville, GA: Mary Vinson Memorial Library/Boyd, 1990.

Bradford, Gamaliel. *Confederate Portraits.* Boston: Houghton Mifflin, 1914.

Bryson, W. Hamilton, ed. *Essays on Legal Education in Nineteenth Century Virginia.* Buffalo, NY: Hein, 1998.

Carey, Anthony Gene. *Parties, Slavery, and the Union in Antebellum Georgia.* Athens: University of Georgia Press, 1997.

Cleveland, Henry. *Alexander Stephens in Public and Private, with Letters and Speeches Before, During, and Since the War.* Philadelphia: National, 1866.

Clinton, Catherine. *The Plantation Mistress: Woman's World in the Old South.* New York: Pantheon Books, 1982.

Cole, Arthur Charles. *The Whig Party in the South.* Washington, D.C.: American Historical Association, 1914; reprint, Gloucester, MA: Smith, 1962.

Coulter, E. Merton. *College Life in the Old South, as Seen at the University of Georgia.* Athens: University Press of Georgia, 1973.

_____. *The Toombs Oak.* Athens: University of Georgia Press, 1966.

Crist, Lynda Lasswell, and Mary Seaton Dix, eds. *The Papers of Jefferson Davis.* Baton Rouge: Louisiana State University Press, 1992.

Current, Richard N., ed. *Encyclopedia of the Confederacy.* Vol. 1. New York: Simon and Schuster, 1993.

Davidson, Grace Gillam, comp. *Early Records of Georgia: Wilkes County.* Vol. 1. Greenville, SC: Southern Historical Press, 1933, reprinted 1968 and 1992.

Davis, Jefferson, *The Rise and Fall of the Confederate Government.* New York: Appleton, 1881.

Davis, Varina Howell. *Jefferson Davis, Ex-President of the Confederate States of America: A Memoir by His Wife.* 2 vols. New York: Belford, 1890.

Davis, William C. *A Government of Our Own: The Making of the Confederacy.* New York: The Free Press, 1994.

_____. *The Union That Shaped the Confederacy: Robert Toombs and Alexander Stephens.* Lawrence: University Press of Kansas, 2001.

DeLeon, Thomas Cooper. *Four Years in Rebel Capitals.* Mobile, AL: Gossip, 1890; reprint, Alexandria, VA: Time-Life Books, 1983.

Dodd, Jordon R. *Virginia Marriages.* Bountiful, UT: Precision Indexing, 1990.

Donald, David Herbert. *Charles Sumner.* New York: Da Capo Press, 1960, 1970, 1996.

_____. *Lincoln.* New York: Simon and Schuster, 1995.

Dorman, John Frederick, comp. *Caroline County, Virginia, Order Book 1740–1746.* Part 3. Washington, D.C.: Dorman, 1970.

Douglas, Henry Kyd. *I Rode with Stonewall.* Chapel Hill: University of North Carolina Press, 1940.

Eisenhower, John S.D. *Agent of Destiny: The Life and Times of General Winfield Scott.* New York: The Free Press, 1997.

Fall, Ralph Emmett. *People, Postoffices and Communities in Caroline County, Virginia, 1727–1969.* Roswell, GA: Wolfe, 1989.

Foner, Eric, and John A. Garraty, eds. *The Reader's Companion to American History.* Boston: Houghton Mifflin, 1991.

Freehling, William. *The Road to Disunion: Secessionists at Bay.* New York: Oxford University Press, 1990.

Freehling, William M., and Craig M. Simpson, eds. *Secession Debated.* New York: Oxford University Press, 1992.

Freeman, Douglas Southall. *R.E. Lee: A Biography.* New York: 1934.

Gallagher, Gary W. ed. *Fighting for the Confederacy: The Personal Recollections of General Edward Alexander Porter.* Chapel Hill: University of North Carolina Press, 1989.

Godfrey Memorial Library. *The American Genealogical-Biographical Index to American Genealogical, Biographical and Local History Material.* Vol. 179. Godfrey Memorial Library: Middletown, CT, 1994.

Hall, Kermit L. ed. *Oxford Companion to American Law.* New York: Oxford University Press, 2002.

Hamlin, Charles E. *The Life and Times of Hannibal Hamlin.* Cambridge, MA: Riverside Press, 1899; reprint, Port Washington, NY: Kennikat Press, 1971.

Heath, Milton Sydney. *Constructive Liberalism: The Role of the State in Economic Development in Georgia to 1860.* Cambridge, MA: Harvard University Press, 1954.

Heitman, Francis. *Historical Register of Officers of the Continental Army During the War of the Revolution, April 1775 to December 1778.* Baltimore: Genealogical, 1982.

Hewett, Janet B. *Supplement to the Official Records of the Union and Confederate Armies.* Wilmington, NC: Broadfoot, 2001.

Hill, Lodowick Johnson. *The Hills of Wilkes County, Georgia, and Allied Families.* Atlanta: Johnson-Dallis, 1922.

Hofstadter, Richard, ed. *Great Issues in American History.* New York: Vintage Books, 1958.

Holt, Michael. *The Rise and Fall of the American Whig Party.* New York: Oxford University Press, 1999.

Johnson, Donald Bruce, ed. *National Party Platforms: 1840–1956.* Urbana: University of Illinois Press, 1978.

Johnson, Robert Underwood, and Clarence Clough Buel. *Battles and Leaders of the Civil* War. Secaucus, NJ: Castle, 1983.

Johnston, Richard Malcolm, and William Hand Browne. *The Life of Alexander H. Stephens.* Philadelphia: Books for Libraries Press, 1878.

Jones, John B. *A Rebel War Clerk's Diary at the Confederate States Capital* [sic]. Vol. 1. Philadelphia: Lippincott, 1866; reprint, New York: Time-Life Books, 1982.

Knight, Lucian Lamar. *Reminiscences of Famous Georgians Embracing Episodes and Incidents in the Lives of the Great Men of the State.* Atlanta: Franklin-Turner, 1907.

Leckie, Robert. *The Wars of America.* New York: Harper and Row, 1968, 1981.

MacDowell, Dorothy Kelley, comp. *DuBose Genealogy: Descendants of Isaac DuBose and Wife, Suzanne Couillandeau, French Huguenot Refugees Who Settled on the Santee River in South Carolina about 1689.* Louisville, KY: Gateway Press, 1981.

Malone, Dumas. *Jefferson and His Time: The Sage of Monticello.* Boston: Little, Brown, 1977, 1981.

Martin, Isabella D., and Myrta Lockett Avary, eds. *A Diary from Dixie, as Written by Mary Boykin Chesnut.* Gloucester, MA: Appleton, 1961.

Martin, John H., comp. *Columbus, Geo. from Its Selection as a "Trading Town" in 1827 to Its Partial Destruction by Wilson's Raid in 1865.* Columbus, GA: Gilbert, 1874; reprint, Easley, SC: Georgia Genealogical Reprints, 1972.

McGrane, Reginald Charles. *The Panic of 1837.* New York: Russell and Russell, 1965.

McPherson, James M. *To the Best of My Ability: The American Presidents.* New York: Agincourt Press, 2000.

Montgomery, Horace. *Cracker Parties.* Baton Rouge: Louisiana State University Press, 1950.

Morris, Roy, Jr. *Fraud of the Century.* New York: Simon and Schuster, 2003.

Murray, Paul. *The Whig Party in Georgia 1825–1853.* Chapel Hill: University of North Carolina Press, 1948.

Nevins, Allan. *Ordeal of the Union: Fruits of Manifest Destiny, 1847–1852.* New York: Charles Scribner's Sons, 1947.

_____. *Ordeal of the Union: A House Dividing.* New York: Charles Scribner's Sons, 1950.

_____. *The Emergence of Lincoln: Douglas, Buchanan and Party Chaos.* Vol. 1. New York: Charles Scribner's Sons, 1950.

_____. *The Emergence of Lincoln.* Vol. 2. *Prologue to the Civil War.* New York: Charles Scribner's Sons, 1950.

Parker, Frank Hudson, comp. *Wilkes County, Georgia, Tax Records, 1785–1805.* Vol. 1. Atlanta: Parker, 1988.

Parks, Joseph Howard. *General Edmund Kirby Smith, C.S.A.* Baton Rouge: Louisiana State University Press, 1954.

Phillips, Ulrich B., ed. *The Correspondence of Robert Toombs, Alexander Stephens, and Howell Cobb.* Washington, D.C.: American Historical Association, 1913.

_____. *The Life of Robert Toombs.* New York: Macmillan, 1913, 1968.

Rable, George C. *The Confederate Republic: A Revolution Against Politics.* Chapel Hill: University of North Carolina Press, 1994.

Reed , John C. *The Brothers' War.* Boston: Little, Brown, 1905.

Remini, Robert. *Andrew Jackson and the Course of American Freedom, 1822–1832.* New York: Harper and Row, 1981.

_____. *Henry Clay: Statesman for the Union.* New York: Norton, 1991.

Rowland, Dunbar, ed. *Jefferson Davis, Constitutionalist: His Letters, Papers, and Speeches.* Jackson: Mississippi Department of Archives and History, 1923.

Schlesinger, Arthur, Jr., ed. *The Almanac of American History.* New York: Putnam, 1983.

_____. *The History of American Presidential Elections, 1789–1968.* New York: Chelsea House, 1971.

Schott, Thomas. *Alexander Stephens of Georgia: A Biography.* Baton Rouge: Louisiana State University Press, 1987.

Seale, William. *The President's House: A History.* Washington, D.C.: White House Historical Association, 1986.

Shyrock, Richard Harrison. *Georgia and the Union.* New York: AMS Press, 1926, 1968.

Small, Samuel L. *A Stenographic Report of the Proceedings of the Constitutional Convention Held in Atlanta, Georgia, 1877.* Atlanta: Constitution, 1877.

Smith, George Burns. *History of the Georgia Militia, 1783–1861.* Vol. 1. *Campaigns and Generals.* Milledgeville, GA: Boyd, 2000.

Smith, Sarah Quinn. *Early Georgia Wills and Settlements of Estates, Wilkes County. Georgia.* Athens, GA: Heritage Papers, 1959, 1994.

Stephens, Alexander A. *A Constitutional View of the Late War Between the States: Its Causes, Character, Conduct and Results. Presented in a Series of Colloquies at Liberty Hall.* 2 vols. Philadelphia: National, 1868–70.

Stovall, Pleasant A. *Robert Toombs: Statesman, Speaker, Soldier, Sage.* New York: Cassell, 1892.

Taylor, Richard. *Destruction and Reconstruction: Personal Experiences of the Late War.* Edited by Richard B. Harwell. New York: Longmans, Green, 1955.

Terrill, Helen Eliza. *History of Stewart County.* Columbus, GA: Columbus Office Supply, 1958.

Thomas, Kenneth H. *The Robert Toombs House, Washing-*

ton, Georgia. Atlanta: State of Georgia, Department of Natural Resources, 1974.

Thompson, William A. *Robert Toombs of Georgia,* Baton Rouge: Louisiana State University Press, 1966.

Trelease, Allen W. *White Terror: The Ku Klux Klan Conspiracy and Southern Reconstruction.* New York: Harper Torchbooks, 1971.

Tucker, Phillip Thomas. *Burnside's Bridge: The Climactic Struggle of the 2nd and 20th Georgia at Antietam Creek.* Mechanicsburg, PA: Stackpole Books, 2000.

Urban, Wayne J. and Jennings L. Wagner. *American Education: A History.* New York: McGraw-Hill, 1996.

Van Deusen, Glyndon G. *Horace Greeley: Nineteenth Century Crusader.* Philadelphia: University of Pennsylvania Press, 1953, 1967.

Warren, Mary Bondurant, ed. *The Chronicles of Wilkes County.* Danielsville, GA: Heritage Papers, 1978.

_____. *Georgia Revolutionary Bounty Land Records, 1783–1785.* Athens, GA: Heritage Papers, 1992.

Watterson, Henry. *Marse Henry: An Autobiography.* New York: Doran, 1919.

Weed, Harriet A., ed. *The Autobiography of Thurlow Weed.* Vol. 2. Boston: Houghton, Mifflin, 1883.

White, Mary H. and John B. Lomax. *William Lomax Family and His Descendants.* Privately printed by John Lomax, 1995.

Whitney, David. *The American Presidents: Biographies of the Chief Executives from Washington through Clinton.* New York: Guild America Books, 1993.

Wilkenson, Warren, and Steven E. Woodworth. *A Scythe of Fire: A Civil War Story of the Eighth Georgia Infantry Regiment.* New York: Morrow, 2002.

Williams, Stephen K., ed. *Cases Argued and Decided in the Supreme Court of the United States.* Rochester, NY: Lawyers Co-Operative, 1885; reprint, 1963.

Woodward, C. Vann, and Elisabeth Muhlenfeld. *The Private Mary Chestnut: The Unpublished Civil War Diaries.* New York: Oxford University Press, 1984.

Young, Jeffrey Robert. *Domesticating Slavery.* Chapel Hill: University of North Carolina Press, 1999.

Electronic Sources

Abbott, John S. *The History of the Civil War in America Comprising a Full and Impartial Account of the Origin and Progress of the Rebellion, of the Various Naval and Military Engagements, of the Heroic Deeds Performed by Armies and Individuals.* N.p.: 1864–1866, page 297n. *http://quod.lib.umich.edu/cgi/t/text/pageviewer-idx?c=moa;cc=moa;rgn=full%20text;idno=ACP5555.0001.001;didno=ACP5555.0001.001;view=image;seq=00000323,* accessed July 17, 2009.

Ammidon, Phillip R. "An Englishman's Opinion." *New England Magazine,* 5 March 1887, p. 478, *http://dlxs2.library.cornell.edu/cgi/t/text/pagevieweridx?c=newe;cc=newe;rgn=full%20text;idno=newe00055;didno=newe0005-5;view=image;seq=0490;node=newe0005-5%3A12,* accessed July 17, 2009.

Appleton, Nathan. *Letter to the Hon. Wm. C. Rives of Virginia on Slavery and the Union.* Boston: J.H. Eastburn's Press, 1860, p. 6, *http://quod.lib.umich.edu/cgi/t/text/pageviewer-idx?c=moa;cc=moa;rgn=full%20text;idno=ABJ4860.0001.001;didno=ABJ4860.0001.001;view=image;seq=0006,* accessed July 16, 2009.

Assumption College. "Eliphalet Nott (June 25, 1773–Jan. 29, 1866)," *http://www.assumption.edu/ahc/Theresa's%20Main%20Folder/Web%20page%20folder/Biographies/Nott%20Bio.html,* accessed July 11, 2009.

Coleman, Ann Mary. *The Life of John J. Crittenden.* Philadelphia: Lippincott, 1873, p. 294, available at *http://quod.lib.umich.edu/cgi/t/text/pageviewer-idx?c=moa;cc=moa;g=moagrp;xc=1;q1=The%20Life%20of%20John%20J.%20Crittenden;rgn=full%20text;idno=ABT3814.0001.001;didno=ABT3814.0001.001;view=image;seq=00000300,* accessed July 16, 2009.

Benjamin, Charles F. "Recollections of Secretary Edwin M. Stanton." *The Century,* 33 (March 1877), 765, *http://dlxs2.library.cornell.edu/cgi/t/text/pagevieweridx?c=cent&cc=cent&idno=cent0033-5&node=cent0033-5%3A12&frm=frameset&view=image&seq=775,* accessed July 17, 2009.

Brahana, Thomas. "The History of Mathematics at the University of Georgia: Teaching, Research and Service," no date, available at *http://www.math.uga.edu/history/,* accessed June 17, 2009, 57–58.

Channing, William Ellery. *Thoughts Selected from the Writings of the Rev. William E. Channing.* Vol. 2. Boston: Ticknor and Fields, 1859, p. 172, *http://quod.lib.mich.edu/cgi/t/text/pageviewer-idx?c=moa;cc=moa;rgn=full%20text;idno=AJK3640.0001.001;didno=AJK3640.0001.001;view=image;seq=00000186,* accessed July 17, 2009.

Clay-Clopton, Virginia. *A Belle of the Fifties: Memoirs of Mrs. Clay, of Alabama, Covering Social and Political Life in Washington and the South, 1853–66,* p. 86, available at *http://docsouth.unc.edu/fpn/clay/clay.html,* accessed July 16, 2009.

Columbia University. "The Campus Business," Presented at the Lawrence University Matriculation Convocation, September 2000," available at *http://www.columbia.edu/~am875/rebell6.html,* accessed June 24, 2002.

Cornell University. "The Constitution and Slavery," *Continental Monthly,* 1 June 1862, 624, *http://dlxs2.library.cornell.edu/cgi/t/text/pageviewer-idx?c=cont&cc=cont&idno=cont0001-6&node=cont0001-6%3A1&frm=frameset&view=image&seq=650* Cornell, accessed July 17, 2009.

_____. "Conversational Opinions of Leaders of Secession." *Atlantic Monthly,* 10 November 1862: 613–623, *http://dlxs2.library.cornell.edu/cgi/t/text/pageviewer-idx?c=atla;cc=atla;rgn=full%20text;idno=atla00105;didno=atla0010-5;view=image;seq=0619;node=atla0010-5%3A14,* accessed July 17, 2009.

Cox, Samuel S. *Eight Years in Congress, from 1857 to 1865. Memoir and Speeches.* New York: Appleton, 1865, p. 27, *http://quod.lib.umich.edu/cgi/t/text/pageviewer-idx?c=moa;cc=moa;rgn=full%20text;idno=ACP4141.0001.001;didno=ACP4141.0001.001;view=image;seq=0033,* accessed July 17, 2009.

Craven, John J. *Prison Life of Jefferson Davis.* New York: Carleton, 1866, p. 172, *http://quod.lib.umich.edu/cgi/t/text/pageviewer-idx?c=moa;cc=moa;rgn=full%20text;idno=ACP4963.0001.001;didno=ACP4963.0001.001;view=image;seq=00000174,* accessed July 17, 2009.

The Demosthenian Society. *http://www.uga.edu/demsoc/,* accessed July 4, 2009.

Ellet, Elizabeth Fries, *The Court Circles of the Republic.* Hartford, CT: Hartford, 1869, 496, *http://quod.lib.umich.edu/cgi/t/text/pageviewer-idx?c=moa;cc=moa;rgn=full%20text;idno=AJA2444.0001.001;didno=AJA2444.0*

001.001;view=image;seq=00000475, accessed July 17, 2009.

Friends of Cemeteries of Middle Georgia, "Memory Hill Cemetery, Milledgeville, Georgia, Tomlinson Fort." *http://www.friendsofcems.org/MemoryHill/SQLSelect2.asp?key=WE052010*, accessed July 7, 2009.

GeorgiaInfo. "Appropriating Money for Georgia's Defense." Act No. 54 of Georgia Legislature, November 16, 1860, *http://georgiainfo.galileo.usg.edu/1860act2.htm*, accessed July 17, 2009.

_____. "Georgia Secession Convention Authorized." Act No. 14 of Georgia Legislature, November 22, 1860, available at *http://georgiainfo.galileo.usg.edu/1860act.htm*, accessed July 17, 2009.

Gihon, John H. *Governor Geary's Administration in Kansas*. Philadelphia: Rhodes, 1857. Available at Google Books, *http://books.google.com/books?id=w3kUAAAAYAAJ&dq=Governor+Geary%E2%80%99s+Administration+in+Kansas&printsec=frontcover&source=bl&ots=VB2PiTo7w0&sig=z6YrRzN0aUFlMIeyIo6KLbsPelM&hl=en&ei=VoNvSqT3CYXusQOG_JDoAg&sa=X&oi=book_result&ct=result&resnum=2*, accessed July 17, 2009.

"Glances from the Senate Gallery." *Continental Monthly*, July 1862, 13, *http://dlxs2.library.cornell.edu/cgi/t/text/pageviewer-idx?c=cont&cc=cont&idno=cont0002-1&node=cont0002-1%3A5&frm=frameset&view=image&seq=21*, accessed July 17, 2009.

Grady, Henry W. "The New South." The *New England Magazine* 8 (March 1890), 88, *http://dlxs2.library.cornell.edu/cgi/t/text/pageviewer-idx?c=newe&cc=newe&idno=newe0008-1&node=newe0008-1%3A13&frm=frameset&view=image&seq=96* Cornell, accessed July 17, 2009.

Harrison, Burton N. "The Capture of Jefferson Davis." *The Century* 27 November 1883, 139, Cornell, *http://dlxs2.library.cornell.edu/cgi/t/text/pageviewer-idx?c=cent&cc=cent&idno=cent0027-1&node=cent0027-1%3A21&frm=frameset&view=image&seq=149*, accessed July 17, 2009.

Houghton, William Robert, *Two Boys in the Civil War and After*. Montgomery, AL: Paragon Press, 1912. Electronic edition from *docsouth.unc.edu/fpn/houghton/menu.html*, accessed July 17, 2009.

"How Stands the Case?" *The United States Democratic Review* 3, no. 9, 8, *http://dlxs2.library.cornell.edu/cgi/t/text/pageviewer-idx?c=usde&cc=usde&idno=usde0003-1&node=usde0003-1%3A2&frm=frameset&view=image&seq=10*, accessed July 7, 2009.

"Index to Land Grants 1&2 1784–1839 Wilkes County," available at *http://files.usgwarchives.net/ga/oglethorpe/deeds/ldgrants.txt,* accessed June 3, 2009.

"Journal of the Public and Secret Proceedings of the Convention of the People of Georgia, Held in Milledgeville and Savannah in 1861, Together with the Ordinances Adopted." Electronic edition available at *http://docsouth.unc.edu/imls/georgia/menu.html*, 3–7, accessed July 17, 2009.

"Journal of the Senate of the State of Georgia, at the Annual Session of the General Assembly, Begun and Held in Milledgeville, 1862." Milledgeville, GA: Boughton, Nisbet & Barnes, 1862, 112, *http://docsouth.unc.edu/imls/gasen62/menu.html*, accessed July 17, 2009.

Mackinnon, Lauchlan Bellingham. *Atlantic and Transatlantic: Sketches Afloat and Ashore*. New York: Harper & Brothers, 1852, 63–65, *http://quod.lib.umich.edu/cgi/t/text/pageviewer-idx?c=moa;cc=moa;g=moagrp;xc=1;q1=Atlantic%20and%20Transatlantic%3A%20Sketches%20Afloat%20and%20Ashore;rgn=full%20text;idno=ABF8697.0001.001;didno=ABF8697.0001.001;view=image;seq=0063*, accessed July 16, 2009.

Matthews, James M., ed., *The Statutes at Large of the Provisional Government of the Confederate States of America*/ Richmond: Smith, 1864, available at *http://docsouth.unc.edu/imls/19conf/menu.html*, 29–30; 42; 52; 158, accessed July 17, 2009.

McCabe, Dabney. *Behind the Scenes in Washington*. New York: Continental, 1873, 193, *http://quod.lib.umich.edu/cgi/t/text/pageviewer-idx?c=moa;cc=moa;rgn=full%20text;idno=AFJ8728.0001.001;didno=AFJ8728.0001.001;view=image;seq=0217*, accessed July 16, 2009.

Montgomery in Secession Time." *Continental Monthly*, March 3, 1863, 361, *http://dlxs2.library.cornell.edu/cgi/t/text/pageviewer-idx?c=cont&cc=cont&idno=cont0003-3&node=cont0003-3%3A16&frm=frameset&view=image&seq=377* Cornell, accessed July 17, 2009.

Nicolay, John J. "Abraham Lincoln: A History. The President Elect at Springfield." *The Century* 35 (November 1887), 66, *http://dlxs2.library.cornell.edu/cgi/t/text/pageviewer-idx?c=cent&cc=cent&idno=cent0035-1&node=cent0035-1%3A9&frm=frameset&view=image&seq=76*, accessed July 17, 2009 .

Parker, Theodore. "The New Crime Against Humanity: A Sermon Preached at the Music Hall, in Boston on Sunday, June 4, 1854." *http://quod.lib.umich.edu/cgi/t/text/text-idx?c=moa;cc=moa;view=toc;idno=ABJ1697.0001.001*, accessed July 17, 2009.

Phillips, Wendell. *Speeches, Lectures, and Letters*. Boston: Lee and Shepard, 1872, 424–425, *http://quod.lib.umich.edu/cgi/t/text/pageviewer-idx?c=moa;cc=moa;rgn=full%20text;idno=ABT7101.0001.001;didno=ABT7101.0001.001;view=image;seq=0430*, accessed July 17, 2009.

"The Presidency and the Review." *The United States Democratic Review* 30 (February 1852): 182, *http://dlxs2.library.cornell.edu/cgi/t/text/pageviewer-idx?c=usde;cc=usde;rgn=full%20text;idno=usde0030-2;didno=usde0030-2;view=image;seq=0190;node=usde0030-2%3A10*, accessed July 16, 2009.

"Recollections of an Old Stager." *Harper's New Monthly Magazine* 48 (January 1874), 254, *http://dlxs2.library.cornell.edu/cgi/t/text/pageviewer-idx?c=harp&cc=harp&idno=harp0048-2&node=harp0048-2%3A12&frm=frameset&view=image&seq=264*, accessed July 16, 2009.

"The Republican A Disunion Party." *The Old Guard* 3 (June 1865), 275, *http://dlxs2.library.cornell.edu/cgi/t/text/pageviewer-idx?c=oldg&cc=oldg&idno=oldg0003-6&node=oldg0003-6%3A8&frm=frameset&view=image&seq=281* Cornell, accessed July 17, 2009.

Russell, Sir William Howard. *My Diary North and South*. Boston: Burnham, 1863, 181, *http://quod.lib.umich.edu/cgi/t/text/pageviewer-idx?c=moa;cc=moa;rgn=full%20text;idno=AAW0172.0001.001;didno=AAW0172.0001.001;view=image;seq=0203*, accessed July 17, 2009.

"Site of Wilkes County Academy," available at *http://www.kudcom.com/www/mark/mark21.html*, accessed June 17, 2009.

"State of Georgia." *Debow's Review* 10 (March 1851), 245–246, for a derogatory description of a Georgia muster. Available at MOA University of Michigan, *http://quod.lib.umich.edu/cgi/t/text/pageviewer-idx?c=moajrnl;cc=*

moajrnl;rgn=full%20text;idno=acg1336.1-10.003; didno=acg1336.1-10.003;view=image;seq=263;node= acg1336.1-10.003%3A1;page=root;size=100, accessed September 16, 2003.

Strahan, Charles Morton. "The University of Georgia." *The New England Magazine*, September 1890, 56, Making of America, Cornell University website, *http://digital.library.cornell.edu/m/moa/*, accessed June 8, 2009.

"The Tariff of 1846." *The American Whig Review* 4 (September 1846), 224–225, *http://dlxs2.library.cornell.edu/cgi/t/text/pageviewer-idx?c=amwh&cc=amwh&idno =amwh0004-3&node=amwh0004-3%3A1&frm= frameset&view=image&seq=234*, accessed July 16, 2009.

Toombs, Robert. "Memorial of Charles C. Jones, jr. L.L.D.: with regard to a subscription on the part of the state to his History of Georgia," at *http://dlg.galileo.usg.edu/meta/html/dlg/zlgb/meta_dlg_zlgb_gb0428.html*, accessed July 17, 2009.

_____. "Slavery: Its Constitutional Status, and its Influence on Society and the Colored Race." *Debow's Review* 20 (May 1856), 581–605, *http://quod.lib.umich.edu/cgi/t/text/pageviewer-idx?c=moajrnl;cc=moajrnl;rgn= full%20text;idno=acg1336.1-20.005;didno=acg1336.1-20.005;view=image;seq=0605;node=acg1336.1-20.005%3A4*, accessed July 17, 2009.

Towle, George M. "Some Secession Leaders." *Harper's New Monthly Magazine* 26 (April 1863), 675, *http://dlxs2.library.cornell.edu/cgi/t/text/pageviewer-idx?c= harp;cc=harp;rgn=full%20text;idno=harp0026-5; didno=harp0026-5;view=image;seq=0683;node= harp0026-5%3A12*, accessed July 16, 2009.

Trollope, Anthony. *North America*. Philadelphia: Lippincott, 1863, 169, *http://quod.lib.umich.edu/cgi/t/text/pageviewer-idx?c=moa;cc=moa;rgn=full%20text;idno= ACP2610.0001.001;didno=ACP2610.0001.001;view=image ;seq=0169*, accessed July 17, 2009.

University Systems of Georgia. "Acts of the General Assembly of the State of Georgia, passed in Milledgeville at an Annual Session in November and December, 1842," *http://neptune3.galib.uga.edu/ssp/cgi-bin/legis-idx.pl?sessionid=7f000001&type=law&byte=21808738&law cnt=137&filt=doc*, accessed July 1, 2009.

Weidman, Budge. "Preserving the Legacy of the United States Colored Troops." No date, available at *http://www.archives.gov/education/lessons/blacks-civil-war/article.html*, accessed July 17, 2009.

Weise, John. *Life and Correspondence of Theodore Parker, Minister to the Twenty-Eighth Congregational Society, Boston*. New York: Appleton, 1864, 223–224, *http://quod.lib.umich.edu/cgi/t/text/pageviewer-idx?c=moa;cc= moa;rgn=full%20text;idno=AGU9018.0001.001;didno= AGU9018.0001.001;view=image;seq=00000239*, accessed July 17, 2009.

"The Whig Convention: The Candidate and Campaign." *The American Whig Review* 16 (August 1852), 101, *http://dlxs2.library.cornell.edu/cgi/t/text/pageviewer-idx? c=amwh&cc=amwh&idno=amwh0016-2&node= amwh0016-2%3A1&frm=frameset&view=image&seq= 107*, accessed July 16, 2009.

Willingham, Robert. "An Overview of Local History." *http://www.rootsweb.ancestry.com/~gawilkes/localhst.htm*, accessed June 3, 2009.

Woodbury, Charles J. "Toombs." *Overland Monthly and Out West Magazine* 7 (February 1886), 125, *http://quod.lib.umich.edu/cgi/t/text/pageviewer-idx?c=moajrnl;cc= moajrnl;rgn=full%20text;idno=ahj1472.2-07.038;didno =ahj1472.2-07.038;view=image;seq=0131;node= ahj1472.2-07.038%3A3*, accessed July 17, 2009.

Young, Lot D. *Reminiscences of a Soldier of the Orphan Brigade*. Louisville, KY: Courier Journal, 1918, 20–21, also available at *http://docsouth.unc.edu/fpn/young/menu.html*, accessed July 17, 2009.

Newspapers

Athens (Georgia) *Southern Banner*.
Atlanta *Constitution*.
Augusta (Georgia) *Chronicle*.
Baltimore *Clipper*.
Columbus (Georgia) *Enquirer*.
Columbus (Georgia) *Herald, Extra*.
Daily Richmond Enquirer.
Dublin (Georgia) *Post*.
Georgia *Telegraph*.
Macon *Messenger*.
Milledgeville *Federal Union*.
Milledgeville (Georgia) *Journal*.
Milledgeville *Southern Recorder*.
National Intelligencer.
New Orleans *Picayune*.
New York *Times*.
New York *Tribune*.
Washington *Daily Evening Star*.

Manuscripts and Personal Papers

Robert Toombs Papers, Hargrett Rare Book and Manuscript Library, University of Georgia.

Edward Alexander Porter Papers, Southern Historical Collection, Wilson Library, The University of North Carolina at Chapel Hill.

John MacPherson Berrien Papers, Southern Historical Collection, Wilson Library, The University of North Carolina at Chapel Hill.

Ralph McGill Collection, Special Collections, Robert W. Woodruff Library, Emory University.

Joseph E. Johnston Papers, Special Collections Research Center, Earl Gregg Swem Library, College of William and Mary.

University of Virginia Faculty Minutes #2328, vols. 1 and 2, Albert and Shirley Small Special Collections Library, University of Virginia.

Union College Student Records, First Term 1827–1828 to Second Term 1828–1829, typescript.

Other

Confederate Generals Speak, CD ROM version, Indianapolis: Guild Press of Indiana, 1997.

Davis, Harold. "The Civil War Career of Robert Toombs." Master's thesis, University of Georgia, 1950.

Medical and Surgical History of the Civil War. Wilmington, NC: Broadfoot, 1991.

Official Records of the Union and Confederate Navies in the War of the Rebellion, Series 2, vol. 3, CD ROM version, Indianapolis: Guild Press, 1999.

Richardson, James D. *A Compilation of the Messages and Papers of the Confederacy Including the Diplomatic Correspondence 1861–1865*. Nashville: United States, 1905, CD ROM version, Silver Spring, MD: H-Bar Enterprises, 1995.

Robert Toombs' Military Service File, National Archives, Washington, D.C.

Simpson, John Eddins, "A Biography of Howell Cobb" Ph.D. dissertation, University of Georgia, 1971.

Southern Historical Society Papers, vol. 28. Richmond, Va. January–December, 1900, CD ROM version, Indianapolis: Guild Press of Indiana, 1998.

The War of the Rebellion: A Compilation of the Official Records of the Union and Confederate Armies Washington: 1880–1901, CD ROM version, Indianapolis: Guild Press of Indiana, 1996.

Index

Page numbers in ***bold italics*** indicate illustrations.